Another
Reformation

Another Reformation

POSTLIBERAL CHRISTIANITY AND THE JEWS

Peter Ochs

B

Baker Academic

a division of Baker Publishing Group
Grand Rapids, Michigan

Published by Baker Academic
a division of Baker Publishing Group
P.O. Box 6287, Grand Rapids, MI 49516-6287
www.bakeracademic.com

Printed in the United States of America

Library of Congress Cataloging-in-Publication Data

Ochs, Peter, 1950–
    Another reformation : postliberal Christianity and the Jews / Peter Ochs.
        p.   cm.
    Includes bibliographical references and index.
    ISBN 978-0-8010-3940-9 (pbk.)
    1. Church—History of doctrines. 2. Continuity of the church—History of doctrines. 3. Israel (Christian theology) 4. Election (Theology) 5. Christianity and other religions—Judaism. 6. Judaism—Relations—Christianity. I. Title.
    BV600.3.O26 2011
    231.7′6—dc22   2011003066

In keeping with biblical principles of creation stewardship, Baker Publishing Group advocates the responsible use of our natural resources. As a member of the Green Press Initiative, our company uses recycled paper when possible. The text paper of this book is composed in part of post-consumer waste.

11   12   13   14   15   16   17   7   6   5   4   3   2   1

For the Ford and Hardy families,
in deep friendship, at the lake

Contents

Acknowledgments   ix

1. Introduction: Christian Postliberalism and the Jews   1

Part 1: American Protestant Postliberalism

2. George Lindbeck and the Church as Israel   35

3. Robert W. Jenson: The God of Israel and the Fruits of Trinitarian Theology   63

4. Arguing for Christ: Stanley Hauerwas's Theopractic Reasoning   93

5. The Limits of Postliberalism: John Howard Yoder's American Mennonite Church   127

Part 2: British Postliberalism

6. Finding Christ in World and Polity: Daniel Hardy's Ecclesiological Postliberalism   167

7. Wisdom's Cry: David Ford's Reparative Pneumatology   195

8. John Milbank: Supersessionist or Christian Theo-semiotician and Pragmatist?   223

9. Conclusion: Christian Postliberalism and Christian Nonsupersessionism Are Correlative   257

Index of Subjects   269

Index of Scripture and Other Ancient Sources   277

Acknowledgements

I offer warm thanks to folks at Brazos Press for their interest, encouragement, and trust in this project. Special thanks go to Rodney Clapp for his wise and patient editorial guidance and to Lisa Ann Cockrel for caring attention to every detail. The design work of Paula Gibson, marketing efforts of Jeremy Wells, and all of the work of the wider Baker Publishing Group staff are also much appreciated

Rather than thank here the many colleagues and students who have nourished this project over its many years, I have cited and quoted these conversation partners frequently on the following pages. And I hope I have been daily thanking my wife, daughters, and those who love them for nourishing what lies behind this book.

1

Introduction

CHRISTIAN POSTLIBERALISM AND THE JEWS

This book introduces and tests one hypothesis: that as demonstrated through the efforts of a recent movement in Christian theology, there is a way for Christians to rededicate themselves to the gospel message and to classical patristic doctrines of the church without at the same time revisiting classical Christian supersessionism.[1]

Here *supersessionism*—or *replacement theology*—refers to a Christian belief that with the incarnation of God in Jesus Christ, Israel's covenant with God was superseded and replaced by God's presence in the church as the body of Christ. Otherwise stated, this is the Christian belief that God's love for the church replaced his love for Israel. Jews of the premodern period and both Jews and Christians of the Enlightenment period—already expressed alarm at this doctrine. They argued that classical Christology was onerous because it was inseparable from supersessionism. Since the Shoah (the term is Hebrew for "Utter Destruction" and is the preferred term for the Holocaust), Christian as well as Jewish concern about supersessionism has grown more urgent. The argument is typically twofold. The first charge is that while classical supersessionism is not itself an expression of racial anti-Semitism, the doctrine has in fact engendered anti-Semitism among Christian populations. In turn, that anti-Semitism has in fact stimulated or justified Christian persecution of the Jews. The second charge is that while Nazism was itself anti-Christian,

---

1. My thanks to Daniel Weiss and Jacob Goodson for helpful comments on this chapter, and to Rodney Clapp for his significant edits.

1

it inherited the anti-Semitism that was a de facto consequence of Christian supersessionism. Thus, whatever its formal, theological justification or non-justification, supersessionism shows itself to be lethal as a public teaching.

After the horrible lessons of the Shoah, what should Christians do about this heritage of supersessionism? Rosemary Ruether's *Faith and Fratricide* offered what I will label the prototypical response of liberal, modernist Christianity.[2] Reiterating the Enlightenment argument, she concludes that Christology itself is the problem: since it necessarily engenders supersessionism, Christians are faced with the either–or choice of affirming classical Christology *or* freeing themselves of the evils of supersessionism.

The premise of this book is that the movement I will label "postliberal Christian theology" offers an alternative to this either–or choice. It offers a way to reaffirm classical Christology while eliding its supersessionism. To be more precise, my basic hypothesis divides into three more detailed hypotheses.

> Subhypothesis 1: There is a logic of postliberal Christian theology according to which the reaffirmation of classical Christology after modernity is inseparably associated with the rejection of supersessionism.

This first hypothesis shapes the way I have compiled the central chapters of this book. To test it, I made a list of what I consider prototypical postmodern theologians: in the United States, George Lindbeck, Robert Jenson, and Stanley Hauerwas; in the United Kingdom, David Ford and Daniel Hardy; plus those among the "next generation" of postliberal theologians who address the issue of supersessionism.[3] I then constructed a vague (not overdefined) model of the patterns of postliberal reasoning that appear in selected writings of all of these theologians. Observing that each of them also argues against supersessionism, I collected and compared their different arguments and constructed another vague model, this time of the shared features of postliberal nonsupersessionism. Finally, I observed that each of these theologians argued for postliberalism in a way that correlated 100 percent of the time with an argument against supersessionism. If the reader wonders why I have not yet defined what I mean by *postliberalism*, it is because I had no clear definition of it throughout the project. I used the term to label whatever appeared, by the end of the project, to be the primary characteristics of the theologians I guessed merited study. By the end of this book—in the epilogue—I shall indeed relent, sum up these characteristics, and then compare them to descriptions some scholars have

2. Rosemary Radford Ruether, *Faith and Fratricide: The Theological Roots of Anti-Semitism* (New York: Seabury, 1974). I comment on Ruether's account of supersessionism in Peter Ochs, "Judaism and Christian Theology," in *The Modern Theologians: An Introduction to Christian Theology in the Twentieth Century*, 2nd ed., ed. David Ford (London: Blackwell, 1997), 607–25 (at 615–16).

3. Kendall Soulen et alia: I review these in the appendix to this chapter.

offered of the "postliberal theologians" (my primary source will be the work of James Fodor).[4]

> Subhypothesis 2: When evaluating a theology that claims to be "postliberal," we can, in a vague sense, "measure" the consistency of the theology's "postliberalism" by testing its nonsupersessionism. A theology that proves to be supersessionist will, on further inspection, prove to have been guided by some model other than postliberalism—that is, by a modern liberal or antiliberal model. Conversely, a theory that proves to be liberal or antiliberal will, on further inspection, prove to be supersessionist.

This second hypothesis offers a means of identifying "exceptions that prove the rule" of the first hypothesis, by alerting us to theologies that are postliberal *except in ways that also correspond to their supersessionism* (or that are nonsupersessionist except in ways that also correspond to their liberalism/ antiliberalism). The hypothesis thus helps us identify persistently liberal *or* antiliberal tendencies within a theology that otherwise promotes a postliberal agenda: if the theology proves to be supersessionist, to that degree it will also display tendencies that work against its postliberalism.

To test this hypothesis in varieties of American Protestant postliberalism, I have added a chapter on John Howard Yoder, of blessed memory. Without explicitly naming it as such, Yoder offers his theology as an equivalent of what I call Christian postliberalism, and he associates that postliberalism with non-supersessionism. In practice, however, his arguments about Judaism include some clearly supersessionist claims. Is this an exception to our rule? I argue that it is not, since these supersessionist claims also lead us to elements of his theology that replay liberal and antiliberal tendencies. To test the hypothesis for varieties of British postliberalism, I have added a chapter on John Milbank. Milbank's critique of modernist and liberal postmodernist thinkers puts him self-consciously in the postliberal camp, albeit in a much more general sense. He is often critical of the others in my collection of postliberals, however, and he is unapologetic about a degree of Christian supersessionism. How then shall I account for his postliberal tendencies? Shall I accept his criticisms and reevaluate my collection as burdened by a combination of persistent liberalism and fideism? Guided by the second hypothesis, I say no, it is more likely the other way around: Milbank's supersessionist claims lead us to elements of his theology that replay liberal and antiliberal tendencies.

> Subhypothesis 3 tests the relative power of postliberal versus liberal versus antiliberal Christian theologies to provide a working alternative to Christian super-

4. James Fodor, "Postliberal Theology," in *The Modern Theologians: An Introduction to Christian Theology since 1918*, 3rd ed., ed. David Ford with Rachel Muers (London: Wiley-Blackwell, 2005).

sessionism. Its three claims are (a) that today's antiliberal Christian theologies bring with them a contemporary version of classical Christian supersessionism; (b) that, as typified by Ruether's analysis, liberal Christian theologies seek a form of nonsupersessionist Christianity but tend to give rise to unintended forms of supersessionism; (c) that postliberal Christian theologies provide the most reliable protection against formal or de facto supersessionism.

Hypothesis 3 cannot be thoroughly tested in this book, since I am commenting directly only on postliberal writings, without comparable text-work on liberal and antiliberal works. Within the limits of this book, I attempt only to show how the postliberal theologians endorse this hypothesis and how their detailed arguments against liberal and antiliberal theologies would enable us to test the hypothesis on another occasion.

What I mean by "postliberalism" will become apparent only through careful study of the works of the postliberal theologians, and there will of course be as many subvarieties of postliberalism as there are postliberal theologians. I am, however, also collecting these varieties from my own limited perspective, and it may help readers if I offer some introductory comments about the generalizations I tend to make about Christian postliberalism.

The Epoch of Postliberal Theology: A Typological Approach

I believe we are now in a new epoch of Christian and Jewish theologies and a new epoch of relations between Christianity and Judaism. According to the typology that informs this book, this is the epoch, at once, of postliberal Christian theologies, postmodern Jewish philosophies, and both Jewish and Christian theologies after the Shoah. Thinking typologically more than historically, I would also label this the third of three major epochs, thus far, in Jewish–Christian relations.

In these terms, the first epoch was and is the Epoch of Formation. This is the time of Jewish and of Christian communal self-definition, when each community defined the other only *as* other—as an offense to its self-definition or a threat to its ideological and social boundaries. The second epoch was and is the Epoch of Assimilation. This is the period of attempts by Christians and Jews to overcome the nastier consequences of mutual exclusion by assimilating their different scriptural traditions to a single religion of reason: a religion of ethics and enlightenment for the new nation-states and market economies of Europe.

The third epoch is the one we have just entered—at least according to the worldview I will attribute to both Jewish and Christian postliberals. This is the epoch of a relationality that invites both critical reason *and* a reaffirmation of scriptural revelation and the traditions of belief and practice that interpret it. This is a relationality, furthermore, that invites Jews to be Jewish in their way, Christians to be Christian in their way, and both to discover some complementary purpose in this relationality itself. The distinctiveness of the third epoch may be captured in this observation: that Immanuel Kant, along with the Neologians and other thoughtful contributors to the second epoch, also sought forms of relation that would enable at least some religious communities to affirm one another's existence. They sought to construct these relations, however, as products of human reason and will, while the relationality of the third epoch is seeded by God alone. As critical thinkers, theologians of this epoch—I will label them "postliberal theologians"—argue against the a prioricity of any universal canon of human reason. They argue that the only reason we share as a species is God's reason, and God's reason is embedded in the orders of creation and the words of Scripture in a way that enables us to observe *that* it is there but not to articulate its universal character through any finite set of humanly constructed propositions. Despite their benevolent wishes, the Neologians and Kantians therefore constructed ideas of relation that tended to reproduce rather than replace the antimonies they sought to resolve.

Postliberal theologians do not, therefore, seek to construct any account of the overlapping purposes of Christianity and Judaism. Nor, however, do they presume that their respective religious pieties need be enacted in the fashion of first epoch "formations": tightly defined by collections of theological propositions that identify the other religion as prototype of what is contrary to the purposes of one's own religion. They believe, instead, that they are called at this time in salvation history to reaffirm the faiths of their primordial communities (rabbinic and early church), to reform their contemporary communities in light of these faiths, *and* to expect that their reaffirmations need not entail denigrating the religious purposes of the other community.

Because it is the focus of this book, I have introduced the third epoch, or Epoch of Postliberalism, with respect to its implications for Jewish–Christian theological relations. This epoch is, however, *not* first and foremost about these relations. It is first and foremost a time when Christian theologians and Jewish theologians both began to observe that their respective communities were no longer burdened primarily by the deep questions that stimulated the second epoch and no longer strengthened by that epoch's answers. On the congregational level, postliberalism's primary question is how to relocate a pattern of religious belief and practice that is free from the regnant antinomy of liberal humanism versus reactionary orthodoxy. On the level of philosophical and theological reflection, its primary question is how to rearticulate the rationality that emerges from out of the scriptural traditions, in place of the regnant dialectic between antimodern skepticism and fideism on the one side and, on the other side, various efforts to reassert the "universality" of rationalist discourses and arguments. Surprisingly enough, this dialectic cuts across secular and religious philosophies.

The Postliberal Critique: A Logical Approach

From a postliberal perspective, the hegemonic modern paradigms of reason (with all their attendant "isms") unraveled because they had completed their time of civilizational utility, not because some new party of thinkers and ideologues foisted a postmodern or antimodern agenda on the West. This argument implies that, against some postmodernist claims, the modern paradigms had their sphere and time of usefulness. To say their time has passed therefore means *neither* that we can now "undo" the "modern error" and "get back to" various premodern orthodoxies, *nor* that we can now construct patterns of discourse and practice that will be free of the "pretensions" or "errors" of modern and premodern civilizations. *Postliberalism* refers to an activity of reformation directed at once to the church or synagogue and to the university (or, more broadly, the *seculum* as a public order). For postliberalism, "reformation" implies both reaffirmation and correction. Like other movements of reform or revitalization, it seeks to criticize certain institutions from within— from *deep* within, that is, which means according to norms embedded within the practices and histories of those institutions, but not necessarily visible to contemporary practitioners and leaders. Postliberals often attempt, therefore, to reclaim what they consider prototypical sources and norms of the church or synagogue and of the university (or seculum) and to offer their criticisms from out of these sources and norms. For this reason, they are not critics of modern or premodern civilization; these civilizations are constitutive of their own "flesh"—their assumptions, languages, and sources of belief. They are critical only of efforts to repair errant social and religious practices today by reapplying rules of reform that were shaped specifically to meet the needs and concerns of an earlier age, modern or premodern. Their surprising discovery is that such efforts tend to display the same logical form, whether they are placed in the service of a rationalist or antirationalist, or a religious or a secular, agenda.

This pervasive logical form is to define one's position as the logical contradictory of a position one is criticizing: for example, defining one's secular postmodernism as the logical contradictory of some religious dogmatism, or one's rational neo-orthodoxy as the logical contradictory of some relativist postmodernism. Such efforts appear to trace steps like the following:

- collecting examples of an offending practice (a, b, c . . . n);
- suggesting that this collection displays a class character that can be defined according to a finite set of propositions, or, in other words, reduced to a relatively simple propositional function [$P = (a, b, c \ldots n)$, where $P = f(x)$];
- promoting another practice (Q) as both the desirable alternative to the offending practice (P) and the desirable means of repairing P (or of repairing institutions that errantly pursue P);

- assuming that Q can also be defined according to a finite set of propositions (which therefore corresponds to another relatively simple propositional function [Q = (x, y, z . . . n), where Q = g (x)]);
- intentionally or unintentionally, therefore, presupposing that Q and P are logical contradictories—in other words, that both P and Q refer to a domain of possible practices (W), such that the domain is served by either P or Q (W = P∪Q), where P ≠ Q.

Applied to the critique of lived practices, the law of the excluded middle, with its attendant propositional calculus, generates what we might call a hermeneutics of war. This is a mode of reparative argument that generates comparable sets of antagonistic postures regardless of the goal of one's argument. It makes secularists, religionists, rationalists, and irrationalists all partners to exclusivist and dogmatic politics and positivist epistemologies. They are positivist because Q is knowable by way of sets of clear and distinct propositions; they are exclusivist because Q ≠ P, which means we know that practices will be either Q or P, that Q is correct and that it excludes P.

Postliberals accordingly get themselves into trouble with either side of the modern dialectic of rationalists versus irrationalists, secularists (or liberals) versus religionists (or neo-orthodox). Since proponents of any one of these four persuasions employ the logic of propositions and excluded middles, they assume that if postliberals object to given Q, then they must be affirming P—if not neo-orthodox, then secular; if not rationalist, then irrationalist, and so on. "Mediators" (to adapt Hans Frei's term "mediating theologians")—like Neologians, Kantians, or some liberal theologians today—also object to these four dogmatisms. They additionally object to postliberalism, however, tending to assimilate postliberalism to an antirationalist neo-orthodoxy. This tendency may be a sign that when push comes to shove, the mediators are more anxious about the ills of religious enthusiasm than about the ills of secular humanism, and more concerned, therefore, to protect the authority and autonomy of human reason than the authority and autonomy of the divine will. We should indeed expect that individual thinkers are most vigilant in protecting against the ills they themselves have suffered and witnessed. One suffered from (or observed those who suffered from) brutal religionists, another from brutal irrationalists, another from condescending rationalists, and so on. This is also to say, however, that there is just so much one can learn from individuals qua individuals. Insofar as an individual's ideology is defined by some reaction to real suffering, it demands attention as a symptom of this suffering, however much it will fail also to serve as a reliable guideline for how to repair this suffering.

To be consistent with their own logic, postliberals cannot be dismissive of those who practice the logics of excluded middles. These may be the logics of war, but they are also the logics of individual suffering. The moment of suffering may even serve as *fons et origo* of the excluded middle. When, God forbid, one suffers, then there *are* only two possible predicates of the world one knows: *in* suffering or *out* of it, either this pain or its cessation. As defined by this suffering, there are only two values in the world: what maintains this suffering and what gets rid of it. As defined by those values, there are only two kinds of actions: those that do and those that do not help relieve this suffering. And there are only two kinds of agents or persons: those who do and those who do not help relieve this suffering. Tragically, therefore, the logic of suffering is also a logic that suffers—that teaches exclusion and consequently can lay the groundwork for more suffering. Otherwise put, the one who suffers, qua sufferer, is not a source of his or her or anyone else's redemption. Postliberalism must take cognizance of this implication of its own logic: one must have nothing but compassion for the *one* who suffers, but one must not learn the logic of redemption—or repair or reform—from the logic of suffering.

In sum, postliberalism emerges as an effort to help repair the kinds of suffering that mark the unraveling of the last epoch of Christianity and of Judaism and that are no longer repaired by the reparative reasoning nurtured by that epoch. How then shall postliberalism turn away from modern logic as a source of instruction at the same time that it turns toward it as a focus of care? Postliberal theologians have answered this question by relocating the relationality that is missing in the dichotomous logics of modernity.

The Postliberal Alternative: A Theo-logic

As noted earlier, the Kantians and the "mediating theologians" recognized the need for such relationality. Their error—according to the postliberals—is that they sought to construct the relationality themselves rather than find it, which means receiving it as gift from the only One who provides the relationality. In different terms, we could say that the "middle" is excluded from modern thinking because it is excluded by the human will and by concepts formulated according to the desires of that will. Kantian and other mediators desire an end to the logic of war but cannot help but reproduce it as a correlate of their very acts of desire. Put in yet another way, these are finite acts offered to take the place of an infinite activity: quite literally, they are sets of finite propositions (from the claim "God is love" to the categorical imperative) offered as substitute for the infinite Word that alone creates, reveals, and redeems.

Modern critics might label this postliberal turn to God "confessional" and therefore inappropriate to "academic" discourse. The postliberal response is that, as used in this way, the term *confessional* belongs to a contrast pair—confessional versus academic—that is meaningful only according to a modern logic of excluded middle. But for the logics that inform postliberalism, the contrast pair "confessional"/"academic" predicates the manner of attention a human being may pay to God, or another point of reference, but it does not characterize the referent itself. To refer to a referent confessionally, for example, may be to refer in light of the referent's relation to me (or to refer "subjectively"), while referring academically may be to refer in light of the referent's relation to other objects of my attention (or to refer "objectively"). Put this way, "confessional"/"academic" and "subjective"/"objective" no longer refer to logical contradictories. On one count, they no longer "refer" at all. According to Friedrich Ludwig Gottlob Frege's very early postmodern distinction between sense and reference, the contrast pair concerns sense and not reference—the mode of attention rather than the object of attention. On a second count, the two elements of this pair are not mutually exclusive; I may consider a referent from the perspectives of its relations *both* to me (as knower) *and* to other objects of my knowing. Frege's distinction represents an emergent critique of modern logic, because it allows us to classify the referent as a *given*, with which we may come into *relation*, but which we cannot *constitute* or "capture" through our conceptualizations of it. It thus exceeds the dichotomizing influences of the human will. The distinction falls short of the later critique we call "postliberal," however, because it does not yet provide a term for relations between sense and reference, or between the referent and its senses. It still displays itself, in other words, in terms of a contrast pair (here, sense/reference), because it still adopts the point of view of the human knower.

Why should modern logic have such a persistent influence? I believe that postliberalism turns on the following hypothesis: that *the issue is not modernity or secularism, per se, but the dyadic[5] logics that inhabit both secularism and the antisecular religious movements that rise up to repel it*. If so, we still need to ask, why should these logics have such a persistent influence in modernity? The postliberal answer rests, I believe, on the following series of axioms through which the logic of postliberalism is received as theo-logic.

Axiom 1 As I have suggested, *the fundamental problem to which postliberalism responds is not modernity or modernism but a more general tendency to reduce the logic that guides our efforts at societal and ecclesial repair to a logic of dyads*. In these terms, a "logic of repair" refers to the underlying rules of reasoning that guide efforts to repair any form of suffering and any form of institutional or societal violence or dysfunction. At issue, in particular, are rules for repairing rules of repair. I will say a logic of repair is "reduced to a logic of dyads" when it portrays any problematic situation as the consequence of some faulty behavior X, which is the logical contradictory of some correct

5. When the lived situation calls for a dichotomous logic—as in the case of suffering—I label the logic *binary*. When binary logics are employed inappropriately, I label them *dyadic*. For a more detailed treatment of this distinction, see Peter Ochs, "Response: Reflections on Binarism," in special issue "Symposium: Pragmatism and Biblical Hermeneutics—The Work of Peter Ochs," *Modern Theology* 24, no. 3 (July 2008): 487–98, available at www3.interscience .wiley.com/journal/120085675/issue.

behavior −X (where X and −X are treated as if they constituted the universe of all really possible solutions to the problem). To repeat what I wrote earlier, postliberalism is critical of dyadic logics of repair, in favor of what we will see is a relational logic of repair.

Axiom 2. Any effort at repair begins with a perception of suffering (or of a problematic situation, to make use of John Dewey's term), *and any such perception is, by definition, governed by a binary logic.* According to this logic, whatever stimulates a perception of suffering also stimulates a desire to perceive the absence of that suffering; the perception of suffering is therefore part of a contrast pair, suffering/nonsuffering, or −X/X.

Axiom 3. For a conceivable set of persons whom we might label "passive ones," the perception of suffering stimulates a desire for nonsuffering but no means of contributing actively to that nonsuffering. If nonsuffering comes, it is unpredictable. For passive ones, life therefore tends to acquire a tragic character, since life often stimulates the desire for nonsuffering but less often satisfies it. For another set of persons, whom we might label "active ones," the desire for nonsuffering stimulates a search for whatever might bring it about. For active ones, the perception of suffering thus stimulates end-directed behavior. The pragmatic philosopher Charles Peirce classified "modern, Cartesian philosophy" as what, in these terms, we might relabel "endless active searching." In Peirce's reading, Cartesian philosophers find no source of relief (either to suffering or the desire to see it relieved) because they trust only what they themselves can see. They see suffering, but they cannot see a way out of it, because, in Peirce's reading, the way out lies within what they cannot see: sources of repair that are embedded deep within the lives, institutions, societies, and traditions of those who suffer.[6] These sources cannot be seen, but they can be accessed in other ways.

The most general logical lesson to draw from axioms 1–3 is that the logic of suffering is not the logic of repair. The logic of suffering is appropriately binary because suffering is perceivable. Suffering is perceived as that which stimulates a desire for its absence; that desire is either present or not present, a sign that suffering is either present (to the perceiver) or not present. In these terms, "active ones" fail to become agents of repair, because they adopt the logic of suffering as if it were also the logic of repair: presuming that the source of repair is perceivable, they fail to locate this source; discounting the nonvisible, they therefore presume that this source cannot be found and that either they themselves must be agents of repair or there are none.

6. See the account of "Cartesian Anxiety" in Richard Bernstein, *Beyond Objectivism and Relativism: Science, Hermeneutics, and Praxis* (Philadelphia: University of Pennsylvania Press, 1983), 8–19. And see the claim that Peirce criticized Descartes for doubting too much and then believing too much, in Susan Haack, "Descartes, Peirce, and the Cognitive Community," in *The Relevance of Charles Peirce*, ed. Eugene Freeman (LaSalle, IL: The Hegeler Institute for *The Monist* Library of Philosophy, 1983), 238–63.

Axiom 4. To become an agent of repair, one must first be able to perceive suffering, which is, in part, to participate in the binary logic of suffering. To move, however, from perception to reparative action, one must also be able *to give oneself to another*, relational logic. Perhaps the most telling axiom of postliberalism is this: one's search for instruments of repair must, if it is to succeed, be guided by a relational (and thus nondyadic) logic of inquiry. Until they are freed from the dyadic logic that enabled them to perceive suffering in the first place, would-be repairers will remain unintentional agents of suffering, or at least agents of nonrepair. This means that efforts of repair require at least two moments of personal transformation: one must first be transformed into a perceiver of suffering (whose sole concern is to transform the $-X$ of suffering into the X of nonsuffering) and then transformed into an agent of rescue (who is prepared to share in some process of repair that has not yet made itself known). But where is this process to be found? How, in other words, is one to leave one logic for another?

Axiom 5. One axiom of postliberal logic is that *one cannot transform oneself. Only the presence of one who suffers can transform a participant in everyday life into "one who perceives suffering"*: the sufferer draws this one out of the monologic of everyday quiet into the dyadic logic of suffering. And only the presence of "one who repairs suffering" can transform this perceiver-of-suffering into an actual agent of repair: the repairer draws this one into the relational logic of repair. In short, it is always some other who is the agent of one's transformation.

This axiom may be illustrated in more concrete terms. Drawing on Dewey's pragmatic analyses of institutions, we might conceive of social institutions as if they were progressively ordered to serve the relative ends of repairing suffering, then of repairing the repair of suffering, and so on. Say we start with the *Lebenswelt*, or the world of everyday practices that includes not only doing this or that but also repairing how one does this or that. A doorknob won't turn, so I oil it. Then I scratch myself, so I put on a Band-Aid. But say I still cannot open the door, or I cut myself badly. We might use the label *service institutions* for the first-order institutions of repair that include the door company I call because I cannot open it myself, and the hospital I run to because I cannot mend myself. But (to follow just one illustrative line of repair), say the doctors do not know how to mend cuts like mine. We might use the label *reparative sciences* for the second-order institutions—like medical schools and research facilities—that recommend ways of repairing the first-order ones. Many disciplines of the academy should serve as reparative sciences for various subgroups of service institutions. But say medical scientists fail to help doctors mend their ways of mending certain injuries. We might use the label *reparative philosophy* for the third-order institution of philosophic metascience that examines the dysfunctions of other academic disciplines and recommends ways of repairing them. Yet again, say the philosophers fail to make such reparative use of their discipline. Pragmatism arose as a means of calling philosophers back to this task. Some pragmatists claimed that the source of this "call" is a rule of common sense—some light of nature, we might say, that most philosophers failed to perceive.

Charles Peirce argued that while many philosophic failings may be repaired by common sense, there are classes of failings that common sense cannot repair.[7] One is the large class of questions over which any generation of philosophers argues interminably, such as questions of the eternity versus contingency of the material world, or of ontological or epistemological realism versus nominalism, or of rationalism versus empiricism, or of the relative power of phenomenological versus analytic modes of philosophic inquiry. Pragmatists read such antinomies as marks of only one mode of reasoning, not of reasoning or of common sense itself. They say that, like suffering, such marks should stimulate philosophers to look elsewhere for help: to look by way of a different logic and different order of reasoning. A more self-evident class of failings is the class of societal and civilizational failings, when "things fall apart" and received systems of language and meaning are sources of more suffering than repair. Within the academic disciplines, these failings are analogous to the epistemological crises that stimulate what Thomas Kuhn labeled scientific "paradigm shifts." Peirce argued that these classes of failings mark the limits of common sense, when philosophers themselves turn to other practices such as mathematics, art, and prophecy for new sources of repair and new insights for how to seek repair.

In his "Neglected Argument for the Reality of God," Peirce recommended "musement" on each order of experience as a means of recognizing the reality of God and of renewing and reforming one's logic of inquiry into the character of God's creation. Elsewhere, he suggested that pragmatism is nothing other than a logical corollary to Jesus's words "Ye shall know them by their fruit." While they do not draw directly on Peirce's work, the postliberal theologians follow an analogous line of reasoning: when philosophers fail to perceive suffering and to reason in response to it, then the Word of God, alone, can call them back to their reparative task.

Axiom 6. Relational logic as theo-logic. As suggested by Peirce's approach, the relational logic of repair is ultimately a theo-logic, since God remains the ultimate source of the pragmatist's calling and of the pragmatic rule for reorienting philosophy to its reparative service.

Axiom 7. Scripture as instruction in reparative logic. God is the source of pragmatic repair, by way of God's Word. Peirce argued as if this meant

---

7. See Charles Peirce's discussions of what he calls "Scotch Common-sense Realism," for example, Charles Peirce, "Issues of Pragmaticism," *Monist* 15 (1905): 481–99, rpt. in *Collected Papers of Charles Sanders Peirce*, ed. Charles Hartshorne and Paul Weiss (Cambridge, MA: Belknap Press of Harvard University Press, 1932), 5:438–63. Also, "Consequences of Critical Common-Sensism" (1905), in 5:502–37.

God's Word in creation as well as (and perhaps even more significantly than) God's Word in revelation or Scripture. I argue, however, that Peirce's logic of science requires grounding pragmatic repair ultimately in the revealed Word: Scripture read as instruction in the logic of repairing conditions of suffering. My account of the reparative order of social institutions identifies the limits of our society's capacity to hear the reparative logic inherent in the laws of creation. These are the laws to which service institutions appeal when they repair everyday problems, to which scientists appeal when they repair failed service institutions, and to which philosophers appeal when they repair failed sciences. But failed philosophies mark the limits of our society's capacities to correct its characterizations of the laws of creation. Pragmatists can repair failed philosophies only if they are graced with instructions that exceed these capacities. Based on Peirce's inadequately developed suggestions on the logic of his argument, and on the logic of its hermeneutical sources in Augustine's semiotics, I argue that these instructions are delivered only by readings of Scripture.[8]

Pragmatism's reparative reasoning is thus a species of scriptural reasoning, which operates by drawing the dyadic logic of any failed practice of philosophy into a transformative relation to the divine Word. This means that a failed philosophic practice provides the context for a reparative reading of Scripture, so that, with respect to this practice (p), a given text or set of texts (S)[9] discloses the reparative meaning p_r (pSp_r). This latter is "the meaning of S *as* a set of instructions for repairing p." For a reparative scriptural reasoning, in other words, a text of Scripture acquires performative meaning as a set of instructions about how to repair the failed philosophic practice. To adduce such a meaning is, for the pragmatist, to repair philosophic practice through the grace and guidance of the divine Word. We may look to Exodus for a prototype of this kind of guidance. "Who shall I say You are?" asks Moses. *Ehyeh*, says God, then *ehyeh imach*, "I will be with you": translated into our vocabulary, "Wherever your understanding of creation fails and you can no longer heal your society's wounds, I will be with you—*ehyeh* will be with you, that Name itself" (see Exod. 3:13–14).

Through the chapters of this book, I will offer more specific illustrations of postliberal Christianity's efforts to repair modern philosophies and theologies through the Name and the Word disclosed in Scripture. These efforts are not displayed by way of the dyadic logic of propositions, as if one could reduce the reparative force of scriptural reasoning to discrete judgments (as if one could claim, "Because He said 'This is My servant, whom I uphold' [Isa. 42:1], we know that Israel should not fret about its suffering"). The efforts

8. See Peter Ochs, "Reparative Reasoning: From Peirce's Pragmatism to Augustine's Scriptural Semiotic," *Modern Theology* 25, no. 2 (2009): 187–215.

9. Or a chain of texts that embeds scriptural texts in a tradition of commentary.

are displayed instead by way of the relational logic that would, for example, bring the suffering of some single group of people to the attention of some particular community of Israel, and bring that community to some particular texts of Scripture, and those texts to the context of that suffering, and that communion of text, interpreters, and sufferers to some series of inquiries, actions, and testings that continues until the suffering is relieved.

Corollary (7a). There is no relationality without God. This is not to declare some sort of occasionalism (that each event of relation displays the consequence of a separate divine act), or some sort of scriptural positivism (that we enter into "true" relations only when we call on the Name revealed in Scripture). It is instead to draw out the theological corollary of postliberalism's pragmatism (axioms 1–6) and its scriptural reasoning (axioms 7–9), or, overall, what we might label its "scriptural pragmatism." It may be useful at this point to illustrate the implications of scriptural pragmatism on two different levels of analysis.

On a *very general level* of analysis, scriptural pragmatism implies that everyday life in this order of creation (*maaseh b'reshit*) includes conditions of suffering and conditions for the repair of suffering. *Suffering* refers, metaphysically, to an event of separation within the relational continuum that characterizes a given order of creation. It therefore characterizes not only the "sufferer," whose separateness is a defining mark of this suffering, but also the continuum, which is actually and not merely nominally interrupted by this event. Epistemologically, *suffering* refers to events that are brought to our attention only by interruptions in our unselfconscious everyday conduct and our unselfconscious activities of cognition. Logically, *suffering* refers to events that we can identify in, and only in, the binary logic of propositions. Theologically, then—and theology shows how all our modes of reasoning are gathered and guided by the scriptural Word—suffering tears the fabric of some order of creation, and the sound of suffering goes up to God and gains God's attention.

Repair refers, metaphysically, to activities that reintegrate the sufferer and a given order of creation. Strictly speaking, this is not the "same" order from which the sufferer was separated: in this context, "sameness" is not part of the elemental vocabulary of postliberal theology, because both the suffering and its repair are matters of relation, not distinct identities. There is no neutral, static perspective from which to imagine that the relationality or continuity of an order of creation was X and remains X. In the words of the rabbinic daily morning prayer service, "God daily renews the order of creation"—and not only daily but also whenever God appears in the Name of *ehyeh imach* to accompany the sufferer. Epistemologically, repair is recognized only "from the inside," as an activity that engages the knower in the relational work of transforming conditions of suffering into conditions, again, of unselfconscious living within some order of creation. Logically, the activity of repair cannot be identified by any discrete series of propositions formed by dyadic logics. It can be diagrammed only through narratives that imitate the activity, thereby providing both illustration and instruction in the practice of repair. Scripture is the prototype as well as the primary book of instruction in how to compose new diagrams of repair, which Peirce calls "existential graphs." Peirce's primary interest was in composing formal diagrams of this kind, including his "logic of relations." Unlike textbooks of modern logic, Peirce's logics are meant to perform, as well as represent, their subject matter. This means that the formal scribblings of a logic of relations remain existentially linked to the context of their composition: like Scripture, a formal logic of relations is not sent off into the world to be read in any way by anyone; instead, it calls its readers into finite sets of relations that bind author, context, and reader together in context-specific ways. In these terms, I believe we may also say that when Scripture diagrams reparative activity, then Scripture functions in turn like a logic of repair. If so, then I may also read the legal midrash (scriptural interpretations) of the Talmud as diagrams of reparative activity. To take another example, I may also read Augustine's *Confessions* this way, and also his *De doctrina christiana* and *De Trinitate*.[10]

In sum, the logic of repair is already a theo-logic, *since we know of no adequate way of analyzing the process of repair without being guided by the reparative logic of Scripture*. All other logics—and thus the logics of all nonpragmatic philosophies—are either reducible to the dyadic logic of suffering or (as employed, for example, in relativity theory and quantum physics) abstracted from their reparative function.

On a *more technical level* of analysis, scriptural pragmatism draws a distinction between two dimensions of relationality. First, the words (and "relations") of creation: scriptural pragmatism refers to the divine Word in the orders of creation as naming both the "relational continuity" we attribute to the worlds of everyday life and the source of reparative logic that is intrinsic to those worlds. Within the "reparative order of social institutions" I described earlier, the words of creation would therefore represent the sources of reparative logic as employed by service institutions, scientists, and philosophers. Second, there are the revealed words (and "relations") of Scripture (axiom 5). Pragmatists are called to repair philosophic practices, however, because our society does not always have access to the reparative potential of the orders of creation. The revealed Word offers instruction in how to repair failed philosophies—including how to repair failed practices of pragmatism. Since pragmatism is a practice of scriptural reasoning, what we call "failed pragmatisms" would also include failed scriptural theologies. For postliberal Christianity, the term *theology* is applied only to practices of scriptural reasoning that are employed to repair failed philosophies.

10. See Ochs, "Reparative Reasoning."

Axiom 8. Modern logic as a falling out of grace or of scriptural in-struction and thus out of the relational logic of God's reparative presence. Why, finally, should modern logic have such a persistent influence in our society? To summarize: On the basis of something like these eight axioms, postliberal Christian theology argues that the issue is not modernity per se but the tendency of modern academics (scientists and philosophers) and modern theologians—both liberal and antiliberal—to adopt the dyadic logic of propositions as a reparative logic. The logical consequence of this move is to reiterate conditions of suffering rather than to remove them. The societal consequence is to leave failed philosophies and theologies un-repaired and thus to leave a legacy of unrepaired sciences and unrepaired service institutions. But in the face of such failure, what could account for the persistence of this modern tendency? There will be many situations in which—and context-specific reasons why—individual thinkers have sought to overgeneralize the function of dyadic logics in this way, thereby displacing relational and, ultimately, scriptural logics from their appropriate places in the academy, the churches, and the social order more generally. But any general account of these errors will have to refer as well to failures of will, and that means to sin. The issue of sin must arise because reparative logic is not just a method but any of an indefinitely large family of methods engendered by scriptural reasoning, which means engendered by attending to the direct presence of God as condition for reparative work. By saying "direct presence," I do not invoke some extrarelational account of religious experience or intuition, for the divine Word is itself God's direct presence in human lives. In Peirce's words, we directly perceive the relational being of God in our midst. Since this being is relational, our perception is irreduc-ible to the form of discrete propositions and articulated only through the relational processes we have associated with reparative reasoning or with more concrete displays of reparative work.

What I call "modern logic" refers to the tendency of liberal and antiliberal philosophers and theologians to segregate realms of "human" and "divine" discourse, to categorize their reparative work as performed strictly within and concerning the human realm, and thereby to lay claim to rules of repara-tive reasoning that can be defined clearly and distinctly. The latter step is the most telling. Whatever the philosopher or theologian's confession—whether agnostic, atheist, or orthodox—this step defines the ultimate source of repair as within our human ken. The postliberal claim is that this step reduces re-parative activity to the dyadic logics of modernity. Whatever these individual thinkers may believe or confess, the logics they practice exclude the elemental marks of pragmatic repair:

   a. context-specificity (that the repair addresses the conditions of suffering
      they are meant to repair);

    b. relationality (that the repair binds together sufferer, agent of repair, and source of repair);

    c. vagueness (that the rules of repair cannot be diagrammed independent of this specific activity of repair); and therefore

    d. recognition of the ultimate source of repair (God).

Secular and some liberal models of repair self-consciously exclude *d* but also tend to exclude *a–c* in the name of "objectivity." Postmodern models tend to exclude *d* but to claim *a* and some form of *b*; they tend to confuse *c* with indeterminacy, overlooking the binding character of both vagueness and relationality. Antiliberal theologians (and, we may add, many contemporary "Christian philosophers") tend to favor a theological positivism that claims *d* while excluding *a*, *b*, and especially *c*. Postliberal theologians argue that by eschewing vague logics in favor of what they consider "clear and distinct statements of their faith," antiliberal theologians deny God a direct place in their professional work. As for those who claim that their discrete theological propositions display God's direct presence, the postliberal theologians call them logically confused, since logical discreteness is a property only of humanly constructed artifacts, as guided by dyadic logics.

    Axiom 9. How, then, does postliberal Christian theology propose to repair the tendency of liberal and antiliberal thinkers to reduce the logic of repair to the dyadic logics of modernity? The answer is *the project of postliberal Christian theology itself* and the subject of all the chapters of this book.

But Why the Jews?

Postliberal Christianity does not first arise out of a concern for the Jews, or out of a direct response to the Shoah. It arises first as a response to the discomforts of, and divisions within, the church in the waning years of modernity—in these years that have displayed the unhappy societal consequences of modernity's dyadic logics. Postliberal Christianity is thus first a movement to recover a voice for the church in the modern academy and in modern secular society; to recover the voice of Scripture within the church; to recover the place of communal discourse and interpretation within the church's reception of Scripture; to recover the place of disciplined reason within the life of each interpreting community of the church; to recover reason's parentage in the Word of God, or Logos; and to recover scriptural reasoning's freedom from subservience to the *ratio* of any single human project (Athenian, French, or Syro-Aramaic, for that matter), including projects that define themselves by rejecting any such project (anti-Greek, antimodern, or antipatristic). Once engaged in this movement, postliberal theologians discover that these activities of recovery lead them, second, to a new relationship with the Old Testament, with Israel's ancient covenant with God, and with the Jews as a religious people during the time of Jesus and into the rabbinic period that continues today.

Having entered this new relationship to the people Israel, these theologians discover that their postliberalism excludes supersessionism. The reason for this is not simply self-evident, and there may be as many paths to reasoning about this as there are postliberal theologians. Before turning to those paths in the chapters to come, I may say this much about the general tendencies of the postliberals. Once having turned away from the conceptualist tendencies of modern theology, they tend not only to recenter their work in traditions of Gospel reading but also to transform the way they read the Gospel narratives. They tend to rediscover each Gospel *as itself* a rereading of the Old Testament narratives of the history of Israel.[11] Why, however, would they not then read the Gospels as an end and a fulfillment of Israel's history? The postliberals tend to observe that their critique of dyadic logics in modernity applies to dyadic logics operative in early Christian exegesis as well. As they see it, one effect of such logics is to reify difference as contradiction—both logical and theo-logical—so that if the Synoptic Gospels as well as Paul draw distinctions between non-Christian Jews and Christian Gentiles, then the one must be unredeemed if the other is redeemed, the one unloved by God as the other is loved. If the logic of postliberalism is to transform contradiction into mere difference, then Jews would remain different from Gentile Christians, but the character of their difference would not be apparent a priori. Some mystery would adhere to that difference ("vagueness" in logical terms), and the mystery would be clarified only through a prayerful and context-specific process of scriptural interpretation, or what I call "scriptural reasoning." Nonsupersessionism would not be the logical contradiction of supersessionism but something else, the character of which would show itself only through the concrete details of postliberal inquiry in its specific historical contexts.[12] For the postliberal theologians described in this book, these contexts are shaped by their individual responses to more events than I can number here, but among them several appear prominent: the waning of modernity, the aftermath of the Shoah, the emergence of a Jewish state, new forms of union and disunion

11. It is misnomer to label postliberal theology "narrative theology," since an interest in narrative textuality is not a source of the movement but only one of its consequences. One might say instead that postliberalism is non-nonnarrativist. Inhibiting modernity's lack of interest in narrative, postliberalism recovers Israel as story but also as history.

12. To be clear about this: If supersessionism is equivalent to the claim that "the church has replaced Israel as God's covenant partner," then the contradictory claim would be that "Israel is God's (only) covenant partner." My point here is that nonsupersessionism is *not* equivalent to the latter claim, although it does not exclude it. Nonsupersessionism is the less-defined claim that "the church has not replaced Israel as God's covenant partner," leaving matters open until a given theologian further defines this claim according to a specific context of interpretation. One postliberal theologian might therefore claim that the church joins Israel, another might claim that there are two covenants, and so on.

within the church, and the new minority status of Christianity within the vast seculum of the West and of the United States of America.

On Face-to-Face Theology

I focus this study on contemporary theologians with whom I have personal contact and can engage in sustained dialogue. I do this because I consider theology a dimension of immediate religious, social, and intellectual life. While theological inquiry must be informed by the long life of a tradition's commentary on revealed Scripture, its criteria for participating in that life belong to the time of a theologian's flesh-and-blood life on this earth, within the concrete movements and ruptures of lived salvation history. I assume that most of us live our lives under the influence of and in dialogue with circles of many others and that these influences and dialogues are manifested not only in articulable words but also through the less discrete ways that we act with one another and in the world. When possible, I therefore prefer to comment on the theologies of people I can talk with and observe over many years and in the context of various circles of fellowship—so that my words, too, are not only "my own." John Howard Yoder, of blessed memory, is the only nonliving subject of a chapter in this book, and I never met him in person. I made an exception in this case because his work provides a rare and critical test for the book's thesis. I have worked closely, moreover, with two colleagues whose lives have been deeply shaped by interactions with him: Stanley Hauerwas (the subject of one of the book's chapters) and Michael Cartwright (with whom I recently coedited a posthumous volume of Yoder's work and in dialogue with whom I have honed many of the theses of this book). Hans Frei, of blessed memory, was another personal acquaintance and is another major influence on my approach in this book. Within the bounds of this book's specific thesis, I believe his approach would fully complement that of George Lindbeck, so I do not devote a separate chapter to him.

Face-to-face inquiry of this kind tends to lead, as well, to communal inquiry. Since some of those I study face-to-face also study others face-to-face, lines of face-to-face study tend to extend into circles and small communities of inquiry.

Overlapping Communities of Christian and Jewish "Scriptural Reasoners"

The voice I speak in this book emerges from out of the discourses of several overlapping communities of Christian and Jewish scriptural reasoners (as well as of a community of Jewish, Christian, and Muslim scriptural reasoning). The Society for Scriptural Reasoning is the largest self-conscious subcommunity of these, bred by many of the theologians examined in this book and many of their students and colleagues, along with complementary groups of postliberal/postmodern Jewish text scholars and philosophers and some emergent groups of postliberal/postmodern Muslim text scholars and philosophers.[13]

These communities are essential, for several reasons, to the thesis as well as the method of this book:

- My interest in postliberal Christianity emerges out of work for over fifteen years in the Society for Textual Reasoning.[14] This community of Jewish text scholars and philosophers is dedicated to postmodern/postliberal theological issues that parallel many of the concerns of postliberal Christianity. Postliberal Christianity therefore interests us, first, as a source of insight and encouragement to support our own Jewish correctives to modernity.

- Jewish "textual reasoners" (as we call ourselves) have discovered, second, that postliberal Christians often show interests that are complementary to our own approaches to modernity. Our mutual interests have therefore spawned dialogue as well as study-of-one-another.

- These dialogues have given rise to the emergent community of Jewish-and-Christian studies we named the Society for Scriptural Reasoning, or SSR (and more recently the SSR was joined, for similar reasons, by a group of Muslim "Qur'anic Reasoners"). Christian members of SSR tend to promote the kinds of postliberalism and nonsupersessionism that are examined in this book. In this sense, the book represents one way that a representative Jewish member of SSR may study the work of SSR's Christian members.

- The book's thesis has implications for more than Christian theology. The way that postliberals couple their high Christology with nonsupersessionism may exemplify a shared hope of Jewish and Christian postliberal theologians: that they may affirm the particularity of their scriptural and liturgical traditions without at the same time delegitimating the other tradition of the One God; or, in the more precise terms of our approach, that, when he delivers his Word to the church and to the people Israel, God does not invoke the human logician's law of excluded middle and declare, "If the church is my covenant partner, then this one that is not the church cannot also be," nor "If Israel is my covenant partner, then this one that is not Israel cannot also be." How we humans are to understand this is another matter.

---

13. See appendix to this chapter, and the book's conclusion, for details about the society.
14. See appendix to this chapter for details about this society.

Appendix: Sources of This Study

My first self-conscious engagement with postliberal theology came in 1987, when I was on leave at Yale to do postdoctoral work in philosophy. I met George Lindbeck and Hans Frei, of blessed memory, for the first time (my previous doctoral work at Yale was only in philosophy) and was immediately eager to work with them extensively. That year—(1987–88)—the Bible scholar Moshe Greenberg happened to be visiting Yale as well. The Yale rabbinics scholar Steve Fraade was also in residence all year. I was very fond of these two scholars of Judaism and felt there might be some unexpected overlap among the ways these two Jewish and two Christian scholars addressed scriptural interpretation. I was happily surprised when all four agreed to meet together a number of times to explore the relation between Greenberg's "holistic" method of Bible interpretation and Frei's "realistic" method.

In this series of meetings, the four spoke and I asked questions and took notes. The result was powerful and formative for me: a discovery of different uses of the term *plain sense* by the group's Jewish and Christian members, but also of a surprising overlap among their strategies and hermeneutics of reading. I continued to examine the area of overlap through the next three years: what patterns of reading it included and excluded, what kinds of scholars shared and did not share in many of the included patterns. I published the results as *The Return to Scripture in Judaism and Christianity: Essays in Postcritical Scriptural Interpretation.*[15] This volume included an introduction in which I proposed a model of "postcritical" hermeneutics, with various Christian and Jewish submodels, and illustrative essays by scholars whose work I believed fit this model. The scholars of Christianity were Hans Frei (edited by Kathryn Tanner), George Lindbeck, David Burrell, John E. Smith (reading Jonathan Edwards), Paul Van Buren, and Stanley Hauerwas; the scholars of Judaism were David Weiss Halivni, Steven Fraade, Michael Fishbane, Moshe Greenberg, Jose (now Yosef) Faur, and Martin Buber (as interpreted by Steven Kepnes). I in no way presumed that the authors would accept being labeled ("postcritical" or otherwise), and many did not. But according to my own criteria, this group displayed to my satisfaction the overlaps I had suspected as well as various differences within the general frame.

I mention all this because the "postcritical" direction of this group anticipates what in the present volume I label *postliberalism.* I confess I do not like either label (my subjects of study tend to object in stronger terms, and indeed I wish the name of one's God or scripture should suffice). But I feel that in the short run such labels are helpful analytical tools for identifying some of the significant interpretive options available to current students and scholars

---

15. *The Return to Scripture in Judaism and Christianity: Essays in Postcritical Scriptural Interpretation,* ed. Peter Ochs (Mahwah, NJ: Paulist, 1993; repr., Eugene, OR: Wipf and Stock, 2008).

of theology and of scriptural hermeneutics. The goal in drawing similarities is not to announce a "club" but to discern distinct patterns of reasoning (and of interpretation and belief) and then to examine and test some of the consequences of different patterns. The results should help students and scholars make more informed judgments.

Jewish and Christian postcritical scriptural interpretation

To help readers of this book make more informed judgments, I shall narrate a little more about that initial group of postcritical scholars and then about the scholars who influenced my subsequent study of "postliberalism."[16] Greenberg introduces his holistic method as an alternative to the "two opposed axioms [that] have served, historically, for the interpretation of the Bible: one theological, the other historical-analogical."[17] He continues:

> The theological [axiom] maintains that without insight gained from faith in the divine origin of Scripture, its message cannot be understood. . . . Historically, the product of this axiom has usually been an exegesis that puts into Scripture what ought to be believed rather than attending to what it says. . . . [The historical-analogical] reaction, which reached fullest articulation in Ch. *vii* of Spinoza's *Theological-Political Treatise* (first printing, 1670), insisted that nothing but what Scripture itself revealed of its sense might be used in interpreting it. The ordinary process of induction, so fruitful for arriving at an understanding of nature, was . . . indeed the only legitimate basis of . . . interpreting the Bible. . . . Having voted for scientific universality, the interpretation of Scripture became linked in the 19th century to the career of literary-historical interpretation at large.[18]

Greenberg's alternative is

> a holistic interpretation, "emphasizing the organic or functional relation between parts and wholes" (Webster). As the religious person approaches the text open to God's call, so must the interpreter come "all ears" to hear what the text is saying. . . . For an axiom he [or she] has the working hypothesis that the text as he [or she] has it has been designed to convey a message. For if it does have design and meaning, they will be discovered only by effort expended to justify such an assumption.[19]

To guard against uncritical acceptance of established or ad hoc readings, holistic interpreters appropriate "something of the historical-analogical [axiom],

---

16. As presented in *Return to Scripture*.
17. Moshe Greenberg, "The Vision of Jerusalem in Ezekiel 8–11: A Holistic Interpretation," in *The Divine Helmsman: Studies on God's Control of Human Events, Presented to Lou H. Silberman*, ed. James L. Crenshaw and Samuel Sandmel (New York: KTAV, 1980), 143–63.
18. Ibid., 143–44.
19. Ibid., 145–46.

namely, the inference from the text itself of principles of its interpretation."[20] The goal is to reconstitute the range of possible significations inherent in the text at the time "when it had reached its present disposition."[21]

As presented in *The Eclipse of Biblical Narrative*, Frei's critique of the tradition of "mediating interpretation"[22] parallels Greenberg's critique of exclusive reliance on either the theological or the historical-analogical axiom. Frei argues that, emerging in the eighteenth century with John Locke and the latitudinarians in England and the Neologians in Germany, interpreters sought to mediate between the hermeneutical and theological extremes of an "orthodox dogmatism and [the naturalists'] radical skepticism about revelation."[23] The mediators tended to insist that belief in the factual occurrences reported in the Bible, especially those connected with Jesus, was indispensable. At the same time they either said or hinted broadly that the religious meaning or truth communicated through these events must be understood by reference to a content of religion and morality broader than the Bible.[24]

Frei argues that the mediators' mediation was illusory, because it retained the hermeneutical axiom that generated the dialectic of orthodoxy-versus-naturalism in the first place. This axiom is that the stories of Scripture point to their meanings referentially but that this reference is ideal, appearing in the text as a token of some universal truths of human experience. Mediators—like Greenberg's modernist readers—locate the meaning of Scripture in a reference that sits "behind" the biblical text in historical events, in authorial intention, or in a conceptual order to which only certain disciplined readers—like the mediators—have access.

Like Greenberg's, Frei's alternative is to relocate meaning within the biblical text in its intratextual context. Following Erich Auerbach, he sought to recover the premodern practice of reading the biblical text as "realistic narrative": a collection of stories that are "history-like," not because they point outside themselves to some antecedent realm of events, but because they portray lives lived in a way that is paradigmatic of Scripture's wisdom and that reshapes the beliefs and actions of biblical readers in accordance with that paradigm.

While similar, Frei's and Greenberg's responses to modernity are not identical. In our conversations at Yale, the subtle differences between them were played out in the two Christian and the two Jewish scholars' subtly different accounts of the "plain sense" of Scripture. As I recall our discussion, Frei and to some extent Lindbeck treated the plain sense of the biblical text *as* its meaning for the authoritative community of interpreters. Greenberg, gener-

20. Ibid., 146.
21. Ibid., 148.
22. Hans Frei, *The Eclipse of Biblical Narrative: A Study in Eighteenth and Nineteenth Century Hermeneutics* (New Haven: Yale University Press, 1974), 60–65, 118–33, 222–24, 255–69.
23. Ibid., 61, 62.
24. Ibid., 118.

ally supported by Fraade, on the other hand, tended to draw a distinction between the plain sense, or *peshat*, and the *performative* meaning of the text for any finite community of believers. The plain sense displays how the text fits together in its intratextual context; it does not legislate any behavior, per se, but sets the conditions for all legitimate readings and interpretation.

These differences between our Christian and Jewish interlocutors in no way inhibited the flow of mutually illuminating dialogue among the four. I therefore sought to identify the shared assumptions that made such dialogue possible alongside the differing assumptions. My first hunch—and the one that led me to propose a "postcritical" approach among both Jews and Christians—was that they shared something analogous to the hermeneutic I had first encountered in the rabbinic studies of Max Kadushin, my teacher at the Jewish Theological Seminary in the early 1970s.

Through a series of six books, published between 1932 and 1987,[25] Kadushin sought to describe the complex conceptual structure of rabbinic Judaism. In his view, the rabbinic exegetes provided the Jewish people with a hermeneutical context for uncovering the performative meaning of Torah for each generation. This meaning, he wrote, was embodied in the practice of rabbinic exegesis itself, so that the patterns of rabbinic exegesis formed the conceptual order of rabbinic Judaism. His central argument was that to observe this order is not to lay claim to any finite system of propositions but (a) to reread each rabbinic interpretation of Scripture[26] as illustrating how some particular set of rabbinic virtues—in his terms, rabbinic "value concepts"—speak to some particular setting of belief, action, and decision making; (b) to behold the rational order of rabbinic Judaism as an "organic" complex of such virtues, in which each virtue had an independent identity but all were interrelated, tending to mix and weave with each other when guiding particular types of belief, action, and decision making; and (c) to learn about the order of rabbinic Judaism not by constructing any formal conceptual model, but by observing all these particular rabbinic interpretations and examining recurring patterns in the ways the virtues interrelated. Primary lessons may be gleaned from the classical rabbinic literatures of Talmud and midrash, secondary lessons from the tradition of rabbinic commentary and decision making that continues through the present day. Kadushin offered his work as an alternative to those who impose extraneous conceptual schemes on rabbinic Judaism *and* those who deny that Judaism displays any conceptual order.

As illustrated in chapter 2 of this book, Kadushin's critique has striking parallels to Lindbeck's critique of interpreters who focus exclusively on the "propositional" or the "expressive" dimensions of scriptural meaning;

25. Kadushin's two most well-known works are *The Rabbinic Mind* (New York: Bloch, 1972) and *Worship and Ethics* (Evanston, IL: Northwestern University Press, 1964).
26. That is, each homiletic interpretation, or what Kadushin termed a "haggadic statement."

Kadushin's analysis of the virtues or value-concepts bears analogies with what Lindbeck labels a "cultural-linguistic" approach to understanding scriptural interpretation.[27] Lindbeck acknowledged these analogies explicitly in an essay he later contributed to a volume I collected, *Understanding the Rabbinic Mind: Essays on the Hermeneutic of Max Kadushin*. The title of Lindbeck's essay, "Martin Luther and the Rabbinic Mind,"[28] intimated the surprising connections we began to examine among certain strains in rabbinic and Christian thought—strains that anticipated and guided our "postcritical" conversations.

After the Yale seminar, I collected more samples of recent Jewish and Christian scholarship that might also bear analogies with Kadushin's approach, and, without ignoring differences, I sought to identify any patterns of inquiry that appeared in most of the samples.[29] My postdoctoral work at Yale focused on Charles Peirce's logical and semiotic studies, and I drew on those studies as resources for disciplined investigations of such patterns of inquiry. My first report on these Jewish and Christian scholars—*The Return to Scripture in Judaism and Christianity*—was therefore both sharpened and burdened by my work on Peirce (sharpened in logical precision and burdened with technical jargon). For example, I claimed that Frei's "mediating theologians" (as well as the interpreters criticized by Lindbeck, Kadushin, and Greenberg) all tended "to reduce biblical interpretation to a dyadic semiotic by assimilating the mediating or modern interpretant to its meaning or referent."[30] According to Peirce, we employ three different classes of sign in our efforts to represent three different types of relation in the world of experience: "monadic" signs represent simple or nonrelational qualities (such as the predicate "____ is red"); "dyadic" signs represent either–or and reactive relations (such as dyadic propositions defined by the transitive verb "____ hit ____," as in "Bob hit Bill"); and "triadic signs" represent genuinely interpretive and dialogic relations or relationships (such as accounts of how two subjects are interrelated by way of a third, as in "____ gave ____ to ____," for example, "Bob gave a gift to Bill," or as in "____ means ____ for ____," for example, "Isaac prefigured Christ in the New Testament"). In the last example, of "meaning," Peirce labeled one term the "sign or signifier per se" (Isaac), a second term the "object or meaning" (Christ), and a third term the "interpretant or context of meaning" (the

27. See chap. 2 in this volume.
28. George Lindbeck, "Martin Luther and the Rabbinic Mind," in *Understanding the Rabbinic Mind: Essays on the Hermeneutic of Max Kadushin*, ed. Peter Ochs (Atlanta: Scholars Press for South Florida Studies in the History of Judaism, 1990), 141–64.
29. Among the essays I wrote on Kadushin's method were "Max Kadushin as Rabbinic Pragmatist," in *Understanding the Rabbinic Mind*; "A Rabbinic Pragmatism," in *Theology and Dialogue*, ed. Bruce Marshall (Notre Dame, IN: University of Notre Dame Press, 1990); and "Rabbinic Text-Process Theology," in *Jewish Thought and Philosophy* 1, no. 1 (Fall 1991): 1–36.
30. Peter Ochs, "Introduction to Postcritical Scriptural Interpretation," in *The Return to Scripture in Judaism and Christianity*, 13.

New Testament). In these terms, my first claim about postcritical interpretation was that the mediating or modern interpreters treated biblical texts as
if their meanings were directly "seen" rather than interpreted, as expressed
by what I am labeling their "dyadic" claims that a given text A simply "is"
(or means) B. For the postcritical interpreters, to interpret a biblical text is
to be engaged in a three-part relation or performance, where a given text A
means (or displays) B (a belief or action or behavioral instruction) for (or to)
C (some "interpretant," which means some condition of knowing or acting,
some personal disposition, some tradition of belief, or some community of
action). In other words, the mediating or modern interpreters treat the biblical
text as if it had a referent independent of any particular interpretant.

My second claim was that postcritical interpreters examine the consequences
of modernity's dyadic interpretation of Scripture and find that dyadic interpreters tend to introduce into Western literature "a series of dichotomizations
that lack warrant in the biblical text—between text and ostensive referent,
between reference and performance, between the intrinsic meaning of the
text and its meaning for the contemporary interpreter; and between literary
and historical, subjective and objective, or scientific and religious methods
of biblical interpretation."[31] My third claim was that postcritical interpreters
locate signs of a "triadic semiotic"—a pattern of interpretive performance
and relation—within the biblical text, in particular "as it is read in the primordial communities of rabbinic or of Christian interpreters. This semiotic
provides general rules of interpretation that, when defined specifically for the
contexts of contemporary study, restore the truly mediational or relational
activities that are missing from modern practices of interpretation. Postcritical scholars define and refine these rules in ways that address" and repair the
specific cases of mediating or dyadic interpretation that concern them. "As a
result, there is no single, postcritical model of scriptural interpretation, but
a family of models each of which may be redescribed in terms of these three
stages of postcritical inquiry."[32]

"Yale" and "Cambridge" schools of postliberalism

While I was working on this "postcritical" project, I joined with a few close
colleagues in Jewish philosophy to form a practice of Talmudic and philosophic study we eventually labeled "textual reasoning." The study partners
were Robert Gibbs and Steven Kepnes and then also Laurie Zoloth and Yudit
Greenberg, then Elliot Wolfson, Aryeh Cohen, Shaul Magid, Jacob Meskin,
Nancy Levene, Susan Handelman, Eugene Borowitz, Michael Zank, and then
an expanding circle. Talmudic literature and traditional practices of Talmudic
study offered prototypes for the kind of study fellowship and dialogue we

31. Ibid. (with some edits added).
32. Ibid., 13–14 (with some edits added).

sought to introduce into our academic as well as denominational work and life. We addressed rabbinic legal argumentation as well as scriptural interpretation, and we sought to re-situate both within our interpretive and performative contexts. These contexts were shaped by a dialectic of postmodern and postcritical approaches to philosophy, textual hermeneutics, and religious social ethics. Our group was animated, in other words, by inner debates between what Paul Ricoeur termed a "hermeneutics of suspicion" and a "hermeneutics of retrieval." Both sides were joined by a single practice of table fellowship and study, by a conviction that only the text on the table before us framed an arena for our inquiries and debates, but that as long as we guarded the material (and lexical) integrity of that arena, this was the appropriate place and time for us to open heart and mind to one another, whether to voice ethical witness, philosophic critique, intertextual discovery, or prayer.

At about the time I completed *The Return to Scripture*, I met Daniel Hardy, of blessed memory, and David Ford at the Center of Theological Inquiry in Princeton (CTI). By the next summer, we began an extended three-way study of Scripture, philosophy, literature, and theology that after about three years generated a practice we called "scriptural reasoning." I shall say a little more about that practice in this book's epilogue. The topic for this section is what I learned about the British, or Anglican, side of postliberalism, which I first thought of as "the Cambridge school." My first impression of the theology I heard from Hardy and Ford (and a few of their Anglican colleagues visiting CTI) was that this was another kind of postcritical interpretation but somehow noticeably different from that of Frei and Lindbeck. During the next year, when I shared my observations with an expanding circle of either the Cambridge group or what I now thought of as the Yale (vs. Cambridge) school, I would be met with protests: affirming the content (if not the label) of what I attributed to postcritical thought, members of either side would claim that *they* belonged to this approach but the other group did not. I began to observe a pattern. Yale seemed to criticize Cambridge for being too tolerant of "naturalism," of extrascriptural "conceptualism," and of assimilating church and state. Cambridge seemed to criticize Yale for being too intolerant, in other words, too bound to language use in general and, more particularly, to the theological discourses of some single denomination, too "sectarian," and thus too inattentive to the church's responsibilities in the broader world, such as attending to the social, political, and economic orders and to the influences and needs of science and technology. A few theologians, like Ford and Hauerwas, seemed less willing to entertain these divides. In Ford's case, I thought this might have something to do with his training at Yale and with Frei and with his doctoral work on Karl Barth. Since many folks told me Hauerwas was "clearly sectarian," it took more time to guess that a strong pneumatology might contribute to his apparent gentleness toward "Cambridge." After learning more about Christian doctrines of the Spirit (perhaps by then I was already in conversation with Eugene Rogers on this topic as well as with the Anglicans), I began to invent the following account, which I have not yet abandoned: call it *a Jewish account of Yale and Cambridge, or why a bird has two wings.*

On either side of the pond, I came to believe, English-speaking postcritical interpretation is self-consciously trinitarian in the manner in which it seeks to repair the ills of mediating or modern or dyadic trends in the church. Either side tends, however, to place greater emphasis on one person of the Trinity rather than the others, and the choice reflects either side's sense of which person is most neglected by the mediating or modernist trends in its neighborhood. The Yale side, I believed, judged that the person of Christ is most neglected by modern movements in the American church, because these movements appeared at the time to be liberal or universalizing, naturalist, overly politicized, and wary of the scriptural canon and doctrine. Yale therefore tended to name Christ as agent of repair, which, I believed, meant that Scripture and *ecclesium* were primary sources of repair: practices of scriptural reading in service to *sola scriptura* and as informed by the life of each finite church community. Cambridge, on the other hand, judged that the Holy Spirit is most neglected by modern movements in the Anglican Church, and the British churches more generally—since (when I learned how better to read such things) a few of those I assumed were Anglican turned out to be British Methodists or Catholics and so on. The Spirit appeared to be neglected by movements that appeared at the time to be overly conservative or neo-orthodox, overly text-centered (on texts of Scripture and of intraecclesial doctrine and *regulae*), and insulated from the political and natural worlds. The church was threatened, at the same, by movements that rejected it because it appeared to display these traits. Cambridge therefore tended to name the Spirit as agent of repair, which, I believed, meant that sources of repair would appear in less predictable places, bearing less recognizable names, except for those already associated with the Spirit in ecclesial history.

This remains my account of what I now call the American and British wings of Christian postliberalism (having at some point come to favor *postliberal* as less ugly and misleading than *postcritical*). I consider them wings, because this bird or angel of repair must at times lean more to one side or the other to do its work; it could not fly at all, however, if either wing were broken by overuse or immobilized by atrophy.

Jewish and Christian postliberalisms

Soon after formulating our initial practice of scriptural reasoning, Hardy, Ford, and I invited a number of friends to join us in forming our first scriptural reasoning fellowship. The friends were Jewish and Christian scholars of Scripture, theology, and philosophy, and our fellowship was a study fellowship patterned somewhat after the study fellowships of Jewish textual reasoning.

Our practices were comparably shaped by Christian postliberal attentiveness to Scripture and community and to spiritual and theological reflection. The Jewish friends were all present or former participants in the textual reasoning circles, which fact encouraged my pursuing further ruminations on a broader movement (or tendency) of Jewish postliberalisms, with its persistent inner dialectic of postmodern suspicion and postcritical resourcement. The initial group of Jewish scriptural reasoners included the aforementioned Gibbs, Kepnes, Zoloth, Magid, and Cohen, along with more recent textual reasoners Randi Rashkover and Martin Kavka, and Cambridge colleague Diana Lipton. The Christian friends were all peers or students of the circle that emerged out of "Yale" and "Cambridge": Nicholas Adams, Michael Higton, James Fodor, Oliver Davies, Susannah Ticciati, Gavin Flood, Ben Quash, Rachel Muers, Tom Greggs, William Young, Chad Pecknold, and more recently Jason Byassee, Jeff Bailey, and Ben Fulford. From the start, we planned for the new Society for Scriptural Reasoning to be a society of Abrahamic reasoning, including Muslim as well as Jewish and Christian Scriptures and scholars. By our third year, 1996, we gathered enough Muslim participants to inaugurate our full plan. I will describe the results in this book's epilogue.

In the years since these early gatherings of scriptural reasoning, I have continued to engage in dialogue with ever-expanding circles of Christian postliberal theologians, testing and reshaping my images of the patterns of postliberal interpretation. Along the way, my primary interlocutors and guides have been the authors collected in this volume, along with their students. In addition to these authors, the most influential guide has been Kendall Soulen. I will conclude this appendix with an overview of what I learned from him. First, of many additional influences, I will name those who, along with the previously mentioned scriptural reasoners, have appeared more often in my footnotes on postliberal Christianity. They are Eugene Rogers, already mentioned as a source of my understanding of pneumatology and of Yale hermeneutics, a longtime colleague and coteacher in Christian and Jewish theology; Robert Wilken, a longtime colleague, a coteacher in classic Christian and Jewish commentary, and a major postliberal scholar in the classic patristic sources; David Burrell, a longtime interlocutor in postliberal approaches to philosophic theology and theo-politics; Scott Bader-Saye, whose significant work on the doctrine of Israel in the church continues Lindbeck's and Soulen's postliberal openings;[33] James Buckley; Gregory Jones; James Fodor;[34] William Placher, of blessed memory; Jay Carter; Douglas Harink, whose work will be cited often in the

---

33. See Scott Bader-Saye, *Church and Israel after Christendom: The Politics of Election* (Boulder, CO: Westview, 1999). I comment on Bader-Saye's postliberal nonsupersessionism in Peter Ochs, "Judaism and Christian Theology," in *The Modern Theologians*, 645–62 (at 652–53).

34. A major resource on postliberalism is James Fodor, "Postliberal Theology," in *Modern Theologians*, ed. Ford and Muers, 229–48. In the epilogue, I draw at length on Fodor's description of postliberalism.

following chapters; Bruce Marshall;[35] Michael Cartwright;[36] William Elkins; Kris Lindbeck; and more recently all the members of the Scriptural Reasoning Research group that met at the Center of Theological Inquiry from 2003 to 2006 (Stacey Johnson, Clifton Black, Rusty Reno, Ann Astell, Kevin Hughes).

In *The God of Israel and Christian Theology*,[37] Soulen introduced his argument for postliberal nonsupersessionism: the plain sense of the entire Scripture teaches that God's identity as the God of Israel is inconceivable apart from the election of the Jewish people (which Soulen identifies with "the people Israel"). Nevertheless, according to Soulen, Christian theology has traditionally assigned to God's interaction with Israel a propaedeutic function within the economy of sin and redemption, serving only to foreshadow God's redemptive work in Christ. This has a doubly unfortunate result. On the one hand, Christians have understood the distinction between Jew and Gentile as a means to the end of Christ's redemption, after which Jewish existence would lack any meaning in God's plan. On the other hand, Christians have tended to make the biblical theme of "creation and consummation" subservient to the biblical theme of "redemption from sin"—rendering Israel's story as one of incomplete redemption from sin. The cumulative result of this misreading is a semignostic distortion of Christian thought that "rejects gnosticism at the level of ontology but not at the level of covenant history."[38] Against this reading, Soulen recontextualizes the economy of sin and redemption within the larger economy of creation and consummation, described now in terms of the canon-spanning story of God's election of Israel as a blessing for the nations. The end and fulfillment of God's consummating work is not to annul the difference between Israel and the nations but to bring both into the "mutual relatedness" and interdependence that is called *shalom* (after Job 5:22–24; Ps. 29:11; 128).[39] Within this context, Soulen depicts Christ as the climactic recapitulation of God's earlier work of redemption on Israel's behalf, for the sake not only of Israel, but also of the mutual blessing between Jew and Gentile.[40]

35. See Bruce Marshall, "Do Christians Worship the God of Israel?" in *Knowing the Triune God*, ed. James Buckley and David Yeago (Grand Rapids: Eerdmans, 2001), esp. 236. I comment on Marshall's postliberal nonsupersessionism in Peter Ochs, "Judaism and Christian Theology," in *Modern Theologians*, ed. Ford and Muers, 645–62 (at 649–51).

36. My work on John Howard Yoder (see chap. 4 in this volume) has been guided throughout by Cartwright. See John Howard Yoder, *The Jewish-Christian Schism Revisited*, ed. Michael G. Cartwright and Peter Ochs (Grand Rapids: Eerdmans, 2003). I comment on Cartwright's postliberal nonsupersessionism in Peter Ochs, "Judaism and Christian Theology," in *Modern Theologians*, ed. Ford and Muers, 645–62 (at 653–55).

37. Kendall Soulen, *The God of Israel and Christian Theology* (Minneapolis: Augsburg Fortress, 1996).

38. Ibid., 110.

39. Ibid., 131.

40. This paragraph is reproduced from Ochs, "Judaism and Christian Theology," 650–51.

In more recent writings, Soulen extends his argument for the "economy of consummation" by exploring the consequences of a nonsupersessionist doctrine of the Trinity. Consistent with both Lindbeck's and Jenson's more recent work, Soulen suggests that the Tetragrammaton, YHVH, remains the name of the God to whom Jesus prays. He says that while Christians have always affirmed in some fashion that "YHVH is the Triune God," they have interpreted the two parts of the affirmation according to the scheme of Old Testament/New Testament, with the result that God's identity as YHVH is left in the past. In place of this, he proposes that Christians interpret the confession "YHVH is the Triune God" according to the logic of "Jesus is the Christ," with the result that both parts of the affirmation speak to past, present, and future.[41]

41. This paragraph is reproduced from ibid., 651.

Part 1

American Protestant Postliberalism

2

George Lindbeck and the Church as Israel

In 2002, I asked George Lindbeck if what we label the "current movement of Christian postliberalism" represents a "reformational movement," and, if so, in what sense. He answered yes, that postliberalism renews the efforts of the Reformers to call the one church to the living Word that should guide it, to reform the Catholic Church and thus prepare the way for the reunification of the church that should be a primary goal soon, in this world and not merely in some distant world to come. He answered, furthermore, that postliberalism revisits and renews the Reformers' call of *semper reformanda*. The goal of reformation is not a onetime correction to be identified simply with the sixteenth-century Reformers' actions or with any effort to renew those particular actions. As they recognized, reformation should be a perennial practice of the church. In every generation, every community within the church should regard itself as standing in direct witness to the life, death, resurrection, and ascension of Jesus Christ, and thereby as under the direct judgment of that witness.[1] This means, says Lindbeck, that the church is always subject to reform. The criterion guiding reform is the incarnate life of God in Jesus Christ, as disclosed in the Gospel witness and as interpreted by way of the evolving history of church doctrine *up through today*. "Today?" I asked. Yes again, he answered, postliberalism may represent a movement of reformation even more radical than that of the Reformers. While renewing the Reformers' doctrine of *sola scriptura*, and of the Pauline doctrine of *sola gratia* before that, postliberalism

---

1. I am consciously wording this phrase as if it were analogous to the biblical injunction placed into the Passover Haggadah: that in each generation, every member of the people Israel should regard himself or herself as having come directly out of Egypt.

calls for a reexamination of how the church shall be guided by its reading of the Gospel witness. Integral to the Gospel witness is the Gospels' reading of the Old Testament, and integral to that reading is the place of Jesus Christ within the salvation history of the people Israel. For Lindbeck, postliberalism calls Reformational churches to greater fidelity to the gospel as scriptural witness, at once, to the life of Christ and the election of Israel.

In this chapter, I introduce Lindbeck's postliberalism as his effort to serve the directive *semper reformanda* within the life of the contemporary church. To ground this introduction, I must turn of course to the themes of his most widely read book, *The Nature of Doctrine*, which remains at the center of academic discussions of postliberal theology. At the same time, there are several reasons why I treat Lindbeck's noted book a little differently from the way it is often treated in such discussions. I am, for one, selectively interested in how Lindbeck's postliberalism engenders his nonsupersessionism, and I therefore place disproportionate weight on this modest feature of his study of church doctrine. For two, I think that both liberal and antiliberal critics of *The Nature of Doctrine* misrepresent Lindbeck's "cultural-linguistic alternative" as a substantive theological claim rather than as a heuristic that is merely instrumental to his scriptural reasoning. Encouraged by other recent postliberal studies,[2] I position this scriptural reasoning back in the center of Lindbeck's argument. In the process, I downplay the role of Wittgenstein's philosophy of language in this argument, and where some philosophical tools are needed, I suggest that Lindbeck's case is better served by Charles Peirce's semiotics. For three, I believe that the theological force of *The Nature of Doctrine* can be measured only if that book is read within the greater corpus of Lindbeck's writings, from before and after the book's publication. Most of these writings belong within the discipline of church history, and most display an underlying concern with relations between the Reformation churches and Roman Catholicism. I therefore believe that Lindbeck's interest in doctrine is best understood—as he reminds us in the introduction to *The Nature of Doctrine*—as an instrument of his ecumenical studies. And I believe that the focus of Lindbeck's *reformational work* is first and foremost repairing the great schisms of the church. This repair begins now with Catholic–Protestant relations, and next it should turn to relations between the Western and Eastern churches; but both now and in the eschatological future, it must also include relations between the church and the people Israel.

For all these reasons, I want to reexamine Lindbeck's study of doctrine as a study of how the church repairs the fissures (the errors, heresies, or sins) that periodically threaten its unity. In his reading, the phenomenon of doctrinal

2. There are many examples, among them Douglas Harink, *Paul among the Postliberals* (Grand Rapids: Brazos, 2003), and George Lindbeck, *The Church in a Postliberal Age*, ed. James Buckley (Grand Rapids: Eerdmans, 2002).

formation is both a *signal* that the church is threatened by some particular fissure and a *means* through which the church seeks to protect itself, then and forevermore, against *this kind* of fissure. I will suggest that for Lindbeck the theological significance of this signal is that the time between the times remains a heterogeneous time: not, that is, a time of living simply in the perfection of Christ's having-come, but a time in which the visible church struggles to enter into that perfection. For Lindbeck, the theological significance of the means—which is the process of doctrinal formation—is that God alone repairs such fissures, through the activity of the body of Christ, as guided by the revealed Word of Scripture. The question of the hour is how to understand this scriptural guidance. For Lindbeck, the process of doctrinal formation is also the process through which the church becomes a community of redemptive readers. When the church sins, it reopens itself to the Word of Scripture as vessel of Christ's correcting and redeeming presence. It then hears that correction as a new instruction about how *not* to interpret Scripture, and it deposits that instruction into the tradition of the church in the form of a doctrine.

And what of today? Based on the broader corpus of Lindbeck's work, on recent discussions with him, and on a good bit of Jewish philosophic reasoning and interpretive play, I propose the following model of Lindbeck's postliberal reformation:

- The goal of this reformation is to repair the schism that both prompted and has been maintained by the Reformation.
- It rereads the Word of Scripture in search of guidance for this repair.
- It receives this guidance as a set of instructions about how not to misinterpret Scripture and thus how not to misinterpret the Reformation doctrine of *sola scriptura*.
- This set includes instructions about how not to avoid reading the Gospel narrative of Jesus Christ as a perennial reading of Old Testament narratives of the people Israel.
- These instructions lead postliberal reformers to identify modern liberalism and modern antiliberalism as Christian heresies.
- Postliberal reformers discover that when freed from both these heresies, they can conduct their redemptive readings of Scripture in a way that draws on the needed resources of both their academic disciplines of study and their ecclesial/theological work in the church.
- Postliberal reformers discover that once they have separated themselves from these heresies, their redemptive reading of Scripture is no longer obstructed. This reading now appears as a contemporary form of the kind of reading they can also rediscover in the hermeneutics of the early church and in later readings that continue that hermeneutics, such as those of Gregory of Nyssa, Thomas, Luther, Calvin, and Barth.

- At the same time, in order to protect this hermeneutical practice from error, postliberal reformers discover that they need to add to it the new doctrine of nonsupersessionism.
- In this way, postliberalism also reforms the Reformation doctrine of *sola scriptura*.

The best way to introduce this model is, I believe, to illustrate its implications for four major axes of inquiry: ecclesiological, scriptural, methodological, and nonsupersessionist. Risking redundancy, I redescribe these axes three times. In the first round, I simply introduce the "primary foci of work" on each axis. In the second round, I examine Lindbeck's method of inquiry along each axis, explaining how the axes of "scriptural" and "nonsupersessionist" inquiry are joined together through much of Lindbeck's inquiry. In the third round, I describe how through each axis Lindbeck seeks to remove obstructions to the reformational work of the contemporary church. After this third round, this chapter concludes with a general model of postliberalism as a reformational practice. I have composed the rest of this book around this model: reading subsequent "postliberal" thinkers as those who extend the model or contradict it (and to that degree "leave the postliberal fold") or offer recognizable alternatives to it.

The Four Axes of Lindbeck's Postliberal Inquiry

Ecclesiological inquiry

This is the main focus of all of Lindbeck's work: historiographic study of ecclesial history, theological study of the meaning of church unity, and what I will call reformational (or reparative) study of the crisis of disunity in the church. Lindbeck's focal concern is how to repair the schism between Roman Catholicism and the Reformation churches.

> The ultimate hope [of the Lutheran Church] is . . . that all Christians in a given place will be joined in a fully united local church, but that is a final rather than proximate goal. . . . Lutherans increasingly understand themselves, just as they did in their sixteenth-century beginnings, not primarily as a church or group of churches, but as a reforming movement within the wider church which was unjustly expelled from the Catholic communion. . . . The reason for Lutheran existence now, and not only at the time of the Augsburg Confession in 1530, is to bring the Reformation understanding of the Gospel first to the Latin church of the West and then to the Church universal.[3]

And, this, as I understand it, remains the goal of Lindbeck's postliberalism.

3. Lindbeck, "The Reformation Heritage and Christian Unity," in *Church in a Postliberal Age*, 70.

Ecumenism is the theological purpose that animates Lindbeck's many years of scholarly writings in ecclesial history. The postliberal theological writings for which he is now best known represent a relatively small and, in that sense, minor component of his academic work. *The Nature of Doctrine* is, of course, the best-known expression of this theological work. Since so much postliberal discussion is about modernity, many readers of that book overlook the fact that its primary focus remains ecumenism. In short, as both ecclesial historian and theologian, Lindbeck is primarily worried about persistent disunity in the church, and his primary constructive effort is to contribute to its reunification. While this chapter, like the rest of this book, will address the integral connection between postliberal theology and nonsupersessionism, it is important to recognize that Protestant postliberals are concerned first about repairing their relationship to Roman Catholicism and only second about repairing their relation to the people Israel. That does not mean that they "put the Jew second" as an ethical concern. It means, instead, that we should not forget the inner-ecclesial movement that animates postliberalism and that may show itself, in the end, to be a primary source for postliberal care for the Jews as well.

Scriptural inquiry

This axis displays the source of Lindbeck's noninstrumental practice for serving the *ecclesium*. Scripture is the church's reformational guide. As witness to the Word of God made incarnate in human flesh, the Christian Scripture is witness against the forces in every age that work against that Word and thus against the unity of the church as the body of Christ. In order to be "catholic" and "ecumenical," a reformational "view of the Church must be biblically warranted. It must, above all, be consistent with the total witness of scripture as this centers on Jesus Christ."[4] Lindbeck thereby reaffirms the Reformational doctrine of *sola scriptura*, but as the basis for reformation, which means as source of the criteria that should guide every generation's efforts to remove obstacles to ecclesial union. *Sola scriptura* is inseparable from the other two "Reformatory 'solas': the solus Christus, [and the] sola fides (which includes the sola gratia)."[5]

Nonsupersessionism

The primary focus of Lindbeck's theological project is the unity of the church. His surprising discovery is that the church can neither repair its relation to the academy nor achieve ecclesial unity until it repairs its relation to the people Israel. The primary reason for this is hermeneutical and theological,

---

4. Lindbeck, "The Church," in *Church in a Postliberal Age*, 147.
5. Lindbeck, "Reformation Heritage and Christian Unity," 60.

not ethical. As we have seen, the second axis concerns refinding Scripture as guide to the church's reformational work. The third axis concerns refinding the people Israel as ground of the church's study of Scripture. This means, in sum, that in order to repair the Catholic–Protestant schism, postliberal reformers need first to repair a hermeneutical schism between the Gospel story of Jesus Christ and the Old Testament narrative of the people of Israel.

Methodological inquiry

This fourth axis of Lindbeck's work is instrumental. Lindbeck discovered that postliberal reformers have a methodological task to perform before they can turn their attention directly to the goal of repairing the Catholic–Protestant schism: to overcome the dyadic divisions that generate antagonisms rather than dialogue between modern academic and church-based theological approaches to Christianity. For Lindbeck, this dialectic distorts inquiry within each of these approaches as well as between them. Within the church, there is an unproductive dialectic between liberal and antiliberal Christianities; within the academy, there is an unproductive dialectic between positivism and relativism. Lindbeck finds, moreover, that these two sets of dyads share a single logical form and perhaps a single ideology: they emerge out of the perennial modern conflict between tradition and individual autonomy, or what often goes by the name of "faith versus reason." In response, Lindbeck's postliberalism offers a way to reintroduce disciplined reasoning into ecclesial discourses, while also reintroducing the concerns of theology into the disciplines of the academy. The modern church has come to fear the academy, and the modern academy has come to fear the church, but Lindbeck's postliberal inquiries should be as acceptable to the church as to the academy.

The Four Axes as Methods of Inquiry

Ecclesiological

Lindbeck's study of ecclesial history is purposive, reparative, and transcendental. The study is purposive because it serves Lindbeck's primary concern, which is the unity of the church as the body of Christ. I call it reparative because he recognizes that the church is not unified. The purpose of his work is to contribute to repairing the disunity in the church, in particular the persistent schism between Reformation and Roman Catholic Christianity. In calling Lindbeck's work transcendental, I refer to the *way* he uncovers practices that he believes would help the church repair this schism. Lindbeck's method is to observe in what sense—however limited—the church *already acts* as if it were unified, then to ask what conditions make this action possible. He reasons, in other words, from actual effect to possible cause, and in that sense his approach is comparable to Kant's transcendental method. He does not ask the question *in general*, however, but only as a way of responding reparatively to a particular crisis—the church's crisis of disunity. In this sense, Lindbeck's transcendental inquiry is not only reparative but context-specific. Peirce introduced the term *pragmatism* to denote this kind of reparative, transcendental inquiry. I therefore find it helpful to label Lindbeck's method *pragmatically transcendental*.

Scriptural

Within his postliberal practice, Lindbeck's scriptural inquiry serves a reformational rather than a formational purpose: providing criteria for his efforts to repair the reformational work of the church. In this way, it joins his nonsupersessionist inquiry as part of his corrective response to the reparative methodologies of the contemporary church (see below, *d*).

Methodological

The question is, how is it possible today to conduct pragmatically transcendental inquiry? Lindbeck's methodological discovery is that two methodological schisms obstruct the capacity of postliberal scholars to carry out the reforms that the church needs today. The most general schism is between the academy and the church as sources of methodology. Under the paradigm of modernity the academy has come to represent a "value-neutral," "scientific," "positivist," "objectivist" approach to inquiry. The church has come to represent a "sectarian," "confessional," "subjectivist" approach. Under the modern paradigm, the academy itself has spawned a schism between several dyadic pairs of methods, among them *Geisteswissenschaften* versus *Naturswissenschaften*, historiographic versus literary/rhetorical science, and, more recently, positivist versus hermeneutical, and within the hermeneutical, furthermore, a priori versus a posteriori, and within the latter, ostensive versus readerly-collusive. For Lindbeck, the method of inquiry needed for postliberalism's reformatory work cannot be divided between any of these alternatives. This means its method must be fully of the church and fully of the academy, fully of "what is" and fully of "our interpretative relation to what is."

This does not mean, however, that Lindbeck's methodology will be a way of *mediating between* the various alternatives of modernity. To seek such mediation would be to construct some mediating third. Rather, Lindbeck's primary methodological discovery is that God alone mediates between the kinds of dyads that typify modernity. However well intentioned and however ingenious, efforts to "repair the breach" through strictly human construction will inevitably repeat the errors they are intended to resolve. That, in fact, is the signal characteristic of modernity: not to have schisms (for this is a feature of all of humanity's sinful history), but to have forgotten the "method" God gave us to repair them. This "method" is nothing other than prayer: our God-gifted capacity to cry to him and confess, "We suffer. We are divided. We have sinned! But we now recognize that we cannot repair this sin, this division, and this suffering without your gracious presence. Help us!" The basis of Lindbeck's method is to identify how the relationship of prayer can enter the reparative work not only of the church but also of the academy, and in a way both church and academy can receive without abandoning their separate identities and inner disciplines.

Nonsupersessionism (emerging out of a reparative hermeneutical history)

In place of a theoretical argument against what he considers the errant modern methods of church and academy, Lindbeck offers what we might label, variously, a "reformational rereading," a "pragmatically transcendental critique," a "Christian genealogical reform," or a "reparative hermeneutical history" informed by Christian reformational practices. All these terms are meant to summon our attention to a kind of inquiry that would include steps like these:

- Reformational inquiry begins with concerns about how certain practices obstruct the reformational life of the church—in this case, certain obstructive schisms within the modern church and academy.

- Analogous to the way that a transcendental (Kantian) analyst reasons from acts or effects of judgment to hypotheses about the possible conditions or cause of the judgment, the inquirer then raises hypotheses about the *historically* antecedent conditions or causes of these problematic practices. This form of historically or genealogically transcendental analysis may also be termed *pragmatic*, since it speculates about the past in order to repair specific practices in the present and future. It may also be termed *a reformational rereading*, since it rereads these schisms within a narrative of ecclesial history and rereads them for the sake of reforming them according to the ideals of ecclesial unity.

- In Lindbeck's case, the analysis moves from these modern schisms as effect to late medieval/early modern disruptions of Christian narrative theology as proximate condition, to prior Christian supersessionism as its functionally ultimate condition. This is the source of Lindbeck's surprising conclusion: replacement theology obstructs the scriptural inquiry that is intrinsic to the reformational practices of the early church.

- As a reparative practice, the analysis ends with a characterization of how we might now imagine these practices if they were performed in accordance with various claims of early Christian thinkers *and* without the obstructive consequences of replacement theology. This characterization integrates the evidentiary work of a church historian with the constructive proposals of a latter-day reformer.

In sum, Lindbeck's diagnosis is that the modern schisms within church and academy can be traced, genealogically, to errant practices of scriptural inquiry; his prescription is to identify and remove the errant practices so that Christian scriptural inquiry can once again do its reformational work on behalf of the unity of the church. There are therefore two correlative aspects to Lindbeck's reformational historiography: a critique of supersessionist scriptural inquiry and a proposal for recovering the nonsupersessionist rule of early Christian hermeneutics.

1. The critique of supersessionist scriptural inquiry. Lindbeck's reformational claim provides the central topic of this book: in order to repair the methodological schisms they inherit, postliberal reformers must first, on one level, repair the aboriginal schism between the church and the people Israel. I must specify that this is only "on one level," because Lindbeck does not intend here something eschatological and theo-political. His discovery is a hermeneutical one. It is that the study of Scripture alone provides both the academy and the church its means of "prayerful" access to the reparative presence of God.

In short, the hermeneutical argument goes as follows. The modern church is unable to protect itself from the various dyads of modernity, because it has lost touch with the reparative practice of scriptural interpretation that is the basis of soteriological work in the early church.[6] To recover that practice is, following Barth, to re-situate Christian theology as a practice of reading the gospel. The gospel that one rediscovers in this way is, as Barth noted, a gospel that is itself a practice of rereading the Old Testament narrative of the salvation history of Israel. This rereading is not a onetime event, however, as if we could say, "Well, the gospel already reread the Old Testament, and by simply rereading the New Testament, we will learn the meaning of the Old." This rereading is instead a perennial event of returning to the plain sense of Israel's story and rediscovering every day what it now means in light of the Gospel narrative of Jesus Christ.

Whether or not it is accompanied by statements about Israel's enduring covenant, this practice of rereading implies that the story of Israel remains integral to Christianity's scriptural witness. The story of Israel remains open as well. It remains open in the sense that no contemporary Christian reader

---

6. In the introduction I drew a distinction between appropriate and inappropriate contexts for drawing either–or distinctions (pp. 6–17, 25–26). I labeled the appropriate ones "binaries," for example, distinguishing in an either–or way the alternatives of "helping" versus "not-helping" a person in danger. I labeled the inappropriate ones "dyads," for example, drawing either–or divisions between political tendencies such as "liberalism versus conservatism" or between genres of academic inquiry such as "materialism versus mentalism."

knows beforehand all that any text of the Old Testament means. Of course, every such text acquires its meaning by way of its relation to the Gospel witness, but that relation cannot be fully defined before each event of reading. Each reading must return to rediscover the Gospel witness, to rediscover the plain sense of the Old Testament as it will be reread in light of that witness, and thereby to disclose the message of Scripture (Gospel and Old Testament) for this day and this context of reading.

Rediscovering the message of the Old Testament, the Christian reader also rediscovers the place of Israel in salvation history. This means that the place of Israel is not yet fully defined. While the Christian reader must say that "Jesus Christ is the Messiah of Israel," no reader knows before the event of reading everything there is to say about the meaning of that sentence now, in the present moment of reading.

2. Restoring nonsupersessionist patterns of scriptural inquiry. I will at this point let Lindbeck speak for himself about the nonsupersessionist hermeneutic that, in his view, animates the early church in its formative years and provides criteria for restoring the church's reformational practices today.

a. The apostolic writers read the Bible of the Jews as Scripture. "The Bible of the Jews, usually in its Septuagint version, was . . . the whole of the Bible for the writers, the so-called apostolic authors, of what later was canonized as the New Testament. . . . Because it was for the first generations of Christianity the only written word of God, [the Old Testament] was the privileged source of the terms, concepts, images and models which they used in understanding Jesus and the Jesus movement to which they belonged. Nor should the influence of contemporary Judaism be forgotten. . . . They assumed that the Old Testament was what was believed and practiced in the Judaism of their own day in which all of them at first had been reared."[7]

b. The anti-Marcionite church identified itself with the story of Old Testament Israel. "It has been [too] little stressed in modern times that the story of Israel as the uniquely Chosen People functioned in the premodern anti-Marcionite ecclesial mainstream as an integral part of the gospel. Jesus's uniqueness was inseparable from that of Israel's Messiah, and Christians thought of themselves as the continuation of the elect people and were deeply influenced both negatively and positively in their relation to non-biblical religions by the Old Testament's communal memories and narratives."[8]

c. The life of Jesus Christ was the climax and summary of Israel's history, but this life thereby provided a hermeneutical rule for reading the Old Testament, not for replacing it.

---

7. Lindbeck, "The Gospel's Uniqueness: Election and Untranslatability," in *Church in a Postliberal Age*, 147.

8. Ibid., 225.

In the early days . . . , it was not a different canon but a distinctive method of reading which differentiated the church from the synagogue. . . . As time went on, an explicit rule of faith and an enlarged canon came into existence. . . . Thus, a certain way of reading Scripture [OT] . . . was constitutive of the Christian canon and has, it would seem, an authority inseparable from that of the Bible itself. To read the Bible otherwise is not to read it as Scripture but as some other book. . . . In light of this interrelation of canon, hermeneutics and the sensus fidelium, the Catholic/Protestant arguments about whether Scripture or the Church [is] prior seem futile. Israel's Scriptures, read in the fashion we have noted, were constitutive of the communities which produced an enlarged canon in order to reinforce their identities against Gnostic, Marcionite and other groups which called themselves Christian. . . . Even though these Old Testament–oriented churches soon became overwhelmingly Gentile in membership, they developed a Christian analogue of the Jewish sense of being a single people. . . . Thus the priority of the Bible seems as plausible as the priority of the Church."[9]

d. *The early church was not, at the same time, innocent of serious errors in the way it read the Bible and in the way it lived according to its reading. The church sinned, just as Israel sinned.* "This is not to deny that the Bible was also grossly misinterpreted: classical hermeneutics is no guarantee of Christian faithfulness."[10]

e. *Nonetheless, the classic pattern of hermeneutics remains the most reliable source for the church's reformational practices.* "The classical biblical hermeneutics as I shall describe it was implicit from the beginning of all mainstream premodern traditions of interpretation. Its main features were articulated already by Irenaeus, but are present in Christian readings of the Old Testament before there was a New Testament, and are in part derivative from the techniques of scriptural interpretation embedded in the Tanakh as these are described by Jewish biblical scholars such as Michael Fishbane.[11] Furthermore, this classic pattern did not disappear with the modern age, even though it did lose scholarly and theological standing and was abandoned by both liberals on the left and fundamentalists on the right. Liturgies retain the pattern, and homiletics continues to be influenced by it. In the United States, if I may judge by the example of some of the students I had had, it remains particularly powerful in black churches."[12]

f. *There are four principal characteristics of this classical hermeneutics.*[13]

• "*Canonical interpretation* [was] a collection of highly diverse literature read as a single work."

9. Lindbeck, "Scripture, Consensus and Community," in *Church in a Postliberal Age*, 204–5.
10. Ibid., 206.
11. Michael Fishbane, *Biblical Interpretation in Ancient Israel* (Oxford: Clarendon, 1985).
12. Lindbeck, "Scripture, Consensus and Community," 234.
13. All the following quotations are from Lindbeck, "Gospel's Uniqueness," 235–36.

- *"Interpretation was guided by what can perhaps best be likened to rules of grammar*, . . . embedded in the speech and practices of the community quite apart from conscious knowledge of their existence, but . . . at times articulated in church doctrine and theological reflection."
- *"Narrative* [had a special place in the] construal of the biblical outlook. . . . The framework consisted of a transhistorical narrative stretching from the beginning of time to its end."
- "The narrative structure is enfleshed by figuration (or, to speak with medieval elaborateness, by typology, tropology and anagogy). In such figural interpretation, analogy and metaphor function both to unify and extend the plain sense."

Lindbeck adds this significant note:

In conjunction with the other features we have mentioned, figuration turns the Bible into a cross-referencing, interglossing semiotic system which can be used even now . . . to assimilate by redescription all the worlds and world views which human beings construct in the course of history. Such grammatical features as the four principal ones just enumerated can remain unchanged even while the lexicon expands indefinitely. . . . Inexhaustible semantic novelty is compatible with syntactic continuity. . . . The Bible is thus its own interpreter, not as bare text but in its classic construal. Although it was the Reformers who first formulated this dictum in opposition to late medieval claims to the contrary, it was implicit in catholic practice from patristic times. The heretics erred, so it was regularly argued, not because they failed to submit to ecclesiastical authority but because they ignored the *scopus* of Scripture as the communally edifying and canonically unified Word from God.[14]

The Four Axes as Ways of Removing Obstructions

Releasing three sets of obstructed possibilities

Let us take stock of what I have suggested so far about Lindbeck's inquiry. According to my model, Lindbeck is an ecclesial historian who conducts his work both within the academic discipline of historiography *and* as contributing to timely, reformational work within the church. The four axes of his inquiry may be re-examined according to the order of this reformational work. From this perspective, the first axis is ecclesiological, because our model suggests that the ultimate purpose of this work is to reunify the church. The second axis is then methodological, because our model suggests that the major obstacle to this reunification is a methodological schism within modern Christian theology. Modern Christian theologians seek but fail to mediate differences

14. Ibid.

in the church, because their efforts at mediation only replicate these differences in new forms. The third axis would be scriptural, because our model suggests that God alone mediates differences within the church and that God is present as mediator in the redeeming Word of Scripture. Lindbeck's non-supersessionism would then constitute the final axis, since the church fails to hear God's redeeming Word if it reads the Gospel message other than as a perennial rereading of God's Word to Israel.

In these terms, Lindbeck's work in the first axis of inquiry depends for its success on his work in the second axis, and then on the third and fourth. In other words, relations between Roman Catholicism and Protestantism can be repaired only once there is some reformation of the church's relation to Israel. In this section, we therefore review the four axes in reverse order, as four contexts for releasing obstructions to the reformational work of postliberal Christianity.

Why is this process described negatively, as "releasing obstructions," rather than positively, as disclosing certain postliberal claims? The answer appeared earlier, in my last description of Lindbeck's "primary methodological discovery: that God alone mediates between the kinds of dyads that typify modernity . . . [while] efforts to 'repair the breach' through strictly human construction will inevitably repeat the errors they are intended to resolve." The end of postliberalism is to help release the mediating presence of God in the scriptural Word and to help release the mediating presence of that Word by removing various obstacles the church has errantly let stand in the way of a reformational reading of Scripture within the life of each Christian community. Human beings encounter the divine Word directly (postliberalism is neither nominalist nor conceptualist), but for that very reason, individual human judgments (of perception, or of cognition more generally) are not adequate representations *or* presentations of that encounter. (If they were adequate, then human encounter would be mediated *through* such judgments and thus no longer im-mediate, or direct. Otherwise put, individual cognitions display a selective, or abstractive relation to the Word as encountered.) Theologians are therefore unable to offer positive judgments about how the Word would in fact mediate. But they can—and must—offer negative judgments about the way that various human constructions *obstruct* the Word's mediating presence. Based on their observations of previous human practices, they can, furthermore, offer positive-sounding judgments about the forms of human behavior that may very well remove or at least lessen these obstructions. That is to say, they may recommend disciplines of social, intellectual, and religious practice that may leave the Word more room to do its work, as it were.

1. Scriptural inquiry: releasing replacement theology (supersessionism) as an obstacle to recovering the Gospels as Scripture. For Lindbeck, the Reformation's doctrine of *sola scriptura* is a necessary but insufficient guideline for completing the work of reformation. It is necessary because the redemptive reading of Scripture provides *the* definitive criterion for ecclesial repair. It is insufficient because it does not by itself protect reformers against certain errors that could possibly arise in the Christian practice of reading Scripture alone, obstructing the very reformational goals of *sola scriptura*. For Lindbeck, this protection is provided by postliberalism's *hermeneutical rule and proto-doctrine of non-supersessionism*. As he has put it most clearly in a 2002 interview, "Christian efforts to forget Israel and thus replace Israel's covenant are co-implicated in Christian efforts to read the Gospel narrative of Jesus Christ independently of reading the Old Testament narrative of Israel, and such readings are the foundation of Christian efforts to read the Gospel narrative as it were a collection of determinate propositions or determinate rules of behavior, rather than as Scripture. *The primary goal of postliberal reformation is to help the church recover its practice of reading the Gospel narrative* as *Scripture.*"[15] As Lindbeck observes Protestant practice since the Reformation, the doctrine of *sola scriptura* does not itself protect reformers against errant tendencies to identify "Scripture itself" *exclusively* with historical-critical readings of the Bible *or* with fundamentalist-literalist readings of the Bible. He argues that adding a proto-doctrine of *nonsupersessionism* would provide this protection.

I have already illustrated key features of this proto-doctrine above, under the heading "Restoring nonsupersessionist patterns of scriptural inquiry."

2. *Methodological inquiry: releasing the dyads of academic positivism versus Christian fideism and expressivism versus propositionalism, as obstacles to recovering the reformational work of Christian scriptural theology.* Lindbeck's comments on this axis of inquiry represent the most well-known and widely cited feature of *The Nature of Doctrine*—in particular, his typology of "experiential-expressivist," "propositionalist," and "cultural-linguistic" theories of religion and of doctrine. Readers would do well, however, to re-situate this typology more broadly within Lindbeck's reformational postliberalism, as well as within his more recent reparative hermeneutical history of the following obstacles to ecclesial reformation.

    a. Reductive uses of historical-critical Bible scholarship. "The first step toward retrieval [of classical scriptural hermeneutics] is to reject the biblical scholars' version of the philosophic category mistake of evidentialism, i.e., the proviso that traditional readings must be supported by historical-critical evidence in order to be accepted. On the contrary, it is wrong for those seeking to work within a tradition to reject its beliefs and interpretations simply because there is no critically available evidence for them. To follow this rule consistently could not help but produce paralysis if for no other reason than that everything we do, say, and think is dependent on inherited background convictions of unknown or unknowable evidential grounding. On the other hand,

15. Interview with the author, November 2002.

it is equally important to take seriously evidence *against* a traditional interpretation. One must weigh the critique and examine the challenged interpretation to see how important it is for the web of belief. When the role of the challenged interpretation is not crucial and especially, as in the case of supersessionism, if it can be shown to conflict with centrally important strands within the tradition, then historical criticism wins."[16]

b. *The historically antecedent loss of the narrative meaning of Scripture.* Reinforcing Hans Frei's argument in *The Eclipse of Biblical Narrative*, Lindbeck argues that historical reductionism is a derivative source of obstacles, conditioned by a late medieval/early modern tendency to forget the narrative meaning of Scripture.

Recent work in the history of exegesis suggests that the crucial change in the modern period has been such neglect. "In realistic narrative of the biblical type, the identity and character of the personal agents with whom they are chiefly concerned (viz. God and human beings) is enacted by the plotted interaction of intention and circumstance. This is the Bible's chief device for telling its readers about themselves, their world, and their God."[17] Lindbeck argues that this loss is directly ecclesial as well as hermeneutical:

> Loss of narrative meaning weakens the glue which holds the canon to-gether and makes difficult the typological use of the biblical stories to shape the present communal and personal identity of Christians. . . . When narrative meaning is neglected, the entire classic interpretive pattern crumbles. It appears that narrative meaning was neglected because it was misunderstood. . . . Instead of asking what the biblical narratives tell about God and human beings and how they are to be used in shaping life and understanding reality, the primary question became whether they are accurate reports of the events of which they tell. The narrative meaning of the stories was confused with their factual (scientific and historical) meaning, and was thereby lost.[18]

c. *Factualist reading replaces scriptural reading.* To replace the now missing relational trustworthiness of narrative, church scholars sought the cognitive certainty of epistemological factualism. Two sorts of factualists emerged—"inerrantists and historical critics":

> The inerrantist tendency was to insist that everything which could by any stretch of the imagination be supposed to be a factual assertion must be so interpreted and accepted as accurate; while historical critics used the

16. Lindbeck, "Gospel's Uniqueness," 243.
17. Lindbeck, "Scripture, Consensus, and Community," 208.
18. Ibid., 208–9.

text as a source of data for reconstructing what could (by the general, and never entirely stable, standards of the day) be plausibly taken to be the originating events, personalities or situations.[19]

In the context of this genealogy, Lindbeck's previous typology of "experiential-expressivism" and "propositionalism" may be reread as identifying two competing models of inerrantist evidence: cognitive and extracognitive judgments of truth.

d. *Modern science, fratricide, and the loss of communal certainties are antecedent conditions for the neglect of narrative meaning.* This claim points to the area of greatest intersection, speculation, and controversy among the leading genealogies of modernism and its errors, including those of Alasdair MacIntyre, John Milbank, Charles Taylor, Richard Bernstein, and Richard Rorty. Joining the fray, Lindbeck and Frei offer speculations that I could not begin to explain, let alone defend, within the limits of this book. Instead, I will simply note the general direction of their argument and its place within my thesis. Citing Frei's work, Lindbeck situates Christianity's turn away from narrativity within the same transitional epoch that gives us early modern nominalism and Cartesian foundationalism. The setting is comparable to what Bernstein dubbed the condition of "Cartesian anxiety": a time of loss of trust in the wisdom and authority of various parenting institutions and of a somewhat frantic searching about for suitable replacements. In Lindbeck's version, "confessional rivalries culminating in wars of religion, on the one hand, and the mentality associated with the development of modern science, on the other, each played a part. The two phenomena are interconnected. Communal certainties were undermined by Christian fratricide . . . and many turned for firm foundations to individual reason and experience."[20] To attend to narrative meaning is, in other words, to trust in the educt of long traditions of reading, and the age of Cartesian anxiety lacked such trust.

e. *Supersessionism is an antecedent condition for removing protections against the loss of narrative meaning.* However modestly it is placed within the structure of this chapter, this claim represents the single most telling piece of evidence we have about the correlation between Lindbeck's postliberalism and nonsupersessionism. According to claims *a–e*, one might conclude that the doctrine of *sola scriptura* should suffice as a corrective against the loss of narrativity in Christian theology: "return

19. Ibid.
20. Ibid., 209–10.

to reading Scripture, and Christian identity will be recovered and the compensatory need for factualism will be removed!" Attending to claim *d*, one must add, to be sure, that such a "return to Scripture" is conceivable only when it is reinforced by certain conditions of communal and epistemological stability. Given such conditions, however, *sola scriptura* would still appear as a sufficient directive to attend to the Bible as it presents itself (narratively, in large part) and not as an instrument of one's a priori schemes or rationalisms. Joining together his genealogy of modernism and his history of Christian hermeneutics, Lindbeck comes to the following, strikingly different conclusion. If *sola scriptura* directs one back to the practice of classical Christian hermeneutics, then yes, it is *possible*, on the basis of that practice, to remember and live according to the narrative meaning of Scripture. It is, however, *not always likely* that one will do so, since the classical practice along with the guiding doctrines of both the early church and the Reformation will not specifically protect one against the temptation to supersessionism. And whatever its ethical implications, supersessionism carries with it one demonstrably heretical hermeneutical implication. By devaluing the scriptural story of Israel, it directs the Christian reader's attention away from the intrinsic theological value of the Old Testament text in its irreducibly many layers of meaning. And it thereby directs the reader's attention away from the story that Jesus read and with which he identified, away from the story that the apostles read in Jesus's name, and away from that dimension of the Gospel narrative that is visible only in the way the living Gospel rereads the Old Testament narrative, not once, but again and again every day. This activity of rereading displays the redemptive energy of Scripture with singular force. Without this dimension, scriptural reading loses much of its capacity to guide the reformational work of the church.

So portrayed, supersessionism does not by itself *cause* intra-Christian fratricide or any of the other challenges of the early modern period. The damage comes instead in the way it removes a significant dimension of Scripture's reformational capacity. Supersessionism does not hurt so much by the bad story it tells as by the redeeming story it *fails* to tell, and more precisely, by the redeeming *practice* it inhibits and obstructs. In this regard, the reformational force of Lindbeck's reading of Scripture has less to do with the semantic "contents" of the scriptural narrative and more to do with the performative force and model of that narrative as an activity of redemptively rereading another narrative. Read in supersessionist fashion, the Gospel narrative lacks dimensions of its own narrativity. Supersessionist reading may therefore contribute to the loss of narrativity, or at least obstruct its reclamation.

In sum, Lindbeck's urgent critique of supersessionism is offered first and foremost as a hermeneutical and christological claim, not an ethical one. It is offered out of concern to restore the redemptive force of the Gospel narrative of Jesus Christ, *not* out of ethical concern for Christian treatment of the Jews; this ethical concern comes as well, but as anagogical confirmation of the hermeneutical claim. In arguing against supersessionism, Lindbeck is not therefore asking Christians to deny their fundamental Christology "for the sake of the Jews"; he is urging them to restore the full scriptural basis for their classical Christology, and only as a consequence of that, to discover that they may also have done something good for the Jews.

3. *Ecclesiological inquiry: releasing the dyads of* sola scriptura *versus* traditio *and of academic study versus ecclesial work as obstacles to recovering doctrinal formation as the reformational activity of the unified church.* We now approach the telos of Lindbeck's postliberal inquiry. He believes that by restoring the patterns of classical scriptural hermeneutics and adding to them the rules of nonsupersessionism, contemporary Christians will be able to recover scriptural inquiry as the source of guidance for ecclesial reformation. To engage in this reformation means both to reaffirm *traditio* and to remove from it any obstacles to the work of ecclesial unity, whose motto is *semper reformanda*. The schisms between Western and Eastern and Protestant and Catholic churches do not constitute *obstacles* to this work, since they are intrinsic to the process of salvation history itself. Instead, they are the primary *subjects* of the work, which is to examine them, understand them, and introduce processes of transforming them from schisms to mere differences within the one church. In the present epoch, there are three primary obstacles to this reformational process. One is a confused holdover from Protestant–Catholic debates: a tendency to dichotomize *sola scriptura* and *traditio*. The ongoing work of reformation presupposes and affirms both of these principles: *traditio* refers to the body of the church itself in its concrete historicity; *sola scriptura* refers to the criteria for guiding reformation within that body.

The second obstacle is a confused holdover from the secularization of the Christian university in modern Europe. This is a tendency to dichotomize academic and ecclesial (alias "confessional") inquiries as if the one were of no use to the church and the other were of no use to the academy. The disciplines of academic inquiry make essential contributions to the work of ecclesial reformation without compromising the integrity of either the academy or the church. For Lindbeck, one goal of postliberalism is to define relations between the academy and the church, preserving their distinctness but without the mutual suspicion and mood of self-protection that currently divides them. Lindbeck argues that historical-critical study and ecclesial historiography make essential contributions to the work of ecclesial reform, including the postliberal efforts to reintegrate *traditio* and *sola scriptura*. It is counterproductive to define these academic studies as somehow competing with the church as opposing sources of authority and knowledge.

The third obstacle is the failure of most modern and contemporary Christian theologies to take responsibility for removing these first two obstacles.

For Lindbeck, postliberalism comes to remind Christian theologians of their reparative task: "When exegesis fails to connect past and present, theology takes up the task. . . . Narrative and typological interpretation enabled the Bible to speak with its own voice in new situations. . . . Now, however, the interpretive direction is reversed: the biblical message is translated into contemporary conceptualities."[21]

Lindbeck's claim cuts two ways. Any crisis in the church will reflect some interruption in the capacity of scriptural exegesis to serve as guide to the work of reformation. Theology emerges in these moments of interruption as the engine of repairing the *process* of reformation; postliberalism is the face of Christian theology in such a moment of interruption today. Theology fails, however, when it mistakes its reparative function for one that defines the foundations of the church, or when it mistakes its work of repairing scriptural inquiry for the reformational work of scriptural inquiry itself. Christian theologies tend to fail in both these ways today, and postliberalism offers criteria for identifying these failures and repairing them.

Lindbeck concludes that when Christian theology recovers its reparative task, it will turn its attention to restoring appropriate working relations between academic and ecclesial inquiry and between ecclesial tradition and scriptural inquiry. These restorations will enable the church to recover its reformational work on behalf of ecclesial unity. *The primary engine of this work is the process of doctrinal formation as the means through which the church in each generation discovers its own errors and uncovers how, in witness to the gospel message, they should be addressed in this particular time.*

Conclusion

Postliberal inquiry as a reparative theory and practice of doctrinal formation

In this concluding section we revisit our point of departure, asking how Lindbeck's theory of "the nature of doctrine" may be re-situated within the context of his postliberal project of reformation. In light of our previous discussion, and within the limited perspective of my *Jewish* philosophic reading, I read his work as an effort to reform contemporary Christian theory and practice of the process of doctrinal formation. This effort could be summarized as generating the following five theses:

- *Semper reformanda*: the purpose of all reformational work is to contribute to the unification of the church, both economically in the unity of the churches and immanently in the unity of the body of Christ.

21. Ibid., 211–12.

- Church doctrines are signposts of moments of radical reformation in the history of the church, moments when the church is called to repair obstructions that have arisen to its perennial work of unification.
- The reformational process of doctrinal formation is a process of rereceiving the Gospel's witness to the life of Christ. It is thus an ecclesial process of rereading Scripture, locating in that rereading the criteria that will guide historically specific activities of doctrinal formation and reformation.
- Postliberalism has proto-doctrinal force as a reformation of the practice of reading Scripture in the contemporary church.
- Nonsupersessionism is a corollary of this reformation.

I conclude this chapter by reviewing some of the implications of these theses. These are my own (potentially idiosyncratic) speculations, gained by interpreting Lindbeck's recent writings according to my interviews of him, my readings of the other postliberal theologians examined in this book, and some of the central dialogues I have recently heard between Jewish and Christian postliberal theologians. I have redacted these implications as if they were subtheses of the previously listed "five theses of Lindbeck's postliberalism." To restate a note from this book's introduction: these subtheses are actually drawn from my readings of all the postliberal Christian theologians, but I apply them here first to Lindbeck's work, since both this book and my own studies of postliberalism began with his work. I return to this list in subsequent chapters, reshaping it each time to reflect the specific emphases of each particular theologian.

A. *Semper reformanda*: the purpose of all reformational work is to contribute to the unification of the church, both economically in the unity of the churches and immanently in the unity of the body of Christ.

1. The church represents the body of Christ as the unity of all empirical churches in each epoch of salvation history; in that unity, the inherited *tradition* of the church represents the collective "ways of life" of the church as it imitates the life of Christ.
2. Within *this* dispensation of Christ, which means within this time between the times, the church does not achieve perfection, which means that perfect unity is not achieved in the body of Christ. The source of that unity is perfectly given in the Gospel witness to the life of Christ; but in its creaturely humanity, the visible church is not fully adequate to the life of Christ within this dispensation. This is, instead, the time of the church's movement toward the full unity of the life of Christ. *Semper reformanda* calls the church to its perennial work of unifica-

tion, continually reforming its tendencies to disunity. Within this dispensation, these tendencies are never absent from ecclesial tradition or practice.

3. I will use the term *general reformation* to refer to the church's perennial work of reforming its inherited traditions and practices according to criteria of ecclesial unity that are displayed in the Gospels' witness to the life of Christ. Scripture displays the criteria that guide general reformation, and I will use the expression *reparative reading of Scripture* to refer to the process through which these criteria are displayed. This is not just any reading of Scripture, but a specific process of scriptural inquiry on behalf of general reformation. This sort of reformation represents the church's regular process of self-criticism, rather than any radical event of disruption and change: the way that ecclesial leaders regularly review and reform the daily practices of the empirical churches in light of the Gospel witness.

B. **Church doctrines are signposts of moments of radical reformation in the history of the church, moments when the church is called to repair new obstructions to its perennial work of unification.**

4. Sometimes, unfortunately, obstacles arise within the process of general reformation itself. The emergence of such obstacles marks times of serious disruption in the capacities of the churches to reform themselves, which means in their capacities to engage successfully in the reparative reading of Scripture. Such times call for what I will label *specific reformation*, or processes of radically reforming how the churches practice their reparative readings of Scripture. Scripture, once again, displays criteria that will guide specific reformation but through a process of inquiry that differs from the reparative reading of Scripture. I will add the expression *reformational reading of Scripture* to refer to the process through which these new criteria are displayed. There is no limit or end to the process of general reformation within this dispensation: the community of churches can always be brought closer to the unity of Christ. Each process of *specific* reformation has a finite end, however, since this is the finite work of repairing specific obstacles that have arisen to the perennial work of general reformation in a particular time.

C. **The reformational process of doctrinal formation is a process of rereceiving the Gospels' witness to the life of Christ. It is thus an ecclesial process of rereading Scripture, locating in that rereading the criteria that will guide historically specific activities of doctrinal formation and reformation.**

5. The goal of specific reformation is to adopt specific church doctrines
   that would remove new obstacles to the process of general reformation.
   In this sense, the process of specific reformation is a process of doctrinal
   formation.
   a. The purpose of doctrine is to restore the capacity of the church to
      engage in the reparative reading of Scripture. Doctrine achieves this
      purpose by identifying how the church may remove specific obstacles
      to general reformation that have arisen in a given time.
   b. While the process of doctrinal formation addresses specific obstacles
      that have emerged at a particular time, this process also contributes
      to the church's overall witness to the gospel of Christ within this
      dispensation. In order to account for this contribution, postliberal
      theologians may want to construct theories—like those offered below
      (see item 7a, b, c)—about the relation between scriptural reading
      and both general and specific reformation.
   c. Any postliberal theory we adopt should redescribe the great events
      of decision making in church history, from the Council of Nicaea
      to the fifteenth- and sixteenth-century Reformation to Vatican II, as
      processes of specific reformation and thus doctrinal formation. As
      will be explained through the postliberal theories of 7a, b, c, these
      processes are strictly "negative" or inhibitory—analogous to what the
      rabbinic sages called "forming fences around the Torah." This means
      that, despite appearances, *church doctrines are not to be taken as
      "first-order" or plain-sense narratives, but rather as narrative-sounding
      formulations of rules for how to avoid misreading the scriptural
      narratives.* In these terms, Nicaea does not reduce the Triune God
      to identities that can be captured in certain discrete propositions;
      instead, it indicates how *not* to misread the relation of Father to Son
      to Holy Spirit as the Gnostics and Arians misread it. This means that
      doctrines offer instructions on how to avoid committing heresies that
      have actually emerged in church history as obstacles to the reforma-
      tional work of the church. The need for such instructions could not
      have been foreseen before the appearance of such heresies (perhaps
      because the scriptural revelation does not come to reduce human
      freedom a priori, or because the creaturely limitations of the visible
      church cannot be predicted before they are manifested).
6. In the terms of item 3a, the Reformation of Luther and Calvin was a
   process of doctrinal formation that addressed specific obstacles that
   emerged in early modern Catholicism to the process of general reformation. Among these were the practice of justification and the relation
   of tradition to the reformational reading of Scripture. To remove these
   obstacles, the Reformers formed or reformed and promoted such doctrines as *sola scriptura*, *sola gratia*, and *sola fide*.

D. Postliberalism has proto-doctrinal force as a reformation of the practice of reading Scripture in the contemporary church.

7. In the terms of subthesis 6, postliberalism represents another Reformation, introducing processes of doctrinal formation that revisit and reform the specific reformations of Luther and Calvin. This is a reform of *sola scriptura* in particular, to articulate lessons learned since the Reformation about how not to read Scripture in the service of reformation. These are the lessons I am summarizing in Lindbeck's five theses A–E and subtheses 1–8.

As noted under item *5b*, this is the appropriate place within my summary to illustrate the kinds of theory that postliberal theologians may want to construct to account for the different roles of scriptural reading in general and specific reformation. I shall illustrate two kinds: a semiotic theory and a more homiletic and heuristic account.

a. *To design* a semiotic theory, it is helpful to distinguish at least four levels of scriptural reading:

- *Plain-sense reading*: the eclectic use of philological, grammatical, rhetorical, narratological, and historical-critical inquiries, as well as reception theory, to augment traditional readings of the intratextual story line of the Old and New Testaments. Since Scripture includes epistolary, poetic, legal, psalmic, parabolic, and other forms of texts in addition to narratives, plain-sense reading may also be said to refer to the intratextual meaning of each text of Scripture in its literary context within the scriptural canon. Since both reparative and reformational uses of Scripture exceed the limits of plain-sense reading, it may be most helpful to provide a strictly semiotic definition of the plain sense as *the material sign-vehicle of all subsequent readings*: that is, as the literal arrangements of verbal signifiers that display any level of interpreted meaning to a given ecclesial community of scriptural readers and interpreters. As a material sign-vehicle, the plain sense may be further defined as *the set of conditions for signifying a certain or circumscribed plenum of possible meanings*. I call this a *plenum* since an indefinite series of meanings may be included within it. While the magnitude of the series is unforeseeable, it may be called *circumscribed*, since the plain sense is also determined in such a way as to reduce possible meanings. These meanings are neither reduced to one set nor opened to an infinite number of meanings. In the helpful terms of Charles Peirce's logic, the biblical plain sense is not fully determined but remains intrinsically *vague*, which means that it displays a potential series of particular meanings, each of whose precise characterizations will become clear only on some future occasion.

- *Formational/traditional (tropological) reading*: the ritualization of scriptural reading as a tradition-determined practice for the religious formation of individuals and the ecclesial formation of communities or groups. This is the dimension of reading that most commentators on *The Nature of Doctrine* associate with Lindbeck's "cultural-linguistic" approach to Christian religion. For them, Lindbeck reads scriptural texts as coded rules for religious and communal formation and maintenance. I would suggest that this is indeed one dimension of Lindbeck's reading, according to which Scripture is enacted through the society-, culture-, and language-specific behaviors of a historically specific community of the church. Here, one may say that Scripture is "performed" rather than "read." Performance means action in the actual world, and this implies selection, choice, and "determination": the reduction of Scripture's plenum of possible meanings to just those meanings that are convertible into rules or patterns of behavior in the world (including all publicly visible liturgical, social, and economic/ecological behavior). In subthesis 1, I identified this dimension with the church as a time-specific "way of life." This also means, however, that subtheses 2–8 address additional dimensions of the church and of scriptural reading.
- *Reparative reading (as a form of typological reading)*: rereading Scripture as a source of more recondite but still publicly articulable guidelines for repairing the kinds of errors that regularly appear in the life of the churches. This rereading represents what we might also label a self-reflective dimension of formational/traditional/tropological reading. Correcting the patterns of behavior that are displayed in the "ways of life" of a particular church, reparative reading must reduce the plenum of possible, plain-sense meanings to those few that would stimulate patterns of effective, reparative action. In terms of the theory of "pragmatically transcendental analysis" I offered earlier (pp. 41–44), reparative reading uncovers rules of repair through a regressive analysis that speculates about the hermeneutically and historically antecedent rules of behavior that we may view as "causes" or "transcendental conditions" of the practices we now consider problematic. This is a pragmatic rather than ontological exercise. Its goal is to recommend readoption of these "causes," now in a contemporary context, as conditions for understanding and then repairing the church's problematic practices. The efficacy of these recommendations must be tested in actual practice: if the problematic practices are repaired, then the recommendation has strength; if the practices are not repaired, then new or modified "causes" must be uncovered and recommended, and so on.

    Some apparent ecclesial errors, for example, may result from conflicts among ecclesially sanctioned practices of behavior ($a, b, c \ldots$).

Guidelines for repairing these conflicts must come from a regressive reading that identifies another level of practices that may function as causes of the problematic practices $(a_{-1}, b_{-1}, c_{-1} \ldots)$. Further conflicts among such "causes" themselves would be repaired through yet another level of regressive reading $(a_{-2}, b_{-2}, c_{-2} \ldots)$, and so on, from levels x_{-1} through x_{-n}. These regressive levels must have some limit, n, which we may identify with the limits of a given ecclesial "way of life" in its historical specificity. I suggest we identify "reparative reading" with "typological reading," because it may be helpful to identify level-n reading with a presentation of the most general scriptural types that define a given way of life: for example, the type of the church as this or that understanding of Christ, or of ecclesial thinking as this or that view of wisdom, and so on.

- *Reformational reading (as a form of anagogical reading)*: rereading Scripture as a source of recondite guidelines for repairing apparent obstacles to the general process of reparative reading itself, which means to an entire church's efforts at general reformation. Such obstacles appear only rarely in ecclesial history, and conscious efforts to remove them represent extraordinary movements of change, or what I label "specific reformation." This kind of radical reformation is stimulated by the judgment of an expanding circle of theologian-reformers that a given church, or aggregate of churches, has exhausted its capacities for removing some set of errors in its everyday life and thus for successfully promoting its general reformation. This is a judgment, in other words, that some entire series of reparative readings has failed $(a_{-1-n}, b_{-1-n}, c_{-1-n} \ldots)$ and that it is therefore time to introduce reforms in the deepest reparative dimensions of some ecclesial way of life: the elemental ways that some church, or aggregate of churches, practices its typological readings of Scripture.

   Reformational reading purports to revisit Scripture's plenum of possible meanings as ultimate "cause" of each system of scriptural types that informs given ways of life in the church. (This is the sense in which reformational reading is anagogical, since it purports to return in some fashion to the "fullness" and thus mystery of Scripture's semiotic generativity.) From out of that plenum, it then rereads its epoch's obstructed practices of general reformation as if they were effects of errant tendencies in some system of scriptural typology. It then purports to reread that system as an errant effect of some aboriginal region of scriptural signification ("possible meaning"). Guided by that region as "cause," or transcendental condition of scriptural practice, it then recommends specific ways of reforming the errant system of typology. This recommendation constitutes what I have called a *process of doctrinal formation.*

As noted earlier, doctrines are *negative* constructs. This means that they do not *determine* (and thereby undo the intrinsic vagueness of) the meaning of Scripture; such determination is strictly the business of formational/traditional/tropological practice. It means, instead, that doctrines identify which specific meanings of Scripture are henceforth to be considered heretical and thus out of bounds as sources of future formational practice. In these terms, the goal of reformational reading is, on the evidence of some rare crisis in ecclesial history, to identify some region of scriptural meaning that should now be deemed heretical and excluded from acceptable sources of ecclesial practice. This region was previously unseen and unforeseeable, except for the evidence of history, which means the appearance of actual obstructions to the ongoing work of general reformation.

> *b. A more homiletic and heuristic account*—The plain sense of Scripture offers the church an indefinitely deep source of guidelines for its everyday life. But the church has discovered that Christians cannot out of their own freedom adopt those guidelines in any possible way they please. As with the sins that exiled humanity from the Garden of Eden, the church has found that its capacities for error exclude its membership within this dispensation from unrestricted use of the plain sense. Without infinite regress, these exclusions could not, by definition, be included in the plain sense itself any more than Adam and Eve could be told, before their sin, that and how they would sin. Only salvation history discloses in unforeseeable ways which ways of reading must be excluded because they have now been seen to engender certain observable errors or sins (or certain obstructions to the work of repairing such errors and sins).

Each major crisis in the church thereby delimits the range of freedom that can and should be permitted in performing and thus delimiting the meanings of Scripture. In his grace and bounty, God grants the church utter freedom initially to live its life in service to the revealed Christ, analogous to the freedom God granted Adam and Eve to live in service to his creative bounty. When Adam and Eve failed, God restrained their behavior in ways that would obviate their worst potential trespass. The process of ecclesial doctrinal formation works, analogously, to rein in the church's freedom in ways that would hopefully obviate the worst potential consequences of misreading Scripture.

For Lindbeck, the history of the church has shown that in its present dispensation the people of Christ are not fully prepared to make the perfection of Christ fully visible in the life of the church. There is no way to see how ready they are beforehand. They must first be sent off into the world with the blessing "Follow me!" And until they freely follow, it will not be apparent what specifically should not be allowed them in their following. Each crisis of the church constitutes a particular display of the incapacity of Christians, in this dispensation, to follow Christ freely without doctrinal limitations.[22]

　　c. Scriptural inquiry in general and specific reformation—My semiotic account suggests ways of distinguishing the reparative and reformational practices of reading Scripture, such as considering the former a species of typology and the latter a species of anagogy. I do not yet have a clear take on how Lindbeck or other postliberals would articulate these differences, but I will speculate that they might build on the following contrasts.

- *Reparative readings in general reformation*: These readings may draw on the discrete narratives of both Testaments, not in their plain sense but topologically, as those narratives disclose time-specific directives for reform.
- *Reformational readings in specific reformation*: These readings may draw on the hermeneutical relations that bind one Testament to the other and, within each, one text to its hermeneutical antecedents— the ways, for example, that the Sermon on the Mount interprets, or hermeneutically binds itself to, the Decalogue; or Deuteronomy to Exodus; or John 17 to Exodus 40.

E. Nonsupersessionism is a corollary of the postliberal reformation.

　　8. As a process of specific reformation, postliberalism introduces a reformational reading of Scripture that concludes with the following recommendation: that the Reformation doctrine of *sola scriptura* is not a sufficient source of ecclesial reform until it is augmented by a doctrine of *nonsupersessionism*. This doctrine excludes as heretical any reparative reading of Scripture that is guided by supersessionist typologies (such as that "Israel is none other than the church") and any reformational reading of Scripture that is guided by a supersessionist hermeneutic.[23] The latter refers to any of the following family of prohibited readings:

22. Which means without the Christian analogue to what rabbinic Judaism calls a "fence around the Torah." Supersessionist Christians have for centuries misinterpreted rabbinic law as a positive instrument of "justification" rather than as a "fence," that is, a means of inhibiting behaviors that have shown themselves to be obstacles to Israel's efforts at reformation.

23. Postliberalism would prove ineffectual if it adopted a form of nonsupersessionism that removed Christianity's own uniqueness and robbed Christians of sufficient reasons to devote their lives to Christian service in particular. For this reason, I have worried that a doctrine of "nonsupersessionism" might seem to leave Christianity too beholden to Judaism: as if, following Franz Rosenzweig's formulation and, to some degree, also Paul van Buren's, Christianity simply offered Gentiles the goods that Jews had and that Gentiles could not otherwise acquire. I wondered if a formulation like "soft supersessionism" might remove Christian triumphalism without also removing the "religious goods" that are unique to Christianity. At the moment, I

- reading the Gospel narrative, or the New Testament more generally, as a self-sufficient Scripture, rather than a necessary part of the canon that includes the Old Testament
- within such an inclusive canon, reading the New Testament as displaying the "fulfillment of the Old Testament," in the sense that one reads the Old Testament, again and again, only in order to understand how it is replaced by the Old Testament, or how Christ replaces Israel, and so on
- reading verses or narratives or textual units of both the Old Testament and the New Testament as if they carried discrete meanings apart from their relations to the other verses and texts of both Old Testament and New Testament; and reading them hierarchically, so that Old Testament texts had intrinsic value but less than New Testament texts (with similar hierarchies within each text)
- reading any scriptural text as a source of reformational guidelines without at the same time reading that text as displaying its guidance *through the way that it interprets or is interpreted by and joins together with another and potentially every other scriptural text.*

There are many reasons for this prohibition, but one reason is central: *supersessionist hermeneutics precludes the possibility of reformational reading itself*! This is because supersessionist hermeneutics does not merely install "the church" as, clearly and distinctly, "what God wants" in place of "Israel." In so doing, *it also installs a way of reading that confuses the practice of formation with that of reformation,* thereby reducing the church to some historically particular "way of life," and a way that no longer has available to it the capacity for radical criticism, repair, and reform. Such a church would no longer have available to it the capacity to read Scripture as the living Word of God. Without that capacity, only God knows what such a church would have available to it.

---

believe my semiotic account might offer a better alternative: that nonsupersessionism is simply prohibited on the levels of reparative and reformational reading, but not necessarily or always from plain sense and formational/traditional readings. This means that it would not necessarily be heretical for individual churches to claim that there are *some ways* in which Christianity repairs some overall errors or inadequacies in Israel's covenant, or for individual church members to act out some sense of Christian superiority. The permissible contexts and conditions for such "soft supersessionism" would be determined by reparative and reformational readings that were themselves wholly nonsupersessionist: that is, that separated themselves from supersessionist typologies and hermeneutics (precluding any effort to "trump" rabbinic hermeneutics by way of christological hermeneutics). If my reflections in this note sound a bit cloudy, that is because they are; I do not yet understand how much a people of flesh and blood needs the self-affirmation of some sort of superiority and how far it can extend hospitality to others without at some point forgetting its creatureliness and claiming for itself the kenotic powers of God.

3

Robert W. Jenson

THE GOD OF ISRAEL AND THE FRUITS OF TRINITARIAN THEOLOGY

Ye shall know them by their fruits" (Matt. 7:16): for Robert Jenson, what Matthew says of the words of prophecy should apply no less to words of theology. Theology is not about some timeless truths of being, but about the lived relations that bind God and church in this world. Except in prophetic or mystical vision, such relations are visible to us only in their fruits, which means their lived effects in this world. For Jenson, the relation of church to God is indeed an eternal relation, but it is not a timeless one, since the eternity of the God of Israel is an eternity that has entered historical time. It enters by way of God's covenant with Israel, among whose fruits is God's redeeming Israel from bondage and thus from death; and it enters by way of God's incarnation in Jesus of Nazareth, among whose fruits is Jesus's resurrection on the third day. If fruits are a relation made visible, then this means made visible to someone: the fruits of God's relation to the church are made known to those who know Jesus as the Christ, which means they are made known to the body of the church. A theology is composed by someone in this body in a certain time and place. I take this all to mean that, for Jenson, the purpose of a theology is to make God's relation to the church visible to the body of the church at a given time and place. To understand and evaluate such a theology is to see how it renders the eternal life of God visible in the body of that church.

To test theology by its fruits is a pragmatic lesson—not in the commonplace use of the term, where *pragmatic* means something like "useful in a strictly materialist sense," but in the way Charles Peirce used the term, to remind abstract thinkers and believers that the fruits of the Holy Spirit are to be eaten in this world as well as the next. Peirce offered a particularly American lesson, bred in Jonathan Edwards's spirit: spirituality must have visible signs in our worldly occupations and affections. In this spirit, Richard Neuhaus referred to Jenson as "America's theologian,"[1] just as Jenson has lent this title to Edwards.[2] To attend in this way to the spirit *in* the flesh is, on the model of Jenson's theology, to trace the dramatic life of the Triune God in the actual salvation history of the church rather than in cognitive ruminations on its purportedly timeless essence. This means, furthermore, to attend to God's suffering with his people as well as to God's glory, which means attending to the sins, errors, and tribulations of the visible church as well as to its perfections. This means that Jenson's theology is decidedly reformational, in service to the sixteenth-century Reformation as an instrument of the perennial reformation of the one catholic church.

In this chapter I introduce Jenson's postliberalism as a pragmatic, trinitarian reformation of the contemporary church. These are my terms, not Jenson's, and, as throughout this book, I am offering my own Jewish philosopher's perspective on Jenson's work rather than some effort to capture "what he is really doing." I present my interpretations in two ways. One is an informal study of what I call the "six axes of Jenson's postliberal inquiry," the other is a more formal presentation of what I call the "ten theses of Jenson's reformational postliberalism," and both draw on a reading of volume 1 of his *Systematic Theology*, augmented by my interviews of him in 2003, by more general readings of his recent essays and books, and by a careful reading of *Trinity, Time, and Church: A Response to the Theology of Robert W. Jenson*, edited by Colin Gunton, of blessed memory. I begin with what I consider the six "axes" or practices of interpretation through which Jenson seeks to repair the overly abstract and spiritualized foci of much Christian theology, including most modern theology and also certain strains of medieval and patristic theology. I use *pragmatic repair* to denote repair that reembodies what has been disembodied; simply to use a less ugly term, I will often replace *pragmatic* with the synonym *reparative*.[3]

---

1. Richard Neuhaus, "Jenson in the Public Square: Thinking the Church," in *Trinity, Time, and Church: A Response to the Theology of Robert W. Jenson*, ed. Colin E. Gunton (Grand Rapids: Eerdmans, 2000), 238–51 (251). Hereafter, references to this festschrift will be to author, chapter name, and pages.

2. Robert W. Jenson, *America's Theologian: A Recommendation of Jonathan Edwards* (New York: Oxford University Press, 1988), viii.

3. I owe this use of the term *reparative* to Nicholas Adams, who heard my studies of pragmatism as most interesting if applied to a more general activity of "reparative reasoning." Adams

Six Axes of Jenson's Postliberal Inquiry

1. Reparative ecclesiology: efforts to repair obstacles to ecclesial unity today

If, in the Augustinian tradition, sin is separation from God, then Jenson might be dubbed an Augustinian of a pragmatist stripe, because he seeks to repair sin that in particular separates the body of the church from its Spirit, and thereby one church from another and from the unity of the body of Christ.

In my interviews with him,[4] Jenson identifies his primary concern quite clearly. "Sin," he says, "is separation, and this applies to *both* parties to [the Lutheran–Catholic] schism." The goal of Luther's *sola scriptura*, he says, is to retain Scripture as *one* of the church's norms; it is the norm of norms but in a way that also serves church tradition and that is compatible with papal authority. Like Lindbeck and in the spirit of Melanchthon, Jenson seeks the reunion of the Reformation and Roman Catholic churches, given "appropriate compromises," and then their reunion with the Orthodox churches as well. The resulting church, he suggests, would reflect both the unity and pluralism of the medieval church and would lack the hierarchical authority that has emerged only since the sixteenth century. Theologians who served such a church would be perennial reformers in the tradition of Gregory and the Nicene repair of Arianism, Augustine and the repair of Donatism, and Luther and the repairs he sought in the liturgy of penance. "Reparative ecclesiology" is therefore another name for Jenson's brand of reformational theology.[5]

We could characterize all six axes of Jenson's inquiry as stages of this reparative ecclesiology. If so, we might identify its first stage with theologians' *coming to attend to these various separations*. As signs of sin, these separations summon theologians to full attention: to do something about this sin, which means to discover how their theological inquiry could itself help repair the separations. In a second stage, theologians *examine the conditions of these separations*, seeking to understand why the church has failed to repair them.

2. Reparative historiography: uncovering sources of the church's inability to repair its disunity

For Jenson, tendencies to disunity may be immanent in creaturely life, including the lives of the worldly churches, but to fail to repair disunity is to fail the

---

formalizes this suggestion in Nicholas Adams, "Reparative Reasoning," *Modern Theology* 24, no. 3 (July 2008): 447–57.

4. At the Center of Theological Inquiry, Princeton, Fall 2003.

5. See axis 5. Jenson would not apply such a mediating term as *pragmatism* to his work. I use the term, nevertheless, to suggest both that American pragmatism is a resource for reformational theology *and* that Reformation theology contributes to this pragmatism, especially in its classical expression in the work of Peirce.

church. In its second stage, Jenson's effort to effect such repair is what I label "reparative historiography": a genealogical search for evidence of what may have undermined the church's capacity to repair itself.[6] Observing how he integrates this historiography with pneumatology, some readers label his work "Hegelian." The label displays two partial truths: both Jenson's and Hegel's reparative histories are also histories of the Spirit, *and* Jenson has studied Hegel carefully. The label is ultimately in error, however, since Hegel's project offers evidence for what Jenson considers one of the telltale obstacles to ecclesial repair: conceptualism, or the tendency to reify abstractions rather than employ them strictly as instruments of repair. For Jenson, Hegel's *Science of Logic* and *Phenomenology* contributes to trinitarian and, particularly, pneumatological inquiry, but only when these studies are re-situated in the reparative ecclesiology that they should serve.

Conceptualism is my term for one of the primary obstacles Jenson uncovers in his genealogy. He judges its primary source to be the Mediterranean church's penchant for Greek metaphysics, which tempts theologians to identify the true with the timeless and the timeless with the abstract and, thus, the conceptual.

> Greece identified deity by metaphysical predicates. Basic among them is time-lessness: immunity to time's contingencies and particularly to death, by which temporality is enforced. . . . The interpretation of eternity as the contradictory of time both established Mediterranean antiquity's spiritual security *and* threatened its specific damnation. . . . Since the relation of eternity to time was grasped by mere negation, the difference between eternity and time could also come to be felt as simple discontinuity between two sorts of reality, in one of which we are confined and in the other of which all life and truth are located. (I 94)[7]

Jenson notes, for example, how this sense of discontinuity underlies the Arians' "especially brusque assertion of God's essential discord with temporal reality" (I 100). The Cappadocians made Nicaea's response to Arius logical and practicable, but, Jenson argues, the metaphysical temptation has continued to revisit Christian theologians ever since. This temptation obstructs the reparative work of the church because it tempts would-be reformers to misidentify "reunification" with a strictly conceptual and spiritual achievement rather than with needed transformations in the concrete life and practices of the worldly churches.

3. Reparative scriptural theology: hermeneutical proposals for recovering scriptural guidelines for the work of reformation

How, then, to render abstract and spiritualized theologies of service, once again, to the concrete work of ecclesial repair? Following Barth in this regard,

---

6. In the study of Lindbeck's postliberalism in chap. 2, this kind of genealogical inquiry is labeled "pragmatically transcendental."

7. Robert W. Jenson, *Systematic Theology*, vol. 1, *The Triune God* (New York: Oxford University Press, 1997), 94. Here and after this volume will be referenced as I + page number.

Jenson's genealogical inquiry comes to rest in the practices of scriptural reading that shaped the early church. For Jenson, this means coming to know the God who redeems by way of the biblical narrative of the life, death, and resurrection of Jesus of Nazareth. To read, study, and have one's conduct shaped by that narrative is to acquire the practices of interpretation and judgment that should guide reformational work today. There is no other way to acquire these practices or to anticipate the shape of this guidance. (Jenson's judgments have support in the rabbinic tradition: *naaseh v'nishmah*, "We will do and we will hear," say the Israelites at Sinai (Exod. 24:7). The Talmudic sages interpret the Israelites to have declared, "We will do what you say, and *then* we will come to understand its meaning" (doing precedes knowing).[8] For Jenson, the unanticipatable consequence of classical Christian practices of reading is to know the God who guides all repair as the Redeemer God of Scripture. It is, furthermore, to know this God as the Triune God who resurrected Jesus from the dead. And it is to know the Triune God as the God of Israel who redeemed Israel from bondage in Egypt.

4. Reparative trinitarian theology: a critique and repair of onto-theology as separating body and spirit and thereby obstructing ecclesial repair

For Jenson, the end of reparative historiography is to rediscover the witness of the early church: that God alone redeems. (To cite rabbinic tradition again, this is the lesson of the Passover Haggadah, whose emblematic midrash is on Deut. 26:8, "'By My outstretched hand I alone redeemed you,' . . . not by the hand of a fiery angel, . . . but I alone.") For Christian witness, this means that the Triune God alone redeems; to share in the work of reformation is therefore to share in the work of the Triune God, and there is no way to share in this work that does not pass through the drama of the Gospel narrative. The first reformational lesson Jenson draws from this drama marks his epistemological and prudential postliberalism: the work of ecclesial repair is obstructed whenever would-be reformers substitute human constructions for the direct presence of the Redeemer God. Finite humanity and finite creaturehood are not the problem, since the very witness of the Gospel is to show how the redeeming God enters into creaturely flesh. The problem is humanity's effort to substitute its own creations for God's, and these creations are *always* formed out of the stuff of concepts. This means, furthermore, that cognition is also not the problem, since human neural processes are creaturely processes. The only problem is humanity's effort to *replace* creaturely processes of living, breathing, desiring, loving, and reasoning, too, with discrete products of individual acts of will, desire, and reason. Since these efforts fail, they are ultimately illusory and thus false; since they, nevertheless, have actual consequences in the world,

---

8. *TB Shabbat* 88a-b.

they are not merely illusory but also destructive and thus evil—matters of sin and not only of error. But how could a creature whose actions require will, desire, and thought *not* sin in this way? Jenson's response has already been given: God alone is Redeemer, and the good news of the gospel is that in Jesus of Nazareth the God of Israel has made redemption from all sin available to all humanity. Jenson's diagnosis of the contemporary crises of the church thereby replays the New Testament's classic diagnosis: sin is separation from God, and the conceptualisms that have infiltrated the modern church separate modern Christians from God's redeeming presence, and this includes separating them from the life of Christ, following which they can breathe, will, desire, reason, *and not sin*, but not following which they most likely cannot. Discovering that both liberal and antiliberal theologies substitute conceptual constructions for certain elements of God's redeeming work, Jenson becomes a critic of both sorts of theology.

Perhaps the greatest challenge for a critic of conceptualism is to account for the generality of norms without appealing to the generality of concepts. Jenson's practice of adopting the gospel as a reformational guide both spreads past his individuality and at the same time serves nothing more than *the particularity* of that gospel witness. "Is this generality?" the philosopher may ask, and Jenson may answer, "It spreads, if that is what you mean." "Is this then nonparticular?" "It is about Jesus and no other, and this gospel and no other; is that what you mean by particular?" One might say that Jenson leaves questions of general and particular to God, not in the sense of throwing up his hands but in the literal sense that the gospel witness replaces such questions and the need for them.

In this way, reparative trinitarian theology classifies large families of either–or questions as appropriate only to specific, creaturely contexts and not to matters of the divine life and Scripture. Among these are either–or questions about Christians and Jews, as if, for example, the salvation of the one compromised the salvation of the other. On this subject, nonsupersessionism emerges as a surprising correlate of Jenson's trinitarian theology.

5. Nonsupersessionism: the surprising discovery that ecclesial repair comes to rest in the hand of a Redeemer God who not only raised Jesus from the dead but also raised Israel from Egypt

Because it emerges from out of his reading of Scripture, Jenson's reparative trinitarian theology comes to rest in the claim that trinitarian belief is not ultimately about some *number* of divine persons. It is fundamentally the Christian belief that God is incarnate in Jesus Christ, which is fundamentally the Christian belief that God has no qualities that we know apart from what both the Old and New Testaments say God does. "God is whoever raised Jesus from the dead, having before raised Israel from Egypt. . . . The church's

Trinitarianism is commonly thought to depart from Israel's interpretation of God. This is the exact contradictory of the truth. . . . the doctrine of Trinity only explicates Israel's faith in a situation in which it is believed that the God of Israel has prior to the general resurrection raised one of his servants from the dead." For Jenson, "All aspects of the Lord's [trinitarian] being appear in Israel's Scripture" (I 63).

While Jenson's nonsupersessionism has doctrinal implications, we are concerned in this section only with its hermeneutical consequences. One premise of Jenson's genealogical inquiry is that efforts to reform the modern church are obstructed by conceptualist efforts to separate body and spirit. As noted earlier, he concluded that efforts to repair those obstructions should be guided by a trinitarian practice of reading Scripture. But he soon added something to this conclusion: if practiced in supersessionist fashion, trinitarian readings will *contribute to* rather than remove these tendencies to separate body and spirit. The reason is that only a conceptualist reading of the Gospel narrative would sever Jesus's divinity from his Jewishness and sever the Gospel narrative of Jesus's life from the Old Testament narrative of Israel's life. Only a conceptualist reading would allegorize the Old Testament narratives, as if the New Testament offered a *pesher*-like "solution" to each element of the Old Testament narrative of Israel's life. Typology is not at all to be avoided, but it names a trinitarian *practice* of reading, not a series of conceptualist pronouncements. A trinitarian reading draws prayerfully on God's direct presence *in* the reading, rather than allowing any set of finite representations to substitute for that presence. And it must be reparative: helping repair separations of body and spirit in the enfleshed lives of individual members of the churches, in institutional practices of the church bodies, and in the broader sociopolitical contexts of contemporary Christianity.

For Jenson, the repair of body and spirit cannot also, through the force of human will and constructions of the human mind, seek to separate the body and spirit of Jesus by separating the life of Jesus, of the apostles, and of the early church from the life of the people of Israel. This does not imply that one must somehow rewrite the Gospel record of Jesus or Paul or other apostles' criticisms of "the Jews who did not follow Christ." Such rewriting would also reflect a conceptual intrusion onto the scriptural record. It implies, instead, that these criticisms are not connected to any soteriological segregation of Jew from Jew, any more than Jenson's efforts to repair the contemporary church imply his segregating the church-that-needs-repair from the church-that-repairs—as if the liberal and antiliberal Christian theologians he criticizes should be booted out of the church. Nonagreement and criticism are internal to the life of Israel and of the church and have nothing to do with supersession and replacement. In a nonsupersessionist reading, the Gospel narrative *does* offer a key for interpreting the Old Testament narrative, but for the early Christians, these interpretations extend and continue the process of reading that is proper and internal to Israel's Scripture. This extension and continuation may not meet with the approval of other groups of Jews then or now, but that disagreement is itself consistent in form with Israel's own scriptural hermeneutic, not opposed to it. Disagreement justifies disagreement in response, but it is no warrant for more than disagreement. Supersessionism *breaks* Israel's hermeneutic and thereby *obstructs* the hermeneutical claim of the New Testament in relation to the Old: replacing not only Israel with the church but also the church's scriptural *claim* on Israel with the pronouncements of some new religion "that knew not Jacob" and had no means of *reasoning* any longer with Jacob. For Jenson, such a religion would be a religion of "timeless, philosophic truths" as foreign to Jesus of Nazareth as it was to his Pharisaic peers and adversaries.

Explained this way, Jenson's nonsupersessionist hermeneutic also gives birth to his nonsupersessionist *historiography*. This means that as he rereads the history of the church in light of his reparative scriptural and trinitarian theology, Jenson evaluates each age of reformation and each obstacle to reformation according to the critical standards of nonconceptualism and nonsupersessionism. Here, for example, are two of his evaluations: (a) *The Old Testament narratives confound the either–or of supersessionism or non-Christology.* "Asked who God is, Israel's answer is, 'Whoever rescued us from Egypt.' . . . To the question, 'Who is God?' the New Testament has one new descriptively identifying answer: 'Whoever raised Jesus from the dead.' Identification by the Resurrection neither replaces nor is simply added to identification by the Exodus" (I 44). (b) *Neither Israel nor the church is fulfilled until the final eschaton.* "The church is nothing other than an appropriate if beforehand unpredictable sidestep in the fulfillment of the Lord's promises to Israel." "The church . . . should regard the continuing synagogue as a detour like herself within the Fulfillment of Israel's hope. . . . Between the end of canonical Israel and the absolute End the church waits by faith in Jesus's Resurrection, and the synagogue waits by study of torah, reading in a way devised by the rabbis for just this situation of waiting" (II 171, 194).[9]

These evaluations are not, in the end, for the sake of generating historical speculations, but for gathering resources for repairing obstacles to ecclesial reformation. The task of repair is to remove conceptualism—whether spiritualist or materialist—from contemporary Christian theology, thereby removing obstacles to the trinitarian practice of Scripture reading as reformational guide; and it is to remove supersessionism from the Christian reading of Scripture, thereby removing obstacles to the concrete and pragmatic practice of reformation.

---

9. "Thus until the Last Judgment and our resurrection, Christ has not yet come in a way that fully consummates Israel's history. It is this in itself rather obvious point that is jointly forgotten by Christian supersessionism and by most attempts to overcome it." Robert W. Jenson, *Systematic Theology*, vol. 2, *The Works of God* (New York: Oxford University Press, 2001), 336. Hereafter, this volume will be referenced as II + page number.

6. Semper reformanda: *the reformational source and force of Jenson's postliberal theology*

We return, then, to the reparative ecclesiology with which I began this review of Jenson's reformational practice. As noted at the outset, Jenson's postliberal project serves both the critical and integrative dimensions of Luther's Reformation: reforming errors in the church while at the same time promoting its catholicity and unity. In an interview,[10] Jenson therefore explains that he serves only one of two kinds of Lutheranism. There are Lutherans, he says, for whom the sixteenth-century events were a "rediscovery of the Gospel: that is, that it was once lost but they refound it and thus refounded the church." This refounding is the Lutheran Church, whose goal is reunification with the Roman Catholic Church but only when it comes to accept Lutheran reforms. But there are other Lutherans—and here he includes himself and George Lindbeck—for whom reformation belongs to the one church as a perennial activity of repair, renewed throughout salvation history. The rules of reformation may be clarified by the sixteenth-century Reformers, but they can be rediscovered throughout ecclesial history, and that means within Roman Catholicism as well.

In my vocabulary, for Jenson to seek both unity and reform in this way is to seek within the church what the classical American pragmatists hoped to fulfill within the practices of science and sociopolitical reform. It is at once to affirm and to reform particular yet age-old traditions, which is possible only if those traditions derive their sustenance and guidance from a source that is itself ever-reforming and ever-affirming. There may conceivably be many such sources, but the only one I am confident in having encountered is the Creator and Redeeming God of Israel, whose Word both generates traditions of human practice *and* calls those traditions to task. Peirce claimed his pragmatism was "nothing but a corollary to Jesus's injunction 'that Ye may know them by their fruit,'"[11] which is but one sign of Peirce's perceiving pragmatism as a reformational philosophy of science in service to the God who creates, reveals, and redeems. Jenson in turn, if I understand him correctly, also associates Jesus of Nazareth with the Word that both generates and reforms traditions of human practices, and this is why I presume to connect Jenson to the American tradition that also produced pragmatism.

There is another American connection worth noting. Lutheran theologians are disproportionately represented among the strongest Christian critics of supersessionism and the strongest advocates of deep theological engagement with Judaism. I have not finished asking why this is the case, but Jenson has offered several strong and complementary hypotheses. One hypothesis applies

---

10. As noted earlier, at the Center of Theological Inquiry, Fall 2003.

11. Charles Peirce, "Search for a Method" (1893), in *Collected Papers of Charles Sanders Peirce*, ed. Charles Harteshorne and Paul Weiss (Cambridge, MA: Belknap Press of Harvard University Press, 1932), vol 5, par. 402n2 (hereafter cited as CP 5.402n2, 1893).

to many schools of Lutheran theology, including both more and less ecumenically minded and both German and American: that I am seeing a Lutheran response to the Shoah, a German Lutheran response in particular. Another hypothesis applies specifically to Lutheran ecumenicists: that just as early Protestant criticism of the Jews was often meant as veiled criticism of Rome, so too more recent Lutheran openness to Rome also carries with it a correlative openness to Judaism. A third hypothesis applies to immigrant American Lutherans in particular: that as relatively recent arrivals to the United States, members of a number of Lutheran churches may identify with other minority religions and ethnic groups, of which the Jews are a prime example. A final hypothesis applies to Lutheran Barthians: that for reasons introduced above under the fifth axis, the Barthian "return to Scripture" also entails a return to the Scripture, and people, of Israel.[12] I sense that all these reasons may apply to the Lutheran postliberals' interests in the Jews. As for why the link between Lutheran postliberal criticisms of conceptualism and of supersessionism, I will conclude this section with an illustration from Jenson's autobiography.

As noted in several interviews, Jenson's autobiography displays a certain pattern of religious and secular learning that corresponds in crucial ways to patterns I have observed in the biographies of the major postliberal Jewish theologians of the twentieth century (Hermann Cohen, Martin Buber, Franz Rosenzweig, and in the United States also Max Kadushin and Eugene Borowitz).[13] Reduced to its elemental correspondences, the pattern is this (where PL means "the emergent postliberal thinker"):

- PL receives a fairly traditional socialization in his or her religion but also with access to Western-style education.
- PL encounters two sets of contradictions: between the institutional practices and what appears to be the deepest spirit of this religion; and between those practices and the criteria for truth and excellence that appear to inform Western canons of knowledge. Juxtaposed this way, the first set of contradictions stimulates interest in the second.
- PL becomes a critical thinker, plunging into studies of Western philosophy, historiography, or social science and gathering from these studies canons for examining the inadequacies in his or her inherited religion.
- PL enters professional life as an academic, working in the university or seminary as a critically minded reformer of the religious tradition:

12. See Peter Ochs, *The Return to Scripture in Judaism and Christianity: Essays in Postcritical Scriptural Interpretation* (Eugene, OR: Wipf and Stock, 2008).

13. I review these in "Rabbinic Semiotics," *American Journal of Semiotics* 10, nos. 1–2 (1993): 35–66; and in "Max Kadushin as Rabbinic Pragmatist," in *Understanding the Rabbinic Mind*, ed. Peter Ochs (Atlanta: Scholars Press for South Florida Studies in the History of Judaism, 1990), 165–96.

- still contributing to the tradition, in other words, but also in service to modern canons of reform.
- PL is gradually disillusioned with these modern canons, discovering within them both internal contradictions and conflicts with the deepest spirit of the religion. This is PL's emergence as a specifically *postliberal* theologian: a reformer, at once, of the religious tradition and of the Western canons of reform.

As he reports, Jenson received his "religious socialization" in a traditional American Lutheran home and seminary. Disturbed by the conventionality of that socialization, and by the lack of critical distance in the seminaries between religious ethnicity and the commanding force of Scripture, he sought "post-ethnic" learning in Continental practice of critical theology (first at Heidelberg and then at Yale). Jenson joined up with Carl Braaten in a cooperative search for "critical norms to evaluate their seminary education." In the terms I introduced earlier, this is Jenson's genealogical inquiry. The primary instrument of their inquiry was a historical-critical study of the sources of their tradition. The inquiry reached its goal with their rediscovering "original Lutheran confessionalism"—a new source of guidelines for their reparative affirmation-and-reform of the Lutheran tradition. They returned from graduate school as reformers, eager to "open the seminaries up" to their historical-critical method and their confessionalist norms. They did indeed make a stir, or perhaps "too much of one," as Jenson recalls in self-effacing fashion. Looking back, he wonders whether *Dialog*, the journal they introduced as an instrument of critical reform, may have been *too* successful in helping stimulate interest in historical-critical methods that he gradually came to doubt. Jenson's gradual disillusionment displayed the sources of both sides of his postliberalism. On the one side, he began to suspect that the historical-critical procedures he learned at Heidelberg and Yale were not merely disinterested tools of reflection, but also expressions of certain culture-specific commitments: the whole complex of modern "conceptualism," as I have termed it above. On the other side and more gradually, he began to suspect that those commitments included supersessionism—most surprising and disturbing, because this was supersessionism from the epistemologically liberal side, from Wellhausen to Harnack and beyond. This leads us to Jenson's practices of postliberalism per se.

In the next, central section of this chapter, we turn to a representative list of what I consider "ten theses" of Jenson's reformational postliberalism. Each thesis is, I trust, true to the plain sense of Jenson's recent writings, but their collection into a single ordered list reflects only my own interests in seeing whether and how Jenson's arguments could be ordered as an argument for reformational postliberalism. I base the list primarily on my reading of Jenson's *Systematic Theology,* volume 1, *The Triune God,* ordered through categories derived from my review of the festschrift for Jenson, *Trinity, Time,*

and Church.[14] Discussion of the first thesis, "what theology is," will be disproportionately long, because it will provide an occasion for illustrating the
central thrust of Jenson's overall postliberal practice.

Ten Theses of Jenson's Reformational Postliberalism

1. *What theology is: "the thinking of the church in its service of its gospel message"—that Jesus is risen*[15]

Jenson characterizes his overall business as theology, and he characterizes
theology as whatever contributes to the efforts of the church to maintain "a
continuing discourse about her individuating and carrying communal purpose"
(I 3).[16] Since the purpose of the church is to maintain "a particular message,
called 'the gospel'" (I 4), theology may be characterized as "thinking what to
say to be saying the gospel" (I 32). The subject of theology is equally "Church"
(or ecclesiology) and "gospel" (or Scripture), for, as Jenson argues, "'Church'
and 'gospel' . . . mutually determine each other" (I 5). Theology may also be
characterized, therefore, as how the church should "get it across . . . that Jesus
is risen and what that means" (I 5).

What, then, is gospel? What is the church? What, furthermore, does Jenson
mean by his references to the classical elements of Christian theology, such as
gospel, Scripture, canon, witness, proclamation, promise, history, tradition,
reformation, doctrine, dogma, and prayer? And what does Jenson mean by
the contemporary terms he uses in his accounts of these classic elements,
such as *practice, speculation, thinking, metaphysical facts, first- and second-
order statements, norms, grammar, hermeneutics, interpretation, the future,
ontology*?

In responding to these questions, my hope is not only to display something of the elemental structure of Jenson's systematics but also to offer an
ordered list of the key elements of his theological postliberalism. To that end,
I will tendentiously explain Jenson's use of these terms as expressions of a
single, central thrust of his postliberalism. As enunciated in thesis 2, this is
to contribute to the unity of the church by helping repair the dis-integrating
tendencies in modern and late medieval theology. I begin here with several illustrations of how Jenson respeaks the elementary terms of Christian theology
in a nondichotomizing fashion.

---

14. Gunton, *Trinity, Time, and Church*. My review of the volume is "A Jewish Reading of
Trinity, Time, and Church: A Response to the Theology of Robert W. Jenson," *Modern Theology*
19, no. 3 (July 2003): 419–28.

15. Braaten's paraphrase of Jenson, Carl E. Braaten, "Eschatology and Mission in the
Theology of Robert Jenson," in *Trinity, Time, and Church*, 300.

16. James J. Buckley, "Intimacy: The Character of Robert Jenson's Theology," in *Trinity,
Time, and Church*, 12.

In modern and at least late medieval usage, many of the terms of Christian theology appear as members of contrast pairs, such as gospel (or proclamation or Scripture) versus ecclesial tradition (or church or doctrine); promise (or spirit or futurity) versus law (or, in this sense, historical tradition or ritual practice); practical versus speculative theology; or ecclesial reformation (or self-correction) versus ecclesial formation (or doctrinal tradition). In Jenson's usage, each member of these pairs retains its difference from the other member, but not as contradictories or poles of a dichotomy. Instead, the two members are also predicated of some single activity of which each is a complementary dimension. I have already mentioned, for example, the complementary relation between gospel and church in Jenson's theology. The gospel is "witness to the Resurrection" (I 12): the apostles' message to the world that "the God of Israel has raised His servant Jesus from the dead" (I 4). The church is the historically continuous community of those who hear the gospel message, believe it, and find themselves under obligation to retell it (I 4): "The church has a mission: to see to the speaking of the gospel, whether to the world as message of salvation or to God as appeal and praise" (I 11). In other words, there is no gospel without the church that speaks it, and no church without the gospel it speaks. They relate, one to the other, as do the Spirit and body of Christ.

Promise and law are another pair of complements in Jenson's theology. If the Word is God's gift to humanity, then "God's gifts are . . . intrinsically bespoken to us, as the church speaks the word of Christ. . . . The kind of speaking that bestows something gratis can be specified: it is promising that does so. Thus the decisive maxim of all the Reformation's theology: God's gifts are *res promissa*, 'the stuff of promise'" (I 13–14).[17] Promises offer assurances about the future; more precisely, "promises not only open a future to our vision but themselves enable that future; they contain and convey the future possibility they signify" (I 15–16). In this conveyance, the promise appears to us, here and now, as the future's gift to the present, declaring, "I am here with you and I will be with you from now until you behold me in my glory." In this way, the promise is both sign of an absent yet anticipated future and also the tangible means through which that future comes to fruition.

> [T]he future that moves a story must somehow be available within it if we are to live the story while it is still in progress, as Israel worshiped her God even while in exile awaiting his salvation or as the church tells the gospel while awaiting the risen Christ's advent. . . . There must be a way in which the closure of death is anticipated, not merely in general but in anticipation of a determinate end. In the gospel, this is done by the making of *promises*; the future that moves the story is available ahead of time in materially specific promises of its coming. (I 68–69)

17. Jenson cites the apology of the Augsburg Confession 4.84.182.

This future therefore lives among us as the gift of God's redeeming presence, and our acceptance of this gift constitutes our faith, "the assurance of things hoped for . . . [and] not seen" (Heb. 11:1, cited in I 68).

From out of the context of a Jewish postliberalism, we would tend to interpret this gift as a sign that the present is also marked by want or suffering: like Israel's bondage in Egypt, in response to which "God . . . took notice of [the Israelites] . . . [and said] 'I will be with you'" (Exod. 2:25; 3:12). In these terms, the promise that is present in Israel's midst transforms Israel from a nation suffering in bondage to one that marches toward the promised land. Jenson's favored characterization of the Triune God is, indeed, the one who, having redeemed Israel from bondage, resurrected Jesus from the dead; in this sense, the Redeemer God appears in the present as the one who brings redemption from suffering. But Jenson tends to avoid the language of suffering, lest (as I read it) we give short shrift to grace, misinterpreting redemption as though it meant release from privation. His strong preference is to speak instead of human sin, but even then to avoid referring to promise as God's promise to release us from sin. In most of Jenson's statements on the subject, redemption appears as our being brought directly to participate "in God's own reality" (I 71). Sin is what keeps us from beholding the gift of promise and thus witnessing this reality's breaking in upon us, and suffering appears as a consequence of our failure to behold what has been given us.[18] "Sin is a fact of humanity's history with God as Scripture narrates it," not a fact of all of creation but only of its human part: "it is what God does not want done [by us]" (II 133). Sin is therefore not a feature of creaturely behavior in itself, some worldly condition that engenders suffering and thereby attracts God's redemptive concern. Sin is a feature only of the relation between the human creature and God: it is about our refusal to acknowledge that relation and thereby acknowledge our more-than-worldly purpose and engagements. In the tradition of Augustine and Luther, Jenson identifies sin with the idolatry of the human "soul's incurvature upon itself" (II 138). This all means that sin does not precede God's promises to us but appears only in our willful refusal to acknowledge that promise when it comes (II 146). Sin would be Abraham's refusing, God forbid, to go forth as God bade him. Since Abraham did go forth, "the Lord reckoned it to him as righteousness" (the Pauline reading of Gen. 15:6).

For Jenson, *righteousness* refers neither to merely worldly virtues (in which case the Genesis text would seem to promote "works righteousness" or creaturely voluntarism) nor to strictly commanded behavior (in which case the text would seem to promote divine freedom to the exclusion of human freedom). Abraham's righteousness, in other words, refers neither to his achieving worldly perfection prior to the encounter with God nor to his overcoming sin only through God's intervention in his life. It refers instead to his successfully

---

18. Out of a Jewish postliberalism, I would read this claim as more ontological than reparative.

overcoming the human propensity to refuse God's promise of a new future. Since it thereby prepares him to receive God's gift, this righteousness must display virtues that are nurtured prior to the gift. But if he interprets Genesis this way, how would Jenson avoid Pelagianism? I take the following argument to be implicit in Jenson's *Systematic Theology*, even if he does not state it in these particular words. The virtues of righteousness must be nurtured through patterns of indirect divine instruction that are implicit in the religious heritage and thus in the religious socialization of every righteous person. Righteousness is in this way an attribute of salvation history, both phylogenetically (in the history of one's people) and ontogenetically (in one's personal history). This is why every Christian is first a member of the people Israel, since it is Israel's praxis that prepares the apostles to behold Jesus's resurrection, and this is why every child of Israel is first a child of the Chaldeans: while Abraham left his parents' home, he also came from that home. For the same reason, it is also why every Christian is also not an Israelite, for the apostles' faith in Christ's promise makes them members of a new dispensation, or new era of salvation history. And it is why every child of Israel is also not Chaldean, for Abraham did go forth: the faiths of Abraham, Isaac, and Jacob made the children of Israel members of a new salvation history.

In this account, salvation history is perennial and heterogeneous. It is perennial since every human belongs to the salvation history of Adam and has the potential of giving birth to descendants who will inhabit the final kingdom. It is heterogeneous because we cannot predict which human being and which human community will be graced with which promise; nor can we predict precisely how one generation's virtues of openness to God's promises will strengthen or not strengthen the virtues of the next generation. There is one salvation history, in the sense that we all begin with Adam and end with the end of days; but there is also more than one, since along the way the "seventy" nations that come from Adam must enter into different and mutually interacting subhistories. The subhistories of Israel and the church may be unusually close—as we will see in Jenson's account—but they are also different, and the difference between Israel's history and that of the Chaldeans appears all the greater in comparison. This is to speak of "lateral" or relational heterogeneity among the subhistories of the one salvation history of Adam. But there is also temporal heterogeneity within each subhistory, or at least within the histories of Israel and the church. To be open to God's promises is to enter into a future that was in some way unforeseeable. It is thus to enter into a history that is at least somewhat new and, thereby, to share in the heterogeneity of redemptive time. This heterogeneity is redoubled, moreover, since the in-breaking of one promise does not preclude the subsequent in-breaking of another. Figural interpretation is testimony to the redoubling of promises, since it reads the in-breaking of at least one promise into Israel's history as anticipation of at least one other.

Let us consider, in sum, what the heterogeneity of salvation history implies about the relation between promise and righteousness. According to this reading of Jenson, righteousness is a human virtue but is enacted wholly for the sake of achieving openness to God's promise. Such an achievement is possible only because the potentially righteous person appears on earth always within salvation history and thus as beneficiary of what rabbinic tradition calls *zekhut avot v'imahot*, "the merit of the fathers and mothers," or what we may describe more broadly as a communal memory of previous promises. A community's encounters with divine promise presuppose, test, and thereby reshape the community's heritage of righteous conduct, or what we call its religious tradition. In these terms, religious tradition enables openness to God's promises, without anticipating, and thereby falsely seeking to delimit, the character of God's in-breaking. This in-breaking is known discursively only through its consequences for reshaping salvation history and religious tradition and thus for reshaping each community's virtues of righteousness. *Righteousness* therefore refers to a community's historically accumulating treasure of wisdom about how to diminish the power of sin and release humanity's in-born capacity to witness God's gifts. This treasure is what Jenson calls law.

"Law" is what Lutherans are said stereotypically to want to oppose to grace and promise. Jenson transforms the meaning of the term in two ways. First, he separates Torah from the category of law, placing it in what I take to be its proper place, the category of Word and thus promise. This means "Torah" as in God's command to Abraham to "go forth," or the command to Moses to lead the people out, or the commandments given to Israel on Sinai (the "Ten Words," *aseret ha-dibberot*, as they are called in the tradition of Israel). Jenson then takes the category of law that remains—works enacted through human will—removes it from the stereotypical dyad of "law/grace," and reintroduces it as the complement of divine promise: the virtues of work that render the human heart open to beholding divine promise and receiving its grace. This means being open to receiving Torah as divine gift (in the case of Israel) as well as to receiving the good news of Jesus's resurrection. Even when separated from Torah, law therefore remains a positive virtue, as the instrument of humanity's preparing the heart as much as it can to receive God's promise. Identifying law with righteousness and with the cumulative treasure of religious tradition, Jenson also redescribes religious tradition as a practice of memorializing the consequences of God's breaking into and in that sense responding to the activities of human righteousness. This means a practice of both remembering and ritually reenacting the events of in-breaking and their consequences for human life. The reenactment takes the forms of both liturgical activity and works of social justice. In both cases, the reenactment also represents a reformation of previous traditions of righteousness, since every in-breaking opens new futures, breeding unforeseeable changes in how the community prepares itself to meet God again. In this way, a community's volitional acts of righteousness may at the same time display the consequences of divine intervention, without compromising either human or divine freedom.

This treatment of law and promise shows how Jenson seeks to transform the apparent contraries of Protestant and Catholic theological relations into complements. We may consider, for example, the stereotypical contraries of practical versus speculative theology, scriptural proclamation versus prayer, and reformation versus doctrinal reaffirmation. Jenson argues that theology is practical, speculative, and hermeneutic. In this way, theology serves both the Reformers' emphasis on practical critique and the medieval Catholic emphasis on theological speculation. "Medieval theology tended to say that theology is a 'more speculative than practical' discipline,[19] Reformation theology the reverse.[20] Identification of theology as thinking about how to speak the gospel—that is how to do something—supports the Reformation answer as the first to be given. Yet we shall see that the older answer is equally necessary" (I 11).

In Jenson's work, theology is *both* practical and speculative because it is *also* hermeneutical. As *practical*, theology serves the mission of the church's proclamation. As *speculative*, it asks what difference this proclamation makes for our understanding of both God and creation, and everything in between. Speculation generates claims about metaphysical and theological "facts." In stereotypical debates from purportedly "Catholic" and "Protestant" positions, the Protestant side discounts such claims as merely dogmatic (as in the Kantian critique); the Catholic side discredits practical theology, in turn, as relativistic. Jenson's response is to locate the ratio of speculative reasoning *in* the gospel proclamation, so that practice and speculation are two interdependent dimensions of the one Word, rather than representatives of two independent spheres in search of a mediator (two spheres of being, that is, when characterized in the language of speculation; or two spheres of authority, according to the language of practice). Theology is therefore always hermeneutical, because it "is an act of *interpretation*: it begins with a received word and issues in a new word essentially related to the old word"; it is "reflection internal to the act of tradition, to the turn from hearing something to speaking it" (I 14). Both practical and speculative theology interpret the scriptural Word *and* reinterpret received tradition and the world according to that Word as norm of action and of reasoning. Hermeneutics is, finally, a *communal* activity. The gospel is spoken to and received by the church, or, as noted earlier, gospel and church "mutually determine each other" (I 5). While individual human beings are indeed instruments of theological activity, there is ultimately no

19. By way of illustration, he cites Thomas Aquinas *Summa theologiae* 1.1.4: "Theology comprehends both [the speculative and the practical]. . . . Nevertheless it is more speculative than practical."

20. To illustrate, he cites Johannes Baier, *Compendium theologiae positivae* (1693), proleg., 1.14.

private practice or private speculation on behalf of the gospel; the individual theologizes as member of the church.

Insofar as it is practical, theology is also *critical*, or *reformational*. "Any 'practical' reflection will be in some degree a critical and self-critical activity, for there is always the possibility that the practice in question is being inappropriately pursued. Thus theology as a practical discipline must always examine the church's verbal and other practice, and its own guidance of that practice, with the question, Does this teaching or other practice further or hinder the saying of the gospel?" (I 11). Practical theology therefore eventuates in some change in church practice. Insofar as it is speculative, theology is also doctrinal, affirming some claim of the church about "what it is to be saying the gospel"—for example, "to be saying the gospel, say 'Jesus is Lord,'" or, following Thomas Aquinas, "'to be saying the gospel, let nothing be said that would imply potentiality in God'" (I 17).[21] Since theology is always hermeneutical, there is, however, no necessary conflict between theology's practical and doctrinal dimensions. The gospel message both affirms our capacity to stand in God's presence and criticizes our failures to be fully open to that presence; it both founds the church and renders it subject to perennial critique. In Jenson's view, theology should thereby always serve the Reformers' rule *lex proclamandi lex credendi*, "the law of proclaiming is the law of believing," as a rule for perennial ecclesial self-criticism (I 13). At the same time, it should always serve the ancient Catholic rule, *lex orandi lex credendi*, "the law of praying is the law of believing," as a rule for perennially reaffirming "the distinguishing regularities in the church's communal life of prayer . . . , [such as] its triune structure" (I 13).

Theology must therefore serve at once the ends of prayer and of scriptural proclamation:

> When the Reformation's rule from proclamation is not followed, theology slips from its assignment. When the catholic rule from prayer is not followed, theology slips from its object, for it is in the church's prayer and praise, in their verbal form and in the obtrusively embodied forms called sacrifice, that the church's discourse turns and fastens itself to God as its object. And it is the ineluctably Trinitarian pattern of the church's prayer . . . by which the church's discourse grasps the resurrection's particular God as the object finally given to it. (I 14)

2. To mend a divided church and contradict a self-contradictory church

The central thrust of Jenson's postliberal project of theology is to mend a divided church and contradict a self-contradictory church, and thus to correct theology in the West, North America in particular, according[22] to readings

---

21. Citing in the first case 1 Corinthians 12:3, in the second case *Summa theologiae* 1.2.
22. I vi, cited by James Buckley, "Intimacy: The Character of Robert Jenson's Theology," in *Trinity, Time, and Church*, 10.

of the scriptural tradition and in light of long traditions of hermeneutical philosophy. In his efforts to mend the church, Jenson becomes "America's theologian" today[23]—doubly so, we might add, since America's *Christian* pragmatic tradition, from Edwards to Peirce, was always to mend divisions within practices and between practice and thinking.[24] In his self-mocking way, Jenson says that as a corrective activity, his theology "dismembers its predecessors and uses the fragments in strange ways." But this is the method of the classical interpreters of Scripture, both rabbinic and patristic: to revere texts by reinterpreting them verse by verse and not just according to their apparent plain sense or whole story. To dismember texts and reread them is itself a discipline taught by Scripture, read as disclosing the identity of God as Jesus Christ.[25] To help restore unity to the church is thus to recommend ways of reforming a divided church in light of fresh interpretations of what the gospel says. This is a political as well as hermeneutical effort, since it is made on behalf of a united church and "a people united in a common spirit, that is, a people who have become a community, is a *polity*" (II 204).[26] At the same time, the scriptural norms that guide reformational theology are also shaped by received tradition and thus by doctrine. To appeal to these norms is to reenact them, and reenactment is ultimately a practice of prayer. This means that Jenson's reformational theology is necessarily Eucharistic: efforts to help unify the church must be guided *by* the unity of the church, and that is the body of Christ that gathers all its members in Eucharistic communion (II 220–27). This communion is *only* local—performed, that is, only within the embodied life of local churches—and this means that the "universal" norm that guides church reform is available only through each concrete locality (II 225). Jenson's reformational theology is written in general terms, but its reformational force would be displayed fully in terms of the communal drama of each local church in its relation to other churches.

3. The weakness of American theology: forgetting history

Jenson seeks to undo the efforts of American theologians to displace the God of history with a generic study of "religion."[27] In Hauerwas's terms, liberal theologians have gone along with the general American presumption that to maintain a pluralistic society, "all strong religious convictions [had] to be relegated to the private realm. . . . Theology in America became anthropology,"

23. Richard John Neuhaus, "Jenson in the Public Square: Thinking the Church," in *Trinity, Time, and Church*, 251.
24. Bruce Kuklick, *Churchmen and Philosophers: From Jonathan Edwards to John Dewey* (New Haven: Yale University Press, 1987).
25. Buckley, "Intimacy," 12.
26. See thesis 10.
27. Colin Gunton, "Creation and Mediation in the Theology of Robert W. Jenson: An Encounter and a Convergence," in *Trinity, Time, and Church*, 81.

and eventually ethics.[28] For Jenson, on the other hand, pluralistic democracy requires public debate on just those ultimate moral convictions that the Enlightenment sought to closet. "The present near extinction of politics in America, the most structurally modern of nations, is often noted. . . . What Americans are likely now to call politics is in fact the functioning of an almost entirely depoliticized collectivity and state" (II 79–80). The reason is that "a polity . . . is the arena in which a community's ethics are done, in which the question is posed, with the possibility of effective decision: What ought our community do about . . . ?" (II 82–83). With the "closing of the polity to the moral discourse that is its own proper matter" (II 84), the polity is longer a polity but the mere instrument of "a mass of petitioners and their interests," manipulated "by professional managers of affairs" (II 80). The alternative, to return to Hauerwas's reading, is what Jenson shares with Barth: a belief "that God matters"[29] and that the place where God matters most is the polity. In Jenson's terms, "the polity is nothing less than the public space in which God calls us to be human in that we call each other to come together in justice" (II 79).[30]

For Jenson, this tendency to forget religious tradition and its gospel norm is, ironically, a tendency to forget the bodily life of the church and think only of its spirit. For as we noted previously (pp. 78–79), the religious traditions of the church represent its evolving earthly wisdom about how the human heart may be cleansed and opened to perceiving gifts of divine promise. Beyond the proclamations of gospel and the developing body of church doctrine, these are practical wisdoms about what particular disciplines of individual, societal, and political life have tended to open the heart to God's presence or to narrow it down. These are accounts of concrete human behavior: how different Christians lived their tradition and how encounters with the divine tested and thereby reshaped their life plans. To forget them is to entrust the care of one's heart to general concepts of Christian practice rather than to the concrete and time-tested wisdoms from which such concepts must be abstracted.[31] In Jenson's use of the term, this is to separate Christianity from law, which, as we have seen, refers to practices that open the heart to the possibility of beholding God's promises.[32] It is therefore to separate Christianity from the body, the

28. Stanley Hauerwas, "Only Theology Overcomes Ethics, or Why 'Ethicists' Must Learn from Jenson," in *Trinity, Time, and Church*, 254.

29. Ibid., 255.

30. Ibid., 259.

31. David F. Ford, *Christian Wisdom: Desiring God and Learning in Love* (New York: Cambridge University Press, 2007).

32. The ninth-century Jewish sage Bahya ibn Paquda called these *chovot halevavot*, "duties of the heart," which he contrasted with *chovot haibarim*, "duties of the limbs," which are mere instruments of the former and which by themselves lack the animating spirit that opens one to see and taste the divine presence. The contemporary Talmudist David Halivni puts it this way: "Some congregants ask, 'Which *mitsvot* [divine commandments] must be observed with *kavvanah* [intentionality]?' And I say, 'All of them! For how can we act in

place of concrete action that Jenson characterizes as "our availability to relation with others": "the personal body is availability to others and to oneself;
the personal body is the reality of the person's history up to any moment;
the personal body is what is seen, . . . the person as an occupant of space"
(II 347); "for Paul a person's embodiment is his or her availability to other
persons and thereupon to his or herself" (II 213). In this reading, the body is
the person's publicness, not his or her privacy. As the wisdom of practice, the
"laws" of the body therefore belong to the public realm, not the private. This
means that they are political: the laws of our availability to others, both to
God (through our openness to his promises) and to other humans (through
our caring and communicative relations to them). The name for the society
of Christian bodies is, of course, the church, which is the body of Christ.

In short, Jenson's theology of ecclesial history is also a theology of bodily
practices, which is also a political theology. The body of Christ is the body
politic: the bodily availability of all Christians to God and to one another in
the church, as well as the availability of the church to all other humans and
to the world. In this way, Jenson counters American religious forgetfulness by
providing an alternative to the Enlightenment's way of separating church and
state. Rather than attempt, in antiliberal fashion, to reverse the Enlightenment, he denies its binarism:[33] the church is neither modern state nor private
confession, neither of the spirit alone nor of the body alone. It is the society
of Christian bodies, the public way that Christians enact their availability to
God and to other creatures.

4. The weakness of Western theology in general: replacing salvation history with concepts of being

For Jenson, American theology's tendency to forget ecclesial history reinforces a more general tendency in the modern West, which is to render both
history and Scripture subservient to ontology. Thus the errors of American
theology share in the errant tendency of post-Enlightenment theologians more
generally to sever systematic and philosophic theologies from their roots in
premodern readings of Scripture and tradition. While first clearly displayed
in the Protestant–Catholic polemics of the seventeenth century,

the more decisive break . . . occurred in the eighteenth century. The European–
North American Enlightenment applied a hermeneutic of suspicion to all received

---

service to God unless we behold God in our actions?' This is to act with *devekut* [or loving
attachment to God], fulfilling the biblical injunction *uraitem*, 'and you shall *see* them'" (in
personal conversation, 2005).

33. As noted in the introduction, I apply the term *binary* to appropriate either–or distinctions
and *dyadic* to inappropriate ones. As in this sentence, I apply the term *binarism* to ongoing
tendencies to generate *inappropriate* distinctions (dyads) out of appropriate ones (binaries). My
assumption is that when binaries get overstated and overextended they become dyads.

wisdom, particularly that propounded by established authorities. Needing a criterion by which to scrutinize the established churches' teaching from "revelation," the Lockeans of the English-speaking world and the "Neologians" of Germany thought to find it in that other theology which Christian theology had itself acknowledged: if there is a knowledge of God natural to our being, this knowledge can be the norm of other purported theology.

What in fact happened therewith was that the West's Mediterranean–pagan religious heritage—truly no more anchored in universal humanity than any other—was elevated to be the judge of its biblical heritage. It took only a few decades for this misstep to evacuate elite theology of its specifically Christian content and, indeed, to repristinate—although often in sadly enfeebled form—the theology of pagan Mediterranean antiquity. (I 7–8)

Jenson's critique is therefore not of ontology per se, but of the modern West's misuse of it as first philosophy and of modern theology's tendency to adopt first philosophies as standards for judging the meaning and truth of Scripture-and-tradition. It is a matter of who is in charge.

In these terms, theology's central challenge is to make sense of classical philosophy's concept of *ousia*, or being, without allowing it to set the agenda for reading Scripture. Of central importance are two attributes of being in the classic readings: substance and the potential for timelessness. James Buckley notes that for Jenson, Christians have tried to meet this challenge in three ways. Some, in particular within Eastern Orthodoxy, allowed questions of *ousia* to apply only partially to God: "God has being but is also somehow 'above it.'" Some "could accept the concept for everything else but deny its application to God, as is the belief [sic] in rabbinic Judaism and among some Christian Heideggerians, risking the confusion of God's nonbeing with violence."[34] Some, finally, reinterpreted "'being to accommodate the gospel,' as did Thomas Aquinas and Gregory of Nyssa—and as does Jenson (I 211–12). To say that metaphysics is accommodated to the gospel is . . . to say that it is normed by the biblical drama of God."[35] In this third way, "the [Mediterranean] culture's

---

34. Buckley, "Intimacy," 19. I report this comparison even though it is overstated and partially unsatisfactory. It correctly reflects apophatic tendencies among the classical rabbinic sages, as well as their great cautions against reducing our scripturally based depictions of divine activity to terms borrowed from philosophy or any of the sciences. These tendencies and cautions are replayed in postmodern Jewish thought, but even then not in a way that "confuses God's nonbeing with violence." Emmanuel Levinas, the implied subject of this attribution, wrote of the violence *not* of nonbeing but of *being*! Beyond this misattribution, the comparison has several more general weaknesses. In addition to overstating the homogeneity of rabbinic thought, it rereads it, anachronistically, in terms of an opposition between *being* and *nonbeing* that is a preoccupation of postmodern Jewish philosophy but not in this sense of the classic sages. It fails, moreover, to translate the cataphatic tendencies of rabbinic Judaism into a comparably contemporary language. Such a translation would bring to light the elements of a *postliberal* Jewish theology that sounds much more like Jenson's Christian postliberalism than any Christian Heideggerianism.

35. Buckley, "Intimacy," 19.

'immutable being' was 'inwardly subverted' by Nicaea's confession that Jesus is God from God, *homoousion* with the Father, as well as by the Cappodocians' theology of Trinitarian hypostases as different subsisting relations."

But "this revisionary reinterpretation of being was incomplete, or flawed. For example, impassible being continued to be presumed (except by neo-Chalcedonians), God's *Logos* was understood as possession rather than communication, and the eschatological character of God's history and therefore the Spirit were suppressed" (I 108).[36] As Pannenberg suggests, this was Augustine's weakness: he conceived of eternity as timeless, but the eternal God "who will be whosoever he will be is not a God to whom time does not matter."[37] For Jenson, even Barth has weaknesses here, since, as Gerhard Forde paraphrases it, "in Barth's Christology, there is a danger that Jesus Christ will become less a concrete historical reality than a timeless Platonic form. The big question is whether for Barth, 'Jesus Christ has become the eternal decree.'"[38] In Forde's words, a "battle between time and eternity becomes the hallmark of Jenson's theology. There is a constant polemic throughout his work against the 'timeless' God of the Greeks. Virtually every theological 'sin' and false formulation can be traced to the intrusion of such timelessness into the theological scene."[39] The concept of substantial being proved to be a comparable challenge. As Forde puts it, Augustine was again one of the culprits, "making the persons functionally the same," sharing the character of "substance" not only with each other but also with creatures—a character that enables us to speak *of* God in the third person, as we also speak of creatures. But this speech creates "a transformation of the biblical discourse about God's Spirit into a stipulation of method for our spirituality."[40] For Jenson, attributing the characters of substance and timelessness to the Divine Being perverts the gospel's message about the identity of God.

5. *The Western theological habit of identifying God with timeless and substantial being must be broken: God makes himself known in historical time*

Any onto-theological claims are derivative of what we know about the Divine Being, and we know God only by way of his revelation in historical time. God's temporal infinity is God's relationality, which is his triune life. In Gunton's words, Jenson's "assault on divine timelessness" is an assault on efforts both to exclude and to limit God's place in time and place—"God is

36. Ibid.

37. Wolfhart Pannenberg, "Eternity, Time, and the Trinitarian God," in *Trinity, Time, and Church,* 65.

38. Jenson, *Alpha and Omega,* 162, cited in Gerhard O. Forde, "Robert Jenson's Soteriology," in *Trinity, Time, and Church,* 127.

39. Forde, "Robert Jenson's Soteriology," 127.

40. Jenson, "Pneumatological Soteriology," in *Christian Dogmatics* 2:126, cited in ibid., 132.

roomy; he can make room in himself if he chooses,"[41] and the room we may call both space and time. For Buckley, Jenson corrects the church's incompletely revisionary interpretation of being by redirecting theology's attention to time: "'the one unavoidable metaphysical fact' is our temporality."[42] "God does not create a world that thereupon has a history; he creates a history that is a world" (II 14). God's "way of being temporal" is, however, "not our way—if it was, God would be identified 'with' our world but not 'by' it" (II 19). The doctrine of God's triune life alone enables the church to assert at once God's temporality and God's infinity. "The triune event is 'temporal infinity.' God in Christ is (here follow Gregory of Nyssa's own words) 'infinite over the past and infinite over the future'" (I 216).[43] In this citation, the triune life is God of the past, the present, and the future.[44]

We might ask if Jenson's emphases are not motivated by the particular contexts of his correctives; to fully hypostatize any mode of temporal being would be to render it substantial, rather than relational, and by Jenson's own rules, he should want to maintain each mode's relationality. *Relationality*, in fact, may be another name for Jenson's notion of "temporal infinity." In Gilbert Meilaender's terms, "individual identity is," in Jenson's theology, "established and lived only in relation. There are no isolated monads who first subsist and then enter into relations with other such monads."[45] Thus, "influenced especially by the Cappodocians' adaptation of that one category of Aristotle's—relation—that was not easily compatible with a metaphysics of substance, Jenson has rigorously developed the notion of a 'person' as a 'subsistent relation.'"[46] In sum, persons achieve their individual identity only in community; for Jenson, this is true of human and divine persons. Past, present, and future would therefore have their identity only in community with one another. In similar fashion, Wolfhart Pannenberg argues, for example, that the

> identity of God belongs first of all to the Father, who is the God of Israel. The Father is prior to the Son. . . . Yet the kingdom of the Father is not only proclaimed by Jesus Christ but also established on earth by the risen Lord and will be consummated by the action of the Spirit. The apparent contradictions between these affirmations can be avoided if the divine identity of the Father is conceived in terms of the power of his future, which is the very source of new

41. Jenson, "Aspects of a Doctrine of Creation," in *The Doctrine of Creation: Essays in Dogmatics, History, and Philosophy*, ed. Colin E. Gunton (London: Continuum International, 2004), 24.

42. Buckley, "Intimacy," 19.

43. Cited by Buckley, "Intimacy," 19–20.

44. Jenson, "Appeal to the Person of the Future," in Robert Jenson and Carl Braaten, *The Futurist Option* (New York: Newman, 1970).

45. Gilbert Meilaender, "A Theology of the Political," in *Trinity, Time, and Church*, 277.

46. Ibid.

events in history, including the incarnation of his Son and the consummation of all creation by the power of his Spirit.[47]

In this argument, Pannenberg and Jenson appear to be at one.

6. To know God's being as God's triune life is to know God in the drama of Israel's Scripture and the drama of God's incarnation in Jesus Christ

God's being in history is a story disclosed to us only by way of God's Word to us, which we call "revealed Scripture." The scriptural Word is God's being in Israel's history (the covenantal life of the people Israel with God), and it is God's being in the history of the church (the incarnation of God's Word in Jesus Christ). To know God's being in human history and in created time is therefore derivative of our knowledge of God's Word in history, which is God's Word in Scripture.

The interdependence of Jenson's trinitarian and scriptural theologies displays his corrective to ontological foundationalism in medieval as well as modern Christian theology. As Buckley suggests, Jenson's innovative assertion of "God's infinite temporality" draws on a "theology of the triune God arising from the biblical drama."[48] This is one of Jenson's distinctive moves, examining the triune life as it is written within the scriptural drama rather than as what some theologians treat as Scripture's ontological or transcendental condition. His theology is biblical and trinitarian at once.[49] In Meilaender's words, "Jenson's attention over decades to the intricacies of Trinitarian dogma has led to a description of God in terms of a threefold mutual agency—of the *dramatis dei personae*, the 'characters of the drama of God [I 75].'"[50] "That God is identified by and with the biblical narrative makes for a circular relation between the two. 'The biblical narrative' is one narrative only as it is about the one God—and God's oneness is the oneness of the narrated Father, Son, and Spirit."[51] God has no qualities that we know apart from what both the Old and New Testaments say God does.[52] As Robert Wilken writes, "When I first read Jenson's discussions of the Trinity in

47. Pannenberg, "Eternity, Time, and the Trinitarian God," 67.

48. Buckley, "Intimacy," 20.

49. Robert Louis Wilken, "Is Pentecost a Peer of Easter? Scripture, Liturgy, and the *Proprium* of the Holy Spirit," in *Trinity, Time, and Church*, 176.

50. Meilaender, "A Theology of the Political," 277.

51. Buckley, "Intimacy," 15.

52. As noted earlier, the triune identity of God is thus none other than the identity of "'the one who rescued Israel from Egypt,' . . . [which] is confirmed as an identification of *God* in that it is continued 'as he thereupon rescued the Israelite Jesus from the dead'" (I 44, cited in C. R. Seitz, "Handing over the Name: Christian Reflection on the Divine Name YHWH," in *Trinity, Time, and Church*, 23).

volume one of his *Systematic Theology*, I was struck by how biblical it was and at the same time how Trinitarian."[53]

In this way, Jenson is particularly radical in his effort to remove philosophic a priorism (scholastic or post-Kantian) as a condition for the reception of Scripture—and as a condition for knowing God. Braaten writes, "In the history of Christian theology, I dare say, this is a Jensonian *novum*. Not even Walter Kunneth or Wolfhart Pannenberg . . . hinged the *identity* of God on the reality of Jesus's resurrection from the dead. I am more than happy to identify myself with this aspect of Jenson's doctrine of God. . . . God is what happens with Jesus."[54] For Jenson, God is thus neither Being *nor* 1, 2, and 3, but the One whose Word enters the world, and the Word suffers there among a humanity that resists it, but those true to the Word follow it and bring about its life on earth.

7. *Since God's identity is as inseparable from the story of Israel as it is from the story of Jesus, supersessionism is as much an assault on the identity of God as on the sacrality of Israel's covenant*

The church's Trinitarianism is commonly thought to depart from Israel's interpretation of God. This is the exact contradictory of the truth. . . . The doctrine of Trinity only explicates Israel's faith in a situation in which it is believed that the God of Israel has prior to the general resurrection raised one of his servants from the dead. (I 63)[55]

For Jenson, all aspects of God's trinitarian being therefore "appear in Israel's scripture" (I 63). Douglas Knight offers a particularly clear statement of Israel's place as the mark of historical temporality in Jenson's ontology as well as his theology: Jenson "has put Israel in her proper place as the object of the election of God and established the Trinity as the tool that keeps theology Christian."[56] "On the modern view we steadily increase our distance from the events of Jesus Christ and leave the church behind just as the church left Israel. Robert Jenson insists however that Israel is not back there, but here; the actual presence of the Jewish people is the theological datum. Her survival is evidence of God's faithfulness."[57] The problem postliberal theologians face is that "the history of the West is the history of the supplanting of the election of this people . . . with a generalized version of the same by which all are indifferently chosen, the concept of God's choosing abstracted to meaninglessness" (I 72). But "if we refuse to acknowledge this people as the elect people, we cannot

53. Wilken, "Is Pentecost a Peer of Easter?" 176.
54. Carl E. Braaten, "Eschatology and Mission," 303.
55. By now the reader will be well aware that I consider this a pivotal claim of Jenson's: I have already cited it above multiple times!
56. Douglas Knight, "Jenson on Time," in *Trinity, Time, and Church*, 71.
57. Ibid., 72.

make a coherent claim on the concept of time" (I 73). Theology must now choose: either substantialism or Israel.

8. The resurrection of Israel is the resurrection of Christ's body—and without this resurrection, being is unredeemed from death

The biblical drama of Israel's rescue is the story of Israel's resurrection from the dead. But "we may not set on one side Israel the nation and on another Israel the Son."[58]

In the resurrection, the created body is redeemed from death. This body is "availability," or what may be brought into relation.[59] The body's "availability is our becoming present for others . . . [and] allowing others to intend us."[60] If "body" is "flesh," then "language is just something that flesh does; the obedient speech becomes obedient practices and forms of life, actualized as human persons."[61] This is a remarkable theological move. Integrating the relationality of flesh and of language, it allows one to read the scriptural Word at once as what the body of Israel *does* in the *mitzvot*, or commandments, and what the body of Christ *does* both in Easter week and in the doings of the church. We return, then, to my opening discussion of law and promise (above, thesis 1). Embodying the scriptural commandments in its evolving body of rabbinic law, Israel prepares itself to receive God's grace, enacting its freedom at the same time and in the same way that it opens itself to receive the promise of God's Word. By accepting its identity *as Israel*, Israel both affirms its life as human creature in God's covenant and dies to its life as *mere* creature. This "dying" is its giving itself to God, who says *lech lecha*, "Go forth," and it goes forth.

Jenson's genealogical critique of modern Christian conceptualism ends by reaffirming what gospel Christianity reaffirmed: the life of Israel with and for God, the life of the body with and for God, and the life of the church as the body of Christ with and for God.

9. The resurrected body of Christ is available to the world at once in the Eucharistic sacrament and the doings of the church

For Jenson, "the one sole object of eternal election is Jesus and his people"[62]— Jesus *as* Israel, that is, but without supersessionism. This election is therefore coterminous with the resurrected body of Christ, which is "received in Eucharist [and] according to . . . recurring passages from Corinthians, is itself

---

58. Ibid.

59. Jenson, "The Body of God's Presence," paraphrased in ibid., 76–77.

60. Christoph Schwöbel, "Once Again, Christ and Culture: Remarks on the Christological Bases of a Theology of Culture," in *Trinity, Time, and Church*, 119.

61. Knight, "Jenson on Time," 77.

62. Geoffrey Wainwright, "*Vera Visibilia*: Robert Jenson on the Sacraments," in *Trinity, Time, and Church*, 293.

identical with the community it creates" (II 221–22).[63] The resurrected body is the church, realized through the sacraments; the doings of the church are thus the doings of Christ's body in its availability to the world, the language of God made flesh.

Christoph Schwöbel suggests that we see here Jenson's Swabian Lutheranism, that "there is no spatial distance to be overcome [in the Eucharist] since there is no space that separates the table of the Lord's Supper and heaven":[64] "Heaven is God's pad within his creation."[65] Does this suggest that if body is availability, then the principle of excluded middle does not apply to God's spatial attributes? Jenson's logic moves this way, and his resultant catholicity[66] may reflect his turn to the Cappadocians and not be merely an effort to "mediate" Lutheran and Catholic doctrines. Along this line, Gunton notes Jenson's sympathy with Cyril's version of the communion of attributes: "By a strong version of the communion of attributes, [Cyril's followers] made the one hypostasis to be the 'synthetic' agent of the whole gospel narrative, both of what is divine in it and of what is human in it, and they identified the eternal *Logos* as himself this hypostasis" (I 133).[67] Further, A. N. Williams notes how Jenson adopts an "operative anthropology" that is more indebted to Aquinas than Luther, but also pronouncing "'the Eastern soteriology' (of theosis) to be 'better than we have thought.'"[68] And as Meilaender stresses, Jenson acquires from the Cappadocians his central notion of the triune persons as relations.[69]

10. The doings of the church are at once Eucharistic and political, delivering God's future to the present

Created being is redeemed from death in the trinitarian-and-biblical drama of the Word made flesh in Israel's covenant and in the resurrection of Christ's body. The fruits of this resurrection are known by the sacraments that make the church and by the political doings of the church that redeem the world. In Jenson's words, "The profusion of the church's mysteries is historically rather than systematically determined and so can be captured by no merely conceptual structure" (II 260).[70] As David S. Yeago suggests, this history belongs to

63. Susan K. Wood, "Robert Jenson's Ecclesiology from a Roman Catholic Perspective," in *Trinity, Time, and Church*, 184.

64. Schwöbel, "Once Again," 117.

65. Robert W. Jenson, *Essays in Theology of Culture* (Grand Rapids: Eerdmans, 1995), 216.

66. Richard John Neuhaus refers to Jenson's "catholic (also uppercase) sensibility," in Neuhaus, "Jenson in the Public Square," 244.

67. Cited in Gunton, "Creation and Mediation," 84.

68. A. N. Williams, "The Parlement of Foules and the Communion of Saints: Jenson's Appropriation of Patristic and Medieval Theology," in *Trinity, Time, and Church*, 191, citing Jenson, *Essays in Theology of Culture*, 109.

69. Meilaender, "A Theology of the Political," 277.

70. Cited in Wainwright, "*Vera Visibilia*," 293.

the political and not merely sacramental life of the church. "As the church is drawn into [its] . . . future by the act of the Spirit, and so becomes a polity, the church . . . becomes the concrete locus where Christ's life is present in and for the world. . . . For Jenson, the church is 'spiritual' precisely *as* 'political,' for the church-gathering act of the Spirit is precisely to form a multitude into a polity by drawing them toward a shared future."[71] In this way, says Yeago, Jenson inherits Dietrich Bonhoeffer and Emil Brunner's efforts to return Reformation theology to political responsibility—in the process also moving it closer to Roman Catholic worldliness. In Meilaender's reading, Jenson's political theology completes his critique of the liberalized church in the West: "The common good is not some pool of goods that flows back in common upon all; [it] . . . simply is that communal life of participation and deliberation";[72] "the question of political hierarchy is [thus also] settled: none will be closer to Messiah than others . . . ; the forum in which the community lives its moral creativity will include all directly."[73]

For Jenson, the church, in sacrament and polity, is thus mission.[74] Not yet the kingdom of God, it is "anticipated eschatology,"[75] "an event *within the event* of the new age's advent" (II 171).[76]

71. David S. Yeago, "The Church as Polity? The Lutheran Context of Robert W. Jenson's Ecclesiology," in *Trinity, Time, and Church*, 203.
72. Meilaender, "A Theology of the Political," 279.
73. Jenson, *Essays in Theology of Culture*, 143.
74. Braaten, "Eschatology and Mission," 305.
75. Ibid., 306 (also citing Pannenberg's "proleptic eschatology").
76. Wainwright, "*Vera Visibilia*," 282.

4

Arguing for Christ

<small>STANLEY HAUERWAS'S THEOPRACTIC REASONING</small>

> Hear this word, you cows of Bashan
> On the hill of Samaria—
> Who defraud the poor,
> Who rob the needy . . .
>
> Amos 4:1 JPS

Stanley Hauerwas argues a lot and in a lot of places. Many of us argue, but very few argue this way.[1] Most of us tend to argue in places of relative comfort, where we think we master the local rules of reasoning, but Hauerwas seems to fight on other people's turf, where he shares few of the local rules and where his arguments are bound to be unpopular. Most of us tend to argue either philosophically, on the basis of what we imagine to be widely shared paradigms of reason, or else territorially, on the basis of assumptions we share with some community. Hauerwas seems to argue both ways at once: addressing the reasonings of some particular group and arguing with them in ways that address both their assumptions and more widely shared norms. Put this way, Hauerwas seems to argue like a philosopher in the tradition of pragmatism, reasoning broadly but from out of the context of local concerns. If that were what he was doing, however, I don't think folks would get angry at him the way

---

1. I am grateful for comments on this chapter from Jacob Goodson and Lindsay Cleveland, and for extensive editing by Rodney Clapp.

93

they do; they would more likely either ignore or thank him. And, of course, he wouldn't be talking about Jesus Christ all the time. I think the prophet Amos offers a closer analogy to Hauerwas's style of argument. But before entering into this comparison in detail, let me preview the overall agenda of this chapter.

This chapter offers and tests a model of Hauerwas's manner of argumentation, which I classify as a type of *theopractic reasoning*. This means a reasoning that is always theological and always attentive to practice. Reading Hauerwas in relation to antecedents in Christian salvation history, I characterize his reasoning as prophetic, pragmatic, retroductive, and Pauline.[2] Toward the end of the chapter I reevaluate these characterizations in light of the previous chapters' models of postliberalism. I conclude that while he shows different emphases, Hauerwas shares in Lindbeck's and Jenson's overall practice of postliberal Christian theology and that his reasoning confirms my thesis that postliberalism entails nonsupersessionism.

A Prophetic Prototype?

Returning, then, to Amos, consider the general impression of these different verses of criticism:

1. He proclaimed:
   The Lord roars from Zion,
   Shouts aloud from Jerusalem,
   And the pastures of the shepherds shall languish,
   And the summit of Carmel shall wither. (Amos 1:2 JPS)

The critical energy may not be so far from Hauerwas's style of criticism. And the standard of judgment belongs to God.

2. Thus said the LORD:
   For three transgressions of Gaza,
   For four, I will not revoke it:
   Because they exiled an entire population,
   Which they delivered to Edom. (1:6 JPS)

The criticism is for specific acts against other people: the ground of judgment may be divine, but the object of judgment is some local human action.

3. Thus said the LORD:
   For three transgressions of Edom,

2. All these terms will be defined in due course.

> For four, I will not revoke it
> Because he pursued his brother with the sword,
> And repressed all pity,
> Because his anger raged unceasing
> And his fury stormed unchecked. (1:11–12 JPS)

The criticism has a repetitious quality: what differs in each case is the particular crime. The punishment fits the crime in some way, which suggests that the genre of divine "anger" may be correlative to the genre of human crime. This point is illustrated more clearly when we compare Amos's prophecy with Hosea's: in Amos's voice the God of Israel speaks anger and fire; in Hosea's, the same God often speaks compassion—"I have had a change of heart. All My tenderness is stirred" (Hosea 11:8 JPS). The simplest explanation is that in one case, Israel has acted with effrontery, and the energy of God's anger mirrors the energy of Israel's sin; in the other case, Israel has already suffered for its sins and lies ravaged, and God's compassion complements Israel's emptiness.

> 4. You alone have I singled out
>   Of all the families of the earth—
>   That is why I will call you to account
>   For all your iniquities.
>   Can two walk together,
>   Without having met. (Amos 3:2–3 JPS)

> 5. Hear this word, you cows of Bashan . . . who defraud the poor. (4:1 JPS)

The criticism belongs to a specific relationship that has a specific history: God and this people walked together before and already came to an understanding that Israel would not act as it now acts. The relationship is therefore characterized by familiarity as well as austere criticism, intimacy as well as irony.

> 6. I will restore My people Israel.
>   They shall rebuild ruined cities and inhabit them . . .
>   Nevermore to be uprooted
>   From the soil I have given them. (9:14–15 JPS)

But the irony ends. The severity of God's judgment remains within this relationship; God thus binds himself to his renewed promise that Israel shall one day merit his full blessing.

Like the philosophic pragmatist, the prophet Amos receives God's voice for the sake of identifying what John Dewey calls a "problematic situation": examining it, diagnosing the source of the problem, and recommending (or commanding) remedial actions. Like Amos, the pragmatist draws on deep sources of reparative wisdom, relevant to many possible needs, but directs this wisdom to the specific problem at hand. Unlike the philosophic pragmatist, Amos names the ultimate source of wisdom "God" rather than "reason" or common sense, and he serves only as witness to the wisdom rather than as active agent.

Does Hauerwas sound more like Amos or like the philosophic pragmatist? The preceding verses from Amos bring to mind the following features of Hauerwas's argumentation:

Critical energy on behalf of divine judgment. The energy is displayed in part by the sheer volume of written and spoken arguments, but also by Hauerwas's willingness to challenge his interlocutors directly.[3]

Considering the relation of divine judgment to historically specific human actions. One of Hauerwas's central judgments is against his colleagues' efforts to generalize beyond the specific contexts of their critical inquiries.

Criticisms offered within relationships of shared history and witness. Hauerwas criticizes his neighbors, not distant strangers. This criticism is thus a mark of some breach in some relationship or in some shared witness; the criticism is a call to both truth (as fidelity to the word) and reconciliation.

Irony, humor, and sometimes sarcasm marking some breach in some relationship. Hauerwas criticizes out of three-part relationships that connect him to certain others by way of their overlapping relations to God. He tends to write without criticism and with less affect when addressing thinkers who tend to be distant from such relations. I read irony, humor, and sarcasm as marks of broken relationships that might nevertheless be one day healed. The more distant the day, perhaps the more biting the sarcasm.

3. As illustrated by his reply to John Cobb: "I simply do not have the basis to know what Cobb seems to know, since I have learned to distrust the very practices that have produced the knowledge he professes. Put differently, I think Cobb would like to be a postmodernist, but he remains caught in the discourse of modernity" (Stanley Hauerwas, *Wilderness Wanderings: Probing Twentieth-century Theology and Philosophy* [Boulder, CO: Westview, 1998, 25]). Or his reply to Gustafson: "I suspect James Gustafson's critique of my work gives voice to the disquiet many feel about the 'newness' of my perspective. By responding to Gustafson I hope to help some readers understand better what I am about. . . . One cannot understand what I am about if one continues to presuppose the dominant philosophical and theological intellectual habits of the past hundred years. . . . As a result, I do not pretend that coming to understand me is easy or without risk but only that such a rethinking is required. I do not expect that those who make the effort will necessarily agree with me, but I do hope that having made the effort they will have learned something" (Stanley Hauerwas, "Why the 'Sectarian Temptation' Is a Misrepresentation: A Response to James Gustafson [1988]," in *The Hauerwas Reader*, ed. John Berkman and Michael G. Cartwright [Durham, NC: Duke University Press, 2001], 91). See below, 122–23nn63–64.

Irony and sarcasm replaced in the end with eschatology—anticipating how lines of relationship, now broken, may touch again in the promised future. I suggested earlier that Hauerwas enters into debates on other people's turf. Now I can refine that suggestion. He debates with others who may share a deeper turf even if they believe their surface differences are all that matters. Hauerwas's strategy may be to engage others long enough on what seem to be their terms that some may be tempted to redefine the debate with respect to some third term not now present that could lie between them. Ultimately, this third is a witness to Jesus Christ, but it may be approached through preliminary witnesses that speak the languages of Hauerwas's interlocutors.

Prophetic Reasoning, Modern and Postliberal

Hauerwas appears to reason like the biblical prophets.[4] Readers may object that Hauerwas often argues in philosophic terms, drawn, for example, from Aristotle's ethics, while a prophetic model should preclude such philosophic practice. In this section, I evaluate the copresence of disciplined rationality and prophetic witness in Hauerwas's pragmatism.

"Ye shall know them by their fruit": reasoning like a pragmatist

In his Gifford Lectures, *With the Grain of the Universe*, Hauerwas draws on the resources of William James to launch a pragmatic critique of modern natural philosophy: there *is* reason for natural philosophy, but "nature" speaks to us (pace J. S. Mill) only by answering questions we ask of it. This is to know the world around us only through our presuppositions and therefore only *as* a supposition. In the vocabulary of Scripture, this is to know the world as *creation*. Hauerwas's argument is that this sort of creation is the most, rather than the least, consistent with the goals of contemporary science. Truth is not a predicate of our immediate intuitions of the world, but only of our relationships with the world. Truth is therefore a predicate of our behavior in the world and shaped through the long run of life in the world. Another word for this shaping is the *personality* we achieve in the world, or what we call *virtues*. Hauerwas's pragmatic theory is that to test the truth of our claims about the world is to test the truth of our virtues.

Hauerwas eventually parts company with James, not because James is too pragmatic but because he is not pragmatic enough! For James, our knowledge of the world is inseparable from the ways we act in it—from our will to believe.

4. Since prophecy has ceased from Israel, it may be anachronistic if not also blasphemous to refer to contemporary styles of argument as "prophetic." We have, however, not ceased to learn about God's ways with the world, and the prophetic texts are sources of evidence of those ways.

James should therefore argue that our knowledge of the world is "traditioned" and that a Christian tradition for knowing the world has no less validity, a priori, than another tradition. Hauerwas argues, however, that James's cultural prejudices led him, for no good philosophical reason, to dismiss specifically Christian presuppositions. James's pragmatism drew on individualistic Emersonian presuppositions that reduced his capacity to evaluate Christian natural philosophic claims. To right this pragmatic wrong, Hauerwas seeks a philosophic account of our presuppositions about the natural world that is not prejudiced against Christian presuppositions. He has no a priori argument to offer about the relative superiority of Christianity as source of our presuppositions. Christianity is to be proved through its practical consequences, rather than through any evidentiary apologetics. This is precisely why Peirce claimed that his pragmatism was "only an application of the sole principle of logic which was recommended by Jesus, 'Ye may know them by their fruits,' and it is very intimately allied with the ideas of the gospel."[5] Peirce's pragmatism displayed both the logic of Jesus's Scripture and Christianity's stake in the logic of scientific inquiry.

In a recent essay, Hauerwas acknowledges the important influence of Victor Preller on the argument of *With the Grain of the Universe*, in particular his affirmative readings of Aquinas and Wittgenstein.[6] Preller (along with, more recently, David Burrell) introduces the best reading of Aquinas as the theological father of Hauerwas's pragmatic theology. As Hauerwas notes, Aquinas did not believe that philosophy derived its validity directly from Scripture. "The principles of other sciences either are evident and cannot be proved, or are proved through natural reason through some other science. But the knowledge proper to [theological] science comes through revelation, and not through natural reason."[7] For Aquinas, therefore, the theologian and the philosopher work independently but learn something significant from one another. Within the environment of contemporary discourse, Preller located Aquinas's philosophic dialogue partner in the Wittgenstein of the *Investigations*.

Three features of Preller's Wittgenstein attract Hauerwas the most. First is his critique of modern philosophy's effort to reduce any lived "system" of life to some finite system of propositions (such as the one portrayed in Wittgenstein's *Tractatus*). The second is Wittgenstein's attention to the wonder of our

5. Charles Sanders Peirce, *Collected Papers of Charles Sanders Peirce*, ed. Charles Hartshorne and Paul Weiss (Cambridge, MA: Belknap Press of Harvard University Press, 1932), vol. 5, par. 402n (future references to this collection will include only volume and paragraph number, as here: 5:402n).

6. Stanley Hauerwas, "Connections Created and Contingent: Aquinas, Preller, Wittgenstein, and Hopkins," in *Grammar and Grace: Reformulations of Aquinas and Wittgenstein*, ed. Jeffrey Stout and Robert MacSwain (London: SCM, 2004).

7. *Summa Theologiae* 1.1.6.2, cited in Stanley Hauerwas, *With the Grain of the Universe* (Grand Rapids: Brazos, 2001), 23.

individual perceptions of the world. The third is Wittgenstein's rediscovering something like this wonder within the linguistic practices that limn everyday social existence. Each of our judgments about the world receives its life not only from what we see but also from the living complex of sociolinguistic practices that enable us to see.

I have on occasion urged Hauerwas to adopt Charles Peirce as his mentor in pragmatism, not James, and I have not received clear resistance. With that modest encouragement, I will suggest that Peirce provides both the pragmatic critique of naturalism that Hauerwas admires in James *and* a nonprejudicial account of the presuppositions of our knowledge of nature: one that not only acknowledges the legitimacy of Christian presuppositions but also grounds pragmatism in the Gospel witness. What, then, of Wittgenstein? I believe Peirce adds something to Preller's Wittgenstein as well. Wittgenstein is a wonderful exponent of Peirce's pragmatism as applied to the philosophy of language use, but he fails to bring forward other features of pragmatism that I believe are necessary for joining philosophic reasoning to prophetic witness. For the sake of brevity, I will focus on one of these features: the capacity to account for and contribute to the power of language communities to change in response to their own failures.

As Preller reads Wittgenstein, our individual perceptions of the world are sources of wonder whose effects on us are displayed through the way we act in the world and toward each other. The instrument of this display is what we call understanding or thought, most broadly put, and the medium of understanding and thought is the language we speak, as embodied in our community of speech and action. In this way, Preller's Wittgenstein speaks of the wonders that enter through the gates of perception into our beliefs and actions and thus our communities of speech and action. The Peirce that I am recommending to Hauerwas provides a complementary account: "The elements of every concept enter into logical thought at the gate of perception and make their exit at the gate of purposive action; and whatever cannot show its passports at both those two gates is to be arrested as unauthorized by reason."[8] Peirce also has much to say about the wondrous features of perception (he call these the elements of "surprise" and "abduction" in our thinking) and about how these features are known through their effects on our understanding ("our logical thought," or our thinking in relation to the world of experience) as it is embodied in our communities of thought and belief. Peirce provides something else, however, that I do not observe in Preller's Wittgenstein: an account of how the wondrous elements of perception and communal practice also emerge as sources of repair and redemption in times of personal and communal shipwreck—when our understanding appears confused, our languages fail to articulate what we experience, and our communities of speech and action appear dysfunctional. In other words, Preller's Wittgenstein helps me account for my community's

8. Peirce, 5:212.

life in the world when we appear to *have* a life in the community, but not when things appear to fall apart—when what we seek is not the order of this world of language and practice, but the transformation of a troubled or even dying world into one in which we may live again.

For Peirce, wonder marks more than one phenomenon. Yes, it may mark the sheer *whatness* of what there is in our world. But it may also mark the terrible *suffering* of our world. And it may also mark the power of *repair* and *redemption* that lies hidden until the wounds of our world break open. I recommend Peirce to Hauerwas, because Peirce's pragmatism offers a cogent philosophic account of these second two marks. I believe Preller's Wittgenstein remains a significant resource when it is extended by this kind of pragmatism.[9]

Marks of Hauerwas's prophetic-and-pragmatic or reparative reasoning

Is Hauerwas therefore a pragmatist? If Peirce is a model, then yes. But is this not to characterize Hauerwas first as a philosopher? No. Peirce's prag-

---

9. "That ye may know them by their fruits." In Peirce's words, pragmatism is nothing other than a logical corollary to these words of Jesus. Agreeing with James's claim that we know what anything or any concept is by observing its effects, Peirce shows that this is equivalent to observing its effects on us (the observers) and thus on our practice or our way of living in the world. This pragmatism builds on several key assumptions: (a) We are not mere spectators of the world. For Peirce, psychobiology, logic, or studies of language use do not warrant the modern presumption that we know the world by gazing at it, as it were, from a distance. (b) The more reliable evidence is that we are first and foremost actors in the world, bundles of habits, each of which links some set of sensory stimuli to some set of actions (some muscular movement). (c) The world is not divided sharply between subjects and objects, knower and the known, mind and matter, the theoretical and the practical, what is active and what is passive. These dyads are unwarranted by empirical evidence. They arise as the consequence of a modern will to believe, which, when granted authority, makes us suspicious of all antecedent sources of knowledge: all traditions are suspect until rendered clear in our own terms, which means until reexamined as objects of knowledge, of we which are the spectators. In this case, the modern prophecy is fulfilled, for now the sources of our knowledge appear as objects of our cognition, and the *cogito* emerges as that-which-cognizes. For the pragmatist, these "objects" are objects of our own intending, rather than publicly observable things or relations. They are, in other words, expressions of our responses to such things and relations, and others cannot perceive these expressions but only their public effects or consequences. The pragmatist's self-appointed task is not to look past these objects of individual intention and will but to offer a means of rendering them publicly meaningful. The means—what Peirce calls "the pragmatic maxim"—is to reread the individual's claims about these objects *not* as claims about the world but as *symptoms* of some event—usually an interruptive or disruptive event—in the relation of the world to a way of knowing that world and acting in it. To read such claims is thus to reread them as effects or consequences of certain events. This reading is therefore a form of retroductive reasoning, from effect to cause: a difficult and fallible form of reasoning, but an urgent one, since if it is successful it will enable us to reread the otherwise private claims of individuals as sources of insight into deep dislocations in the ways we know and act in the world. The pragmatist's task is to teach us how to generate testable hypotheses about the meanings of our otherwise private claims, the epistemological dislocations that may underlie these claims, and, ultimately, how these dislocations may be repaired.

matism emerged out of his reparative critique of the modern philosophy of science. Appropriate to its object, Peirce's pragmatism is thus articulated in the language of philosophy, but there are other ways to speak pragmatically. Our study of Amos's words suggests, in fact, that pragmatism may have a prophetic lineage. And this may as well be the as-yet-unspoken implication of Peirce's Matthean emblem: Jesus says, "Ye may know [the truth of prophecies] by their fruits." Consider, therefore, the fruits of Amos's prophecy.

Amos's Reparative Reasoning

Amos's prophecy appeared on the occasion of major crises in the nation of Israel. The *first mark of pragmatic reasoning*—or what we may more felicitously call *reparative reasoning*[10]—*is reasoning in response to a profound interruption in one's community of speech and action.*

In Amos's reasoning, the next mark is to diagnose the source of this interruption, which Amos finds to be both external to the community (such as the earthquake of Amos 1 or, we may add, the Assyrian invasion of Isaiah 28 on) and internal (the behavior of Israel as a nation, and Judah). (Were the source merely internal, there would be no clear public evidence to capture the nation's attention; were the source merely external, there would be reparative action to take.) *The second mark is thus to read a material threat to the nation as symptom of an as-yet-invisible disorder within the national community.* Reasoning from consequent (threat) to antecedent (disorder) is a species of what Peirce calls "retroductive reasoning" or "abduction" (his favorite name for the way one reasons from the threat to a plausible vision of what can be done about it).[11]

The third mark is another level of retroduction: reading the disorder in the nation as symptomatic of the nation's collective sin or error. (Indeed *chet,* "sin" in Hebrew, is literally "missing the mark.") This prophetic retroduction is neither a strictly human activity of diagnosis nor a strictly divine disclosure through the prophet's voice (as through Balaam's ass).

The fourth mark is a moment when the prophet's reasoning and God's voice are mutually indistinguishable. This is a mark to reconsider in treatments of philosophic pragmatism: at a certain point, pragmatic reasoning summons the divine voice and proceeds—if at all—only by way of this voice. To be sure, this is the mark that modern philosophers refuse to acknowledge, as if they had indubitable grounds for knowing a priori that the realms of science and the divine do not mix.[12]

10. As noted in chap. 2, I owe this use of the term *reparative* to Nicholas Adams, who interpreted my studies of pragmatism as most interesting if applied to a more general activity of "reparative reasoning." Adams formalizes this suggestion in Nicholas Adams, "Reparative Reasoning," *Modern Theology* 24, no. 3 (July 2008): 447–57.

11. Retroduction is a fallibilistic form of what Kant called "transcendental reflection."

12. One lesson of Peirce's "Neglected Argument for the Reality of God" is that a certain level of retroduction does, in fact, summon what he calls "the reality of God." This retroduction gen-

The fifth mark may illustrate an immediate occasion for the Matthean formula: the prophet's public proclamation. "He proclaimed, The LORD roars from Zion, shouts aloud from Jerusalem. . . . Thus saith the LORD: For three transgressions of Damascus, for four, I will not revoke it" (Amos 1:2–3 JPS). Here, the public is told for the first time that a material threat is, in fact, symptomatic of an inner disorder and that the disorder is symptomatic of their collective sin.

The fifth mark thus implies a sixth: this proclamation is a call for public action. To say there is sin here is to say that if the sin is removed, there may be hope for relief from the disorder and thus from the external threat the nation now suffers. God alone decides, so that pragmatic "repair" is at best only probable.

Hauerwas's Reparative Reasoning

The six marks of Amos's reparative reasoning may also be observed in Hauerwas's. For economy of reporting, I will look for the most part to a single essay by Hauerwas for illustrations of these six marks: "What Could it Mean for the Church to Be Christ's Body? A Question without a Clear Answer."[13]

Mark 1: Responding to profound interruptions in a shared tradition, community, or relation. Hauerwas frames his essay as a commentary on how the Feast of the Ascension is observed in the village of Sneem, Ireland. What does it mean, he asks, "to dress up young girls to become brides of Christ"? According to the essay, it means that following Christ means joining the body of Christ, and that is not something one can do with mind and spirit alone; the body matters. A subframe for the essay displays another way the body matters: in this case, the body of Hauerwas's own feelings, relationships, reactions. As on many occasions, he offers the essay in part as an argument against his critics—in this case, against two friends who have, in his opinion, mischaracterized his work as "proposing that the Christian community focus on its own identity" (21).[14] His self-defense will complement his reflections on

---

erates the broadest hypotheses we have about the order of the entire universe—"all the universes of experience"—within which we may include major paradigm shifts in science. "Musement" on the reality of God thereby underlies the logic of science. This is a central claim in Peirce's pragmatic logic of science, but the modern philosophers who otherwise draw on Peirce's contributions to logic tend selectively to discount this one part of his logic. In this way, they preserve the modern dyads and repress Peirce's more medieval and scholastic-like assumption that the hypotheses that lead modern science rest on the foundation of a theological witness. In the case of Amos, there is, in other words, a prophetic voice that is at once fully human and fully divine.

13. Stanley Hauerwas, *In Good Company: The Church as Polis* (Notre Dame, IN: University of Notre Dame Press, 1995), 19–31. I am not suggesting that these marks are definitive of Hauerwas's work, only that they may be observed in his work.

14. The friends are William Placher and George Hunsinger, who offered their comment in an introduction to one of Frei's essays in *Hans W. Frei, Theology and Narrative: Selected Essays*, ed. George Hunsinger and William C. Placher (New York: Oxford University Press, 1993), 213–14.

Sneem, since his account of the church as a body will be offered as an alternative to both individualistic and communitarian accounts.[15]

Within these frames, Hauerwas delivers the central lesson of the essay: his theological writing is offered only in response to what he believes are profound interruptions in the life of the church today (and over the past decades). For Hauerwas, a *theological lesson is made in response to something really practical and really wrong; otherwise it is not a theological lesson but some spiritualized meditation.* What's really wrong is that the unity of the church—and thus the unity of the body of Christ—is threatened by the regnant theo-political paradigms of how to live in the church and how the church lives in the world. What's really practical is that these paradigms, while articulable in the languages of academy theology, are defined only as they are lived day to day.

Mark 2: diagnosing both external and internal conditions of the interruptions. Hauerwas's theopractic reasoning turns on the claim that threats to the unity of the church today are not mere accidents of history. They are, more significantly, symptoms of recent Christian commitment to a series of dichotomous paradigms: divided, for example, between loyalties to faith or reason, body or spirit, ethics or liturgy, Rome or the nation-state, individualism or communitarianism, Jew or Greek, *sola scriptura* or *traditio.* Hauerwas therefore writes, for example, of the inseparability of body from church: "*Lumen Gentium*[16] quite rightly assumes that questions about the status of the church as 'the body of Christ' are inseparable from questions of government. Such a practice is necessary for a reading of the Pauline stress on the body if we are to avoid the ontology of the body so characteristic of liberalism—i.e., that my 'body' is an instrument for the expression of my 'true self'" (24).[17]

15. This element of personal defense brings to mind another trait of prophetic reasoning: the prophet's identifying personal self with prophetic mission, where the bodily state of the prophet is evidence of perception of the conditions to which God's Word responds. Hauerwas dramatizes this materiality by speaking in a "down-home" voice replete with a "Texan's cuss words." I imagine that this drama is meant to counter the contemporary church's tendency toward spiritualization.

16. *Lumen Gentium* ("Light of the Nations"), the Dogmatic Constitution on the Church, was promulgated by Pope Paul VI on November 21, 1964. It is one of the primary documents of the Second Vatican Council.

17. Hauerwas writes, moreover, of the inadequacy of "Rome" of itself to serve as a model of ecclesial politics: "Catholicism is not only what it is because of the Reformation, but Catholicism is what it is because it has also been produced in reaction to modernity. . . . I am thinking of the concentration of administrative power that seemed necessary to counter the rise of the modern nation-state. . . . I assume that Rome has no built-in immunity to such processes" (*In Good Company*, 27). Hauerwas cites the following claim of Barth's against the dyads that persist within the Reformation as well:

Within the organized unities of the Evangelical Churches, we are faced with the fact of pietistic-rationalistic Modernism, with its roots in medieval mysticism and the humanistic Renaissance. . . . [A]t this point, in its opposition to Roman Catholicism

Hauerwas's secondary claim—and the theme of much of his writing—is that such dyads inform academic theology and ecclesial scholarship as well as individual and institutional practices in the churches. This means that Hauerwas's critics will be those who, thinking within those dyads, mistake his critique of binarism per se with what they fear is a critique of the dyadic pole they endorse.[18] Assuming that he is endorsing the opposite pole, they therefore tend to respond with some aggressive defense of one against the other. As illustrated in this essay, Hauerwas often returns the aggression: offering them a carefully drawn nondyadic argument that is also spiced, in places, with a more dyadic-sounding rhetoric of defense. He writes, for example,

> I have, after all, been labeled a "sectarian fideistic tribalist" who is calling for the church to beat a retreat from the world. (20)

> I must be more emphatic in my rejection of the description of being a communitarian. (25)

Interlocutors may choose to respond reactively to the rhetoric or more soberly to the argument. Either way, Hauerwas's response may confound their habits of separating theological and philosophic analyses from moral and religious judgment (mark 3), separating rational argument from theological witness (mark 4), and separating argument from concrete practice (marks 5–6).

Mark 3: reading inner disorder as a symptom of sin and moral trespass. Hauerwas's claims about threats to the unity of the church lead to claims about who is responsible for these threats: the members of the church. I believe Hauerwas responds to such questions in the tradition of Amos. For Amos, each nation is responsible for its behavior: if it sins against God's will, the nation will suffer; if it repents of its sins, it may win relief from its suffering and regain the Creator's blessings. Unlike "blood guilt," Amos's theodicy cannot be justified on the basis of merely efficient causality. As in the words of Amos 3:8—"The lion has roared—who will not fear?" (NIV)—natural causality is Amos's metaphor for the indirect rule of divine justice: God alone judges if and when a certain act of sin or of repentance will bear its good or evil fruit. Hauerwas's theodicy appears to be analogous to Amos's. To hold each church member responsible for contributing to the unity of the body of Christ is to make a claim not of efficient causality but of divine justice. It is to argue that (a) the unity of the church is threatened by dyadic paradigms of

---

and to Protestant Modernism, evangelical faith is in conflict with itself. (Karl Barth, *Church Dogmatics* 1/1, trans. G. T. Thomson [Edinburgh: T&T Clark, 1936], 36, quoted in ibid., 27.)

18. As noted in the introduction, I apply the term *binary* to appropriate either–or distinctions and *dyadic* to inappropriate ones. As in this sentence, I apply the term *binarism* to ongoing tendencies to generate inappropriate distinctions (dyads) out of appropriate ones (binaries).

Christian life; (b) church members have the freedom to affirm such paradigms or not; and (c) to affirm them is sin (threatening the unity of the body of Christ intentionally or unintentionally).

Mark 4: where divine and human voices meet. This is the defining—and most challenging—mark of Hauerwas's theopractic reasoning, for it answers what I take to be the bottom-line question: what, after all, is nondyadic in Hauerwas's own reasoning? The answer is that the nondyadic elements of his thinking are elements in which divine and human voices cannot be distinguished. Readers committed to dyadic paradigms will object. Rationalists may protest that this claim of copresence is itself a theological claim, since it introduces God into what we know only in human terms. Fideists may protest that this claim of copresence is itself a rationalist claim, since it implies that theological judgments are marked by human finitude and cannot therefore refer infallibly to God. I understand Hauerwas's overall response to be that the claims of both faith and reason are copresent in the nondyadic elements of his reasoning *and* that nondyadic claims can be proved "only by their fruit."

If asked, for example, if the church is a community of persons or part of Christ, Hauerwas answers, "What is crucial . . . is not whether the church is primarily understood as 'the body of Christ' or 'the people of God,' but whether the practices exist through which we learn that our bodies are not 'ours'" (24).[19] Our bodies are not our own because we have been given a new body by the Spirit (1 Cor. 6:12–20). The Spirit does not render us all-spirit, however, but body-and-spirit or body-with-others and others-with-God: all these are what I mean by nondyadic relations, manifested in the nondyadic practices of communities of persons, prototypically the body of Christ. To say that this body includes individual bodies is to say that it lives historically, extended through time and space. Only in space-time can the human and divine share in one body. "I seek therefore not for the church to be a community, but rather to be a body constituted by disciplines that create the capacity to resist the disciplines of the body associated with the modern nation-state and in particular the economic habits that support that state" (26).

As illustrated in Hauerwas's writing, the claims of nondyadic reasoning cannot be directly affirmed or formulated through the series of dyadic reasonings that we tend to author as individuals. Nevertheless, nondyadic reasoning includes individual reasonings within its movement, for each individual reasoning marks a particular space-time, by way of which it opens nondyadic reasoning to its place within concrete history. And why do individual reasonings fill this unique role? In Peirce's terms, it is because "the individual [may

19. To me, "not ours" implies that, as strictly individual reasoners, we can cognize only one of these options at a time, which is to reduce their unity to something it is not; reasoning outside our individuality, in a greater reasoning, we can share in a nonreductive, nondyadic reasoning. This reasoning is not not-ours; it is fully ours and not-ours, present to what is human of us and what is divine with us.

be] marked only by ignorance and error." While overstating his point, Peirce uncovers the defining lesson of marks 1–4: *individual reasonings, alone, bear witness to profound interruptions in a given tradition and community; therefore, individual reasonings alone occasion prophetic witness and pragmatic repair.*[20] For this reason, prophetic-and-pragmatic reasoning may be redescribed as the species of nondyadic reasoning that interprets individual reasonings as marks of societal distress and that initiates a society's reparative response to such marks. Such reparative reasoning appears in the form of particular projects of repair, each of which bears marks comparable to those I have attributed to Amos and, now, to Hauerwas.

Hauerwas names the ultimate source of repair Jesus Christ, fully human, fully God. He implies that this repairer (redeemer) is not outside of our reasoning but is the ground of reparative reasoning in the church; this ground should be summoned directly in times like this, when members of the church may forget that this ground is not only implicit in their power of reasoning but also available to them as an active agent of repair. Jesus Christ is the identity of the God "who comes when we call." In "What Could It Mean for the Church to Be Christ's Body?" Hauerwas emphasizes the embodied character of the Redeemer as a corrective to spiritualizing tendencies in the church today. To bear witness to the embodied Christ is to bear witness to the God who can redeem his creatures because he is already present in and to the individual of flesh and blood whose cry (and whose reasoning) he hears as a call for societal repair.[21]

Returning to our discussion of Preller's Wittgenstein, we need to address one more challenge posed by mark 4. Preller provided Hauerwas with a philosophic warrant for knowledge claims about the divine–human encounter: christological presuppositions are as valid as any other successful ground of language use, where "success" is measured by sustained use. While acknowledging this warrant, I suggested that Preller's Wittgenstein fails to provide Hauerwas with an account of how language systems may be transformed in response to catastrophic change. Mark 4 is evidence that Hauerwas relies on such an account and that it is grounded in a Christology that is at once prophetic and pragmatic. In this account, therefore, *Christology* refers to the source not only of some Christian "language game" but also of the repair and renewal of any distressed or moribund Christian language game. It refers, in other words, to the source of Christian reparative reasoning, public knowledge of which is as reliable as any other reparative practice. As we have seen, such knowledge

---

20. The individual claim appears prototypically as a cry: "and [the Israelites'] cry for help from the bondage rose up to God" (Exod. 2:23 JPS). See David Ford's extensive account of "the cry" in his *Christian Wisdom* (Cambridge: Cambridge University Press, 2008).

21. Judaism includes a comparably embodied understanding of God, whose Word is embodied in Torah. My understanding of Torah is the source of my reasoning, analogically, about Hauerwas's understanding of Christ.

is displayed in nondyadic reasonings, of which each claim is irreducible to the dyadic, either–or terms of everyday language use. In Peirce's terms, such claims are "irremediably vague," which means that (a) these are truth claims about actual entities in the world, but (b) they do not predicate either one of any pair of dyadic attributes of those entities, except (c) in relation to an individual observer, so that an otherwise "vague" (or partially indeterminate) claim about some entity is made determinate only in relation to a given subject or observer. In plain-speak: one may say "Christ shall redeem us from this distress," but most details about how specifically Christ "redeems us" are offered only with respect to a historically specific event of repair or redemption, as disclosed by a particular witness. For Peirce, and I trust for Hauerwas, these epistemological rules apply comparably to christological and scientific claims about what is there in the world and how it may be repaired.[22]

22. For Hauerwas, spiritualism reduces "body" to an idea rather than to that which is directly encountered in the world. For him, "body" and "spirit" appear as correlatives in the world, much as Aristotle claimed. Peirce liked to say that all actually existing things are vague, because we can never say of something we encounter out there in the world that we know with utter certainty that it is X or Y. We can say this only of something we ourselves have constructed or defined. Peirce also liked to say that *God* is the ultimately vague name, since it names that which we believe exceeds the limits of any of our concepts or definitions. To say something is vague, however, does not mean we can say either nothing about it or anything we want about it. An entity that really exists has really knowable properties. Vagueness is one such property. It means that the entity's "own" character is irreducible to our dyadic concepts and, therefore, that our dyadic distinctions say more about us than they do about the entity we seek to know. It also means that there is more to know about this entity. According to Peirce and consistent with Hauerwas's reasoning, the Matthean formula tells us how to know more: "ye shall know them by their fruits." That is to say, the characters of the entity are not displayed overtly to us in this moment but only by the consequences (fruit) of our relation to the entity over time into the future.

Will we one day know if the entity is X or Y? That is not the right question, since it remains in dyadic form. The Matthean formula implies that our knowledge of the entity is relational. The question is not "What is it?" but "What is its relation to me or us in a certain point in space-time?" It is therefore appropriate to claim that "at this space-time C, it displays the character X to this observer O." It is consistent with the vagueness of an actual entity to say of it, "It is cXo" (but not "It is X"). That is real knowledge and a really warranted claim. Such a claim can be offered, moreover, not only about things in the world but also about God. There is no false presumption in the claim, "At this time and place in my life (my community or our tradition, and so on) God is (or names) a frightening being." Since the claim is about the relation of that term to me at this time, I am the one who is privileged to make the claim. This does not mean that the claim is self-evident, since I may on further consideration change my mind and say something like, "Ah, now I see I didn't mean 'frightening' but 'unknown.'" The perceptual evidence that leads me to say, "God is now X to me," is not defined by the dyad "either I know this certainly or I do not have grounds to make any claim." It is defined, instead, by the rule of any empirical claim: I am certain that I have these feelings or sensations, and I think (believe or strongly hypothesize) that they tell me this (that the dog is black, that it is raining, that the divinity is frightening). In each case, subsequent feelings or sensations can lead me to refine what I think (no, now I think that the dog is really dark brown, that you are just watering the lawn, that God's distance fills me with awe): there need not be any change in the sensory evidence per se, but only in its relation to what else I encounter in space-time. In sum, our immediate encounter with God in the

Mark 5: public proclamation. And mark 6: call to public action. Does the Christian reparative reasoner encounter Jesus Christ in Scripture or in "experience" (reparative engagement with real problems in the world)? For Hauerwas, as I read him, such a question replays one of those modern dyads. As reparative reasoner, Hauerwas encounters Jesus Christ as always in Scripture and in the world. This also means that Scripture cannot be defined, dichotomously, as "this book of words here" as opposed to "this Christ who lived there" (or "who lives in my heart and practice"). Like any real entity, Scripture is encountered as a vague entity, identified only in its relation to the knower in space and time. It carries additional significance as both a thing in the world and a word: a message sent from one to another, like a letter addressed to the reader. Whoever the sender, such a message has at least four elements: the "signifying thing" (like black ink on parchment that signifies something to someone), the person who sends the message (or many persons, each defined only as a being who can communicate to another being), the person who receives it (or many persons), and its "meaning" (what the receiver understands the message to be). Scripture carries additional significance as a word understood to be sent by God to the community covenanted with God. For Christians (particularly postliberal and most patristic Christians) as well as Jews, "Israel" is the prototype of such a community. The church is grafted onto Israel and its covenant, becoming thereby another recipient of God's Word. While not all postliberal scholars make this distinction, it seems to me that Israel's Torah remains the prototype of Scripture for postliberal (and others forms of) Christianity as well as for Judaism. Gospel and New Testament are Scripture of a different sort: received by the church not as divine revelation, per se, but as the apostles' divinely inspired witness to the life of God incarnate in the Jew Jesus Christ. Jesus interprets his life as an interpretation of the Torah; Paul follows suit, so that by declaring Jesus's life a fulfillment of Israel's covenant, the New Testament becomes not only a "completion of" but also a reading of the Old Testament. Scripture also has significance as a "face" of God: a manifestation of what God does among us and thereby a primary means of entering into intimate relation with the One who redeems and repairs.

For Christian reparative reasoners, the Gospel narrative is witness to the source and paradigm of reparative reasoning; participating in that paradigm, they become members of the Redeemer's body. As a Jewish reader, I find a parallel in classic rabbinic teachings about Israel's relation to Torah as God's revealing and redeeming Word. In the Exodus narrative God hears Israel's cries and delivers his saving Word on behalf of Israel. For the rabbinic sages, Torah offers instruction in how to serve as agents of Israel's repair. For the

---

world is like our encounter with anything: there are some sensations or feelings or intuitions. The difference between one category of entity and another comes in the fruit, or how our immediate sense comes into relation with who we are, where we are, and what else we encounter.

medieval kabbalists, those who participate in the Torah are agents, as well, of *tikkun olam*, or the repair of God's creation overall. To study and interpret Torah (*l'drosh et ha-torah*) is also to act in the way of Torah as an agent of repair and redemption in this world.

Trinitarian and ecclesial reasoning. How, then, by way of reading Scripture, do Christians participate in Christ's reparative presence? Hauerwas offers a concise response in an earlier essay:

> In this transformation of the disciples we see the central theme of the Gospel. To be a disciple of Jesus it is not enough to know the basic "facts" of his life. . . . Rather to be a disciple of Jesus means that our lives must literally be taken up into the drama of God's redemption of this creation. That is the work of the Spirit as we are made part of God's new time through the life and work of this Jesus of Nazareth.
>
> That is why the Trinity is such a central affirmation to sustain the Christian life. The Trinity is not metaphysical speculation about God's nature in and of itself but rather is our affirmation that God has chosen to include us in his salvific work. . . .
>
> At Pentecost God created a new language, but it was a language that is more than words. It is instead a community whose memory of its Savior creates the miracle of being a people whose very differences contribute to their unity.
>
> We call this new creation *church*. It is constituted by Word and sacrament, as the story we tell, the story we embody, must not only be told but enacted. . . . In the enactment, in baptism and Eucharist, we are made part of a common history that requires continuous celebration to be rightly remembered. . . . Through this telling and enactment we, like Israel, become a people who live by distinctively remembering the history of God's redemption of the world.[23]

Christians thus enter the work of reparative reasoning by becoming disciples of Christ and members of the church as the one body of Christ. This also means that Christians becomes disciples of Christ by entering the work of reparative reasoning. Reparative reasoning is thus trinitarian and ecclesial reasoning as well. Mark 5 names the moment of this reasoning that proclaims who and what will be the source of repair. Hauerwas's writing and teaching appear to constitute the marks of proclamation in his reparative reasoning. Mark 6 names the call to action that completes his individual projects of reasoning: calling himself and other members of the church to follow Christ in the work of repair. What follows this call is beyond the limits of his distinct contribution to reparative reasoning, for it belongs to the work of the church and of salvation history.[24]

23. "The Church as God's New Language," in *Scriptural Authority and Narrative Interpretation*, ed. Garrett Green (Philadelphia: Fortress, 1987), 184–85; rpt. in Berkman and Cartwright, *Hauerwas Reader*, 148–49.

24. The moments of divine–human relation, of proclamation, and of a call to action appear so closely interconnected that I am unable to illustrate each one separately.

Reasoning with Israel. As "What Could It Mean" progresses from its narrative of Sneem through its diagnosis of the sources of disunity in the church, Hauerwas draws the story of Israel increasingly into his reparative reasoning. I believe the reason is that for Hauerwas, Israel is the ground of one's embodiment in the church, and this essay looks to the body as means of repairing an overly spiritualized—and rationalized—church. This does not imply some dichotomy of Israel/body versus church/spirit, since Hauerwas reads body and spirit as always integrated. When the church is unified, then it should be as embodied as Israel is embodied. When it is not unified, then it is disembodied, and what it is missing is not its body in a literal sense (for that cannot be removed), but its memory of how to practice embodied religious life.[25] I assume that for Hauerwas the term *the body* does not refer to any separable entity but is shorthand for the wisdom and events that embody Christian practice in the world.[26]

> Like the Jews, Christians are called to be a community and a people capable of remembering: indeed this is their first social task. . . . But the "social ethics" of the church is not first of all what the church can or should do to make the societies in which it exists more just. The church does not *have* a social ethic in that sense, but rather the church *is* a social ethic as it serves this or any society by first being the kind of community capable of nourishing its life by the memory of God's presence in Jesus Christ.
>
> But if that is the case, the great social challenge for Christians is learning how to remember the history of the Jews, as part of and as essential to our history. Such remembering cannot be based on feeling guilty about the Holocaust, since guilt soon fades or becomes a substitute for honest appraisal. Rather, we must learn to remember with the Jews a history that certainly includes the Holocaust because we are learning that the Jews are our partners in discerning God's way in the world. To learn to remember in this manner is a radical political act in that it must of necessity change our understanding of the Christian community and its relationship to our world.[27]

In a note to this comment, Hauerwas cites with favor the following comments by André Trocmé:

25. Thus from another essay: "The church, therefore, is not some ideal of community but a particular people who, like Israel, must find the way to sustain their existence generation after generation" ("The Servant Community," in Berkman and Cartwright, *Hauerwas Reader*, 383).

26. Thus the "body" is not something that "I *have*" (*In Good Company*, 24). To repeat the statement quoted above: "I seek, therefore, not for the church to be a community, but rather to be a body constituted by disciplines that create the capacity to resist the disciplines of the body associated with the modern nation-state and, particular, the economic habits that support that state" (26). This sentence associates the term *body* with what is constituted by disciplines of practice.

27. Stanley Hauerwas, "Remembering as a Moral Task: The Challenge of the Holocaust," in *Against the Nations: War and Survival in a Liberal Society* (Notre Dame, IN: University of Notre Dame Press, 1992), 61–90 (75).

The more the strict monotheistic faith in the God of Israel is exalted, the more visible becomes the thought of Jesus Christ. Let us never forget that the God of Jesus Christ was the God of Israel. The Christian faith dissolves into mythology as soon as it no longer leans upon Judaism. Nothing can be lost by rejudaizing Christianity. Judaism is the point of departure for all research destined to rediscover the Jesus of history.[28]

There is an additional way to understand Hauerwas's *remembering* Israel. As noted earlier, Hauerwas's reparative reasoning moves from symptoms of disunity in the church to hypotheses about the sources of this disunity and resources for repair. I noted that this reasoning locates causes or antecedents *within* rather than outside of the tradition marked by these symptoms of disunity. This "look within" lends prophecy its moral and religious force, so that, through prophets like Amos, Israel is commanded to take responsibility for whatever it suffers.[29] A defining mark of Peirce's pragmatism is the difference between "taking responsibility" and being named "efficient cause." If Israel takes responsibility for its being attacked by Assyria (Isa. 10:5), this does not mean Israel has been identified as the efficient cause of its own suffering. Nor does it mean that its guilt is a mere metaphor for its free choice to make each suffering a condition for moral action. These two alternatives belong to a dyadic analysis of the Deuteronomic theodicy, and they are inadequate to a pragmatic reading of the Matthean formula.[30] There are two complementary

28. André Trocmé, *Jesus and the Nonviolent Revolution* (Scottdale, PA: Herald, 1973), 2, quoted in Hauerwas, "Remembering as a Moral Task," n. 33. Hauerwas adds, "Fortunately Trocmé's views have found expression in John Howard Yoder's widely read *The Politics of Jesus*" (Grand Rapids: Eerdmans, 1972).

29. It is not sufficient to attribute such self-critical diagnostics to the Deuteronomic theodicy of reward and punishment, in which Israel may seem to have attributed each of its misfortunes to some occult trespass of its own. On such a view, Deutero-Isaiah's "Suffering Servant" marks a wholly transformed theodicy, in which the immensity of the destruction of the Temple overwhelms Deuteronomic logic, forcing the prophet to recognize a wholly new source of Israel's misfortune: not its own sins but those of the nations. I am not convinced, however, that these two theodicies are so extremely different. As suggested earlier, Amos's theodicy reasons from material effect to moral-spiritual antecedent, not to material cause, so that Israel's suffering still belongs to the order of divine will and divine choice. While Deutero-Isaiah's God may have more compassion for Israel and perhaps less hope for its neighbors, it is still he who puts the weight of the nations' sins on Israel's head; it is no law of nature. For both prophets, Israel is responsible for its actions whether or not it bears guilt for prior faults; the responsibility is a matter of divine choice. Peirce's pragmatic reasoning follows a similar logic. While William James and some other pragmatists may have reasoned from material effects to material causes, Peirce thought a lot more was going on in an antecedent than may on a given occasion have appeared to dribble out in some material consequent. For him, a material effect may be symptom of an antecedent whose spiritual-mental-and-material complexity could only be imagined—or, we might say, could only be hypothesized by a wise and experienced observer and diagnostician, rather than some mechanical meter.

30. William James's "The Tigers in India" illustrates a dyadic type of pragmatism that appears to identify pragmatic meaning with mere efficient cause. Hauerwas is right to reject this side of pragmatism; the problem does not arise in Peirce's pragmatism.

pragmatic readings: that Israel's sins engender the possibility of (or cannot prevent) Assyrian oppression and that God reads Israel's sin as a reasonable warrant for sending Assyria against her:

> Ha! Assyria, rod of My wrath,
>   In whose hand, as a staff, is My fury!
>   I send him against an ungodly nation,
>   I charge him against a people that provokes Me.
>
> Isaiah 10:5–6

Isaiah tells us unambiguously that Assyria's will works only in the world of efficient causality, governed by its perverted and unseeing intelligence, which would of its own impulse lead it against Israel and all surrounding nations:

> His mind harbors evil designs;
> For he means to destroy,
> To wipe out nations, not a few,
>   For he thinks,
> After all, I have kings as my captains!
>
> Isaiah 10:7–8

Divine causality, in other words, reads out of and acts into the world of efficient causes but neither belongs to that world nor warrants each causal chain in that world. Yes, God creates a world of efficient cause, but no, occasionalists err if they say God reasserts his will on behalf of each act in that world. Yes, he neither sleeps nor slumbers, but he speaks his will through words rather than brute force, and these are not mere words like ours, but efficacious words whose force is displayed in each event of this world, but whose character we cannot simply infer from those events. To see God's hand in the events of this world is to read these events by way of imaginative hypothesis making ("retroductively," in Peirce's terms). Trying to see God's hand is thus a precarious enterprise, since it passes through a faculty—the imagination—that at some levels is inseparable from the realm of fantasy. Sober folks warn wisely against "religion," because they accurately observe the fairy-tale dimension of religious imagination. But, seeking at all cost to protect us from illusion, sober folks err when they suppress the imagination in favor of a world of "strict reality." The result is the more damning illusion that we live in a world of merely literal causes and effects, in which all nondyadic relations are deemed unreal.

Hauerwas offers his theopractic reasoning to repair Christian institutions that have been reordered and thus disordered by sober folks of this kind *and* by their complements—the antiefficient yet equally dyadic thinkers who have, perhaps out of feeling hearts but weak minds, sought to reclaim the realm of religion by defining it as *not of this world at all* but of *another*. They claim that to enter this "spirit world" we must pass by the world of efficient causality altogether, entering instead through stories of another world. Hauerwas believes he inherits a church overpeopled by both sober folks and fantasy folks, disintegrated into mutually delegitimizing camps of materialists and spiritualists. His practice of retroduction belongs to neither camp (however much each camp sees his work as handiwork of the other), because each part of it is nondyadic, linking some mark of distress in the churches' this-worldly life to some point of distress in the relation of Christ's body to the triune life. In his terms, this triune life is the life of the Redeemer who is with Israel in its suffering and with his Son in his suffering and with the poor in their suffering; to invoke this life is to invoke the One for whom each mark of distress is a call for his redeeming work.

What does this invocation mean, practically, for the future life of the church? Hauerwas's response (his second level of retroduction) is to link God's redeeming presence, per hypothesis, to a set of recommended behaviors in the churches. These correspond to the prophet's call for Israel to repent and to the pragmatist's theory about how a society in distress may reawaken its deepest and neglected habits of belief to repair the elemental conditions of social life. I believe that Hauerwas reads the story of Israel and the life of the Jews as marks of how, God willing, the churches may be repaired today. I imagine that his reasoning (retroduction) proceeds through successive cycles of the six marks: moving from symptoms of ecclesial distress to visions of ecclesial repair, then repeating the movement again to disclose successively "deeper" levels of antecedent church practice. Through such cycles, he would uncover elemental challenges to church unity complemented by elemental rules of ecclesial repair. To some degree, the order of this reasoning would reverse the order of salvation history. If, for example, Hauerwas sought rules for repairing confusions about the relations of Son and Holy Spirit to Father, then his reasoning might lead to claims about the Council of Nicaea. If, however, he sought rules for repairing confusions about body and spirit, then his reasoning might lead to earlier portrayals of the church as Israel and thence to the life of Israel itself. This does not mean Israel as some nation outside of the church or as a metaphor for some Jerusalem of the spirit. This comment from an Orthodox website may well capture the force of Hauerwas's retroduction:

> God working in history, "salvation history," is the characteristic mark of every aspect of our faith. The Church's task, therefore, is both to preach and present what God has done, what God is doing and what God will do to save and re-create. The Church, being the Qahal, the Ecclesia, stretching back to the dawn of time, therefore includes all the righteous as saints, both before and after the coming of the Messiah. So, in the Orthodox Church, the patriarchs, prophets, kings and righteous ones of the former covenants are all gloriously commemorated in our Calendar. They also partake of Christ. As Jesus Himself said to his fellow Jews:

"Your father Abraham rejoiced that he was to see my day; he saw it and was glad." The Jews said to him, "You are not yet 50 years old, and you have seen Abraham?" Jesus said to them, "Truly, truly, I say to you, before Abraham was, I am." (John 8:56–58)

The Orthodox Church, therefore, includes all the salvation history of the Jews, because this was the Church before Christ. Unlike the west, therefore, we do not say that the Church was born at Pentecost. The Church was born in the Garden of Eden! We recall that St. Irenaeus represented the Fathers generally by saying that in Christ, the whole of Creation has been recapitulated.[31]

The statement captures many features of Hauerwas's references to Israel, except that he introduces salvation history not as a grand narrative but as a means of uncovering resources for repairing specific ailments. He concludes that for what ails it today, the church needs the medicine of Israel's narrative, re-membering its primordial calling as an assembly grafted onto the covenanted people and guided by God's revealed Word. In this view, to forget Israel is to forget some of the defining elements of church life; to re-member Israel is to reaffirm dimensions of the church that are always Israel. For Hauerwas, this is not "Judaizing" but a means of reaffirming what it means to be disciples of Christ.[32]

Why does Hauerwas bother with the Jews since rabbinic times? Is not Israel of Scripture enough? Hauerwas appears to reason, with Lindbeck, that Israel-likeness alone would offer a necessary but not sufficient resource for repairing dyadic tendencies in the church today. I do not have any neat formula to suggest here, but the following elements appear to be ingredients in Hauerwas's reparative attention to the Jews:

- Observing Jews today means perceiving the historical reality of God's promises. This is a vital exercise for stimulating Christians to remember daily that the God of the church is the God who fulfills his promises. This practice strengthens Christian will to turn aside from the temptations of both sobriety and fantasy, to attend instead to the corporeal Jesus Christ.
- For Hauerwas, the communal form of Diaspora rabbinic Judaism introduces Christians to several features of church life after modernity, many of which correspond to Yoder's Anabaptist model of the Israel-like church: Christianity as a minority religion, guided by a politics of ecumenical

---

31. The Orthodox website (www.orthodox.clara.net/index.html) of the Community of St. Aidan, Clare Road, Levenshulme, Manchester, participant in the Antiochian Orthodox Deanery of the United Kingdom and Ireland.

32. Since the life of Israel belongs, for the most part, to the Old Testament narrative, this dimension of Hauerwas's retroduction replays aspects of the Reformation doctrine of *sola scriptura* (but see below, 124–25).

life and various forms of settlement with non-Christian neighbors and powers; Christian communal life within a broader secular polity, centered on study, social practice, worship, and scripturally grounded witness.

> Christians in the West are just beginning to live the way Jews have had to live since Christians took over the world by making Caesar a member of the church. Put simply, we must learn from Jews how to survive in a world that is not constituted by the recognition, much less the worship of our God. In the process, Christians may not only learn from the wisdom Jews have hewn from their struggle to survive Christianity, but we may even learn that our destiny is inseparable from the destiny of the Jews. I am convinced, however, that Christians cannot learn that lesson if, in an attempt to appear tolerant, we pretend our ethics can be divorced from the conviction that God through Jesus' life, death, and resurrection has made us nothing less than heirs of Abraham. Accordingly, I believe Jewish theological readings of Christianity must face the challenge that the existence of Christianity is not a mistake, but rather one of the ways God desires to make his covenant with Israel known to the nations.[33]

- The rabbis' scriptural hermeneutic (midrash) and their Scripture-based social law (*halakhah*) remind Christians how to recover two defining practices of the early church. Midrash reads individual biblical texts as always authoritative but always "vague," here a technical term for the fact that each text delivers a clear meaning only as applied to some historically specific context. A different context will disclose a different dimension of meaning. This is not relativism but an understanding of the Bible as God's living speech to Israel.[34] Halakhah provides guidelines for determining how biblically based rules of practice get practiced in historically specific contexts of life. The wisdom here parallels that of midrash: God's will must be enacted in the concrete details of everyday life, and it takes a prayer-filled heart, a world-wise mind, and a humble sense of human fallibility to hear how that will may be spoken to each context of life.

> The New Testament obviously includes, particularly in the letters of Paul, an ongoing critique of the law. Paul says that those in Christ have "died to the law" so that they might "belong to him who has been raised from the dead," and so "bear fruit for God" (Rom. 7:4–6; Gal. 2:19). Now that Christ has come, those who still try to keep the law (by being circumcised or maintaining ritual purity) cut themselves off from Christ and lose his benefits (Gal. 5:2–6). Yet, as Bruce Marshall maintains, these New Testa-

---

33. Stanley Hauerwas, "Christian Ethics in Jewish Terms: A Response to David Novak," in *Christianity in Jewish Terms*, 294.

34. Stanley Hauerwas, *Unleashing the Scripture: Freeing the Bible from Captivity to America* (Nashville: Abingdon, 1993).

ment passages are not "again the law itself, but against treating the law and its observance as the way to salvation," a view that is not incompatible with the understanding of the law within Judaism. Marshall notes that Jews understand "their obedience to the commandments as acts of gratitude and thanksgiving to God for his electing love towards the Jewish people, and not as a means to salvation or so some other end."[35]

- While necessary for its own sake, this discipline of learning from the Jews also helps Christians repent, in part, of the sin of anti-Jewishness.

  Put as starkly as I can put it: if Christian envy of the Jews is ever so effective that we are able to destroy the last Jew from the face of the earth, then God will destroy the earth. Our God is not some generalized spirit, but a fleshy God whose body is the Jews.[36]

Reasoning like Paul: Apocalyptic Pragmatism

There is only one step left in my review of the marks of Hauerwas's reparative reasoning: to identify what ecclesial model Hauerwas adopts for reasoning like the prophets and the pragmatists and with Israel. I trust he would say the apostle Paul! In *Paul among the Postliberals*, Douglas Harink suggests that Hauerwas joins all the postliberals in adopting Paul as his primary teacher. In light of Harink's work, I would dub Hauerwas's Pauline reasoning "apocalyptic pragmatism," where the term "'apocalypse' is shorthand for Jesus Christ. In the New Testament, in particular for Paul, all apocalyptic reflections and hope comes to this, that God has acted critically, decisively, and finally for Israel, all the peoples of the earth, and the entire cosmos, in the life, death, resurrection, and coming again of Jesus."[37] Drawing illustrations from Harink's reading of Galatians (with supplementary comments from J. Alexander Sider), I will comment on five marks of apocalyptic pragmatism in Hauerwas's reading of Paul, roughly corresponding to the six marks of Hauerwas's prophetic pragmatism.

1. Apocalyptic pragmatism overall

Hauerwas imitates a Paul (a) whose attention is drawn to specific wounds in historically specific communities of the church; (b) who diagnoses each wound as symptom of a community's turning away from disciplined discipleship in

35. Hauerwas, "Christian Ethics in Jewish Terms," 137, citing Bruce Marshall, "Christ and the Culture: The Jewish People and Christian Theology," in the *Cambridge Companion to Christian Doctrine*, ed. Colin E. Gunton (Cambridge: Cambridge University Press, 1997), 381.
36. Stanley Hauerwas, "Jews and the Eucharist," in *Disrupting Time: Sermons, Prayers, and Sundries* (Eugene, OR: Cascade, 2004), 42.
37. Douglas Harink, *Paul among the Postliberals* (Grand Rapids: Brazos, 2003), 68.

favor of merely human desires; (c) who searches (retroductively) for deeper
sources of repair within the church, the most profound wounds leading him
to the deepest sources of repair; (d) who encounters the apocalypse in his encounter with Jesus Christ as redeemer or ultimate source of repair for wounds
that cannot be mended by any creaturely means; (e) who therefore calls the
wounded community to repent of its divisive ways, while recognizing that
repentance is not a matter of human will alone: the community's errors have
exposed a wound in the creature qua creature, and this can be mended only
when the human community finds its prayer is met by divine grace. Perhaps
Paul's most general lesson in pragmatism is this:

> For I consider that the sufferings of this present time are not worthy to be com-
> pared with the glory which shall be revealed in us. For the earnest expectation of
> the creation eagerly waits for the revealing of the sons of God. For the creation
> was subjected to futility, not willingly, but because of him who subjected it in
> hope; because the creation itself also will be delivered from the bondage of
> corruption into the glorious liberty of the children of God.
>
> Romans 8:18–21

Perhaps Hauerwas's most general Pauline lesson is this: "Christians are the community of a new age that must continue to exist in the old age" (2 Cor. 5:16–17).[38]

2. Attention to specific wounds within specific communities of the church

The paradigm here is general to Paul's mission: Paul addresses each of his
letters to a specific community of the church in response to specific threats to
this community's identity as member of the church.[39] The letters are therefore
explicitly reparative and context-specific, each letter offered (a) to a specific
community, (b) as a reparative word, and (c) on behalf of the Redeemer. Thus,
"I am astonished that you so quickly desert him who called you in the grace
of Christ and turn to a different gospel, not that there is another gospel, but
there are some who trouble you and want to pervert the gospel of Christ" (Gal.
1:7). Here Hauerwas echoes Yoder's Pauline attention to historical context.
Sider states the case elegantly:

> When the apostle Paul wrote in various contexts throughout the epistolary
> literature of the New Testament about the diversity of spiritual gifts within
> the Christian movement, he was not (only or merely) making the point made
> since within humanistic anthropologies that each person is unique. . . . Paul
> rather, says Yoder, organizes his discussion of the ecclesial recognition of each

---

38. "The Servant Community," in Berkman and Cartwright, *Hauerwas Reader*, 379.
39. Compare mark 1, above.

member around the diversity of gifts, not simply as an awareness of ubiquitous unique qualities, but as social functions appropriate to the body of Christ and (therefore) empowered by the Holy Spirit. This, in turn, makes sense only within a context of dialogical vulnerability.[40]

In Paul's manner, Hauerwas's aim is "to remind Christians that we are in a life-and-death struggle with the world."[41] In Harink's words, "Such a struggle, or warfare, is always engaged in the specific awareness that real enemies pose real threats."[42]

3. Diagnosing each community's distress as a specific case of failed discipleship

Several submarks merit attention within this one.[43]

a. Each case displays symptoms of divisiveness that extend from everyday social phenomena to the community's sharing in the elemental wounds of creation itself. Thus, "Formerly, when you did not know God, you were in bondage to beings that by nature are no gods; but now that you have come to know God, or rather to be known by God, how can you turn back again to the weak and beggarly elemental spirits, whose slaves you want to be once more?" (Gal. 4:7). And, "You were running well; who hindered you from obeying the truth?" (Gal. 4:9). As for divisiveness, Hauerwas offers "What Could It Mean" as a critique of tendencies to define ecclesial practices by such dyads as Israel's covenant against the church, communal versus bodily life, or theology versus ethics.[44] Sider devotes his book specifically to Yoder's critique of such dyads:

> John Howard Yoder . . . probed deeply into the wound left in the con-
> temporary Christian conscience by the opposition between holiness and

---

40. J. Alexander Sider, *To See History Doxologically: History and Holiness in John Howard Yoder's Ecclesiology* (Grand Rapids: Eerdmans, 2011): 180. He adds, in a helpful note, "The rule of Paul (1 Cor. 14) builds on the vision of the diversity of gifts attested by the church's practice of the fullness of Christ by prescribing a model for intra-ecclesial dialogue that foregrounds listening to others so as to ensure the acknowledgment of each member's gifts within the body. Both practices function on the assumption that because the Holy Spirit is present and active in the gathered community, the best way to discern the will of God is through patient attentiveness to the voice of each member" (180n39).

41. Stanley Hauerwas, "The Christian Difference," in *A Better Hope*, 36, cited in Harink, *Paul among the Postliberals*, 67.

42. Harink, *Paul among the Postliberals*, 67.

43. Compare marks 2 and 3, above.

44. Against tendencies to divide faith versus works or Israel's covenant versus the church, Hauerwas argues that "the body that the church becomes . . . cannot be less than the body of Israel" (31). The essay as a whole is a critique of efforts to divide communal versus bodily life; here, as throughout his work, Hauerwas "refus[es] to distinguish between theology and ethics" (21).

difficulty. In the chapter of Yoder's monumental book, *The Politics of Jesus*, entitled "Trial Balance," he delineated a series of dualisms that seem fundamental for Christian theology and repeat the opposition between holiness and difficulty. Moreover, each requires unfaithfulness of the Christian. Among the dualisms, Yoder contended that "the systematic tradition tells us we must *choose between the political and the sectarian*."[45]

In "The Servant Community," Hauerwas offers a comparable critique:

> The scandal of the disunity of the church is even more painful when we recognize this social task [that the "church is a social ethic"]. For all too often it appears that we who have been called to be the foretaste of the peaceable kingdom fail to maintain unity among ourselves. As a result we abandon the world to its own devices. The divisions I speak of in the church are not only those based on doctrine, history, or practices, important though they are. The deepest and most painful divisions affecting the church in America are those based on class, race, and nationality that we have sinfully accepted as written into the nature of things.[46]

b. The wounds are prototypically political, such as the separation of merely human rule from the rule of God's Word. For Harink, Paul's apocalypticism is prototypically political, as illustrated in Yoder's efforts "in *The Politics of Jesus* to persuade readers that the writings of the New Testament present Jesus as 'a model of radical political action,' that is, as the normative bodily enactment of God's political will for God's people."[47] For Yoder, this political will now requires Christians to renounce Constantinianism, which is to renounce direct participation as Christians in the mechanisms of nation-state governance. Following Louis Martyn, Harink reads such a politics as apocalyptic, since "Paul's talk of principalities and powers cannot be less than talk about the social and political shape of human existence. . . . So too, God's conquest of the powers in the cross of Christ, as the *apocalypse*, must be at least about the reshaping of the sociopolitical character of the community of the cross."[48] Paul's politics is thus eschatological as well, since "although the heavenly Jerusalem *has come*, it remains appropriate for the writer to remind the Hebrews that they have 'here . . . no lasting city, but . . . are looking for the city that *is to come*'

---

45. Sider, *To See*, 3n50, citing Yoder, *Politics of Jesus*, 105; emphasis original. Sider adds, "The other dualisms include the following: the choice between the Jesus of history/Jesus of dogma, prophetic witness/institutional stability, external/internal reign of God, and the individual/social" (103–8).

46. "The Servant Community," in Berkman and Cartwright, *Hauerwas Reader*, 513.

47. Harink, *Paul among the Postliberals*, 106–7, citing Yoder, *Politics of Jesus*, 2.

48. Harink, *Paul among the Postliberals*, 119.

(Heb. 13:14)." Hauerwas's political theology, says Harink, shares this apocalypticism with Paul and Yoder:

> Right now the American church is under submission to "a yoke of slavery," "fallen away from grace," caught up in a dual allegiance to Christ and the liberal polis, and therefore standing under God's apocalyptic wrath, a situation in which "Christ will be of no benefit" in the coming judgment (cf. Gal. 5:1–5). Hauerwas seeks nothing less than the conversion from apostasy, the holiness, of American Christianity, which will come only with the flat-out rejection of the liberal state and its claim to be another or better gospel.[49]

c. The wounds are ultimately those for which there is no mere creaturely remedy.[50] There are several submarks of this characteristic:

- Remedies cannot be reduced to what serves the needs and discourses of individuals alone. "I cannot imagine any teacher who is serious who would allow students to make up their own minds."[51] Readers do not need reminders of Hauerwas's manifold criticisms of Enlightenment individualism. These, says Harink, come in the spirit of Colossians 2:8: "Beware lest any person spoil you through philosophy and vain conceit." Sider notes, "The rule of Paul is in fundamental continuity with MacIntyre's assumption that specifically human flourishing relies on acknowledgment of what he calls 'the virtues of acknowledged dependence.'"[52] Peirce writes of this kind of dependence when he refers to "the individual ego" as known only in "ignorance and in error"[53]—not that the individual has no worth, but that its worth is to call tradition and community to attention: something is wrong here! The community's task is to respond by way of what Peirce calls the "social logic" of repair.[54] In Hauerwas's terms, this is the logic of Jesus Christ: "Faith for Paul is not some mystical transformation of the individual; rather it is to be initiated into a kingdom. Faith is not belief in certain propositions, though it involves the attitude and passion of trust. Faith is not so much a combination of belief and

49. Douglas Harink, "Apocalypsis and Polis: Pauline Reflections on the Theological Politics of Yoder," 13, available at http://brandon.multics.org/library/misc/harink1999apocalypsis.html#_ftnref11.

50. Compare mark 4, above.

51. Stanley Hauerwas, "Christian Schooling, or Making Students Dysfunctional," in *Sanctify Them in the Truth*, 220, quoted in Harink, *Paul among the Postliberals*, 77.

52. Sider, *To See*, 210, citing Alasdair MacIntyre, *Dependent Rational Animals: Why Human Beings Need the Virtues* (Chicago: Open Court, 2001), 68.

53. C. S. Peirce, "Man's Glassy Essence" (1892), 6:270–71.

54. C. S. Peirce, "Grounds of Validity of the Laws of Logic" (1868), 5:354.

trust, as simply fidelity to Jesus, the initiator of God's kingdom of peace."[55]

- Remedies cannot be reduced to rational principles. Hauerwas argues that one of the greatest failings of the modern church is to seek to comprehend Scripture and doctrine through strictly "rational" principles.[56] I believe his lesson is that there is no need to call on God when creaturely reasoning will suffice: if the door is broken, the carpenter or locksmith will do. To call on God is to give witness to a wound for which there is no creaturely remedy. This is to appeal not to unreason, but to the One who alone has the power to reform and renew our very capacity to reason. Kantian rationality, for example, does not trump the gift of God's Word, because the autonomy that Kant associates with rationality must be read instead as a mark only of that gift:

> Kant . . . argued that autonomy consists of doing our duty in accordance with the universal law of our being. Such an objection, however, fails to appreciate that for Christians freedom is literally a gift. We do not become free by conforming our actions to the categorical imperative but by being accepted as disciples and thus learning to imitate a master. Such discipleship can only appear heteronomous from the moral point of view, since the paradigm cannot be reduced to . . . principles known prior to imitation.[57]

- Remedies invoke the rule of love, which humans acquire as a grace. Sider observes,

> Yoder's account of the essentially communal embodiment of holiness in the rule of Paul (open meeting) and the fullness of Christ (diversity of gifts) could be paraphrased as commentary on Paul's exhortation in Romans 13:8, "Owe no one anything, only love one another." Here Paul subtly draws attention to our propensity to assume that the graciousness of love is dissociable from our normal contexts of negotiating with others, with owing people something. Prima facie, this makes some sense. Love characteristically happens to us.[58]

In the same spirit, Hauerwas writes, "For Christians, marriage is not ultimately where one learns what love is about; indeed, the 'love' that Christians share in marriage is made possible because we have first been loved by God."[59]

55. "Peaceable Kingdom," in Berkman and Cartwright, *Hauerwas Reader*, 139.
56. See the discussion of mark 2, above.
57. "Christian Life," in Berkman and Cartwright, *Hauerwas Reader*, 225.
58. Sider, *To See*, 196.
59. "Radical Hope," in Berkman and Cartwright, *Hauerwas Reader*, 513.

d. Uncovering deeper sources of repair within the church. The repair is ultimately apocalyptic, which means it comes only through encounter with Jesus Christ.[60] In Harink's words,

> Paul himself is the servant of only one apocalypse, one theme, one gospel, one God, the Father, and one Lord, Jesus Christ ([Gal.] 1:1–5). It is this Jesus Christ and God the Father "who raised him from the dead" who commissioned Paul as messenger of the singular gospel, the gospel of deliverance from "the present evil age" ([Gal.] 1:4). God's deed in raising Jesus from the dead is precisely that which determines the present time of Paul's speech and sets it off from that other time which is also still "present" but no longer determinative, the evil age of the old creation.[61]

Harink notes that while "Hauerwas rarely declares his own apocalypticism explicitly," his clearest declarations come through others whom he cites with favor. One of these is William Stringfellow, who identifies three features of apocalypticism, each of which should ring familiar to Hauerwas's readers: apocalypticism (1) reminds us of the "intrinsically political character of salvation"; (2) rejects notions of the cosmos as "a seamless web of casual relations"; (3) sees "God's creation [as] caught in a dramatic and final battle" in which God accomplishes the decisive victory in the death and resurrection of Jesus, leaving us free to participate in this victory rather than to try to accomplish it ourselves through optimistic social engineering or cynical violence. Such participation is the very meaning of the Christian community."[62]

e. A call for the wounded community to repent of its divisive ways and thus lend itself to God's will in Jesus Christ.[63] Human works, and thus works of the law taken only as works, will not suffice to bring Christ's reparative presence. "Behold, I Paul say to you that if you get circumcised, Christ shall profit you nothing. For I testify again to every man that is circumcised, that he is a debtor to the whole law. Christ is become of no effect to you, whoever of you are justified by the law, you are fallen from grace" (Gal. 5:2–4). Harink explains: as "Martyn notes, 'From the epistle's beginning to its end, Paul draws contrasts not between two human alternatives, such as works and faith, but rather between acts done by human beings and acts done by God' ([Gal.] 1:1, 6:15)." Harink adds, "God's apocalyptic act of new creation reveals that the

---

60. Compare mark 4, above.
61. Harink, *Paul among the Postliberals*, 72.
62. Ibid., 74–75, citing Hauerwas's discussion of William Stringellow in Stanley Hauerwas, *Dispatches from the Front: Theological Engagements with the Secular*, rev. ed. (Durham, NC: Duke University Press, 1995).
63. Compare marks 5–6, above.

Galatians could not have contributed by their own actions to their rescue and rectification."[64]

In the spirit of this reading of Paul, Hauerwas criticizes Reformation tendencies to read "justification by faith" literally, as if it inserted a wedge between the human realms of action and belief. He devotes "What Could It Mean" to an alternative reading: that the suffering of which we speak cannot be repaired by mere human works, but by God alone. When the reparative Word comes, we shall serve it with body and soul, faith and works. Thus, "quite simply, faith is our appropriate response to salvation, and it is fundamentally a moral response and transformation."[65]

Conclusion

Having framed and tested several models of Hauerwas's theopractic reasoning, I turn to a final question: does my detailed model of Lindbeck's and Jenson's postliberalism (the subject of chap. 2 and 3) apply as well to Hauerwas's theopractic reasoning? My concluding response is yes: while Hauerwas's postliberalism displays distinctive marks, these are all compatible with my model of Lindbeck–Jenson's *semper reformanda*.[66] In this final section, I note how the marks of Hauerwas's reasoning complement and also extend this model.

1. *Semper reformanda*: the purpose of all reformational work is to contribute to the unification of the church, both economically in the unity of the churches and immanently in the unity of the body of Christ.

Affirming this doctrine, Hauerwas attends in particular to its empirical fruit—unity within and among the empirical churches—rather than offering conceptual or extrascriptural claims about the character of this unity. His work also shares in the perennial work of unification, implying that perfection is

64. Harink, *Paul among the Postliberals*, 79.

65. "Peaceable Kingdom," in Berkman and Cartwright, *Hauerwas Reader*, 139. This quotation leads to the one offered earlier: "Faith for Paul is not some mystical transformation . . ."

66. Lindbeck's focus is on scriptural hermeneutics, ecclesial history, the practical force of church doctrine, and its capacity to evolve in response to each major challenge to ecclesial unity. In response to the challenge posed by modern supersessionism, he seeks reforms in the doctrine of *sola scriptura* that would lend nonsupersessionism doctrinal status. Jenson shares in Lindbeck's doctrinal claims and reforms, while devoting more attention to trinitarian theology and the dramatic character of the triune life of God in the world. While devoting his primary attention to ecclesial practice rather than doctrine, Hauerwas also affirms these claims and reforms. As for general or systematic claims, he offers these in only two ways: regional criticisms of the modern church, as tending to disintegrate the unity of the body of Christ; and a witness to the life, death, and resurrection of Jesus Christ, as narrated and proclaimed in the New Testament, defended in church doctrine, and encountered in what one might call the living rule of Christian theopractics.

not achieved within this dispensation. Some critics call him a "sectarian," or one who believes his sect could achieve perfect unity.[67] Hauerwas answers them by arguing for the fallibility of theological claims: "Theological convictions inextricably involved truth-claims that are in principle open to challenge. . . . Indeed, I have avoided all appeals to a Kuhnian-like position (with which Kuhn may unfairly be identified) designed to protect theological convictions from possible scientific challenge."[68] Tied to fallibility is *vagueness*, and tied to vagueness is *relation*: Hauerwas's church lives in relation to contingent space-time as well as to other communities in that space-time. This kind of relationality is incompatible with a perfectionist sectarianism. For Hauerwas, finally, the perennial work of reformation is grounded in the Gospel witness to the life of Christ. Among the postliberals, his work offers a model of the reformational, reparative reading of Scripture: what I have called the marked of his pragmatic or reparative reasoning.[69]

2. Church doctrines are signposts of moments of radical reformation, when the church is called to repair obstructions to its perennial work of unification.

Lindbeck argues that church doctrines answer problems that arise in the very definition of the church as the body of Christ and of what it means

67. James Gustafson was a primary critic of this type. Hauerwas notes that:
Gustafson began his critique by reporting that he discovered some enthusiasts for my work among theologians from the Church of Scotland and the Church of England, as well the Roman Catholic Church. Gustafson described this enthusiasm as a "seduction" and advised that anyone tempted to follow me give some consideration to the incongruities between the "sectarian ecclesiology" I represent and the ecclesiology represented by their more traditional churches. . . . Gustafson develops this broadside by suggesting that my sectarianism reflects the position of certain "Wittgensteinian fideists," such as Paul Homer and George Lindbeck, who allegedly hold that the language of science and the language of religion are totally incommensurable. . . . In opposition to this view, Gustafson argues that insofar as religion and science are rational activities, it must be possible in principle to subject theological claims to correction and revision in terms of what we have learned from the social and physical sciences. . . . [Gustafson holds, moreover,] that my sectarian tendencies are based on the theological assumption "that God is known only in and through history, and particularly through the history of the Biblical people culminating in the events of Christ and their effects. In Christian sectarian form God becomes a Christian God for Christian people: to put it more pejoratively, God is assumed to be the tribal God of a minority of the world's population." (Hauerwas, "Why the 'Sectarian Temptation' Is a Misrepresentation," 91–95, citing James Gustafson, "The Sectarian Temptation: Reflections on Theology, the Church, and the University," *Proceedings of the Catholic Theological Society* 40 [1985]: 93.)
68. Hauerwas, "Why the 'Sectarian Temptation' Is a Misrepresentation," 98. Hauerwas continues, "Certainly I do not believe, nor did Wittgenstein, that religious convictions are or should be treated as an internally consistent language game that is self-validating" (99).
69. See mark 1 of Hauerwas's reparative reasoning, above.

for Christians to live according to Scripture's narrative of the life of Christ. While they appear in propositional form, these propositions are not meant to mirror reality but to signal how the church should protect itself against any historical tendency to obscure or obstruct that reality. For Lindbeck and Jenson, postliberalism protects the church against modern tendencies to apply the doctrine of *sola scriptura* in dyadic ways. Hauerwas's theopractics shares in this kind of doctrinal reform, attending in particular to ways of reforming the lived practices of *sola scriptura* and justification by faith.[70]

3. The reformational process of doctrinal formation is an ecclesial process of rereading the Gospels' witness to the life of Christ. This rereading uncovers historically specific guidelines for doctrinal reformation.

Hauerwas shares in this reformational process when it is understood pragmatically—judged, that is, only by the way it contributes to changes in the body of church practice. As he argues in *With the Grain of the Universe*, reformational theologians are like experimental natural scientists, offering falsifiable theories to account for what they observe (in this case, in ecclesial practice) and testing their recommendations empirically (in this case, testing any proposed reforms according to their capacity to repair problematic practices).[71]

4. Postliberalism has proto-doctrinal force as a reformation of the practice of reading Scripture in the contemporary church.

This item captures Hauerwas's reformational practice more directly than discussions of doctrine, since for him the doctrinal rules of the church are embedded in the narrative of Scripture, and reforms in doctrine mean reforms in how the churches read Scripture and practice what they read. In these terms, we could confirm that Hauerwas also contributes to another Reformation, sharing in processes of revisiting and reforming the ways that Luther and Calvin reformed the churches' reading of Scripture.[72]

5. Nonsupersessionism is a corollary of the postliberal reformation.

Hauerwas's work confirms my thesis that postliberalism entails nonsupersessionism, as illustrated in his treatment of Judaism in "What Could

70. As illustrated in mark 5 of Hauerwas's reparative reasoning, above.
71. As illustrated above, Hauerwas, like the pragmatists, criticizes modern natural philosophy not for its empiricism but for its rationalism and thus its failure to attend to the empirical world. See mark 4 of Hauerwas's reparative reasoning.
72. As illustrated in mark 5 of Hauerwas's reparative reasoning and in mark 3c of his apocalyptic pragmatism, above.

It Mean . . ."[73] Reading Hauerwas leads me to add several marks of postliberalism that, while possibly less explicit, may also be observed in Lindbeck's and Jenson's writings, as follows.

6. Where divine and human voices meet.

Hauerwas, Jenson, and Lindbeck all locate Scripture as the paradigmatic place of theological encounter: Scripture as witness and proclamation, Scripture as intimate relation to God and covenant, and Scripture as rule for action in the world. At the same time, none of the three reads Scripture as text-alone. The text is instead the ineliminable face of a body that extends into sacramental intimacy and sociopolitical practice.[74]

7. Reasoning like Paul: apocalyptic pragmatism.

All three theologians lay claim to the postliberal reading of Paul, from historiography to scriptural hermeneutic to theopractics. The dramatic characterizations of apocalypticism fit Hauerwas more than the others. Jenson comes next to mind, especially in his eschatology of time and of death. All three share, textually speaking, in Paul's recognition of Jesus Christ as the apocalypse; of the three, Lindbeck stays the closest to Thomas, perhaps, in his trust of canonical and systematic discourse as means of articulating that recognition.[75]

8. Human works will not suffice to bring Christ's reparative presence.

All three theologians seek to correct spiritualizing and thus dualistic implications of the doctrine of justification by faith. Obedience to biblical law brings sanctification if it is obedience to the divine will and thus an opening to the divine presence, rather than a pursuit of justification. God alone repairs, but the body of Christ cannot enter the world without embodied practice.[76]

---

73. As illustrated in mark 5 of Hauerwas's reparative reasoning, above.

74. By way of illustration: on Lindbeck, see his critique of mediating theology and thus his claim that "God alone" repairs, chap. 2, pp. 37, 41, 47; on Jenson's scriptural pragmatism, see chap. 3, pp. 65–74; on his critique of mediating or conceptual theology, see chap. 3, pp. 65–66; on Hauerwas's account of divine-human intimacy, see above, mark 4 of theopractics; his overall apocalyptic pragmatism, pp. 116–23.

75. By way of illustration: on Lindbeck's attention to doctrinal reform, see chap. 2, pp. 37–38; on Jenson's Pauline account of the availability of the resurrected body of Christ, see chap. 3, pp. 89–90; on Hauerwas's overall apocalyptic pragmatism, see above, pp. 116–23.

76. By way of illustration: on Lindbeck, see his critique of intellectualization, chap. 2, p. 76; on Jenson, see his argument that the triune God alone redeems, chap. 3, pp. 67–68, and on the embodied character of the divine life among us, chap. 3, pp. 87–88; on Hauerwas, see his apocalyptic pragmatism, above pp. 116–23.

5

The Limits of Postliberalism

JOHN HOWARD YODER'S
AMERICAN MENNONITE CHURCH

Preface

On March 16, 2007, Eastern Mennonite University held a conference on John Howard Yoder's *The Jewish–Christian Schism Revisited*, which was coedited by Michael Cartwright and me.[1] We had added extensive commentaries to the volume, mixing words of appreciation for Yoder's work with some words of caution. This chapter mixes praise and caution as well. I will argue that the dominant voice of *The Jewish–Christian Schism* (hereafter *JCSR*) is both postliberal and nonsupersessionist but that a secondary yet clear voice in Yoder's work is nonpostliberal and non-nonsupersessionist. I will argue that by providing the exception that proves the rule, Yoder's secondary voice confirms the overall thesis of part 1 of this book: that there is a strict correlation between American Christian postliberalism and nonsupersessionism. Whenever Yoder's work is other than postliberal, then, despite his intention, his work proves to be non-nonsupersessionist.[2]

1. I am grateful for comments on this chapter from Tommy Givens, Andrew Black, and Jacob Goodson, extensive commentary from Daniel Weiss, and extensive editing by Rodney Clapp.
2. Let me add another note about that wonderful conference at Eastern Mennonite University, a day of gentle albeit intense interaction with Ray Gingerich, Mark Nation, Alain Epp Weaver, and many other insightful participants. One effect of the day was to open my mind to a more complex reading of Yoder and thereby to moderate as well as complexify the theme of this chap-

This chapter has three parts. I begin, in part 1, by reviewing the conclusions I drew from the EMU conference. Part 2 overviews the significant marks of postliberalism and nonsupersessionism in Yoder's work; its purpose is to justify placing Yoder's work in the general family of American postliberalism. The material for this part is gathered broadly from different writings of Yoder's and from secondary writings by my principal teachers in the ways of Yoder: Douglas Harink, J. Alexander Sider, Michael Cartwright, Mark Nation, Alain Epp Weaver, and, of course, Stanley Hauerwas. Part 3 articulates my argument about the relationship between postliberalism and nonsupersessionism in Yoder's work. The argument has four steps. Step 1 overviews the marks of Yoder's postliberalism that have been already introduced in parts 1 and 2. Step 2 illustrates these marks. Step 3 identifies marks of nonpostliberalism in Yoder's writings. This step should be noncontroversial, since Yoder does not profess postliberalism or any self-defined movement of theology. Step 4 examines marks of non-nonsupersessionism in *JCSR*. This step should indeed be controversial, since my conclusion will appear to contradict some of Yoder's claims to have found a way past the Jewish–Christian schism. I hope to show how the nonpostliberal tendencies in Yoder's reasoning lead him to draw non-nonsupersessionist inferences from his nonsupersessionist observations about first-century Judaism and Christianity. Since Yoder was an uncommonly self-conscious thinker of extraordinary clarity, I do not expect that he would be surprised by the elements of my analysis. I assume he would argue that the claims I label "supersessionist" belong in fact to what is most deeply Jewish. I would reply that God alone sees what is "most deep" and that to be too clear about what God alone knows is, to that extent, to supersede Scripture's witness to Israel's covenant. I expect, of course, that Yoder would come back with some surprising retort, cogently argued, and I have no doubt of Yoder's intention to care for Israel's covenant and for the Jews. My concerns are only with the logical details and consequences of his writings, not with his intentions.

The Arguments of Yoder's *The Jewish–Christian Schism Revisited*

Without presuming to reconstruct Yoder's authorial intentions, I read the words and logical force of *The Jewish–Christian Schism Revisited* as generating three broad arguments.[3] I offer only few words on the second two arguments, since they are the major focus of this chapter as a whole.

---

ter. As you will see in a moment, I still argue that Yoder's tendency toward nonpostliberalism corresponds to his tendency to non-nonsupersessionism. But I hope that the lessons I learned that day at EMU render my argument more gentle and discerning.

3. By the end of our day of study at EMU, most of us seemed to agree that *The Jewish–Christian Schism* displayed three different purposes. These purposes were voiced by Mark Nation and

1. The central argument is for and about the church, not the Jews

Yoder argues for the truth of the radical Anabaptist witness to Christ as a means of correcting errors in most Reformation as well as Catholic theologies.[4] For Yoder, Nicaea is itself problematic, since it already replaces Jesus's scriptural voice with the conceptual doctrines of a religious orthodoxy, and since its gathering of bishops already legitimates a form of the Constantinianism that Yoder believes undermines the politics of Jesus. JCSR contributes to Yoder's corrective search for pre-Orthodox and pre-Constantinian witnesses to the politics of Jesus Christ. In this sense like Lindbeck, Jenson, and Hauerwas, Yoder reencounters the Jesus of history and Scripture and, by way of this, reencounters Jesus's Jewish flesh. In the gospel of Jesus and the hermeneutic of Paul, he rediscovers what he believes was clear to the very early church: that Jesus's words always reread Israel's Torah, which means that they *continually* read those words as well as reading them through their fulfillment in Christ. The hermeneutical lesson is that "fulfillment" does not mean supersession, as if the "solution" to each verse of the Old Testament were simply "Jesus Christ!" The lesson is that Jesus's life, death, and resurrection reread in everrenewable and surprising detail all the details of ancient Israel's narrative.

So why is this discovery not primarily *about the Jews*? Because it is the end-point of Yoder's search for the witness behind Nicaea, and the lesson is not all that far from Jenson's claim that the Trinity means no more than that the God who redeemed Israel from bondage in Egypt also resurrected Jesus from the grave. In Yoder's terms, "What Saul or 'Paul' did was not to found another religion but to define one more stream within Judaism [and within '*Pharisaic* Jewry']."[5] "Neither Jesus nor Paul nor the apostolic communities rejected normative Judaism."[6] Whether grafted in or in the flesh, this people Israel is therefore the one whom God redeemed and ever will redeem from bondage and whose Messiah is Jesus Christ.

For Yoder, there is one covenant, continuous from Old to New Testament, and it is not superseded by Nicaea or any subsequent council or dogma. In these terms, repairing the Jewish–Christian schism is, first and foremost, not

---

received broad support from many of the conference participants. The way Nation orders these three dimensions or purposes enables us, I believe, to see that Jewish–Christian relations may not be the primary issue in Yoder's writing, so that the first issue in our minds should not be Yoder's literal nonsupersessionism or non-nonsupersessionism. It should, instead, be his postliberal-like effort to enact another reformation and reclaim the Christ of early, pre-Constantinian Judeo-Christianity. In that spirit, I present Nation's overview here as a statement of three dimensions of Yoder's performance in *JCSR*.

4. To paraphrase Mark Nation (and I did not hear much objection at the conference to his claim).

5. John Howard Yoder, "What Needs to Change," in John Howard Yoder, *The Jewish–Christian Schism Revisited*, ed. Michael G. Cartwright and Peter Ochs (Grand Rapids: Eerdmans, 2003), 32. (Hereafter, references will be to *JCSR*.)

6. Yoder, "'It Did Not Have to Be,'" *JCSR*, 49.

about repairing relations between Jews and Christians but about reuniting the divided body of Christ. Yoder's central concern is to argue that the free church vision is appropriate to the church as a whole. His goal is therefore to argue, against the Reformation and what he considers Catholic orthodoxy and Nicaea, that the purpose of Christianity is displayed normatively and most clearly in the practices of the first generations of messianic Jews or Nazarenes. These were Torah-observant Jews of the first and second centuries who recognized the resurrected Jesus Christ as the Messiah of the Jews. With the Jeremiah of 29:7, these were Jews of perennial exile who abandoned claim to any land and sought to live among the nations as lights to the nations, claiming the light of Torah to be incarnate in the flesh and word of Jesus of Nazareth. This, for Yoder, is the radical Anabaptist vision, and it displays the authority of the revealed Torah of Sinai, the life, death, and resurrection of Jesus, and the apocalyptic theo-politics of the apostle Paul. For Yoder, this is primordial Christianity, and it is challenged only by something added onto Christianity: the theological orthodoxy of Christian bishops who gathered for the sake of an ecclesial political unity that lacks warrant in the words of the Gospels and in Pauline proclamation. This means that if Yoder writes primarily about the "Messianic Jews" of the first centuries, this need not directly imply supersessionism, because it need not be about the Jews per se. It is about the church and its self-understanding. It may of course have implications for how the church regards the Jews who are not messianic, but this is a second and separate question that need not be mixed with Yoder's first purpose.

In this way, Yoder reads the efforts of the early Anabaptists as what I am labeling "another reformation":

> When the magisterial Reformers spoke of the medieval Church as having lost the way . . . they had in mind . . . the development of the Papacy and unbiblical doctrines of sacraments and Salvation. The deviation they deplored had not taken place before the sixth century, since these "Reformers" did not intend to abandon the great creeds of the fourth and fifth centuries, or the achievements of Constantine, Theodosius, and Justinian in creating the Christian Empire. The "radicals" of the Reformation on the other hand dated the "fall" earlier, beginning at the latest with the persecution of dissenters at the order of Constantine, and perhaps much earlier at the death of the last apostle.[7]

Yoder's argument in part 1 of *JCSR* is that at the time of this death "Christians" were still "Jews," so that in part 2 he might argue that by dating the "fall" that early, the Radical Reformers had in effect recovered Jewish Christianity. Yoder has, moreover, no brief against Old Testament law, so long as the landed polity of Israel—with its national bureaucracy, temple, and

---

7. Yoder, "The Jewishness of the Free Church Vision," *JCSR*, 107.

priesthood—arc items only of a previous history and a present-day figure.[8]
He adds that there is no reason for Jews to fear or obstruct members of the
Jewish community who witness the apocalypse in Jesus Christ and who seek
to proclaim and evangelize it.

Yoder does not ignore the fact that "the free churches of the sixteenth century did not see clearly enough to transcend the popular antisemitism of their
times."[9] He argues, nonetheless, that these churches were "like the Jews" in
their behavior, so it remains the work of contemporary Anabaptists not only
to continue this likeness but also to fight anti-Semitism and supersessionism.
The point, again, is not for the sake of Jews per se but for the sake of the
truth of Scripture's witness. "Why," he therefore asks, "not let the Jews be
themselves?"[10] Why, in other words, argue against the Constantinianism (or
what he calls the "Christianity") of early rabbinic Judaism as well as against
the Constantinianism of the fourth-century church? Because, he says, the
issue is not "provincial" or "particular" but concerns the universal message
that joins Jews and Christians. In "The Forms of a Possible Obedience," he
argues that this is the message of a messianic Judaism that the Anabaptists
rediscovered: "In a form befitting their century . . . the Anabaptists were able
to rediscover and realize a functional equivalency of the original messianic
Jewish universalisms, as of the original Jewish messianic pacifism, which
had characterized the earliest churches, which had later been abandoned by
both the anti-Judaic Catholicism of 'Christendom' and (to a lesser degree)
by the defensive Judaism of the Mishnaic codification."[11] I believe this suf-
fices to illustrate Yoder's primary goal of advancing a single vision for the
church.

2. The second argument is to overcome the historical schism between the Jewish people and the church

This argument is the primary topic of this chapter, because it is the context
for Yoder's offering both postliberal, nonsupersessionist claims and non-
postliberal, non-nonsupersessionist claims. As Alain Epp Weaver writes in
an overview of *JCSR*, "Just as there were a variety of Judaisms in the first
centuries of the Common Era, so today [Yoder contends] there are a plurality
of Judaisms and Christianities.[12] Yoder believed that highlighting the plurality
of 'Judaism' then and 'Judaism' and 'Christianity' today would facilitate a

8. Daniel Weiss suggests that Yoder's reading of Jeremiah works if and when it is applied
strictly to Jeremiah's end-time visions as well as to the Pauline assumption that the church has
entered the end-time ("'The Yetzer Hara Will Be Uprooted': Recovering Paul's 'Rabbinic' Messianism," manuscript).

9. Yoder, "Jewishness of the Free Church Vision," 109.

10. Ibid., 113.

11. Yoder, "Forms of a Possible Obedience," *JCSR*, 129.

12. Yoder, "Jewishness of the Free Church Vision," 111–12.

rapprochement between Jews and Christians, as Christians came to understand themselves as part of a Jewish conversation and debate."[13]

3. The third argument is that Christians need to care for the Jews after the Nazi Holocaust

Mark Nation suggests that a third argument lay wholly unspoken behind the words and energy of *JCSR*. According to Nation, Yoder traveled to Germany in 1949 specifically to check on the condition of Jewish refugees. Nation suggests that Yoder was profoundly marked by the reality of Jewish suffering in the Nazi Holocaust and that these feelings underlay the more literal dimension of his argument in *JCSR*. Yoder was deeply committed to removing supersessionism from the church and helping undo the wounds and distance that have separated Israel and the church for two millennia. As Yoder writes in *JCSR*: "It does make a difference, even for today, if as a matter of fact for generations non-messianic and messianic Jews and messianically missionized Gentiles could continue to read the *Tanakh* together, to pray together, to break bread together, and to consider themselves as part of one people of God, however strained and threatened, one family of Abraham under the heels of the emperors of Persia or of Rome."[14]

When I turn to examine Yoder's non-nonsupersessionism it is not, therefore, as a mark of his intention but only of the logical force of his second argument in *JCSR*.

Significant Marks of Yoder's Postliberalism

Stanley Hauerwas often speaks of himself as a student of John Yoder. This attention has helped stimulate a broader community to read the works of this Mennonite thinker, and Hauerwas's reading has led to Yoder's current reputation as one of contemporary Christianity's foremost theologians. Another consequence is that scholars who count Hauerwas among the postliberals have begun to count Yoder among them as well, and this accounting has obvious implications for the current study. Having argued that Hauerwas, Jenson, and Lindbeck share a broader postliberalism, shall I now argue that Yoder shares in it as well? If so, will his work also confirm the "postliberal formula," that postliberalism entails nonsupersessionism? The initial evidence would lead me to say "yes and yes." As I will note, Yoder's work exhibits the characteristics I have associated with Hauerwas's "apocalyptic pragmatism," and his work

13. Alain Epp Weaver, "John Howard Yoder's 'Alternative Perspective' on Christian–Jewish Relations," *Mennonite Quarterly Review* 79, no. 3 (July 2005): 2, available at www.goshen.edu /mqr/pastissues/july05eppweaver.html.
14. Yoder, "'It Did Not Have to Be,'" 62.

tends to illustrate the six marks of Hauerwas's "reparative reasoning," as well as the four broad marks of the Jenson–Lindbeck understanding of "reformation." Yoder's work is reparative, and he seeks to repair the church, to locate the agent of repair in Jesus Christ, who is known by way of the scriptural witness, and which witness is inseparable from the life of Israel. *JCSR* appears moreover to state the case for nonsupersessionism as forcefully as Lindbeck's studies of the church as Israel. To illustrate my overall portrait of Yoder's postliberalism, I turn to two different but complementary accounts by Mark Nation and Douglas Harink.

1. Marks of a radicalized Anabaptist theology

Mark Nation notes that in his years of graduate study in Basel, Yoder joined a "Concern group" of seven Mennonite grad students who, in Yoder's words, came to the conclusion "that if we were to make sense of North American Mennonitism, it would have to become more Anabaptist, more radical, more self-critical, less mainstream Evangelical, less institution centered."[15] Their vision radicalized what they had learned from their teacher Harold S. Bender, according to whom "the Anabaptist Vision" is marked by the following characteristics:[16]

- discipleship "as a concept which meant the transformation of the entire way of life of the individual believer and of society so that it should be fashioned after the teaching and example of Christ"
- "a new concept of the Church as created by the central principle of newness of life and applied Christianity"
- "the Ethic of Love and Nonresistance as applied to all human relations"[17]
- "the call to Discipleship belongs within the context of the church"— whose organization should be "solid and accountable" but unrestricted by "legalism"[18]

---

15. Mark Thiesssen Nation, *John Howard Yoder: Mennonite Patience, Evangelical Witness, Catholic Convictions* (Grand Rapids: Eerdmans, 2006), 20, citing John Howard Yoder, "1980 Autobiography," transcript of an autobiographical tape (made by Yoder for James McClendon Jr., in possession of Nation), 1. Nation notes that to disseminate their own more radical take on this vision, the Concern group published a periodical named *Concern*. In a 1957 issue, Yoder identified these as the group's primary concerns ("What Are Our Concerns?" as summarized by Nation, *John Howard Yoder*, 45–46).

16. Nation, *John Howard Yoder*, 15, citing Harold S. Bender, "The Anabaptist Vision," *Church History* 13 (March 1944): 3–24.

17. Harold S. Bender, "The Anabaptist Vision," in *The Recovery of the Anabaptist Vision*, ed. Guy F. Herschberger (Scottdale, PA: Herald, 1957), 42–43, 47, 51; emphasis by Nation. In Nation, *John Howard Yoder*, 15.

18. Nation, *John Howard Yoder*, 45, citing John Yoder, "What Are Our Concerns?" *Concern*, 1957, 27.

- "the Local congregation is the primary locus of discernment and authority"
- "the Bible functions as the authority of the church"[19]
- the church remains distinct from "the world" as "that which was not the church"
- "the Church is to be led by the Spirit and to be missionary"

The Free Church, further, should be ecumenical. From his graduate student years, Yoder's radical Anabaptist vision therefore already anticipated several marks of the Christian postliberalism we have seen in Hauerwas, Lindbeck, and Jenson. Like these postliberals, Yoder practiced theology as an instrument of repair and reform rather than as a source of icons that represent or mirror the divine life. Theology therefore belongs to Christian life; Christian life means living as disciples of Jesus Christ; such a life is lived in the context of the church, which begins in the local congregation and extends to ecumenical participation in the unity of the body of Christ and in the extensive, Spirit-led mission of the church. Like the postliberals, Yoder argued that Scripture is arbiter of what it means to live as disciples of Christ. As for the relation of church to world, the postliberals may be positioned along a continuum whose limits are, on one side, an immanent conception of the divine life within the world and, on the other side, a radically transcendent conception of Christ as not of this world. As a group, the postliberals would tend, with Karl Barth, toward the transcendent side, a vision of the scriptural Word as absorbing the world rather than being absorbed by it. At the same time, the postliberals display a more embodied pneumatology than we observe in Barth.[20] They are far more engaged with the economic than immanent life of the Trinity, so that the most systematically trinitarian theologian among them, Jenson, also speaks in the most radically immanentist terms: "The only Logos or Son we . . . may reckon with is the Suffering Servant, . . . exiled, and trampled, crucified. . . . The Logos that God speaks to command heaven and earth into being is no other Word than the Word of the cross, the Word the Father speaks by the mission, death and resurrection of Israel [in Egypt, and so on] and this Israelite."[21]

---

19. "However," notes Nation, "as soon as [Yoder] made this claim, he intentionally avoided tying it to any particular *theory* of authority: 'Our only conclusion for the moment is that there is as yet no satisfying doctrine of Biblical authority. . . . The first question for us is what the Bible says, not a doctrine of authority,' as 'a concept which means the transformation of the entire way of life of the individual believer and of society so that it should be fashioned after the teaching and example of Christ.'"

20. As Barth is portrayed, for example, in Eugene Rogers, *After the Spirit: A Constructive Pneumatology from Resources outside the Modern West* (Grand Rapids: Eerdmans, 2005).

21. Robert W. Jenson, "The Hidden and Triune God," *International Journal of Systematic Theology* 2 (Dec. 2002): 7.

While he speaks the most often of "the Bible absorbing the world," Lindbeck appears closest to Thomas in tolerating more give-and-take between the empirical churches and the worldly society that surrounds them. Among the postliberals, Yoder and Hauerwas appear to share the most radical suspicion toward "worldly powers and principalities" and yet also the most worldly interest in the material consequences of discipleship. In this sense, the Anabaptist pole of postliberalism is more suspicious of both worldly politics and otherworldly philosophies, while the Lutheran pole moderates such suspicion for the sake of its concern for the ecumenical unity of the church. In Harink's reading, the Anabaptist logic of Yoder/Hauerwas is the most apocalyptic of the postliberals, attentive to the worldly details of a *new* world.

2. Marks of an apocalyptic, Pauline theopolitics

In Harink's reading, *The Politics of Jesus* displays Yoder's Pauline apocalypticism applied to the practical work of Christian theopolitics. Adopting Harink's terminology, and drawing as well from the commentaries of Nation, Sider, Cartwright, and Hauerwas, I would consider the following to be the leading marks of Yoder's mature theopolitics.

First, *a critique of individualism, otherworldliness, and spiritualism in the church and a critique of any Christian accommodation to worldly powers and principalities*. As Harink argues well, this dual critique displays the two sides of Paul's apocalyptic. As I discuss later, this dual critique could breed a dualism of the modern or gnostic sort. In this section I note how *The Politics of Jesus* offers its dual critique in nondualistic ways. According to Harink, Yoder offered his theo-politics to correct a strong tendency in Christian social ethics—both recent and classical, liberal and conservative—to read Jesus's concrete social politics as only "the symbolic or mythical clothing of his spiritual message."[22] In this view, Paul transmuted Jesus's societal vision into an account of the inner life of the individual person *coram Deo*. In spiritualized readings of Luther, for example, justification by faith concerns a radical change in ontology that mysteriously bypasses material and social behavior.[23] To refute this tendency and these readings, Yoder offers "*The Politics of Jesus*. . . . Against them Yoder proposes and defends the 'alternate hypothesis that for Paul righteousness, either in God or in human beings, might more appropriately be conceived as having cosmic or social dimensions.'"[24] Yoder shows how such readings may be corrected by recovering the Gospel's and

22. John Howard Yoder, *The Politics of Jesus: Vicit Agnus Noster*, 2nd ed. (Grand Rapids: Eerdmans, 1994), 6–7, quoted in Douglas Harink, "Apocalypsis and Polis: Pauline Reflections on the Theological Politics of Yoder, Hauerwas, and Milbank," 4, available at http://brandon .multics.org/library/misc/harink1999apocalypsis.html#_ftnref11.

23. Harink, "Apocalypsis and Polis," 4.

24. Ibid., 5, quoting Yoder, *Politics of Jesus*, 215.

Pauline portrayal of Jesus as a political actor rather than an otherworldly one. He explains that because Jesus and Paul reject the "powers and principalities" of this sociopolitical world, readers may errantly assume that Jesus belongs to a wholly immaterial realm that they can nonetheless "think" by way of their own immaterial spirit. More learned readers may avoid this error, Yoder adds, but cling instead to an exaggerated apophaticism: identifying Paul's teaching with a rejection of this-worldly powers in favor of what will come in ways that surpass all knowing. For Yoder, both misreadings are corrected by recovering the gospel as *positive* political instruction, where the church is polis and following Jesus Christ means introducing the politics of the church into this world.[25]

Thus, second, *repairing the church means recovering Scripture's witness to the church as the body of Jesus Christ and to discipleship as participating in that body by building the church into this world.*

> For Yoder, ecclesial life is concrete political life in the other world that becomes this world when Christians follow after and embody Christ. The Jesus Christ who is witnessed by way of Scripture is thus not only of Scripture as a text, but also of the world that comes into being when the church acts as the church: when members of the Church are united in both theo-political service and sacramental communion. "Christian social ethics [is thus] a task of reading and re-reading scripture."[26]

For Yoder as for Paul, the church is the site of God's apocalyptic mission to rescue cultures, communities, and cities from their enslavement, and to form and transform them to serve the one Creator God. And for Yoder as for Paul, the church shares in this mission in the confidence of God's apocalyptic triumph over enslaving powers and ideologies. The church begins its life in that fissure which the proclamation of the gospel splits open within a given social and cultural context, and there it shapes a living sign of what a society and culture might become if it acknowledges the reign of Jesus Christ.[27]

---

25. In Harink's words,
On this understanding, for Paul justification is an *intrinsically and explicitly* social and political doctrine, of which the *ekklesia* of God is the most immediate and direct correlate in human life. One can thus speak as justly of "the politics of Paul" as of the politics of Jesus, a politics rooted firmly in a narrative about the "faithfulness of Jesus Christ" (*pistis Iesou Christou*), the messianic agent of God's new political order, about God's conquest, through the cross of Christ, of the rebellious "principalities and powers" which hold peoples in bondage, and about the creation in Christ of a new *polis* in which enemies are reconciled and believers are called into a new social order governed by the pattern of Jesus Christ. (Harink, "Apocalypsis and Polis," 7)

26. Ibid., 3, paraphrasing John Yoder, "The Authority of Tradition," in *The Priestly Kingdom: Social Ethics as Gospel* (Notre Dame, IN: University of Notre Dame Press, 1985), 63–79.

27. Harink, "Apocalypsis and Polis," 9.

Third, *the paradigm and goal of reparative work are thus apocalyptic.* Harink's strong thesis is that *The Politics of Jesus* embodies Paul's apocalyptic theo-politics. This thesis enables Harink to account for several key features of Yoder's vision: *service to both sacramental and political life; the nondu-alistic duality of a materiality that is, however, not of this present world; an ecclesial politics that is in the world but not of worldly powers and princi-palities.* In Harink's terms, "'Apocalyptic mission' is a way to characterize [Yoder's theo-political] thinking": "The meaning of this phrase is perhaps best captured by phrases in the titles of other works by Yoder: *The Priestly Kingdom, The Royal Priesthood, For the Nations.* Yoder stresses that God's invasion of the cosmos in Jesus Christ creates a people whose calling and task is to live amidst the nations for the sake of the nations, as a *paradigmatic sign* of humanity's and creation's destiny, and to do so as witness, servant, exemplar, and intercessor."[28]

Fourth, *the church is in the world but not of this world, political but not of worldly politics.* For Yoder, Paul's critique of worldly "principalities and powers" is, in Harink's terms, not a rejection of worldly institutions, since the principalities and powers are "analogous to the concrete 'structures'— religious, intellectual, moral, political, economic—within which human beings live, and without which they cannot live."[29] While "these powers/ structures were created by God for human welfare," they have, however, "rebelled against God's purposes and now hold human beings in bondage."[30] To serve God's purposes again they must be saved, and God saves them "through the faithfulness of Jesus Christ, in his defeat of the powers through submitting to them in his crucifixion."[31] Paul's critique is thus a call to join the body of Christ, so that in joining this body the children of Adam will resist the world's fallen powers and place all aspects of their creaturely lives in God's service.

---

28. Ibid., 5.

29. Ibid., 7, citing Hendrikus Berkhof. Daniel Weiss suggests that this reading of Paul applies only in the time between the times; in the final end-time, there will be no place for polity. See Weiss, "'The Yetzer Hara Will Be Uprooted.'"

In the chapter on "Christ and Power" in *The Politics of Jesus* Yoder expresses his indebt-edness to Berkhof, *Christ and the Powers* (Scottdale, PA: Herald, 1962), which Yoder himself translated from the Dutch. A clear statement of Yoder's use of the concept of the powers in relation to the questions of "Christ and culture" as posed by H. Richard Niebuhr may be found in "How H. Richard Niebuhr Reasoned: A Critique of *Christ and Culture,*" in Glen H. Stassen, D. M. Yeager, and John Howard Yoder, *Authentic Transformation: A New Vision of Christ and Culture* (Nashville: Abingdon, 1996), 31–89, esp. 68–71. For a helpful brief summary of Yoder's thought on the powers, see Marva Dawn, "The Biblical Concept of 'the Principalities and Powers': John Yoder Points to Jacques Ellul," in *The Wisdom of the Cross: Essays in Honor of John Howard Yoder,* ed. Stanley Hauerwas et al. (Grand Rapids: Eerdmans, 1999), 168–80.

30. Harink, "Apocalypse and Polis," 7.

31. Ibid.

Fourth, *the church must be apart from the world, not sectarian or against the world.* Therefore, "the relationship of the church with the structures and orders of the wider world must not be that of indiscriminate opposition but of critical discernment. . . . For Yoder the possibility of agreement, co-operation and participation in the structures of the wider world cannot be ruled out a priori. Yoder is consistent in stressing this point against what has often been charged as 'sectarianism.'"[32]

Fifth, *Yoder thus affirms Anabaptist radicalism while resisting Anabaptist tendencies to dualism.* Yoder's early, gentle parting from his teacher Harold Bender may anticipate what Harink considers his wariness of Anabaptist tendencies at times to divorce justification by faith from material action and thus to draw an inappropriate divide between the realms of spirit and of practical law and politics: "Against what may be an historic Anabaptist tendency to read the church/world relationship in terms of an apocalyptic dualism, Yoder wants to stress, precisely through his apocalyptic theology, the creational continuity of the church/world relationship."[33] Harink argues that Paul, by analogy, sought to lead the Corinthians away from a spirit–body dualism toward this sort of being in the world but not of the world.[34]

Sixth, *the church is for the nations, not of or against them.* For Yoder, the church should serve, like the Jews, as "a light to the nations," standing apart from their worldly powers and principalities as a paradigm of how else to live in the world. Even the sacraments have this paradigmatic function for those outside the church per se: "[E]ach of these practices can function as a paradigm for ways in which other social groups might operate. . . . [T]hey are accessible to the public. People who do not share the faith or join the community can learn from them."[35]

32. Ibid.
33. Ibid., 8.
34. Harink explains:
The Corinthian believers . . . viewed their freedom as separate from the body, whether social or personal. . . . Paul responds that the Corinthian body, whether social or personal, must itself be brought into submission to Christ, re-ordered according to his own pattern of self-abasement and self-offering, in order to make visible the social body of Jesus Christ in the midst of the Corinthian polis. The body, its functions and its needs—eating and drinking, sexual intercourse, social intercourse—is precisely the site of God's reclamation of Corinth in Jesus Christ, made possible by his conquest of the powers that hold Corinth and its people in bondage. (Ibid., 8)
Harink says his reading of 1 Corinthians is inspired by Dale B. Martin, *The Corinthian Body* (New Haven: Yale University Press, 1995), and Richard B. Hays, *First Corinthians* (Louisville: John Knox, 1997).
35. John Howard Yoder, "Sacrament as Social Process: Christ the Transformer of Culture," in *Royal Priesthood: Essays Ecclesiological and Ecumenical* (Grand Rapids: Eerdmans, 1994), 369. Harink draws his account of the sacraments from this essay and from John Howard Yoder, *Body Politics: Five Practices of the Christian Community before the Watching World* (Nashville: Discipleship Resources, 1992).

Finally, *the church is in exile among the nations.* Yoder's church is in exile in the sense of not serving worldly powers and in that sense not "possessing the land." At the same time, its exile is *among* the nations, with them. "How pointedly, and at what points [the alternative social and political ethics of the Christian community] will set us at odds with our neighbors, will of course depend on the neighbors."[36]

3. Apocalyptic postliberalism

This account of Yoder's *apocalyptic, Pauline theopolitics* fills in something otherwise missing in my account of Yoder's radicalized Anabaptist theology: evidence that his theology is introduced as a context-specific corrective to specific ills of the empirical church, rather than as a context-neutral proclamation. Yoder's critique of Christian individualism, otherworldliness, spiritualism, and Constantinianism complements the pragmatism I attributed to Hauerwas, Jenson, and Lindbeck. This means that Yoder also seeks the unity of the body of Christ. As he suggests in "The Nature of the Unity We Seek: A Historic Free Church View," Yoder shares the postliberals' sense that the unity of the church imitates the unity of Scripture and that this unity is realized in discipleship. He displays a more radical sense, however, of the demands of unity, beyond those of sacrament and doctrine. In Nation's reading, Yoder identifies three such demands. One is *conversation*: "True conversation exists only where there is movement toward agreement, motivated by appeal to an authority recognized by both parties."[37] For Yoder's free church, this authority is "*Christ himself* as he is made known through Scripture to the congregation of those who seek to know him and his will."[38] A second demand is *supranational*: "It would be hard to find a more flagrant implicit denial of the givenness of Christian unity than the churches' unhesitating consent to nationalism in its demonic military form."[39] A third demand is for *discipline*: "the Church cannot but be a disciplined fellowship of those who confess that, if there be one faith, one body, one hope, there must also be one obedience."[40]

Yoder's attention to the body—individual, social, and political—belongs to the postliberal vision. Like Hauerwas, he devotes much more energy to theopolitics than do Jenson or Lindbeck, but the general model of life "in the world but not of the world" is embraced by all the postliberals. The differences are matters of emphasis and degree, and this applies as well to what Harink calls

36. Yoder, "The Hermeneutics of Peoplehood: A Protestant Perspective," in *Priestly Kingdom*, 43, quoted in Harink, "Apocalypsis and Polis," 7.
37. Yoder, *Royal Priesthood*, 223, quoted in Nation, *Apocalypsis and Polis*, 88.
38. Ibid., 88, quoted in Ibid., 89.
39. Ibid., 226, quoted in Ibid., 90.
40. Ibid., 28, quoted in Ibid., 90–91.

Yoder's Pauline apocalyptic: the criterion governing all postliberal reforms is the revelation of God in the life, death, and resurrection of Jesus Christ.

Significant Marks of Yoder's Nonsupersessionism

Lindbeck seeks ways to overcome the doctrinal schisms that divide Lutheran and Catholic churches, Eastern and Western rites, and also what some consider the conflicting covenants of ancient Israel and the church as the New Israel. In these terms, Yoder's *The Jewish–Christian Schism Revisited* appears to serve Lindbeck's goal, since Yoder seeks to demonstrate that the schism did not have to be and that we may therefore *undo* it by promoting mutually affirming forms of Judaism and of Christianity.

Yoder first notes the commonplace definitions that have underwritten almost two thousand years of mutual enmity:

> 1. There was first of all a base line of "normative Judaism." . . . It was essentially the same as that codified two centuries later in the *Mishnah*, except for its being at home in Palestine. For these purposes "Judaism" means both a *position*, i.e., a religious synthesis of beliefs and practices, and a *population*, which we might more precisely call "Jewry." Both the positions and the population were relatively homogeneous.
>
> 2. Jesus rejected normative Judaism and was rejected by it. That reciprocal rejection is not a misunderstanding or a tragic fluke, but a proper and necessary response, befitting the real positions of both "sides." There was a necessary antagonism between what Jesus was saying and the Judaism which he attacked.
>
> 3. The apostle Saul/Paul again rejected Judaism and was rejected by it.
>
> 4. Christianity as such is defined by these two successive rejections, not by its commonalities with Judaism. The many convictions which were still held in common by Christians and Jews around 100 CE . . . do not contribute as fundamentally to the definition of Christianity as do the points involved in the double rejection summarized above. The rejection is *doubly* double: Jesus and Paul rejected Judaism, and Judaism returned the compliment.[41]

Yoder then offers step-by-step arguments—historical, textual, political, and theological—about why this schismatic model no longer stands the tests of historical evidence and theo-political wisdom. His preface and first chapter overview the following essentials of his argument:

1. First corrective
   a. There was no such thing as normative Judaism. Jewry as a population was a great number of very diverse people. Their "convictions" were

---

41. Yoder, "'It Did Not Have to Be,'" 47.

scattered across a broad and messy spectrum within which various people projected various normative visions.[42]

b. The collapse of the Jewish governments in Palestine . . . meant that the definition of Jewish identity after the year 70 would have to come from somewhere else than from the bearers of civil government. That was not too tragic, since there had not been a completely viable independent Jewish civil government since 586 BCE.[43]

c. Not until the end of the second century of our era can the historian say that there existed a single definition of Jewishness claiming normativity. It acquired an institutional definition in the networking of the rabbinate, and an intellectual vision in the codification of the Mishnah. . . . Yet those beginnings . . . were smaller in constituency and weaker in terms of inner coherence than were the "Christians" at that time. Even once codified, the Mishnah was not immediately "received" (in the strong technical sense) from Babylon to Barcelona. It needed to be propagated and to make its way in the synagogues, just as the Christian gospel before it had had to do.[44]

2. Second corrective

a. If, then, the very notion of a "normative Judaism" as backdrop and interlocutor for Jesus and Paul does not hold water, the whole picture must be redrawn.[45]

b. *Neither Jesus, nor Paul, nor the apostolic communities rejected normative Judaism.* . . . If there was no such thing as normative Judaism no one could have univocally rejected it or been rejected by it. But the point is far more fundamental. What Jesus himself proposed to his listeners was nothing other than what he claimed as the normative vision for a restored and clarified Judaism, namely, the proper interpretation of the Jewish Scriptures and tradition for this present, in the light of the New Age which he heralded.[46]

c. There is in the Gospel accounts of the ministry of Jesus nowhere a rejection of Judaism as a stream of history or a group of people. With

---

42. Yoder, "What Needs to Change," 31. Yoder continues: "This diversity had been there for centuries. Some of the bearers of these conflicting normative claims tried to discipline the others, the 'zealous' ones after the mode of Phinehas (5) in fact doing so by the sword, but the people they disciplined were still Jews. That was in fact why the Zealots claimed the right to exercise the discipline."

43. Ibid., 31–32.

44. Ibid., 32.

45. Yoder, "'It Did Not Have to Be,'" 49.

46. Ibid., 49. Yoder adds: "Jesus rejected certain other teachings, and he scolded certain other people, as did all Jewish teachers, but he never granted that the traditions and the people he was challenging or reprimanding were qualified interpreters of Torah. He claimed that he himself represented that, and that those other teachers were misled and misleading in their contrary efforts to interpret the tradition."

regard specifically to the law, Jesus's attitudes are all affirmative. He said he had come not to destroy the law or even relax it—but rather to fulfill it. He claimed to defend its intent against interpretations which would destroy its meaning or dull its edge. He appealed both to the historical experience of Jews and to their canonical writings to authenticate and illuminate everything he taught. He placed himself completely within that context.

d. At points where Jesus entered into debate, it was a debate about the proper meaning of the Jewish Scriptures and traditions, never an effort to relativize or deny that heritage. . . . Similarly, the apostle Saul/Paul never surrendered his claim that a true child of Abraham must share the faith in the son of the promise made to Abraham.

e. Paul debated head-on against certain ways of applying the Jewish heritage to the Diaspora situation, especially with regard to how much of the Jewish lifestyle should be expected of proselytes and of God-fearing adherents of the synagogue who did not become full Jews. That was a debate which had been going on already generations earlier, a debate provoked within Diaspora Judaism before Jesus, by its extensive success in attracting to the synagogue community sincere seekers of non-Jewish blood. . . . Paul's advocacy of a relatively liberal attitude toward these people without a Jewish ancestry was one of the positions which had already been taken in those earlier discussions. It was in no way an un-Jewish or anti-Jewish position. Paul was the great Judaizer of the Gentiles.[47]

3. Third corrective

a. *The Jews did not reject Christianity.* . . . Judaism as a system of beliefs and practices did not reject Christianity as a belief system. Nor did Jewry as a body of people, or most of their institutions, reject believers in Jesus as a people. The Temple at Jerusalem was open to believers in Jesus until its destruction.

b. Outside of Jerusalem the social context of the believing community was the synagogue. Until the end of the first century (at the very earliest hypothesis) there was no general expulsion of Christians from synagogues. . . . To be a Jew and to be a follower of Jesus were not alternatives. *Tertium Datur.*

c. The accounts in the New Testament of what could authentically be called persecution of believers in Jesus by Jews are very few. In the cases we do have, the agents of such mistreatment are generally not the most morally qualified representative leaders of the Jewish community.[48]

47. Ibid., 49–50.
48. Ibid., 51.

The Overall Force of Yoder's Argument

Yoder's argument complements the following features of Lindbeck's non-supersessionism, which I take as a prototype.

1. The genealogical movement of religious repair, from current divisions back to aboriginal schisms

Like Lindbeck, Yoder reasons from current conditions of disunity in the church to antecedent sources of unity and thus repair. Along his genealogical movement toward these sources, he—like Lindbeck—also uncovers antecedent sources of potential nonrepair, such as antecedent marks of schism and thus disunity. The surprising mark of both Lindbeck's and Yoder's genealogies is that each turns to the Jewish–Christian schism as a problem rather than as a norm. This means that each of their genealogies is fundamentally reformational, since each must invoke Scripture afresh as the source of nonsupersessionist claims that have no precedent in the councils of patristic Christianity but that, according to them, are true to the practices of primitive Christianity.

2. A scripturally grounded reform

Yoder's and Lindbeck's nonsupersessionism reinstitutes Scripture reading as an irreplaceable feature of Jesus's work and Paul's ministry: Jesus's work on earth can be understood only in relation to Israel's covenant and Scripture. It is by no means sufficient to read the Gospels as a once-and-for-all-time rereading of the Old Testament, the way, for example, the Dead Sea Scroll commentary on Isaiah specified a single *pesher* or allegorical "solution" to the identity of the Teacher of Righteousness. For Lindbeck and Yoder, Gospel is a perennial rereading of the Old Testament, through which the Spirit draws new readings out of the Old Testament into the present day of the church. That is the hermeneutic of nonsupersessionism: not because it lessens the Gospels' unique message, but because it retains Israel's covenant and Scripture as part of the ever-living alphabet of that message.

3. A depth-historiographic rereading of the context of Scripture

Yoder practices what I consider a distinctly postliberal manner of historical scholarship, comparable to what I have called "depth historiography" in the practice of the Talmudic historian David Weiss Halivni.[49] Such historiography begins with text-historical study as the scholar's means of

---

49. See Peter Ochs, "Talmudic Scholarship as Textual Reasoning: Halivni's Pragmatic Historiography," in *Textual Reasonings: Jewish Philosophy and Text Study at the End of the Twentieth Century*, ed. Peter Ochs and Nancy Levene (Grand Rapids: Eerdmans, 2002), 120–43.

making claims about what I label the "plain-sense history" of Scripture and early scriptural commentary: these are claims that can win general approval from the scholarly community. The "depth historiographer" then accepts an additional responsibility, to answer certain questions that are of urgent significance for the current life and identity of his or her religious community but for which the text-historical evidence provides no clear answer. In this case, the depth historiographer proposes a historical claim that is most consistent with the plain-sense evidence and most responsive to the community's urgent questions.

Yoder articulates his depth historiography this way: "We do violence to the depth and density of the story if, knowing with the wisdom of later centuries that it came out as it did, we box the actors of the first century into our wisdom about their children's fate in the second."[50] Yoder assumes we need to begin with plain-sense history ("to get the facts straight") but that we must seek, in addition, "to put ourselves so effectively into the psychic skins of the actors of those days that we can say that the history looks open: it could've gone otherwise."[51] As I understand it, this is to learn about ourselves now by imagining ourselves in their skins then. With appropriate warrants in recent rabbinic scholarship, Yoder argues that the Judaisms of the Roman era were pluriform and that proto-rabbinic Judaism competed for religious authority among several other forms, including the Nazarenes (or followers of Jesus) and other messianic movements.[52] There is no evidence of a single "normative Judaism" in this era. Yoder's broadest conclusion is warranted as well: there is no clear evidence that early Christianity rejected "Judaism" or that first- and early second-century Judaism rejected "Christianity."[53] Yoder rereads what we take to be early Christian–Jewish invectives as, therefore, intra-Jewish invectives, typical in energy and acerbic tone of intra-Jewish debates of these early centuries. This means that it would be anachronistic to claim that "the

50. Yoder, "'It Did Not Have to Be,'" 44.

51. Ibid.

52. Ibid., 46–49. Yoder draws on recent historical evidence that Jewry from the first century BCE through the second century CE included diverse communities with a broad range of religious observances. Recent rabbinic historians from Jacob Neusner on have successively complexified the claims of an earlier generation, from G. Foote Moore on, who tended to read the culture of a later Talmudic Judaism back into Mishnaic Judaism and then read the culture of Mishnaic Judaism back into the competing movements of Jewry under Roman rule. In light of this historiographic reform, it is possible to reconsider, for example, the more Greek-friendly Judaisms of Alexandria and Antioch as of continuing value as models for how Judaism can frame itself within Mediterranean and later civilization. As Yoder argues, it is also possible to reconsider first-century Nazarene Jews as not merely nonrabbinic but one of the ways that Jews lived their convictions.

53. Ibid., 49–51. The implications are that Jesus's work took place within the people Israel and within the Judaisms of his time; that Paul extends a messianic Judaism to the Gentile nations as his way of practicing Judaism; and that the Gospel of John did not seek to condemn "the Jews" in general but only a certain part of what he took to be the Jewish establishment (ibid., 50–51).

Jews rejected Christianity."[54] Many Jewish movements rejected the claims of many other Jewish movements but without rejecting the membership of the other claimants in the people Israel.[55]

> 4. Adopting this depth-historiographic reading as his form of reparative genealogy[56]

Yoder's depth historiography serves as his way of practicing the genealogical phase of postliberal reparative reasoning. By reading plain-sense history, he locates antecedent sources for repairing contemporary crises in the church. By reading depth-historically, he is able to recommend how to identify these, *specifically*, as sources for repairing crises that he diagnoses in the church today. Depth-historical clams of this kind are probabilistic rather than certain, vague (or subject to definition in the act of application) rather than clear and distinct. The claims are, in this sense, logically "triadic"—(1) claims that display their (2) definite meaning and validity only with respect to (3) their specific context of application—rather than dyadic (either–or claims that are clearly true whatever the context, so that competing claims are clearly false).[57] When understood in this sense, Yoder's depth-historiographic claims complement postliberal doctrines of nonsupersessionism.

> 5. Contributions to postliberal Jewish–Christian dialogue

When adopted according to these caveats, Yoder's historiography contributes to the postliberal pursuit of a reparative dialogue between contemporary Christianities and Judaisms. This pursuit entails

> a. a new kind of Christian openness to dialogue with Jews and Judaism
> b. a postliberal openness to theological dialogue in general
> c. an openness that meets the needs and crises of this particular time in history
> d. a rediscovery of scriptural study as the basis of such a dialogue
> e. a rediscovery of community as the context for scriptural study and thus of intercommunal study as the basis for Jewish–Christian dialogue
> f. a practice of "depth historiography" as a contribution to intercommunal study of Scripture

54. Ibid., 51.
55. Paragraph drawn from my commentary on ibid., in *JCSR*, 67.
56. What I called "the genealogical movement of religious repair, from current divisions to aboriginal schisms" (above, item 1, p. 143).
57. For an account of how I employ the terms *dyadic* and *binary* in this book, see the introduction.

g. a recognition of the vagueness and fluidity of both Jewish and Christian self-definitions

Marks of Non-postliberalism and Non-nonsupersessionism in Yoder's Work

Now comes the turning point in this chapter and in this book as a whole. I will argue that *JCSR* exhibits a mix of both postliberal and nonliberal theology and of both nonsupersessionism and non-nonsupersessionism. I will argue, furthermore, that this feature of Yoder's work confirms my book's overall thesis: there is a direct correlation between postliberalism and nonsupersessionism, so that the presence or absence of one is directly correlated with the presence or absence of the other. Yoder's work is the exception that proves this rule, since the very places where he fails even if unintentionally to achieve nonsupersessionism are also places where he exhibits non-postliberal practices of reasoning. I present this argument in three steps. First, "the data": marks of non-nonsupersessionism in Yoder's text. Second, "an explanatory account": a hypothesis that these marks are the fruit of Yoder's reasoning from apparently nonsupersessionist premises to supersessionist conclusions, by way of non-postliberal practices of reasoning. The "culprit," in other words, is a practice of non-postliberal reasoning that undercuts nonsupersessionism. This account includes two subarguments: (2a) "non-postliberal reasoning in Yoder's corpus" and (2b) "non-nonsupersessionism in Yoder's corpus." Third, I argue that (2a) leads to (2b).

1. *"The data": marks of non-nonsupersessionism in* The Jewish– Christian Schism Revisited

Yoder's profound contribution to nonsupersessionism is to retrieve dimensions of Judaism that Christian supersessionists have for generations identified as beyond the pale of Judaism and disclosed only in the New Testament, such as dedication to life in exile outside the land, nonviolence, openness to mission work among the nations, and suspicion of state power and authority as well as of priestly authority and exclusivism. However, Yoder has also—unintentionally, I presume—defined these dimensions in strict ways that obscure rabbinic Judaism's tendencies to offer its claims vaguely, subject to context-specific interpretation. Excluding its opposite, Yoder's praise for one dimension of Judaism has the effect of condemning another dimension as if it were "not worthy of being Jewish." The result is a partial delegitimization that functions as a degree of non-nonsupersessionism.

Yoder's grounding argument is that there is no single historical type of Judaism, that Judaism has therefore no single norm, and that Judaism is not, therefore, only rabbinic Judaism. Yoder employs his historiography for more than relativizing purposes, however. He also argues that there is another Judaism, underexamined by rabbinic historians, that merits our attention not merely as one additional possibility among others but also as a privileged possibility: the Judaism that was most true to the God of Israel and most resistant to humanity's perennial tendency to replace the one invisible God with earthly gods of their own fancies, gods of landedness, statecraft, nation building, or of antimissionizing halakhic life. The result of Yoder's reasoning is, I believe, both self-contradictory and non-nonsupersessionist (however unintentionally).

It is self-contradictory because Yoder claims, on the one hand, that we cannot "recuperate the narratives of communities which died out"[58] and that there was no single Judaism in the first century,[59] but, on the other hand, that we should recognize diasporic, "Jeremianic" Judaism as the essential thrust of first-century Judaism.[60] It is non-nonsupersessionist because it valorizes only the one variety of Judaism that anticipates Yoder's free church. It selectively delegitimizes the Judaism that achieved major influence in second- and third-century Jewry the same way the Christianity of Nicaea achieved major influence among the competing Christianities of the first through third centuries. It may be liberating to disclaim rabbinic Judaism as the only possible model of Jewish life. But it is non-nonsupersessionist to delegitimize major tenets of rabbinic Judaism as a worthy focus of most Jews' devotion and study since the third century. We therefore have reason to be wary of the way Yoder seeks to legitimize the Jesus movement, as if Jesus and then Paul's followers were as already as influential within the various first- and early second-century Judaisms as were the movements gathered around Hillel and Akiva. Beginning with the Jeremiac model of exile, I note here five features of early Judaism that Yoder identifies as essential to Judaism and to Christianity.

A. Judaism is Exilic: The Jeremiac Model

The concluding chapter of *JCSR*, "See How They Go with Their Face to the Sun," is a stylistically powerful reading of the Jewish writer Stephan Zweig's poem/drama *Jeremiah*, composed during World War I. For both Zweig and Yoder, Jeremiah 29 warrants the desire to join Israel's fate directly to the universal goal of redeeming humanity and thereby to avoid the embarrassment of the people Israel's landedness. For both Zweig and Yoder, there is no middle between Israel's exilic separation from the land and the Maccabees' nationalist strategy for remaining in it. There is therefore no medium between Israel's two roles as embodied Word to the nations (for what is light but a trope for the divine Word?) and as a prototype of humanity's recalcitrance. For both

---

58. Yoder, "It Did Not Have to Be," 57.
59. Ibid., 58.
60. The claim of his subsequent chapters.

Zweig and Yoder, the tragic consequence of this tension corresponds to the tragic image we have of the face of Jeremiah.

Jeremiah 29:7 embodies Yoder's vision of both a free Judaism and the free church: "Seek the welfare of the city where I have sent you, and pray to the Lord on its behalf, for in its welfare you will find your welfare." In Yoder's reading, the "dynamic English equivalent" is, "Seek the salvation of the culture to which God has sent you. . . ."[61] Reading Israel's *galuth* (Diaspora) as a figure of "the Christian attitude to the Gentile world," Yoder links the pacifist ethos of early Christianity with the "ethos of Jewry."[62] From Yoder's perspective, the story of Babel in Genesis 11 voices the experience of the Babylonian captivity. Rejecting what he regards as the "palestinocentric reading" of Jewish history, Yoder contends that the captivity has proved to be constitutive of Jewish identity. The Jews were scattered for mission just as seeds are broadcast "to bloom where they were sown."[63] Exilic Judaism is therefore not merely compatible with "messianic Judaism" but also completed in it.[64]

61. Yoder, "See How They Go with Their Face to the Sun," *JCSR*, 202n60. This reading can be questioned at several levels of exegetical and hermeneutical inquiry. While it serves Yoder's desire to clarify the missiological vocation of the exilic community, it does so by collapsing into a monologic what can arguably be said to be a much more complex set of concepts beginning with but not limited to the meanings ascribed to the Hebrew word *shalom*.

62. Ibid., 191.

63. Ibid., 197.

64. Yoder continues:

Within this missionary vision, the role of "seeking the welfare of that city" becomes quite concrete, both in real experience and in legends which reflect, interpret, and in turn further foster that experience. What we might call the "Joseph paradigm" became a standard type. In three different ages and places, the same experiences recur in the Hebrew story. Joseph, Daniel and his three friends, and Esther all found themselves involuntarily at the heart of the idolatrous empire. Each ran the risk of faithfulness to their people and to the revealed will of the one true God, when their civil disobedience could have cost them their lives. Each was saved by divine intervention, with the result that the pagan tyrant was converted to the recognition of the one true God, vindicating them against their enemies, and giving Jews a role in running the empire. . . . In all the different ways represented by Sadducees, Pharisees, Maccabaeans and Essenes, Jews in Palestine had no choice but to define their identity over against the dominant Gentiles, and to be divided from one another by their conflicting responses to that challenge. On the other hand, the synagogues and the rabbis in Babylon, and in the rest of the world where the Babylonian model was followed and the Babylonian teachers were consulted, were spared that selfdefeating distraction, so as to enter creatively into the Jeremianic phase of creating something qualitatively new in the history of religions.

Somewhere, some time, in the Jeremianic setting, there arose what I claimed above was the most fundamental sociological innovation in the history of religions, namely, the culture of the synagogue. There is here no priest accredited by his qualification to administer cultic ceremonies. There is no high priest mandated by the emperor. Precisely because the Jerusalem temple is not portable and its functions not replaceable, what Jews gather around elsewhere will be not an altar but a scroll. The legitimacy of the local gathering depends on no central hierarchy, although its fidelity to the message of the scroll may be served by a

B. Judaism is not, therefore, a religion of any land

For Yoder, the next step is not to claim, like the Mishnah *Pirke Avot*, that Judaism may thrive outside the land as well as within it. He claims instead that Judaism fulfilled its mission to depart from the land and adopt Diaspora as its home. Life in *galuth* or Diaspora[65] is not without its dimensions of profound and painful alienation. Psalm 137 has become for us the prototypical expression of that suffering: "How can we sing Zion songs in a strange land?"

> Yet, painful as the question is, that is what the Jews learned to do, and do well. It may well have been in this age of Galuth that the Psalter began to form as a central identity resource, part of the canon, beside the Torah. The very possibility of the mocking challenge, "Sing us one of the songs of Zion!" (137:3 RSV) presupposes the awareness on the part of the "captors" that despite having no temple, the Jews had an important worship life of their own.[66] Even that experience reinforces their identity.[67]

Michael Cartwright argues that Yoder's diasporic model of Judaism is supersessionist:

> Yoder . . . understands that in order for his argument to be persuasive he has to show the books of *Ezra* and *Nehemiah* have no real bearing on [the argument about Jeremiah]. . . . [To do so, he] gesture[s] to the work of . . . Stephan Zweig, whose vision of the return is metaphorical only. . . . Unfortunately, Yoder consistently renders Zweig's metaphor monologically, thereby ignoring other ways in which the metaphor of *galut* registers in the texts of the Hebrew Bible.[68] . . . [Yoder's] principal agenda through [the next section] is to attempt to delegitimate the significance of the role of Ezra and Nehemiah in the canon of the Old Testament. . . .
>
> By breaking the *triad*—Torah, land, and people—in this way, Yoder has constructed a conception of Jewish peoplehood that gathers around the reading and interpretation of a text "which can be copied and read anywhere."[69] . . .

---

rabbi trained in a school. Any ten households qualify as a local cell of the worldwide people of God. Since what they do when they gather is to read together, a canon of scriptures must develop. There will be no orally transmitted mysteries reserved to the initiated. (ibid., 186)

65. Yoder notes: "Etymologically these terms, one Hebrew and one Greek, both mean simply 'scattering.' Those with a view of the past as ideal will give them the negative overtones of 'exile' or 'banishment.' For Jeremiah it is mission. (The Greek form includes the sense of broadcasting seed.) The Jews were sent there to identify their own welfare with that of that place, to bloom where they were sown." (ibid., 197)

66. Yoder notes, "We might compare this to the way in which white Americans' awareness of the power of the spirituals and of blues has contributed to both the viability and the self-respect of African-Americans." (ibid.)

67. Yoder, "See How They Go with Their Face to the Sun," 185–86.

68. Michael Cartwright, "Afterword: If Abraham Is Our Father . . . ," in *JCSR*, 219.

69. Cartwright cites Yoder from Leroy Friesen, *Mennonite Witness to the Middle East*, rev. ed. (Elkhart, IN: Mennonite Board of Missions, 2000 [orig. 1992]), 64.

By making the "return to Zion mythic," Yoder effectively disengages from the deeply rooted complex of Jewish theological claims that see the land of *eretz yisrael* as the locus of the sacred and thereby displaces the theological unity of election, covenant, and God's promise of redemption from exile.[70]

For Cartwright, in sum, Yoder offers a reasonable argument for *galut* as a Jeremiah-inspired model for Christianity but broadly overstates the status of *galut* within first- and second-century Judaisms. To identify Jewish and Christian models in this way is to predefine the judgments of the living community of Israel, and this is non-nonsupersessionist.

c. Judaism is nonviolent and separates itself from any dealings with worldly powers and principalities

Yoder's vision of exilic Judaism corresponds to several characteristics of rabbinic communal life in Diaspora. In Yoder's terms, these characteristics are as follows:

- The primary vehicle of identity definition is a text which can be copied, and can be read anywhere.
- The ground floor of "worship" . . . is reading and singing the texts.
- A valid local cell of the world Jewish community . . . can exist wherever there are ten households. No priesthood, no hierarchy is needed. If they can afford a rabbi, his role is that of a scribe, rather than that of prophet, priest, or prince.
- The international unity of the people is sustained by intervisitation, by intermarriage, by commerce, and by rabbinic consultation, needing no high priest or pope or king to hang together.
- Although there is plenty of material, and plenty of freedom, with which thinkers over the centuries can develop Jewish philosophical systems (cosmological, mystical, linguistic, scientific), the ground floor of identity is the common life itself, the walk, *halakah*, and the shared remembering of the story behind it.[71]

I agree that this list captures central features of Diaspora Judaism, with the exception that this Judaism never understood itself as the only legitimate form

---

70. Cartwright, "Afterword," 219–20. Cartwright continues, "How do we account for Yoder's misreading of the texts in this regard? From the perspective of the Israeli scholar and peace activist [now at Hartford Seminary] Yehezkel Landau—who knew Yoder personally and greatly admires *The Politics of Jesus*—Yoder 'magnifies the prophetic dimension of Jewish vocation' and in so doing displaces the integral relationship of the prophetic vocation to the priestly role. From Landau's perspective, the priestly/prophetic vocation of the people of Israel 'has everything to do with sabbath, but does not make *galut* a normative existence.'"

71. Yoder, "See How They Go with Their Face to the Sun," 187.

of Jewish life.[72] For Yoder, however, this is the only legitimate model of Judaism and the only alternative to "Constantinianism," whether Christian (of which the prototype is Catholic Rome or any Reformation analogue of a Christian nation-state) or Jewish (of which the contemporary prototype is Zionism, and the ancient prototype is Maccabean Israel). Yoder's non-nonsupersessionist tendency lies not in what he admires about rabbinic Judaism but in what he strictly excludes from it.

Yoder's vision of messianic Judaism overlaps in one way with what we know about proto- and exilic rabbinic Judaism: the rabbinic sages sought to promote peace and to avoid violence, anger, and killing. These were ultimate goals, however, rather than clear and distinct rules. Understood broadly, rabbinic Judaism never abandoned the covenant between the God of Israel and the people Israel *as* a people. Rabbinic Judaism never separated this peoplehood from its earthly embodiment in a people joined by quasi-kinship bonds, shared memory, and shared languages, practices, and physical space. Until the twentieth century, most European Orthodox Jews rejected efforts to construct a Jewish state before the days of the Messiah. Even they, however, still hoped to return to the *land* of Israel as a worldly home. While the diasporic rabbinic Judaisms tended to presume that exile would remain until messianic time, not all privileged exile as the Jewish condition for this world. Many appear to have accommodated themselves to exile until a return was possible and warranted. A dialectical relation between exile and landedness is therefore more representative of classical Jewish life and belief than any clear and unchanging choice *for* one against the other.[73]

72. Daniel Weiss objects to my claim here, since rabbinic Judaism foresaw a return to the land only in the end-time. I argue, however, that rabbinic claims are framed in a theo-political environment in which a return appeared utterly impractical and that the claims remained untested until Jews judged that a return was practicable in this world. I argue, second, that Yoder did not imagine an end-time that could include the rabbis' predominant sense of Israel's ultimate return to political hegemony in the land. There are indeed some parallels between the rabbis' sense of Israel's indefinite exile and Yoder's model of permanent exile, but these remain separate streams of belief. (See the following note.)

73. Consider, for example, this sampling of the range of rabbinic views about the exile Israel suffers in this world:

(a) "Exile atones for sins" (Makkot 2b, Sanhedrin 37, etc.): This is the most general interpretive tendency, to rule that one who commits certain kinds of sin is exiled: for example, one who kills accidentally is exiled to a city of refuge. By extension, the exiles of communities of Israel were interpreted to be punishments for collective sins.

(b) Israel remains in exile until the Messiah comes (Sanhedrin 98a):

> Johanan also said: The son of David will come only in a generation that is either altogether righteous or altogether wicked. "In a generation that is altogether righteous,"—as it is written, "Thy people also shall be all righteous: they shall inherit the land for ever" (Isa. 60:21). "Or altogether wicked,"—as it is written, "And he saw that there was no man, and wondered that there was no intercessor" (Isa. 59:16).

In this sense, Yoder's exclusive choice *for* an exclusively exilic Judaism shares the same logic as the Maccabees' and Zealots' choice *for* an exclusively nonexilic Judaism of land and national power. The logic of either–or is not a logic of peace, whatever the content of the choice. As exhibited, for example, in the philosophies of Ahad Ha'am and Mordecai Kaplan, a more likely contemporary Jewish model is both-and, not either–or. These two envisioned a "cultural Zionism" or "civilizational Judaism" that valued corporate Jewish life, including life in the soil of Israel, but without formal nation-state self-governance.[74]

(c) God regrets having made exile (Sukkot 52b):

> Four things does the Almighty regret having made: Exile, the Chaldeans, the Ishmaelite and the Evil Inclination. . . . "The Exile," since it is written, "Now, therefore, what do I here, says Adonai, seeing that My people is taken away for nothing?" (Isa. 52:5).

(d) The end of exile is near (Makkot 24a–b):

> Rabban Gamliel, Rabbi Elazar ben Azariah, Rabbi Yehoshua, and Rabbi Akiva . . . on another occasion . . . went up to Jerusalem. When they got to Mount Scopus they tore their clothes and when they got to Mount Moriah, they saw a fox coming out of the Holy of Holies. They all cried, and Rabbi Akiva laughed. They asked him, "Why are you laughing?" He responded, "Why are you crying?" They said, "Foxes are now walking in the place about which it says, 'the stranger that comes close shall die' (Num. 1:51), shall we not cry?" "For that reason I am laughing," he said. "There is a verse that states, 'I brought faithful witnesses, Uriah the Cohen, and Zechariah ben Berachiyah' (Isa. 8:2). What is the connection between Uriah and Zechariah? Uriah lived during the first Temple and Zechariah during the second, but the verse implies that the prophecy of Zechariah is dependent on the prophecy of Uriah. Uriah says, 'Because of you, Zion will be plowed over like a field' (Micah 3:12). Zechariah says, 'Once again old men and women will sit in the streets of Jerusalem' (Zech. 8:4). Until the prophecy of Uriah was fulfilled, I was worried that the prophecy of Zechariah will never happen. Now that the prophecy of Uriah has been fulfilled it is certain that the prophecy of Zechariah will surely be." They said to him, "Akiva, you have comforted us, Akiva, you have comforted us."

(e) The end of exile means a rebuilding of Israel's polity, not an end of political rule (Maimonides, Mishneh Torah, Law of Kings 11:4):

> A king will arise from the House of David who delves deeply into the study of the Torah and . . . observes its commandments. . . . [He will] build the Temple and [then] gather in the dispersed remnant of Israel. At that time, we will all proceed to the Land of Israel in the actual sense in the true and ultimate Redemption, led by Messiah. May this take place soon.

(f) When Israel is exiled, God is exiled (Megillah 29a):

> "The Divine Presence was exiled with them . . . , and will return with them." The verses cited are, however, more comprehensive, implying that not only did the Divine Presence accompany the Jews into exile, it is in exile itself, and is in need of "salvation," as it were.

Once again, I am mildly skeptical about diasporic rabbinic claims that Israel will remain in exile "until the Messiah comes," since these claims were not tested by empirical evidence that any ingathering was practicable. My argument is not that most traditional Jews before the nineteenth century sought a this-worldly messiah like Bar-Kokhba, but only that traditional Jewish attitudes toward exile versus landedness should not be overdefined: dogmas about exile represented directions of theodicy rather than context-independent and impermeable doctrines.

74. See Mordecai Kaplan, *A Religion of Ethical Nationhood: Judaism's Contribution to World Peace* (New York: Macmillan, 1970), and Ahad Ha'am (Asher Ginzberg), *Nationalism and the Jewish Ethic* (New York: Schocken, 1962).

Seeking to serve both the spiritual and material ideals of Judaism, they would have made more compelling dialogue partners for Yoder than Stephan Zweig.

For the overall movement of rabbinic Judaism, the path to peace cannot be defined before the fact in the clear and distinct ways that Yoder recommends; it must take its shape within the tragic contours of the Jewish community's life in this world. The rabbinic sages require each person's protecting his or her own body as well as that of the neighbor, since each body is God's creature and "one does not reject one soul for the sake of another soul" (*eyn dochim nefesh mipney nefesh*; Sanhedrin 72b).[75] Except in certain situations, one may defend one's own life even through the use of force, but it is impossible to predict beforehand what this should mean in each individual case. There is a clear preference for avoiding violence but no clear-cut dogma for or against

75. While the rabbinic sages privileged nonviolence and nonkilling, their position cannot be captured in any single concept like "pacifism" or even "peace." Consider, for example, this sampling of the range of rabbinic views about killing:

(a) *Self-defense is justified:* In the case of a thief invading a private home at night (Exod. 22:1–2), "the Torah decreed, 'If he comes to kill you, kill him first'" (Sanhedrin 72a; cf. BT Berakhot 58a and 62b).

(b) The case of the *rodef*: even without warning, one may kill a person if that is the necessary means of keeping that person from killing another (the guilty party is called a *rodef*, or one who is in the act of "pursuing" another to kill him or her; Sanhedrin 73a):

> *Mishnah:* The following must be saved [from sinning] even at the cost of their lives: he who pursues after his neighbor to slay him . . .
>
> *Gemara:* Our Rabbis taught: whence do we know that he who pursues after his neighbour to slay him must be saved [from sin] at the cost of his own life? From the verse, Thou shalt not stand by the blood of thy neighbor (Lev. 19:16).

(c) There are three (and only three) cases in which one should sacrifice one's life (from Sanhedrin 74a):

> R. Johanan said in the name of R. Simeon b. Jehozadak: By a majority vote, it was resolved in the upper chambers of the house of Nathza in Lydda: Every [other] law of the Torah, if a man is commanded: "Transgress and be not killed" he should transgress and not be killed, excepting idolatry, incest [which includes adultery], and murder.

(d) But one must not substitute another's life for one's own (Sanhedrin 74a):

> A man came to Rava and told him that the governor of the city had ordered that he [the man] slay a certain man or himself suffer death, and Rava said to him: "Rather than slay another person, you must permit yourself to be slain, for how do you know that your blood is redder than his, perhaps his blood is redder than yours?"

(e) In "lifeboat" situations, however, your own blood is not less red than his or hers (from Bava Metzia 62a):

> Two people were traveling, and [only] one of them had a canteen of water. [There was only enough water so that] if both of them drank they would both die, but if one of them drank [only] he would make it back to an inhabited area [and live]. Ben Petura publicly taught: "Better both should drink and die than that one see his friend's death," until Rabbi Akiva came and taught: "'Your brother should live with you' (Lev. 25:36)—your life takes precedence over the life of your friend's."

(f) One may say the general rule tends to be *eyn dochim nefesh mipney nefesh*, "One does not reject one soul for the sake of another soul" (Sanhedrin 72b).

pacifism in general, and there is significant room for dialogue between Yoder and religious Jews on such questions.

D. Judaism is open to mission work among the nations

There is historical warrant for Yoder's claim that the rabbinic sages reduced Judaism's missionary impulse partly in reaction to Christianity's missionary zeal. But Yoder strongly overstates the case when he concludes that "the Judaism of Jeremiah, of Hillel, of Jesus, and of Jochanan ben Zakkai was a missionary faith" but the "rabbis by the time of the Mishnah abandoned their missionary openness, leaving that function to the messianic Jews [i.e., the Christians]."[76] Yoder's claim could be misread as a warrant for delegitimizing Mishnaic Judaism, interpreting its legal teachings and its protective care for the people Israel as mere reactions against the ascendancy of Christianity. Indeed, Yoder infers from his own insight that "nonmissionary Judaism is a product of Christian history," and this "Christianization" of Judaism culminates, negatively, in Zionism. But even when it had missionizing tendencies, early rabbinic Judaism remained protective of Israel as a separate people and of Jerusalem as a center of Jewish religious life. The rabbinic sages recognized that Judaism could be characterized at once by the religious ideals of centrality *and* noncentrality, landedness *and* nonlandedness, group particularity *and* universality.

E. That Judaism is not specifically rabbinic (Mishnaic and Talmudic)

There is scholarly evidence to support Yoder's claims that there were many varieties of Judaism in the first century, including early Christianity, and that exilic rabbinic Judaism shares deep commitments with early Christianity. However, there is *not* strong evidence to support his effort to minimize the proto-rabbinic direction of late Second-Temple Judaism. Nor is there historical evidence to support his claim that "messianic Judaism" was as representative an option within post-70 Judaism as what would become rabbinic Judaism. Further, there is not evidence to support his claim that radical "pacifism and universalism" are defining attributes either of proto-rabbinic Judaism or of subsequent exilic rabbinic Judaism. There are indeed individual sages who articulated pacifist positions, but these remain within the hermeneutical framework of a pluralistic and dynamic movement of argument that keeps many positions in dialogue at the table of study.

2. An explanatory account

Here I hope to offer a reasonable account of the relationship between Yoder's non-nonsupersessionism and his non-postliberalism. I offer this account through two subarguments.

76. Yoder, "Jewishness of the Free Church Vision," 105–6.

A. NON-POSTLIBERAL REASONING IN YODER'S CORPUS

In this section I collect samples of Yoder's non-postliberal tendencies, so that in the next section I can test whether these tendencies are associated with his non-nonsupersessionism. I observe a modest but strongly developed line of non-postliberal reasoning that runs through Yoder's *JCSR* as well as *The Politics of Jesus* and other writings. This reasoning displays a modern tendency to mistrust all inherited traditions, which means, in Cartesian or Lockean fashion, to overly trust direct disclosures of knowledge (what postmodernists since Wittgenstein have called a "foundationalist" or "intuitionist" tendency). This is associated with a tendency to draw stark distinctions between true and false judgments and to assume that what appears to be the contrary of a true judgment must be a false judgment. It is also associated with a tendency toward uncompromising judgments. This latter tendency both reinforces and is reinforced by a doctrine of fulfilled or messianic time. This eschatological reasoning retains a modern timbre, in that its end-time visions tend to be conceptually clear and distinct.

I call this tendency "modern" because I see no strong antecedents of it in premodern Christian traditions,[77] other than various Gnostic and Marcionite movements, and Yoder is clearly free of the latter. The logic of this reasoning is, however, consistent with that of various Lockean movements, Neologians, and others. Cartwright therefore argues:

> More generally, while not falling captive to overstated patterns such as Thorlief Boman's conception of the Hebraic and the Greek "minds,"[78] Yoder used phrases

77. Daniel Weiss suggests that Paul's writings may be as clear and distinct on such matters as Yoder's, so that we may indeed find premodern prototypes for such binaries. Here clarity is a consequence of the arrival of the end-time, rather than modern conceptualism; the dogmas of classical Judaism would also become clear and distinct in the end-time so that an end-time Judaism would draw the sharp distinctions I am challenging. My reply is that it may be more helpful to read the New Testament writings as animated by a dynamic interplay of contrary influences: Semitic textuality on the one hand, Hellenic logics on the other (to which we may add the more complex hermeneutics of Homeric interpretation and more complex logics of the Stoa, and so on). Yes, Paul displays tendencies to end-time clarity but also to the polysemy of epistolary rhetoric. I have the easier case to make, since it is proved by any degree of indefiniteness in these writings.

78. In chap. 6, n9, Yoder clarifies the difference between his own position and that of Boman: I am not espousing a permanent ethnocentrism, in the style of Thorlief Boman, with Hebraic thought forms always sacred and safe and Greek always pagan. My objection is not to entering the Hellenistic world as a cultural arena. Jews had been doing that long before Jesus and Paul. Paul did it again, with no sacrifice of his Jewishness or his faithfulness to Jesus. What is to reject [sic; to be rejected] is the subsequent abandonment of Jewish substance, as the "apologetes" succeeded the apostles and the goal of insight displaced that of obedience.

Yoder's shorthand reference to Thorlief Boman is a gesture toward the latter's study *Hebrew Thought Compared with Greek* (Philadelphia: Westminster, 1960). Yoder provides a fairly nuanced discussion of the difference between his version of "biblical realism" and Boman's position in *To Hear the Word*, 136–39.

like "the Christ of Byzantium" as a catchall designation for dismissing classical Catholic and Protestant conceptions of the life, ministry, death, and resurrection of Jesus. Yoder rejected these conceptions because they constitute "the abandonment of Jewish substance," substituting "insight for obedience."[79] Yoder also associated patterns of error in Judaism with the Constantinian legacy insofar as he believed that "the Davidic Project" to constitute a monarchy in Jerusalem was prototypical of Christian forms of faithlessness. Thus, he argues that "the error of the age of Samuel"[80] is repeated in variant forms of Constantinianism that evolve over the course of the history of Western Christianity. By contrast, free churches would bear witness to a different conception of divine rule, which Yoder found most aptly adumbrated in the prophecy of Jeremiah.

If Cartwright is correct, how do we account for Yoder's mistrust of almost all modern forms of Protestant and Catholic traditions? One possibility is that Yoder believes the church is now so corrupt that nothing short of total "renewal" is sufficient. Another possibility is that there is an unhappy tension between Yoder's critique of modern foundationalism and his espousing a christological intuitionism: a claim that members of the free church have immediate intuitions of what the Christ of Scripture demands of them, whether these demands are for "anti-Constantinianism" or for the "Jeremianic turn." Claims of this kind would be foundationalist.

Earlier I labeled Yoder's study of Christian and Jewish history both "reparative genealogy" and "depth-historiography."[81] If my account has any merit, then we might read Yoder's mistrust of antecedent traditions as a tendency to promote his genealogy and depth historiography in a foundationalist-like way. This is to read every antecedent source of current church practice as comparably divisive and thus as a source of nonrepair. The implication is that unless the church is irreparable, the Christian genealogist must have unmediated access to the apostolic witness. If so, Yoder's genealogy imitates a Cartesian pattern of doubt and belief: either our knowledge is wholly unreliable or it must be grounded in some immediate, inerrant intuitions. One possibility, therefore, is that Yoder's modernist tendency has a Cartesian or Lockean pedigree. An alternative possibility is that things are as Yoder appears to claim

---

79. Yoder, "The Restitution of the Church: An Alternative Perspective on Christian History," *JCSR*, 143.

80. Yoder, "Earthly Jerusalem and Heavenly Jerusalem," *JCSR*, 163.

81. By reading plain-sense history, Yoder locates antecedent sources for repairing contemporary crises in the church. By reading depth-historically, he is able to recommend how to identify these, *specifically*, as sources for repairing the crises that he diagnoses in the church today. These depth-historiographic claims retain the status of "reparative abductions," which means claims that are probabilistic but not certain, vague (or subject to definition in the act of application) and not clear and distinct—in this sense logically "triadic" (or [1] claims that display their [2] definite meaning and validity only with respect to [3] the specific context of application) rather than dyadic (that is, either–or claims that are clearly true whatever the context, so that competing claims are deemed clearly false).

and that the free church is privy to a direct rewitnessing of Christian origins. A third possibility is that Yoder's claim belongs, like Lindbeck's, to another reformation: not that all church traditions are suspect, but that all are in need of revitalization and repair by way of a reformatory rereading of primitive Christianity's reading of Scripture. Yoder's reasoning approaches this, but clear differences remain. Lindbeck rests his reparative genealogy in a reading of Scripture that remains vague and subject to further dialogue in a way that is not apparent in this aspect of Yoder's reasoning. Lindbeck, for example, does not know fully what will and ought to come out of Jewish–Christian scriptural dialogue, but Yoder does.

I therefore find the first possibility to be the most convincing. This hypothesis is also strengthened by an element of Yoder's theology that I have not yet mentioned: his Anabaptist account of the fall. In *The Politics of Jesus*, Yoder writes,

> Unfortunately . . . we have no access to the good creation of God. The creature and the world are fallen, and in this the powers have their own share. They are no longer active only as mediators of the saving creative purpose of God; now we find them seeking to separate us from the love of God (Rom. 8:38); . . . we find them holding us in servitude to their rules (Col. 2:20). . . . These structures which were supposed to be our servants have become our masters and our guardians.[82]

While Yoder acknowledges that "the workings of the Powers is not simple something limitlessly evil, . . . [as] they continue to exercise an ordering function," nonetheless, the powers have rebelled, and the work of Christ in this world is to defeat these powers and subject them to the will of God. Richard Mouw, who has famously engaged Yoder in an extended Reformed–Anabaptist dialogue, identifies the Anabaptist doctrine of the fall as a traditionally Calvinist view, but radicalized:

> [T]he Anabaptist position is not one that Calvinists denounce because it is so alien to their own view, but rather because it represents very real tendencies that they fear within themselves. . . .
> Calvinism is well known for its stark portrayal of the human sinful condition. . . . The Bible gives us reason to think that sin actually perverted the creation in significant ways. The theology of the "principalities and powers" which Professor Yoder has done much to sensitize North American Christians to, is one important vehicle for understanding this distortedness. More generally, biblical Christianity must promote an awareness of the "cursedness" of the fallen creation. To be sure, Jesus came to the creation to lift the curse of sin. . . . But as the writer to the Hebrews observes, while God placed all things originally under the dominion of humankind, "as it is we do not yet see everything in subjection" to human beings—"but we see Jesus . . . crowned with glory and honor because of the suffering of death" (Heb. 2:8–9).

82. Yoder, *Politics of Jesus*, 141.

In effect, then, the Anabaptists as represented by Professor Yoder are posing questions to Reformed Christians about the radicality of human sin, and about the radicality of the work of the Savior who came to rescue the creation from the cure of that sin. What did the fall do to the creation, . . . to human noetic and volitional capacities?

It seems obvious—to Professor Yoder and to me—that these are very Reformed questions. But they are also very Anabaptist questions.[83]

Such a radicalized view of the fall could underwrite Yoder's mistrust of antecedent traditions and his need for a wholly non-tradition-based corrective. However, while acknowledging this Anabaptist and, in Mouw's sense, Reformed theology of the fall, I remain unconvinced that such a theology is itself independent of Cartesian or Lockean-like influences. Because this theology lacks the tolerance for vagueness that I am more accustomed to seeing in primitive Christian and patristic scriptural hermeneutics, I am led to suspect a modern source.

Yoder's foundationalist line of historiography, complemented by this radical soteriology, appears to generate dyadic claims. In Cartwright's terms,

According to Yoder, those Jews and Christians who have voluntarily committed themselves to reconciling with their enemies . . . are in the best position to know the true meaning of texts such as Galatians 4:25–26 or Jeremiah 29:7. When this kind of position is taken within the horizon of a doctrine of the perspicuity of Scripture . . . , it results in the kind of dichotomized reading of texts that ultimately is not peaceable precisely because it eliminates ambiguities in the text at the cost of the very identity of the ones to whom the text ostensibly refers.[84]

Cartwright offers this illustration:

The way that Yoder goes about affirming the "Abrahamic model" as constitutive for Jews and Christians alike involves narrating the history of Jewish peace witness in a way that is determined by the Anabaptist tradition. As a result, the very coherence of the Jewish people turns out to be reliant upon "the free church vision." . . . Here [Nicholas] Lash's counsel about the *provisionality* and *instability* of the "middle distance" perspective is useful to bring into view. . . . According to Lash, it is precisely when we forget that our very categories have been "shaped by the tradition that precedes us that we are most likely to err in

83. Richard J. Mouw, "Abandoning the Typology: A Reformed Assist," *TSF Bulletin*, May–June 1985, 8–10.

84. Cartwright, "Afterword," 229. Cartwright adds this illustration of Yoder's binarism: Here, then, we see an instance in which Yoder elects to eliminate the "darkness" of a particular set of biblical texts in favour of a reading that provides clarity, albeit at the cost of excluding other possible readings of the texts in question. Interestingly enough, in this particular context, what is bypassed by this conception is the very set of canonical and/or covenantal contexts that could provide the organic link to Rabbinical Judaism. (229n103)

our attempt to offer theologies of history."[85] Yoder's apparent failure to take the measure of the limitations of the Anabaptist tradition of hermeneutics leads him to be blind to the displacing effects of those same categories of reasoning.

This way of explaining the problem accounts, in part, for what turns out to be *non-non-supersessionism of Yoder's project*.[86]

Part of the postliberal critique of modern thought is that neither the things of the created world nor the messages of God's revealed Scripture are adequately "captured," represented, or defined by humanly constructed claims. *Conceptualism* refers to efforts of individual thinkers to bracket this critique and present their conceptual constructions as if they were reliable representations of God's creating and revealing Word. Overall, Yoder is a strong critic of conceptualism in modern and ancient sources. His critique of Constantinianism, for example, is in part a critique of its conceptualism:

> What we then find at the heart of our tradition is not some proposition, scriptural or promulgated or otherwise, which we hold to be authoritative and to be exempted from the relativity of hermeneutical debate by virtue of its inspiredness. What we find at the origin is already the process of reaching back to the origins, to the earliest memories of the event itself, confident that that testimony, however intimately integrated with the belief of the witnesses, is not a wax nose, and will serve to illuminate and to adjudicate our present path.[87]

Yoder also criticizes conceptualism when it appears in what he considers the modern forms of Constantinianism: efforts to identify Christianity with any of a variety of global institutions, from the market economy to various military, industrial, economic, and political vehicles for controlling human behavior on a mass scale.

Nonetheless, Yoder's dyadic line of reasoning is accompanied by its own series of conceptualist claims, such as this one:

> In a form befitting their century, and within the limits of their capacities and opportunities, the Anabaptists were able to rediscover and realize a functional equivalent of the original messianic Jewish universalism, as of the original Jewish messianic pacifism, which had characterized the earliest churches, which had later been abandoned by both the anti-Judaic Catholicism of "Christendom" and (to a lesser degree) the defensive Judaism of the Mishnaic codification.[88]

Neither true nor false, Yoder's notions of "universalism" and "messianic pacifism" overgeneralize trends in rabbinic thinking that the rabbis refuse to

85. Citing Nicholas Lash, *Theology on the Way to Emmaus* (London: SCM, 1986), 219n14.
86. Cartwright, "Afterword," 229.
87. Yoder, *Priestly Kingdom*, 70.
88. Yoder, "The Forms of a Possible Obedience," *JCSR*, 129.

define in clear and distinct ways. Yoder's conceptions of the Jewish values of exile and mission are comparably conceptualized in a manner that is strange to both biblical and rabbinic discourse.

B. NON-NONSUPERSESSIONISM IN YODER'S CORPUS

Neither this chapter nor this book concludes with any proof that postliberalism and nonsupersessionism fulfill a divine will. I cannot therefore say that Yoder is simply wrong (or un-Pauline, unscriptural) to integrate dyadic lines of reasoning with postliberal-like claims. I hope only to have shown that he does this. In this section, I offer no more than a reasonable hypothesis about how Yoder could conceivably have drawn non-nonsupersessionist inferences from nonsupersessionist premises. I offer four illustrative possibilities.

- First, dyadic reasoning from "there is historically no single, normative Judaism" to "rabbinic Judaism is not authoritative" or "rabbinic Judaism is a fall from what Judaism ought to be."

Following a dyadic line of reasoning, Yoder argues that both Nazarene and Jeremianic Judaism are "earlier" and thus have more claim to normativity than the rabbinic Judaisms of the Mishnah and Talmuds. As noted earlier, Yoder addresses the "missionary" character of these "earlier" Judaisms as a case in point: "The Judaism of Jeremiah, of Hillel, of Jesus, and of Jochanan ben Zakkai was a missionary faith," but the "rabbis by the time of the Mishnah abandoned their missionary openness, leaving that function to the messianic Jews [i.e., the Christians]."[89] On one level, postliberal Jews might find this claim energizing as a claim of depth history, stimulating them, in this age after the Shoah, to help renew Judaism as a mission to the world. On another level, however, Yoder's readers could also take his claim as a warrant for delegitimizing Mishnaic Judaism.[90]

- Second, dyadic reasoning from "Judaism can live in exile" to "Judaism is exilic per se" or that "Jeremianic Judaism" is Judaism per se, or is God's will.

Yoder's model of "Jeremianic Judaism" illustrates what I labeled his "foundationalist" line of genealogy. After identifying early exilic Judaism as his source for repairing Constantinian Christianity, he constructs a clear model of "exilic Judaism" as his definition of a reunified Jewish–Christian witness. His next step is to delegitimize features of both Christianity and rabbinic Ju-

---

89. See 154n76.

90. As I suggested earlier, this is to judge the legal teachings of the Mishnah and its protective care for the people Israel as mere reactions against the ascendancy of Christianity.

daism that fall outside the boundary of this model. He then argues that exilic Judaism is not merely compatible with "messianic Judaism" (the Nazarene tradition of Jewish messianism), but completed in it:

> This is not to lower our sights or to retract our proclamation. It is to renew the description of Jesus crucified as the wisdom and power of God. This is the low road of general validity. . . . It thereby frees us to use any language, to enter any world in which people eat bread and pursue debtors, hope for power and execute subversives. The ordinariness of the human Jesus is the warrant for the generalizability of his reconciliation. The nonterritorial particularity of his Jewishness defends us against selling out to any wider world's claim to be really wider, or to be self-validating. . . . There is no road but the low road. The truth has come to our side of the ditch. . . . The real issue is not whether Jesus can make sense in a world far from Galilee, but whether—when he meets us in our world, as he does in fact—we want to follow him. We don't have to, and they didn't then. That we don't have to is the profoundest proof of his condescension and thereby of his glory.[91]

Yoder has, in other words, identified, before the fact and independent of any historical complexities, the one way in which Jewish life would fulfill Jewish expectations: to live in exile, imitating in its nonterritoriality the humility of Jesus on the cross. Yoder's foundationalism is not displayed in his adopting the Gospel narrative as the standard for human life on earth; belief in this narrative is not "foundationalist," because the narrative's meaning is neither directly intuited nor articulated in clear and distinct propositions. Yoder's foundationalism appears instead when he offers such propositions about Israel's life: that Jewish life in exile is a direct illustration of the meaning of Jesus's narrative. The problem is in the clarity and finality of this claim.

- Third, dyadic reasoning from "Judaism is non-violent" and "Judaism can stand outside of worldly powers and principalities" to "Judaism is

---

91. Yoder, *Priestly Kingdom*, 62. Cartwright offers this critical commentary:
At the risk of belaboring the obvious, this vision of human enactment of God's peace stands in an uneasy relationship with many aspects of the Jewish tradition. The "dividing wall" that is destroyed is often said to represent the wall of the Temple in Jerusalem that separated the Court of the Gentiles from those "inner" courts where Jewish women, men, and priests were permitted to gather in worshiping God. More scandalous still, from a Jewish perspective, is that the Temple in Jerusalem has been supplanted by a "new temple" that comes about through the cross of Jesus Christ and incorporates the human society of the reconciled company of Christians and Jews. Moreover, the new "dwelling place for God" has no space other than that of those who gather in reconciliation, and it has no tradition given the abolition of the commandments, Torah, etc. In the process of such shifts, the covenantal basis of Jewish identity also is eclipsed in a way that breaks apart of the trilateral unity of land, God and people. (Cartwright, "Editors' Introduction," *JCSR*, 11)

pacifist" and "Judaism, like the Free Church, will not involve itself with land, state, or world powers."

The illustrative text here is "See How They Go with Their Face to the Sun," Yoder's effort to identify Stefan Zweig's exilic Jeremiah with the essential posture of Judaism and thus of the free church. This Jeremiah is, however, only one mark of Jewish life or even of Jeremiah's own life, since his concession to exile appears to have been pragmatic. To essentialize this partial Jeremiah is to reason outside the context-specificity and multivalence of Scripture's witness in favor of the clarity and distinctness of modern hermeneutics.[92]

For postliberal Jews, life is no longer defined by the clear and distinct alternatives that tended to define Jewish political existence in late modern Europe. That existence ended, literally and metaphorically, in the Shoah. Postliberal Judaism emerges as an early phase of Judaism's rebirth after the Shoah. As in previous rebirths—after both *Chorbanot* (destructions of the ancient temples), after the Expulsion from Spain, and after comparable disasters in Jewish history—we may expect that this one, too, will lead to transformations in the religion of Israel. After previous traumas, Israel eventually recovered its trust in the body of its covenant, which is nothing other than the written Word of Torah. But that body was filled, each time, with the spirit of a new reception of Torah, a new midrash or way of reliving the tradition of being Jewish in a new historical setting.

The stark separation that both Yoder and conservative Zionists assert between exile and land is a lingering mark of this recent and continuing period of transformation. It is not a mark of our future, however, and it is in this sense not prophetic. The voice of prophecy begins with visions of the separation that Israel is about to suffer between its body and spirit, but it ends, each time, with a vision of the new heaven and new earth that are about to be realized in the next epoch of Israel's religious life. This is a religion in which Israel's body and spirit will be reintegrated once again—albeit, we fear, not forever, since the cycles of Israel's history do not appear to be over.[93]

- Fourth, dyadic reasoning from Judaism's scriptural and covenantal premises to various clear and distinct definitions of the essence of Judaism.

Within his dyadic line of reasoning, Yoder's effort to undo the Jewish–Christian schism has less to do with dialogue between Judaism and Christianity than with a unified and clear vision of messianic Judaism:

92. As I note earlier, both Zweig and Yoder offer foundationalist claims about the normative character of Israel's exilic life.

93. The last three paragraphs were excerpted, with some revision, from my commentary on Yoder, "See How They Go with Their Face to the Sun," in *JCSR*, 203.

Only when it is a fact that Jewry and paganism are set at one (are "atoned"), only when Jew and Gentile are eating at the same table and lovingly adjusting their lifestyles . . . , only then can it be said to the powers that peace is God's purpose. . . . How does our life reenact the melding of two histories and two cultures? Where does our banqueting celebrate the new humanity created by the crosses of our time breaking down the walls of our time so that the cosmic powers of our time can see what God is about?[94]

Cartwright responds that, in Yoder's vision,

dialogue between Christians and Jews can take place within the horizon of the "good news" that a new social and historical possibility has been disclosed that makes it possible for them to embrace a new reality. They, like the apostle Paul, no longer have to regard one another from a "human point of view"—as "Jews" and "Gentiles" but rather can operate out of the horizon of 2 Corinthians 5:17—"The old has passed away; behold the new has come." Accordingly, "Jew" and "Gentile" are (unstable) sociological constructions to be overcome, not constitutive identities that have stability that inheres in traditioned practices and narratives.[95]

In the end, I measure Yoder as a great friend of the people Israel and a profound resource for postliberal thinking, Christian and Jewish as well. I do, however, wish that his students and disciples could accord his words no less than the humanity and fallibility we Jews tend to assign our biblical heroes, Moses included. Fallibility may be the issue that separates postliberal nonsupersessionism from that part of Yoder's reasoning that rejects postliberal ways of reading Scripture and in so doing engenders a non-nonsupersessionism. For this aspect of Yoder's reasoning, Christ encountered directly replaces the Christ of Scripture—the one who is read and interpreted in community and, thus, vaguely.

94. John Howard Yoder, "The Burden and Discipline of Evangelical Revisionism," in *Nonviolent America: History through the Eyes of Peace*, ed. Louise Hawkey and James Juhnke (North Newton, KS: Bethel College, 1993), 22.

95. Cartwright, "Editors' Introduction," 11.

Part 2

BRITISH POSTLIBERALISM

6

Finding Christ in World and Polity

Daniel Hardy's Ecclesiological Postliberalism

Preface

The previous chapter was about the radical Anabaptist Yoder, and there may be no stronger contrast within the postliberal fold than between Yoder's anti-Constantinianism and Daniel Hardy's Anglican ecclesiology.[1] Here is a fitting first test of Anglican postliberalism: does the "Anglican settlement" that underlies Hardy's, David Ford's, and John Milbank's theologies display Constantinianism or some third postliberal option between anti- and pro-Constantinians? From across the broad range of Hardy's theological reach—from pneumatology and science to trinitarian scriptural theology to theopolitics—I focus this chapter on his ecclesiology as the most efficient way of conducting this test. My thesis is that the Anglican settlement allows Hardy to forge a nonmediating relationship between the body of Christ and "worldly powers and principalities." With the term *nonmediating* I mean to invoke Hans Frei's critique of "mediating theologies" that engage worldly powers by compromising their fidelity to Christ. I will argue that, like Frei, Hardy places loyalty to Christ first, so that his engagement with worldly powers comes not by compromise, but by way of God's presence in the world. I will acknowledge, at the same time, that Hardy's Anglican settlement is at odds with at least the Hauerwas–Yoder

1. I am grateful for helpful comments on this chapter by Micheal O'Siadhail and Andrew Black and editing by Rodney Clapp.

wing of the postliberal movement, if not also in tension with the Lutheran wing. In Yoder's terms, Hardy is clearly Constantinian. Hauerwas's terms would be more nuanced: Hardy may risk accommodation by paying too little regard to the withering power of human sin.[2]

Part 1 of this book has, I believe, laid out the theological program of the postliberal Christologists. With Daniel Hardy, I introduce the program of the postliberal pneumatologists. This chapter focuses on three features of this pneumatology. The first is ecclesial history, or what I will dub "found theology." For Hardy, one of the wisdoms of Anglicanism is to trust that Christ's work begins with whatever one finds in the world, rather than beginning with theological concepts that precede the world and require the world to reshape itself in order for Christ's work to begin to be done. American critics might call this accommodation to the world, but I will argue that it is a different yet complementary way to place the world under the care of the divine Word. Anglican historiography is a piece of this "found theology," because it matters to the church where it has been in the world and what has actually happened to its members in history. This historical awareness also breeds a sense of contingency or "particularity" in a sense that is closer to Anabaptist consciousness than either British or American postliberals would tend to acknowledge. This does not mean "sectarian closure" or "relativism." Instead, it means a theological fallibilism that disclaims prior conceptual certainty and trusts that God's work is enacted through the Spirit's presence in the world rather than through prior verbal proclamations by Christ's disciples.

The chapter focuses, second, on Hardy's philosophic account of what it means to know and to live in the Spirit. To know in the Spirit is to know contingently. This is to know in relation to one's found history and thus contingently and fallibly. But it is also to know in direct relation to God, so that cognitive fallibility is a loss only of isolation—the flip side of the gain of intimacy with God. This, one finds, is intimacy with Christ, whose body is the church, which is the wisdom of society, whose source of unity and repair is the Eucharist.

The chapter's third pneumatological focus is on the power of the Spirit to heal disunity in the church (schism) and between the church and Israel (supersessionism). Hardy's account illustrates that British and American postliberals both seek to repair supersessionism but in notably different ways. As I read it, American nonsupersessionism arises primarily out of christological efforts to protect the hermeneutics of *sola scriptura*. I believe this is the same reason that it is theologically more challenging for American postliberals to extend

2. Richard Mouw may be a helpful third interlocutor: defending a form of Calvinism that has Anabaptist-like clarity about humanity's fallen condition while allowing a less predefined arena for ecclesial engagement with the world. He might be gentler on Hardy. See, for example, Richard J. Mouw, "Abandoning the Typology: A Reformed Assist," *TSF Bulletin*, May–June 1985, 7–10, and Richard J. Mouw, *When the Kings Come Marching In: Isaiah and the New Jerusalem* (Grand Rapids: Eerdmans, 1983).

the same invitation to Muslims. As evident in their hearty participation in various societies of scriptural reasoning, Lindbeck, Jenson, Hauerwas, and their students and peers do indeed engage Muslims as well as Jews in intimate scriptural dialogue. But I believe it is a more challenging theological move for them to make, since the Jews enter into their theology *ab initio* with the flesh of Christ and the text of Scripture. On the other hand, I think it is more challenging for the Anglicans—and British postliberals more generally—to lend the Jews a privileged place as if already almost inside the body of Christ and, correspondingly, easier for the Anglicans to lend Muslims the hospitality they (the Anglicans) lend the Jews. I believe this is because Anglican nonsupersessionism arises out of pneumatological efforts to meet Christ, as it were, wherever and however he appears. Unlike the Americans, Anglican nonsupersessionists might therefore argue as follows:

- that Jews and Muslims come in first by the Spirit rather than by the Son;
- that this coming-in belongs in part to Anglican national responsibility to care for all citizens of the settlement (state), while American anti-Constantinianism brackets any political responsibility for the other "churches";
- that all creatures, nations, and denominations come under the mystery of Christ's care and thus merit care by Christ's disciples;
- that "foundness" is a pneumatologically valid criterion for measuring the divine will, so that, for example, unpredictable friendships among some group of Christians, Jews, and Muslims may be a sign of the Spirit's call;
- that, at the same time, Anglican nonsupersessionism is also strengthened by the scriptural concerns that are central to the American postliberals; in that sense, Jews hold a special place in the church, while the national settlement provides a comparable place for the Muslims.

"Found" Theology: Hardy's Historical and Empirical Pneumatology

In April 2004, Daniel Hardy delivered a remarkable lecture at the University of Virginia on the topic of theopolitics. He began by relating what he observed when he stood at Thomas Jefferson's Rotunda, the defining mark of Jefferson's architecture for the school. From the Rotunda, Hardy looked south across "the Lawn," UVA's main campus, bordered east and west by lovely brick dormitories and apartments, toward what in Jefferson's vision should have been the unenclosed wilderness beyond. In the last century, however, UVA's planners had closed off this southern view to obtain more building space; now the Rotunda faced a large classroom building rather than open forests. Hardy commented that for him both the original vision and this cutoff symbolized the difference between American and Anglican understandings of our place in God's creation. For the American Jefferson, he said, reason is a human construct, informed by a priori principles inherent in our being or "nature." This means that the other "nature" we find out there is ultimately unknown and threatening: in Jefferson's time, the place of potentially unfriendly indigenes of the Americas and untamed wildlife and climates. Nature is beautiful, to be sure, but also sublime and dangerous; it can be cognized only to the degree that it is domesticated, and it is domesticated only by human rationality. Hardy suggested that whatever the immediate purpose of UVA's building classrooms across that open space, the resulting enclosure symbolizes this failing of Jefferson's American standard of rationality: that nature is acceptable only when it accommodates our rational constructs. When nature displays its fury, we would judge it irrational and close it off, limiting reason's gaze to what lies within our precincts. Hardy argued that Anglicanism has a different vision.

For Anglican theology, reason does not begin with itself, but with the "found objects of the world" (my term), or what Hardy called "whatever we find before us." Look at English gardens, he said; they are not all preplanned, but a settlement between wildness (foundness) and a sampling of our loves and preferences. We must not, in other words, expect the world to behave in accordance with our strictly human rationality. For English folk shorn of the church, this may breed a gnarly skepticism. But, said Hardy, for English folk inside the church, the world "out there" is not some independent "nature," but God's creation and creatures, and we and our reasonings belong among them. In this case, reason is not something defined a priori within us; it is nothing less than the Logos, God's Word as it continually creates the world and as it is revealed to us in Scripture and in the body of Jesus Christ. Our employment of reason is thus a relational affair: we participate in rationality through both worldly wisdoms, such as science and the arts, and the revealed wisdoms that are embodied in Scripture and in lives lived in *imitatio Christi*. The worldly and revealed sources of rationality are deeply bound up one with the other.

Hardy concluded that, were he Anglican, Jefferson would more likely have constructed his school *in* the world, not facing out at it. "In the world" would mean *in intimate relation and dialogue with what he found already there*: not looking eclectically with his brilliant mind's eye at what classic Rome, contemporary Europe, and the colonies recommended as a new and neoclassical design, but observing what relations were already enacted among Virginia's colonists, the indigenous populations, and the witness of the church. Were Jefferson Anglican, furthermore, he would have worked out of the church-and-world body, not as an independent inventor.

This long anecdote will, I hope, offer readers some visual imagery to accompany the following review of Hardy's more systematic treatment of found theology. I think of "found theology" in the sense of "found objects," a term in recent American English to refer to things that we stumble upon by chance but then take note of and decide to use for some purpose. I hear the term used most often to describe works of sculpture, all of whose materials are "found" (from driftwood to scrap metal), or paintings in the style of collage or mixed media. Philosophers might associate the term with Martin Heidegger's notion of *Dasein*, or the existence we know, as *Geworfenheit* or "thrownness": in other words, "being" does not come to us predesigned, but encountered as it is thrown at us. We might call it "found being." I confess I thought of Hardy's thought as "found theology" before he reminded me of the title of his book, which I had just read, *Finding the Church*. Before turning to what he says in that book, I want to begin with brief words of my own about what Hardy "finds."

As I have read and listened to him, Hardy finds the church, rather than choosing or "constructing" it. Within that church, he finds Scripture. He finds a community of persons gathered around Scripture to study, discuss, and embody its wisdoms. And he finds a Eucharistic practice through which God finds him and his ecclesial community and through which God finds his church and his humanity and his creation. I take these to be Hardy's elemental findings: Scripture in the church, church in the world, and God who finds the church and its members through Eucharistic practice. There is much more to find within each of these elements.[3] Hardy finds the church in some space-time and history and in relation to himself and his cohorts.

For Hardy, the Anglican Church comes *from* somewhere and develops through time. Beyond its antecedents in the early and medieval church, this means that the church arises specifically within the history of England, often traced from the Augustinian mission of 597, the selection of the See of Canterbury as the mother church of England, and, more generally, the Anglican Settlements beginning in 1534. For Hardy, the settlements refer both to the earlier church–state agreements through which the church was founded and to the subsequent evolution of these agreements. In this view, the Anglican Church is fully of God incarnate in the body of Christ and fully in the world, political and natural. Regardless of whether its origins include Erastian doctrines (that in relation to the church, the state may enjoy privileges analogous

---

3. One might say "finding" is an Anglican transcendental, in the medieval sense of "transcendental." For Hardy there is a Coleridgian analogue of the transcendentals: what Coleridge called "conceptions," not in the modern philosophic sense of cognitive constructions, but in his Anglican version of Christian Neoplatonism. It is helpful to mention such "conceptions" at this point, lest we imagine Hardy's findings to be of the more skeptical Humean variety. This is, indeed, empirical theology. As in the empirical sciences, however, empiricism need not be divorced from realist ontology. In more common terms, one can find the church by looking around with one's eyes and mental vision; reasoning is as much an instrument of finding as are the senses, the heart, fellowship, and prayer. Hardy's findings integrate science and prayer in a way that is uncommon among the American postliberals we have met, suggesting that this Anglican theologian will also find in Christian life much more of the world and of other peoples and faiths than we are likely to encounter among postliberal Yale or Barthian cohorts.

to those of the Davidic monarchy in ancient Israel), the Parliament's 1534 statute of royal supremacy assigned Henry VIII the position of supreme head of the Church of England. The statute evolved, however, so that Elizabeth's Religious Settlement reduced her position to "supreme governor" of the church and established the central governing bodies of what remains the Anglican Settlement. Of particular note for Hardy is Richard Hooker's contribution to the Elizabethan Settlement. In opposition to both Rome and the Elizabethan Puritans, Hooker (1554–1600) maintained the authority of Scripture but non-exclusively, since it is balanced by the complementary authorities of church tradition and doctrine and by the reasoning that enabled church leaders to discern how Scripture and tradition address present-day issues. Hardy follows Hooker in the manner of Newman, Coleridge, and Nouwen.

To find the Anglican Church in history is, for Hardy, also to find it within the social and political realities of the world. From page 1, *Finding the Church* is thus shaped by Hardy's response to what he considered the ecclesial crisis of his day: "Anglicanism today is at a critical juncture in its history. . . . What is required is that it should understand and follow its special calling in the purposes of God for the world."[4] At the Lambeth conferences of 1998, 2000, and 2001,[5] Hardy saw the church leadership nearly split in half by controversies over issues of gender, especially the admission of openly gay men into the priesthood. His deepest concern was not the issue itself but the primates' failures to employ the gifts of the church in the ways they addressed the issue. He therefore devoted his book to identifying these gifts: the ecclesial practices through which the Anglican Church embodies the unity of Christ.

If I followed my pragmatist's instincts, I would conclude that the purpose of Hardy's theology was repair, and the norm of repair was participation in the unity of Christ's body. In this case, we might number "repairing the churches" among his elemental "findings." Over more than fifteen years of conversation, however, both he and David Ford sought consistently to wean me from what they considered my overuse of pragmatism as an elemental rule of theology. They agreed that Christian religious life as well as theology is devoted to service, and that includes the service of repair. But in this sense similar to Barth,[6] they argued that God repairs only by way of God and only as measured by God, and they feared that my pragmatism sought to premeasure what God would do. Their alternative is suggested by the first book they coauthored, *Living in Praise*. Displaying the Pentecostal force of their Anglican spirituality,[7] the

4. Daniel W. Hardy, *Finding the Church: The Dynamic Truth of Anglicanism* (London: SCM, 2001), 1.

5. Meetings of the primates, or church leaders of the worldwide Anglican Communion, under the leadership of the archbishop.

6. Hardy would indeed not want to draw any further analogies.

7. David F. Ford and Daniel W. Hardy, *Living in Praise: Worshipping and Knowing God*, 2nd rev. ed. (Grand Rapids: Baker Academic, 2005).

book situates worldly service in doxology—in much the way, I would agree, that rabbinic morning prayer situates the work of petitionary prayer in the "Psalms of Praise" (*pesuke dezimra*) that initiate the prayer service. The book's lesson, as I read it, is that we will have eyes to see the suffering around us only to the degree that we are open to God's presence and that we might share in healing that suffering only to the degree that God has drawn us to his service. While I cannot gainsay these cautions about my pragmatism, I also observe that Hardy typically presented his theological writings as ways of responding to specific problems in the church. Shall I therefore label him "pragmatist" or not? I will conclude that Hardy offered his theology in the service of repair but recognized the Holy Spirit rather than the human reasoner as the one who discerns the place of suffering and the source of healing.

To complete this sampling of Hardy's findings, we might add three more: human history, other peoples and faiths, and creation. For Hardy, human history is one context of church history. The Anglican Settlement is a strong reminder that, unlike the Catholic Church and most Reformation churches, the Church of England attaches itself to a worldly polity and—in Hardy's terms—shares responsibility for the welfare of all citizens of that polity. This raises the question of peoples and faiths outside the church, since these citizens include Baptists and Buddhists, atheists, Jews, and Muslims. The subjects to whom the church is responsible are not determined a priori; they come as history has led them. It is only one or two steps from there to the rest of humanity, since there is no predicting whom history may lead to the polity's—and the church's—doorsteps. How specifically to relate to this or that person is a matter for more detailed study of church doctrine and law. For now, I want simply to note the place of contingency in the Anglican Church's dealings with the world. To serve the themes of this book, I will look more closely at one contingency in particular: how this Anglican theologian encounters Jews and Muslims.

In earlier chapters we have seen that American postliberals "find" the Jews in Scripture. While refinding Christ after modernity, they rediscovered Jesus's Jewishness and the permanent place of Israel's story within the hermeneutic of Jesus's gospel. From this perspective, theological relations between Christianity and the Jews were defined a priori by the dual canon of Old and New Testaments. For the same reason, American postliberals have a more difficult time finding warrants for theological dialogue with Muslims. Since Muslims are not explicitly part of the Christian canon, Christians must look for warrants outside the explicit sense of Scripture, somewhat analogous to the challenges traditional Jews face in finding warrants for theological dialogue with Christians. Hardy's Anglicanism offers another route to these theological dialogues: to engage whomever one finds in a manner called for by Scripture, church, and the Eucharist. This "calling" introduces the pneumatological context of Hardy's relation to Jews and Muslims.

In his earlier writings Hardy takes note of the Bible's witness to Israel's covenant, and his work in both church and academy was marked by hospitality to persons from all faith communities. As far as I am aware, however, Hardy's deep experiences of interreligious theological dialogue took place independently of any a priori plan. A few of us Jewish philosophers happened to meet him and enter into discussions that disclosed some overlapping approaches to religious study and practice in the modern world. These discussions led to friendships, and the friendships led to deeper conversations, and these led to projects of shared study that resulted in what we later called the Society for Scriptural Reasoning (SSR). I happened to have an observant Muslim graduate student, Basit Koshul, with whom I entered into lively discussions of Kant and of Scripture. He then invited me to visit his community of young Sunni professionals who met regularly to study the philosophy, poetry, and theology of the great Pakistani intellectual Mohammad Iqbal. I joined their studies on a few occasions, during which we collectively observed several analogies between their Muslim and my Jewish approaches to religious study and practice in the modern world. Hardy and Ford expressed great interest in this emerging discussion, and soon other Jewish and Christian members of our previous dialogue group joined this new dialogue. It was then that we named our group SSR—an inter-Abrahamic group for the study of Scripture and philosophy—with Hardy as the senior member of our leadership group. I interpret this account to suggest that Hardy "found" himself in theological dialogue with Muslims just as he does with Jews. There are differences, which I find helpful to attribute to differences between his Christology and pneumatology. In his Christology and study of Scripture, Hardy is closer to the American postliberals in the way he "finds" the Jews within the Christian canon. In his pneumatology and theological encounters in the world, he is unlike the Americans: entering into comparably deep theological exchanges with both Jews and Muslims.

Encounters with the world include those with the world outside of humanity, although *outside* would not be the right term to use within Hardy's theology, since humans are, after all, made up of the stuff of the material creation. Unlike the Americans, Hardy devotes acute theological attention to the material world and the sciences that examine it. The vocabulary of *God's Ways with the World* shows the influence of twentieth-century physics, biology, sociology, and mathematics, and more recent essays such as "Receptive Ecumenism" (hereafter RE) display Hardy's vision of an integrative, Eucharistic ecclesiology of the heavenly, natural, and social worlds.[8]

---

8. See Daniel Hardy, "Receptive Ecumenism: Learning by Engagement," in Paul Murray, ed., *Receptive Ecumenism and the Call to Catholic Learning: Exploring a Way for Contemporary Ecumenism* (Oxford: Oxford University Press, 2008), 428–41. See the Receptive Ecumenism website, www.centreforcatholicstudies.co.uk/?cat=6.

Redemptive Ecclesiology: A Philosophy of the Spirit

My discussion of "found theology" has been an introduction to Hardy's pneumatology in somewhat everyday terms. In this section, I turn to two illustrations of Hardy's own pneumatological vocabulary: three chapters from *Finding the Church* (*FC*) and his essay "Spirit of Unity—Reconcile Your People!" (SU).[9] The latter offers what I consider the most comprehensive overall statement of Hardy's pneumatology. I begin with a long quotation from SU, followed by commentaries on this and on *FC*:

> Even to utter such bidding to the "Spirit of Unity" is to make certain suppositions. They do not have the character of axioms from which we then make derivations; they are more like a pre-theoretical awareness of "significant form" from which we operate.[10] But in so speaking, we do operate from a certain conditionality in which we find ourselves. In other words, and in a very fundamental sense, we "speak that which we do know, and testify that which we have seen" (John 3:11).
>
> Now what is this conditionality? As soon as we begin to answer, we are driven to a full description of the life of God with his creation which it is very difficult to state without begging many questions. . . . [A] more energetic way of speaking would be to say: "there is that which moves toward and in us and thereby joins us to its own movement, which is the Spirit of God."[11] . . . The Spirit is not less than God himself in his action for us, and the Spirit is near and moves within us to draw us to unity with God. . . .
>
> Taking this one step further, we can see that this conditionality has implications for the nature of God. It implies the movement of the wisdom of God who is in and through the activity of the Spirit, as that within which we operate. So, the "stirring of wisdom to be in being present with us" is the conditionality within which we find ourselves existing; and that conditionality enfolds us in the self-constitutive activity of God. Properly speaking this is a Trinitarian movement by which the Spirit is the stirring of the wisdom which is God to be fully himself (the Fatherhood of God) by being fully present with us (in the Son).
>
> [This] fullness is one of movement, not of state: the Spirit stirs God to be fully himself, and this is his unity. Likewise, it is in being drawn into unity with God that we are brought to our fullness. We do not thereby achieve a fixed or selfsame identity; our identity is contingent upon God's movement to bring us

9. Daniel Hardy, "Spirit of Unity—Reconcile Your People!" (Commission on Faith and Order, World Council of Churches, Würzburg, Germany, 1989).

10. Hardy notes that "even such awareness is dynamic, occurring within an interaction between the perception of significant form and the history of life, the 'significance buried in events.'" See Daniel W. Hardy, "Christian Affirmation and the Structure of Personal Life," in *Belief in Science and Christian Life: The Relevance of Michael Polanyi's Thought for Christian Faith and Life,* ed. Thomas F. Torrance, 71–90 (Edinburgh: Handsel Press, 1980).

11. Cf. Daniel W. Hardy, "Rationality, the Sciences and Theology," in *Keeping the Faith: Essays to Mark the Centenary of Lux Mundi,* ed. Geoffrey Wainwright, 274–309 (Philadelphia: Fortress / London: SPCK, 1988), which discusses the position of Jesus Christ as formative in this movement.

into his own fullness. So there is, properly speaking, a "stirring" by which God is fully himself—in wisdom and goodness—and it is that same stirring by which we are fully ourselves. . . .

In spatial terms, there seems to be a distance, not between God and us, but between what may be called "reality" and "appearance," that which God has brought and that which appears to us. In terms of movement, there seems to be a "movement" in us which yet does not "work" in us. Perhaps these disjunctions are necessary for us to be fully free, to give us the space (privacy) and play in which to initiate. But by asking the Spirit to reconcile, we are freely opening ourselves to, and involving ourselves in, what is brought to the Spirit's stirring which is already in God's work for us. More than that, we thereby open ourselves to the conferral of the Spirit as a real movement in our very particularity. (SU, 1–3)

1. Empirical contingency and transcendental presupposition (SU + FC 3)

In other words, and in a very fundamental sense, we "speak that which we do know, and testify that which we have seen" (John 3:11). (SU, 2)

The Spirit is encountered in its contingency, which means that it is knowable, but only through its effects, which are as visible in the world as the world itself. The effects of the Spirit include human actions. There are certain patterns of inquiry that enable humans to search from effect to cause and offer *abductions*—probable, nonnecessary, but testable observations—about the characteristics of Spirit as ground and presupposition of our actions. Such abductions enable us to "see" the Spirit, not face-to-face but through the "shadow" or "back" of our visible behaviors. This form of encounter is analogous to the way we acquire a sense of our individual personality and assumptions: not seeing but inferring via hypothesis and then reconceiving in response to new experience. It is therefore analogous to the way, according to the philosopher Immanuel Kant, we know the individual things of the world. He argues that while we cannot observe these things directly, from the *way* we see them we can infer the "spectacles" through which alone we see them (he calls these the "transcendental conditions" of our knowledge of the world). We may therefore have probable, abductive knowledge of the Spirit as it is displayed, as well, in actions other than our own. Just as the psalmist exclaims, "The heavens declare the glory of God," the work of the Spirit appears through all the patterns of relation we may observe among the elements of God's creation. This abductive knowledge of the Spirit bears the label *pneumatology*.

Hardy thus shares Emmanuel Levinas's sense of the immemorial: the bases of our actions lie in conditions that precede and ground our capacity to think and conceptualize. These conditions are therefore "precognitive" but not unknowable. Knowledge of them is simply of a different sort from direct perception or rational inference. It is a posteriori the way that empirical science is a posteriori: reasoning from effect to cause, it offers us probable knowledge of such laws of creation as gravity or the speed of light. This probability may be of a very high degree, enough that we bet our lives on it: that the ground will remain under my feet after the next step, that there will be new life and death, that the Spirit will bring us knowledge of God's very Presence, and that this Presence may heal us in times of distress.

2. Correlativity

The epistemological language of a human being's searching "from effect to cause" serves as a philosophic introduction to Hardy's trinitarian exposition. If so, the next question to ask is, "On what basis does the human being first guess or imagine what the cause might be?" From Hardy's trinitarian perspective, the answer is, "Through the Spirit, by way of the abductions to which it gives rise": "'there is that which moves toward and in us and thereby joins us to its own movement, which is the Spirit of God.' . . . So there is, properly speaking, a 'stirring' by which God is fully himself—in wisdom and goodness—and it is that same stirring by which we are fully ourselves."

Like the Jewish philosopher Hermann Cohen, Hardy describes our knowledge of God's identity as *correlative* to our own identities, and our identity as correlative to God's.[12] Like Cohen, furthermore, Hardy reads this pattern of correlation as a prototype for all social relations and, in fact, all relations among the creatures of this world. The Anglican theologian adds something, of course, since he reads the triune life of God as not only the prototype for correlation but also the activity that underlies all relations. And he gives special place to the Spirit as calling both God and creature to this activity.

3. Ecclesial soteriology: redemptive work in the church

[B]y asking the Spirit to reconcile, we are freely . . . involving ourselves in what is brought to the Spirit's stirring which is already in God's work for us. More than that, we thereby open ourselves to the conferral of the Spirit as a real movement in our very particularity. (SU, 1–3)

If by way of the Spirit our actions are correlative to those of God, does God accompany us in our suffering? Citing Exodus 3, Hardy replies that *ehyeh imach*, "I will be with you," belongs to God's very self-identity. I trust Hardy thereby affirms the reading of the psalmist, "I will be with you in [your] suffering." Would he also affirm this addition by the rabbinic sages (in the midrash *Exodus Rabbah*): "I will suffer with you"? I read Hardy's broader corpus of writings as consistent with the following claims: (a) the christological inference that by way of Christ's suffering, God is present with humanity in its

12. For a full account of correlativity in Hermann Cohen and a host of related thinkers, see Robert Gibbs, *Correlations in Rosenzweig and Levinas* (Princeton: Princeton University Press, 1994).

suffering; (b) the pneumatological inference that this presence is redemptive: by way of the Spirit, God appears as our Redeemer, not just eschatologically but also in the contingencies of our worldly lives; (c) that we are redeemed in relation to God's unity, which is the unity of the body of Christ; (d) that our suffering is a mark of disunity in our relations to the divine Unity, and to be redeemed is to be brought from such disunity to Unity; (e) that "being brought to such Unity" is neither a direct consequence of human works nor an event of divine will that appears independent of our actions.

The single most instructive illustration of these claims may be located in the contexts within which Hardy employs the terms *extensity* and *intensity*. Read as abstract terms within Hardy's theological vocabulary, *extensity* characterizes our place in this world as finite creatures, and *intensity* characterizes the point of contact between divine and human action. Read again, however, in light of when and where he uses them, these terms refer to vectors in Hardy's soteriology: *intensity* names the direction we turn to gain access to God's redemptive presence, while *extensity* names both the place of relative absence out of which we seek him and the direction we turn either to do his work in the world or to flee from doing it:

> Human beings live in extended time and so learn of the movement of God's truth and holiness to them in the course of time. But there is another kind of "extensity": [that] of the situations in which they live. . . . We need [thus] to learn to think of Christian faith as by nature spread out, as something extended by its "spread-out-ness." (*FC*, 109–10)

Here Hardy refers to extensity as the worldly and contingent place of Christian life and service, so that "the Church is a complex of people faithful in very different situations throughout history" (*FC*, 110). But this same extensity is also a source of our potential "distraction" from God's will:

> This, perhaps, explains why the loss of intensity afforded by the high views of revelation and church in the Reformation and Counter-Reformation could lead so easily to preoccupations with conquering the world for commercial gain . . . [or] with divisions between us. (*FC*, 112)

When he reflects on the vacuity of such preoccupations, Hardy is wont to refer back to "intensity" as now a source of repair: "For all the potential distractions of our extensity, we may also live in the intensity of God's gift of truth and holiness, in the inner dynamic of the wisdom of God. . . . Such a way of living can carry us deeper into the meaning of the Word of God in Scripture and its manifold presence in the living tradition of church life" (*FC*, 111).[13]

13. Hardy continues, "Properly speaking, the intensity of wisdom needs to be pursued within worship, where the interwoven involvements of God, community, world and self are most fully

To live is thus to live in extensity and intensity, but to live only in extensity is to live outside of God's unity. Any redemptive movement from disunity to unity is a movement from extensity to intensity, so that the "place" of redemption is a place where intensity enters our extensive lives. Hardy observes that for ancient Israel, this place was identified with the Temple, the Tent, and access to Torah. For the church, this place is reidentified with life inside the body of Christ, archetypically in the practice of Eucharist. For Hardy, Eucharist is the name per se of God's redemptive presence in the life of the church. A full account of soteriology is thus a full account of the place of Scripture, church, and human life in the Eucharist.

4. Eucharist: center of an ecclesial pneumatology (from FC conclusion)

(a) Individual suffering is a soteriological category only in the context of social and political life

Unlike the pragmatists, Hardy does not adopt a biological model for "repair" as a species of stimulus and response. Instead, he adopts a *theo-social* model of repair (my term) as a mending of relations in light of the triune life. For Hardy, this model neither reduces soteriology to the terms of worldly sociology nor spiritualizes sociology by restating it in strictly theological terms. Instead, the model applies correlatively to intratrinitarian and interhuman society. The treatment of individual human suffering is correlative to the treatment of societal disunity, and, in the "other" direction, to the treatment of bio-organic disorder and disunity. Hardy's soteriology therefore applies to a series of correlations: the organism understood as a society of material elements (protoplasm and such), whose unity and disunity is correlative to that of the human person as a society of relations (cognitive, emotive, and such), in turn correlative to that of a human society, to societies of society, to broader patterns of relation in the created universe, and so on to the society of divine persons. The Spirit displays itself as the correlation of correlations, animating and guiding all relations and relations of relations.

> Is human agency even conceivable without reference to radical responsibility to and for others? In an era of radical fragmentation, the availability of a stable, unifying yet dynamic, exocentric rightly formed and responsible spiritual self has become highly important. ("Theology and Spirituality," FC, 100–101)

> A primacy is therefore accorded to social life, one difficult fully to appreciate in the context of the individualistic culture of today. ("Truth, the Churches," FC, 137)

---

expressed, where the spread-outness of life *in situ* is returned in thanks and the compassionate gift of truth is most fully realized" (FC, 112).

It is worth remembering that before the last 200 years, referring to "I" or "me" meant something different. Before, it was assumed that an "I" was always inter-woven with "we" and "me" with "us." The "I" was simply not divided off, but was an extension of the "we," the two fused together. ("Jesus Said," *FC*, 221)

(B) Church is society

"The Church," writes Hardy, "is a society, [which] is meaning—potentially wisdom—structured in social terms" (*FC*, 238). The center and guide of this structure is "intensity of meaning," which is the presence of the Spirit, society's access to the triune life of God. In this world, however, the structure remains fragile—a balance, one may say, between the centrifugal pull of the Sprit and the centripetal pull of extensive life in the world (239).

By way of the Spirit, the triune Life of God is thus architect of the unity of human society (241). One may thereby attribute to Hardy another kind of Enlightenment: the light of God shines through the unity of any society; in God's light, displayed through the Spirit, the church structures its own meaning. The dynamic source of this structure is the sacramental life of the church, of which the Eucharist is prototype (242). Eucharistic worship is the practical activity through which the triune life of God becomes active guide to the structuring of Christian society, within which the redemptive actions of God will take place for the church.

(C) Eucharist is the practical activity that founds church society

To observe how the Eucharist guides the society of the church is not to study doctrine but to attend to actual ecclesial practice. The Eucharist "is historically particular, theoretically infused practice that is also normative for the social performance of meaning as referred to God through Jesus Christ, and thus an anticipation of God's eschatological purposes" (*FC*, 243–44).

> The Eucharist is an embodiment of all the dimensions of human existence in the world; biological, physical, historical circumstance, personal participa-tion, social relations, political configuration, economic exchange, and cultural formation—in a forward trajectory anticipating the good of all people and things. . . . The Eucharist is [thus] . . . a comprehensive event or performance of social meaning. . . . The Eucharist is . . . more akin to a dramatic performance than to a verbal statement. It preserves the characteristic dynamics of God's relations to the world in exemplifying them, not by stating them as if we were outside of them observing them. (244)

While some of these characteristics may be articulated in general, Hardy ar-gues that the Eucharist makes itself known in the strictly local context of its performance. "It faces those present, within their particular circumstances, with themes and counter-themes of human existence, and stimulates them to a new course of social life—a new enactment of meaning that approximates to goodness in their place" (247).

(d) Eucharistic practice is incomplete in this world

Hardy identifies Eucharistic practice only as performed within the contingencies of particular ecclesial and social contexts and only as correlative to its empirical and spiritual consequences. This means that in this time between the times, Eucharistic practice is not wholly independent of what happens in the personal lives of members of the Eucharistic communion and therefore of what remains incompletely realized in those lives. "While the Eucharist always brings to light the mutual involvement of the drama of human life with God's work, this is *always as history*. . . . The good that is sought is always 'surrounded, attacked, and relativized by other goods and values'" (247).[14] The Anglican Church may be unique in the way it recognizes this contingency:

> Here is where the Eucharist . . . differs strongly from conceptions of it in Roman Catholic, Orthodox, and Reformed traditions. For, in different ways, those traditions suppose that the Eucharist manifests—visibly or invisibly—the already-complete action of God in human life in the Church. The conception of the Eucharist here, however, is of the in-folding of human social meaning with God's, whereby human social meaning does not lose its character as fragile, incomplete, and forward-moving even as it is drawn by God toward the eschatological finality of God's work. (*FC*, 246)

Not untypically, Hardy's account of this eschatological intensity leads to reflections on what, removed from this intensity, waits for redemption.

(e) The Eucharist is a source of redemption and repair

Unlike that of the pragmatists, Hardy's account of loss or suffering and repair or redemption begins with the source of redemption rather than the fact of loss. There is no "natural" account of loss, as if the creaturely world possessed intrinsic standards for measuring its soteriological "needs." Loss and what is needed to redeem it are both made evident by the light of God's saving presence, displayed with increasing intensity in humanity, in the people Israel, in the narrative of Jesus's life, death, and resurrection, and in the "holiness" or "the intensity of God's presence" that is disclosed in the sacraments and realized in the life of the church as the body of Christ. Hardy writes that this holiness displays "purity," "capacity to maintain its fullness according to its own kind, without reference to—or collapse into—other kinds" (*FC*, 9). Holiness "resists comprehension in the other terms normally available," including "the ontological . . . the cosmological . . . and the historical" (9). Within

14. Hardy cites Hans Urs von Balthasar, *Theo-drama: Theological Dramatic Theory, Vol. 1: Prolegomena* (San Francisco: Ignatius Press, 1988), 413ff.

the biblical traditions in particular, "we meet something much more full, a holiness filled with the perfection of wisdom and goodness and therefore beautiful: "The law of the Lord is perfect, reviving the soul . . ."" (FC, 11–12, citing Ps. 19). "Here, holiness and God are mutually defining. God is a holy God" (FC 12, citing Josh. 24:19). Received through "the Word of God and the Spirit of Life," holiness emerges as "a relational propriety that capacitates or invests human beings with intimates of itself—its propriety—by which they can identify it" (FC, 13–14).[15] Holiness may thereby become a characteristic of human as well as divine being: what Hardy characterizes as a "new intensity" that appears within the communion of the church. "This is seen most dramatically at Pentecost, where there is for the disciples an immense change simultaneously in the intensity and extension of life in Christ with God" (FC, 135). Hardy refers to the breaking-in of this intensity as the condition for all worldly repair and spiritual redemption, since the Spirit lives in us through relations and as relationality, through society and *as* society. Hardy's pneumatology thereby diverges from most American postliberalisms, since he will not segregate sociopolitical life from the reach of the Spirit and of the church. I therefore infer that his fairly ubiquitous criticisms of sociopolitical, ecclesial, and theological practices are *not* his means of identifying what, after Dewey, we might label "problematic situations" in need of repair. They are, instead, his means of identifying institutional practices that *obstruct the reparative and redemptive work of the Spirit in our lives.*

5. Addressing obstructions to the redemptive work of the Spirit

The telos of Hardy's reparative writing is to recommend ways of removing obstructions to the work of the Spirit, rather than ways of directly repairing loss. In this way Hardy's work is pragmatic to a degree, but without the pragmatists' presumption that we rather than God can measure where God's reparative work is needed. Obstructions to the work of the Spirit are removed by the Spirit's own bidding and guidance. I find three of Hardy's writings most helpful for discerning what he means by "obstructions" and how he believes we can contribute to the Spirit's work of repairing them. In the essay "Spirit of Unity,"[16] he argues that the church has imbibed a modern "binary thinking"[17] that obstructs the redemptive agency of much theological and ecclesial work. In the essay "Redemptive Ecumenism," he (literally) diagrams the place of God's redeeming Spirit in human society and examines how our access to that place is obstructed by ecclesial disunity

15. Paraphrasing Jonathan Edwards, "A Personal Narrative," in *A Jonathan Edwards Reader*, ed. John E. Smith et al. (New Haven: Yale University Press, 1995), 293.

16. The focus of his essay is a remarkable series of diagrams of the church's "social transcendental": his depiction of the center of intensity that guides repairs of this divisiveness.

17. What, throughout this book, I label "dyadic thinking."

and ecumenical schism. In the concluding chapters of *Finding the Church*, he attends specifically to disunity and schism in the Anglican Church today, concluding with a reparative response that provides concluding images for this chapter. In the limited space of this section, I hope to draw out of these three writings a single portrait of how Hardy concludes his ecclesial soteriology. It is an account of the Holy Spirit's double gift to the church: enabling it to see what obstructs its life and work today and empowering it to contribute to the repair of those obstructions.

(A) APPEALING TO THE SPIRIT

For the church to repair itself is for it to join the work of the Spirit. But how is it possible to teach the ways of the Spirit to a church whose practices obstruct them? Hardy's overall soteriology is set in this double bind: obstructions to the work of the Spirit are also obstructions to joining the Spirit's efforts to remove obstructions. Hardy offers a doubled response: (i) to be reacquainted with the Spirit is to be introduced to a condition of knowing rather than to be offered knowledge directly—the Spirit moves, as it were, behind us; *and* (ii) this condition of knowing is specific to the context of our obstructions—the Spirit draws us both to the absolute source of repair and back again to the concrete place of life and obstruction. Soteriology is thus an indirect affair, shuttling back and forth between heaven, doubled as place of critique and hope, and earth, doubled as place of life and obstruction. Hardy calls this *double engagement*.[18]

Whatever society we inhabit and seek to comprehend and measure, "we can only begin from where we are" (*FC*, 241). According to Hardy's rule of double engagement, this "from where" is specific at once to our societal home in this world and to the Spirit who is its architect. In this way unlike the American postliberals, Hardy seeks a double engagement between his ecclesiology and his general theory of society: a double presumption that human society has to do with the life of God and that the life of God has implications for the character of human society. Hardy's ecclesiology is always local to his account of a particular church in the Anglican Communion but, at the same time, always general not only to an account of the universal church but also to an account of human sociality. He therefore presumes that his ecclesiology is insufficient if it does not also help him more subtly understand the community of Israel or the sociopolitics of Thomas Jefferson's Virginia. "It should be self-evident," he concludes, "that we are only at the beginning of realizing the full scope of the meaning of society as found in God" (*FC*, 241). Hardy has in mind not only the triune sociality

---

18. "How is it possible to be positively Christian in such a way as to include but also transcend the particularities of different churches?" He answers, "The way forward lies in a *double engagement*, of denominations and theologies with each other on the one hand and . . . with the vitalities of modern life and understanding on the other hand" (*FC*, 127–28).

of the divine persons but at the same time the sociality of every gathering of human beings.[19]

(b) Doubly bound obstructions facing the church today

Hardy's account of soteriology is thus both top-down and bottom-up: arguing at once by way of concrete illustration and by way of the immanent Trinity. Typically, his account responds to recent crises in the Anglican Communion, examining possible sources of obstruction at once in classical formulations of church life, in the influence of the modern West, and in the contingencies of recent ecclesial politics. Here are illustrations of these three sources.

Obstructions in the Anglican Communion. Hardy's writings on the church often begin and end with his reflections on the Anglican Communion's seemingly irreconcilable debates about the status of homosexuals among the clergy. While attending to the detailed arguments and to the historical events that stimulate them, his primary concern is more general: the fact that a church that gives witness to Christ in scriptural study and worship appears to enlist neither as a vehicle for resolving the debates and reconciling the opposing parties. What has obstructed the capacity of the church to practice what it preaches? Hardy notes that the Communion is sharply divided both in these debates and in its criteria for resolving them. On the one side are those who "see the Bible and the apostolic tradition . . . in hierarchical and sequential terms," so that Christian faith is enacted "juridically": the rules of faith are announced in the Bible, articulated in the tradition, and defined and defended through reason (*FC*, 146). On the other side are those who see "the Bible and the apostolic tradition as providing the historical origins and provenance of the multiple dimensions of Christian faith today, now to be explored through varieties of experience [several of which are mutually fruitful]" (*FC*, 146). For this "integrationist" standpoint, Christian faith is enacted pluralistically and inclusively, with a minimum of centralized controls. Hardy argues that disagreements between these two standpoints cannot be resolved until the antagonists acknowledge that each of their standpoints derives its merit from service to a "greater 'common ownership' of the Anglican Communion."[20] This is not service to a single polity or office but to the body of Christ itself, which means to a revitalized commitment "to our common identity in Jesus Christ, our baptism in the Trinitarian name, and in our recognizability to each other as mediating Christ to each other. These are the 'essentials' in which our primary

19. And perhaps also of other creatures as well, since subatomic particles, for example, also participate in the divine work of creation, if not directly in the divine image.

20. "Beyond that which can be brought about through the Archbishop of Canterbury" (*FC*, 149). Hardy explains, in more detail, that the erosion of common ownership has led the Communion to overweigh the authority of a single office, in the process lessening common ownership even further—and thus lessening loyalty even to the authority the Communion has invested in the archbishop.

and precious unity consists" (FC, 149–50). Hardy argues, in other words, that differences within the Communion are now so great that they would simply be reproduced through any action by the current church polity—or through any effort of mediation—that was not part of a general revitalization of the fundamental purposes of the Communion. But to what ecclesial model shall the Communion turn to guide this revitalization?

Perennial obstructions in the church. Hardy acknowledges that both in the last century and in the last twenty centuries, the church has modeled schism as much as it has modeled the unity of the body of Christ. In the twentieth century, "ecumenicity . . . is sadly lacking. . . . The one church has become many, a church related even in multiplicity has been replaced by disconnected ecclesial unity and the churches have been displaced from the public domain. . . . Often the rationales offered for the churches have disallowed mutual understanding and respect except where imposed by other parties" (RE, 428–29). Hardy suggests that the divisions emerge out of the practical effects of two ideals of classical Christianity. One is the effort to achieve a perfect Christianity, leading, in practice, to deep disagreements about just which Christianity is most "authentic."[21] The second is the mission to draw all humanity into love of Christ, which, in practice, is a mission to bring the church's witness into the seculum. In modern times, this has meant bringing the church into close contact with the "rapidly spinning vortices of modern civilization" and, thus, the double bind that defines modern church life: if the church ignores the modern world, it fails in its mission to the world; if it learns to speak to the modern world, then it learns to speak by way of radical dichotomies that militate against the content of its witness. The result, he writes, is three levels of obstruction that beset the modern church.

Obstructions in the modern church. On one level, congregants and clergy alike tend to think and speak in terms of modernity's radical dichotomies, as if they needed to choose, for example, between "stability" and "change." On another level, churches portray their relation to modernity in terms of these dichotomies: typically, the "church" comes to symbolize "stability" against change, implying not only "continuity" but also "conservatism." On a third level, the church may seek to draw on its own resources to overcome such dichotomies. This, says Hardy, is the right idea, except that the churches tend to have forgotten what it means to turn directly to the Spirit as source of redemption. In practice, they continue to speak of the Spirit only by way of the modern divisions. By way of illustration, Hardy notes the tendency of recent ecclesiologists to universalize norms that are specific to the practices of a single church or denomination. This is to begin appropriately with regional

---

21. "From the start, the church marked its identity in Christ through a linear continuity in doctrine, ecclesial forms and practices that were taken as necessary to authentic Christianity. . . . The main divisions occurred within these continuities: the schisms the East and West and as defined by the reformation in Europe and in England" (RE, 429–30).

church practice but then, out of a misplaced anxiety, to build purportedly global models out of merely regional accounts. The anxiety is to seek "universal" warrants for norms that are encountered more locally. This is a modern anxiety that arises when, having displaced the Spirit, modern ecclesial thinkers seek to find in purported "universality" the assurance their forebears would have sought in the Presence of the Spirit.

Hardy analyzes this modern anxiety similarly to the way the philosopher Richard Bernstein analyzed what he dubbed "Cartesian anxiety" and John Dewey before him called "the quest for certainty." This is Descartes's search for an "Archimedean point" on which to ground a new certainty and new science. The search, writes Bernstein, is only as passionate as the anxiety that stimulates it: a dread that, without such certainty, "madness" will overtake us; it is either–or, madness or rational certainty. Hardy adds that when the church acquires its place in modern civilization, it also acquires this anxiety. Although knowing God in the Spirit means knowing God's creation without madness or rational certainty, the modern church comes to speak of this knowledge in terms of the modern either–or. Modern Christian rationalists say that we encounter God either by way of rational certainty or through the madness of unreason. Modern Christian antirationalists say we encounter God either unpredictably (through radical unknowing) or through the tyranny (in this sense, madness) of some humanly constructed system of ideas.

(C) The Spirit's redoubled work in the modern church

In each case, Hardy's accounts of obstruction lead directly to his accounts of repair. The previous paragraph ended, for example, just at the transformative moment where one account—in this case, of worldly obstructions—leads to the next.

Addressing obstructions in modern civilization. For Hardy, the alternative is not to ignore these opposing mind-sets—for that would be to ignore the worldly setting of the church today—but to teach to them in ways that might lead, indirectly, to the mediating work of the Spirit. To illustrate, he considers what it means to teach about the Spirit to science-minded thinkers divided into camps who adopt either a strictly "unifying" or a "diversifying" model of knowledge. The unifiers favor "a unified empirical-theoretical explanation of the world," which they love to express in clearly defined formulas; the diversifiers emphasize "complexity, diversification, . . . [and a] concern for life, . . . freedom and relationalities," which they portray through broader theories of life and normative action (SU, 5–6). Hardy addresses them both through a sympathetic account of the place of unifying and diversifying modes of explanation in contemporary science and theology.[22] He illustrates how

---

22. Drawing, for example, on recent texts in systems theory and in evolutionary biology, Hardy speaks of "the energetics involved in the development of dynamic order" and the way

these modes are treated sometimes as complementary and sometimes as contradictory. In the latter case, scientists and theologians construct monolithic accounts of "Unity" or "Diversity" so that the sum total is a complex account of unity-and-diversity. He suggests that many readers will also be familiar with accounts of natural phenomena that appear to balance these two tendencies, such as studies of the ecosystem that examine both unities and diversities of individual organisms, species, and laws. He notes that such phenomena appear to transform what we see as "opposites" into complementary elements of a dynamic order. Hardy concludes by writing of the Spirit in analogous ways. When considered with respect to unity, the Spirit's identity is distinguished from those of Father and Son, and it is recognized through its discrete actions in the world. When considered with respect to diversity, the Spirit is known through its complex relations with Father and Son and with the creatures of the world. When considered in ways that balance these two perspectives, the Spirit appears as a movement of reconciliation among the persons of God and the creatures of the world, in the latter case transforming potentially opposing forces into complements (SU).

Addressing obstructions in the church. Hardy's ecclesial pneumatology culminates in his recommendations for repairing the church today: the modern church in general and the Anglican Church as his primary example. Stated abstractly, it is a recommendation for transforming potentially opposing forces in the church into complements. The agent of transformation is the Spirit, the Reconciler; the means of access to the Spirit is the Word, embodied in Scripture, Eucharist, and the full life of the church, local and universal. The Reconciler of the one and many is encountered by way of "the Christ who lives in me" (Gal. 2:20). To live both here in the worldly church and also there in the body of Christ is to enjoy and suffer "the determinative change [that] has come about through being 'crucified with Christ,' in whose cross there is a reversal of the human abuse of all that is 'in the flesh' and even the revocation of 'nature's' corruption" (FC, 130). But Hardy is wary of the church's tendency today to proclaim the Word too simply and too triumphantly. He cautions that to overcome its obstructions, the church must avoid what we see most strongly in the vision of Hegel: a tendency to overunify and thus absolutize our vision of the church, as if there were one grand formula for fulfilling what it means to live in Christ. It must also avoid the opposite tendency: to abjure all theological language and speak only in the most local terms about specific actions that need to be taken in specific churches in their time in place. As noted earlier, Hardy's alternative is a *double engagement* of the church universal and the many local churches, attending at once to the "Christ in me" in this specific space-time and also in all time within the inmost life of God.

---

that systems (biological and other) emerge in relation to their environments by balancing energy (associated with growth and complexity) and order (associated with stability and simplicity).

Hardy's primary warning is that our attachment to both the one and the many cannot be mediated by acts of the human will; the Spirit alone mediates. Many obstructions in the modern church are, in fact, expressions of generous human efforts to heal and mediate; but, however well-intentioned, the human will cannot provide this kind of mediation. The task of the human will is to make a choice for Scripture, Eucharist, and church life—to leave other concerns behind, in other words, and "follow him." The rest is up to the Spirit: to guide us through the word of Scripture, the activity of communion, and the life of the church. Many details in Hardy's writings concern ways in which we may simply obstruct or inhibit our openness to this work.

As noted earlier, Hardy offers his account of the Eucharist as a prototype for all forms of reparative work. In a way that is reminiscent of Talmudic thinking, Hardy employs the name of a particular activity (in this case, Eucharistic communion as enacted in specific congregations) to refer to a general type of action that can be repeated both in ways we readily recognize (such as different practices of Eucharist) and in ways we would not otherwise recognize (analogous uses of the term). This is a much broader illustration of his method of double engagement. It means that on one level, the church will be repaired only if it literally revitalizes the way Eucharistic communion is practiced in each church. On another level, it means that the church will be repaired only when the activity of the Spirit that we know prototypically in the Eucharist is reiterated in every dimension of church life. And, more than that, it means that the world will be repaired only when that activity of the Spirit is reiterated in every activity of every human society. This does not mean that redemption awaits all humanity's converting to the Anglican community or to Christianity more broadly defined. It means that what Hardy recognizes within his denomination's experience of communion must, he believes, have an analogue in the way that the Spirit visits each human community, however differently each community may name and recognize these visitations. On the one hand,

> that involves recognizing the Eucharist as a complex patterning of particulars, in which particular people "return" from their "spread-out-ness" in particular situations to gather and give thanks, and thereby to be renewed, in this particular setting by these particular actions and words in this sequence in this particular time-scale, and then "resume" life in their particular situations. (FC, 246)

On the other hand,

> the Eucharist is a full exemplification of the dynamics of the truth of divine life in full engagement with social meaning, where the freedom of God capacitates—forms and energizes—human freedom. . . . If we accept that the Eucharist is itself an enactment of the economy of God in world history . . .

we find there a Trinitarian God who is himself—maintains the consistency of his life—in restoring the dynamics proper to human life in the world. (*FC*, 249)

For Hardy, any repair of human sociality is, therefore, a repetition of the type he names "Eucharist." Because this is a pneumatological claim, it generalizes beyond the province of the church per se. It therefore speaks, in different ways, to what is reparative in my Judaism or in my friend's Islam. Typical of both Talmudic and figurative thinking, this kind of generalization displays what the philosopher Charles Peirce calls "indefinite growth," as opposed to abstract "universalization." This means that the type will reappear in various analogous ways, but not in ways that we individual thinkers can anticipate. The Spirit alone discloses the analogue. Hardy's ecclesiology, therefore, has a powerful generalizing force, but we individual readers do not have the power on our own to foresee what the next example will look like. It is something that will have to happen somewhere else, and only after it happens may we be able to recognize it and exclaim, like Jacob, "God was in this place and I did not know it."

6. *Obstruction, schism, and postliberalism*

The fact that Hardy theorizes by typology rather than generality is itself a fundamental lesson in his ecclesial soteriology. It teaches that the Absolute is agent as well as source of redemption and that the human will obstructs rather than contributes to this agency. To this extent, Hardy's typological soteriology complements the work of his American peers. His practice differs from theirs in the way he invites his readers to draw analogies beyond his Eucharistic examples. This invitation marks Hardy's distinctly Anglican rather than American approach to the challenges of supersessionism and schism. In this concluding section, I suggest that Hardy's diagnosis of schism in the Anglican Church introduces all the terminology we need to identify his responses to ecclesial schisms, the schism between church and synagogue, and inter-Abrahamic schisms as well.

(A) Transforming schisms into complements

Hardy's Eucharistic typology marks his response to schisms not only within the Anglican Communion and among the worldly churches, but also between Christianity and Judaism and among the three Abrahamic traditions. While his responses overlap in various ways with those of the American postliberals, the integrative character of his response is a distinct mark of his Anglicanism. For the Americans, ecumenical schisms are repaired through the unity of the body of Christ; the Jewish–Christian schism is repaired through the unified canon of God's revealed Word; and there is no general repair of the Muslim–Christian schism. My overview of Hardy's response to schism will therefore also provide a helpful summary of similarities and differences between American and Anglican postliberalisms.

(B) Repairing intra-Christian schisms

As illustrated in the previous section, Hardy's soteriological goal is not to undo differences and identities, but to see competitive differences transformed by the Spirit into complementary routes to divine service. In the fractious Lambeth conferences he attended, Hardy urged the practices of shared Eucharistic communion and scriptural study as setting the conditions for appropriate dialogue and argument. He worked not to promote one opinion on the various issues before the primates, but to promote fidelity to one Spirit as the host of ecclesial exchange across differences. He pursued the same end in his ecclesial work on interdenominational schism. Rather than argue for the unification of all empirical churches into one catholic denomination, he worked for the double engagement of the many churches *as we find them* into one body of Christ: not only one worldly institution and bureaucracy of Christians but complementary institutions of service, and dialogue in the Spirit and in the name of Christ.

The American postliberals share Hardy's sense that church schisms today reflect both perennial and specifically modern tendencies to disunity. For both Americans and Anglican postliberals, the modern church errs when it assimilates revealed discourses to the divided discourses of modern thought; it errs as well when it unwittingly reinforces modern dyadic thinking in the very act of promoting a single antimodern vision of the church, pitting church against modernity or religion against the world. Both Americans and Anglicans, furthermore, promote Scripture and sacrament as resources for repairing these errors. Their differences are complementary. The Americans devote relatively more attention to Christology—in this case, to reunite Christian thinking to practices of scriptural study and communal life. The Anglicans attend relatively more to pneumatology: in this case, to reintegrate church and world, *ecclesium* and *polis*. When tempted by the logics they seek to repair, the two postliberal movements may tend to criticize each other: Americans accusing the others of naturalism (assimilating church to world and to polity), Anglicans accusing the others of sectarianism (isolating their church from the world and from other churches). By their own better standards, the two should read each other's work felicitously, noting that Americans specialize in *ressourcement* (recovering the resources of early Christian practices of scriptural study and communal life) and Anglicans specialize in *adjornimento* (rereading today's worldly and political life by way of such practices).

(C) Repairing the Jewish–Christian schism

Hardy applies the same general soteriology to his efforts against Christian supersessionism and for intimate theological dialogue and overlapping theopolitical work among Jews and Christians. On one level of double engagement, to be sure, this does not mean that he seeks to unite Jews and

Christians in the one body of Christ. On another level, however—and here, to avoid misinterpretation, we must reason very carefully—Hardy does indeed extend his Eucharistic typology to relations between Judaism and Christianity. On a second level of engagement, Eucharist is a type of the communion of Jews and Christians in the one Word of God. Hardy celebrates the different characteristics of Jewish and Christian scriptural tradition and practice as the "found" identities of these two servants of God in the world. But he also celebrates the one Spirit that draws them together into fellowships of dialogue and argument about the Word and about how it shall be embodied in the world. He does not know where such fellowship leads, since its future is known by God alone. But he knows the Word that calls Abraham to go forth also calls the church; and he knows that those who are called will find each other on the way. Like American postliberals, Hardy finds the Jews in the scriptural canon, and much of his intimate theological dialogue with Jews begins with shared scriptural study. From this christological perspective, he overcomes supersessionism because the canon affirms God's promise to the Jews a priori. Hardy also finds the Jews in a second way, however: in the Spirit's contingent actions in history that have led Jews and many others to the precincts of the Anglican Church and that have, in particular, led Hardy to a fellowship circle of Jewish and Christian scholars. From this pneumatological perspective, he overcomes supersessionism because, through its unpredictable actions, the Spirit has led Hardy this way. Hardy's soteriology of double engagement requires attending to both of these mutually reinforcing perspectives.

(D) Repairing intra-Abrahamic schisms

American postliberals tend not to share Hardy's second pneumatological response to schism. For this reason, they tend not to share in the depth of his theological engagement with Muslims as well Jews. For both Americans and Anglicans, there is a modest christological basis for engagement with Muslims: since Islam is a religion of the Abrahamic covenant and the book, Christians will find that much of the Qur'an revisits familiar narratives and tropes. The primary basis for Anglican–Muslim dialogue is, however, pneumatological, with little parallel in American postliberalism. The same fellowships that led Hardy, contingently, into theological dialogue with Jewish theologians also opened him—and his Jewish peers—to comparable dialogue with Muslim theologians. As noted earlier, these fellowships generated the inter-Abrahamic Society of Scriptural Reasoning, of which Hardy was cofounder and senior mentor. His intimate theological dialogue and close friendship with Muslim, Jewish, and Christian peers is a model of the double engagement that he espoused in his Christian ecclesiology and embodied, as well, in his inter-Abrahamic practice.

Conclusion: Marks of Anglican Postliberalism

I find the following marks of what we may call Anglican postliberalism in Hardy's theology. These marks correspond to marks of American postliberalism and thereby justify my placing these two submovements—American and Anglican—within the same family. Differences between the submovements reappear within each mark. The work of postliberalism is as follows:

- to practice theological writing as reparative reasoning;[23]
- to repair disunities, dislocation, and divisions in church and in society;
- to read these disunities ultimately as divisions in the body of Christ, so that the goal of repair is to contribute to the unity of the body of Christ;
- to initiate repair with two simultaneous directions of reparative work:
  ◊ to examine disunities and divisions within their social contexts, but also extending from there to the church as a whole and to the world, and
  ◊ to reaffirm the norms of reparative work, as introduced, for example, within the Anglican Settlement, in classical church doctrine, and in the scriptural record of God's triune work in the world;
- to integrate these two directions of work in the dynamic activity of repair I have called "reparative genealogy," redefined here within the terms of Hardy's pneumatology.

The genealogy moves from phenomena of disunity to a pneumatological account of what aspects of Christian witness and work are responsible for repairing them. It moves, at the same time, to consider obstructions that undermine the church's capacity to enact this repair and to consider resources for repairing these obstructions.

Hardy peers behind the Anglican Settlement just as the Americans peered behind the Reformation. Both Anglican and American postliberalisms therefore turn back to reparative resources in the early councils, and behind them in the early church and ultimately in the New Testament and Old Testament narratives.

Hardy offers a unique account of the epistemological, hermeneutical, and theological characteristics of the final step in this reparative genealogy. Like the Americans, he employs this last step as a final source of norms and guidelines for repairing the disunities that mark and stimulate his entire genealogy. In my own terminology, his genealogy is ultimately pragmatic, since it is a project of

23. As noted in chap. 2, I owe this use of the term *reparative* to Nicholas Adams, who heard my studies of pragmatism as most interesting if applied to a more general activity of "reparative reasoning." Adams formalizes this suggestion in "Reparative Reasoning," *Modern Theology* 24, no. 3 (July 2008): 447–57.

disciplined—and prayerful—reasoning adopted for the sake of repairing contemporary conditions of social and religious life. Hardy does not use the term *pragmatic*, since he finds its references reductive and perhaps materialistic. He recognizes that Charles Peirce claimed to ground his pragmatic reasoning in an activity of "musement" that generated a deep and encompassing "abduction" about the reality of God as ground of all our "universes of experience" and of any repairs that may be made in them. Hardy notes, however, that Peirce must have adopted the term *abduction* from Coleridge, for whom it also referred to the product of musement, but with ontological implications that appear to be bracketed in Peirce's account. In Hardy's pneumatology, abduction discloses God's capacity to attract all worldly and social institutions toward the eschatological direction enacted in his triune work. For Hardy, this abduction marks the telos and resting place of reparative genealogy. One cannot say, formulaically, that the abduction begins "here" and ends "there." Nonetheless, it is when the genealogy enters into scriptural study that the abduction begins to display its prototypical characteristics, for which Hardy has invented or borrowed several very effective terms. First is *abductive attraction*, which refers, in this context, to the way scriptural reading begins to disclose God's reparative work in relation to the specific conditions of disunity that have stimulated this entire genealogy. Second and third, *dynamic relationality* and *nonlinear dynamics* are terms drawn from contemporary physics to refer to the plentitude of God's work: that Scripture discloses not only an Israel-specific and a church-specific soteriology, but also a complementary account of creation appropriate for physicists as well as Bible readers. This is science, but not positivism, since abduction discloses the creative and reparative activity that animates the cosmos as well as the triune life and thereby doubly obligates the believer to hope for and participate in this cosmic and divine work of repair.

Hardy also claims that abduction engages reparative reasoners in the "social-triune transcendental," suggesting that abduction introduces reasoners to the transcendental conditions of reparative knowledge and behavior. In this sense, to be *introduced* means to be initiated and habituated into a practice. For Hardy, another term for this initiation is *worship*, so that abduction is both scientific reasoning and worship. Hardy means that, as in sacramental worship, this worshipful, reparative reading of Scripture must be social. However solitary the initial stages of reparative genealogy may be for a given reasoner, genealogy becomes a social affair when it enters into the domain of scriptural study. To study Scripture reparatively is to participate by way of Scripture in triune patterns of face-to-face relationship. This activity of social relation becomes then the immediate environment of initiation into the transcendental conditions of repair. Abduction is thus a genealogical, reparative, scriptural, transcendental, and social affair.

A fellowship of reparative scriptural study is a society situated somewhere in history. To engage in reparative abduction is thus to engage in some historically marked project of repair: not "the one" authorized work of repair, but one way of repair that issues appropriately out of scriptural study. Abduction is therefore of the cosmos and of God, but also fallible: not because it may have been performed errantly, but because abduction is always of the creature as well as of God, and the creature is always fallible. This means that no abduction is self-legitimating, any more than any prayer is self-fulfilling no matter how piously it may be voiced. Abductions must be tested. In this case, testing means engaging in the all-the-more-creaturely activities of institutionalizing one's abductive recommendations for how to repair a divided society and a divided church. These repairs must actually be undertaken, which means that, for Hardy, there is no way for the disciple of Christ to worship apart from the world. The sacrament of Eucharist has its place within the church building. But abductions emerge from out of the sacramental life to repair socially specific relations and institutions. Hardy's reparative pneumatology therefore becomes a practical ecclesiology. The richest evidences for how Hardy understands reparative abduction are displayed in his time-specific accounts of disruptions in the Anglican Communion, in 2000 and 2001, for example. Those of us who read Hardy from out of very different social and religious contexts, have nonetheless much to learn from his Anglican-specific account. The Absolute, we might say, is disclosed rather than hidden in the particularities of historical life.[24]

24. See Daniel W. Hardy, with Deborah Hardy Ford, Peter Ochs, and David Ford, *Wording a Radiance: Parting Conversations on God and the Church* (London: SCM, 2010).

7

Wisdom's Cry

DAVID FORD'S REPARATIVE PNEUMATOLOGY

One ubiquitous characteristic of David Ford's work has been joy: the joy of the Spirit's outpouring in all of creation, in prayer, song, speaking, love, friendship, feasting.[1] His writing, social action, and institution building seem to sweep folks up in an embrace of praise.[2] In Ford's prose, even the word *cry* means the cry of joy before it means the cry of suffering. But the cry of suffering is always folded in there too, and this is most evident in Ford's more recent work, in particular his *Christian Wisdom: Desiring God and Learning in Love.*[3] The central texts of the book are Job and Luke-Acts; the central focus is the reparative spirit of wisdom that, we pray, emerges in the face of severe trauma to repair affliction—however little it can smooth over worldly suffering.

In this chapter, I focus on the reparative pneumatology that emerges out of the center of *Christian Wisdom*: not because it captures some center of all of Ford's work, but because it illustrates one deep part in a vivid and comprehensive way. This illustration also speaks directly to the themes of *Another Reformation*, since in his near-identification of Job and Jesus Christ, Ford uncovers an intimate place in his work where Jew and Christian commune

---

1. After Emmanuel Levinas, Ford also writes of *jouissance*.

2. I am grateful for helpful comments on this chapter by Tom Greggs, Jacob Goodson, and Rebekah Eklund, and editing by Rodney Clapp.

3. David F. Ford, *Christian Wisdom: Desiring God and Learning in Love* (Cambridge: Cambridge University Press, 2007).

deeply and where the American and Anglican wings of Christian postliberalism beat in near-harmony.

Wisdom's Cry: A Commentary on Selected Chapters of *Christian Wisdom*

In Ford's theological writings, the Spirit's superabundance is displayed through a variety of faces, each one naming a locus, manner, and mood of God's fluid presence. Some faces, like "Feasting," "Praise," and "Song," recur in Ford's work as names of perennial features of life in the Spirit. Others, like "Face" itself, come to name the primary foci of Ford's theological vision over a period of years: the impress of the Spirit in his thought and action. In *Christian Wisdom* (hereafter *CW*), Wisdom names herself as one of these defining tropes, and "the Cry" accompanies her as a newly added feature of life in the Spirit.

> The more I have searched for Christian wisdom, the more I have been struck by its core connection with cries: . . . in joy, suffering, recognition, wonder, bewilderment, gratitude, expectation or acclamation: and cries of people for what they most desire—love, justice, truth, goodness, compassion, children, health, food and drink, education, security, and so on. Christian wisdom is discerned within earshot of such cries, and is above all alert to the cries of justice. (4–5)

"Wisdom's Cry" names the current focus of Ford's pneumatology: a study of the Spirit's redemptive work in the world, as if to ask: when severe trauma and affliction have interrupted life's joys, how can the Spirit do its work again, reintegrating worldly being, creature by creature, into friendship with the Creator and communion with the chorus and community of all his creatures?

From one perspective, *CW* offers a systematic theology of the "incarnate Spirit," a term that may be appropriate to Ford's account of "wisdom Christology" (chap. 5) or of the Spirit as known in this and that place in the body of Christ: when, for example, Ford writes of "Jesus, 'full of the Holy Spirit,'" who "led by the Spirit (Luke 4:1) spends forty days fasting in the wilderness" (158), or when he writes of "the church [as] a school of desire and wisdom" (254), the "church being 'built together in the Spirit into a dwelling place for God'" (John 2:22) (257). From another perspective, *CW* is a commentary on Scripture: on Luke, Job, John, and on various ways that the Gospel narratives read and reread the Hebrew Scripture. If I refer to *CW* as a "systematic pneumatology," it eschews the form of "system" that generally appears in a "systematic theology." Such systems often trace a line of movement from one theological concept to another, but *CW* is the kind of system that traces a movement of the Spirit from one scriptural reading to another. In *CW*, the theological reasoning emerges only out of scriptural reading. While all postliberal theologies, British and American, are based in Scripture, relatively few postliberal writings are structured as scriptural commentaries in the manner of *CW*. It is therefore a prime illustration of scriptural reasoning—in this case, pneumatological reasoning emerging from out of scriptural reading to generate what Ford calls wisdom.[4] From a third perspective, *CW* is an account of Christian discernment, of how Christ's disciples discern the movement of Spirit in this world of human suffering and divine blessing. As in all of Ford's work, *CW* pulsates with expressions of the superabundance of this blessing. The abundance does not, however, deflect Christ's disciples' capacity to hear the cries of those who suffer. In *CW*, discernment is the capacity to hear such cries and to respond to them from out of the abundance of God's blessing. When "wisdom cries in the street," *wisdom* names both capacities. I would misrepresent the commentarial form of Ford's pneumatology if I traced its "system" through any form other than a commentary on his writing.

Introduction: wisdom calls

There is a primary theology that can be distilled from reading and rereading the Bible. . . . It might be described as "scriptural-expressivist" in its concern to draw from reading scripture a lively idiom of Christian wisdom today. . . . It is "postcritical" in its attempt to do justice simultaneously to the premodern, modern, and late modern . . . taking seriously the critiques of Christianity generated in recent centuries, but not letting them have the last word. It might be termed a "theology of desire and discernment" in its attempt to unite in a God-centred discourse the love of wisdom and wise loving. It is also a "theology of learning in the Spirit" . . . [which] learning is dialogical and collegial, located in theological communities, understood as "schools of desire and wisdom." Above all, the schooling is in loving God for God's sake. (Introduction, 3)

Page 3 of *CW* names the central themes of Ford's book as a whole. Wisdom is both the subject and the consequence of "reading and rereading the Bible." Ford's reading has an "archaeological interest" in biblical wisdom as understood by the earlier communities of Israel and of the church, but his primary attention is on how these understandings have been received through the ages, today in particular. This is how Ford explores what he calls a "scriptural expressivism": the scriptural texts trace the life of the Spirit within the canon and trace it anew within each community that receives it. Ford's reading is thus "postcritical," since it is informed at once by what academic scholars tell us about the contexts of earlier communities of reading and by the cries that call us to reread Scripture today. "Wisdom calls" readers to discern their existential responsibilities today and to allow their discernment to be shaped

---

4. In correspondence, Tom Greggs adds a helpful suggestion: "Attending to pneumatology may lead one to read scripture in a certain way. . . . Is this not what Christians mean in speaking of scripture as inspired or God-breathed (*theopneustos*), as in 2 Timothy 3:16?"

by the scriptural Word. This shaping is God's love, as is our manner of responding to the world's cries.

For Ford, discernment is cousin to desire, since God shapes our discernment by shaping what and how we desire. The shaping is therefore limned by the fleshly economy of cause and effect but as complementing the economy of attraction and love. Ford's way of introducing his account of wisdom leads me to think of Jewish kabbalists' accounts of the relation between God's overflowing wisdom, *chokhmah*, and divine discernment, *binah*. *Chokhmah* connotes the divine overflow, received all at once as a plenum of insight. *Binah* connotes the intellect's capacity to discern how and where wisdom works in this world. Ford introduces "wisdom" as both superabundant (the object of desire) and discerning (the activity of reasoning, shaped by the Word).

Chapter 1: wisdom cries

Wisdom is a mother with many children, and Jesus suggests he himself is one of them. (15)

Ford's comment is his gloss on Luke 7:35: "Wisdom is vindicated by all her children." For Ford, the "all" implies that many children are in the family: Jesus, John the Baptist, all of the disciples, and those to follow. "Wisdom" is the name Ford applies to the Spirit in CW, but Wisdom itself has many identities. If each name—whether of a type or of a person—is an embodiment of the Spirit, then an "incarnational pneumatology" is one that narrates the movement of Spirit from body to body and name to name. In classical Hebrew, "child—*ben* if male, *bat* if female—refers to 'what issues from,'" and this can mean either a child of human flesh or other forms of issue, including what issues from a rational premise. The conclusion of a syllogism is thus the child of its premises: the premises are father (*av*) or mother (*em*) of the inferences drawn from them. In this way, Ford's commentary has a pedigree in ancient Jewish thinking as well as in his Christian thinking. Wisdom hands herself over to her children, who embody her, descend from her, can be inferred from her, and are the consequences of her in history. A Hebrew word for a series of such handings-over is *mesorah*, "tradition," from the root *masar*, "to hand over or transmit." Ford's commentary explores and reverberates with the various sets of possibilities that are marked by any biblical word or phrase, and this applies both to the Greek of Gospel and Septuagint and the Hebrew of Tanakh. In the case before us, the reverberations are among Sonship, the unfolding of history and of reasons, tradition as a chain of transmission, and the generations of children that flow from parent to child to child.

The cry of blessing is fundamental to wise discernment. (16)

If wisdom moves from one body—or event or occasion for handing over—to another, then the place of each one is marked by what Ford calls a cry. There are cries of blessing, joy, affliction, wonder, discovery, and renewal. Each one marks the irrefutable fact that something has happened and things are not now what they were. We do not, however, know clearly what the mark signifies, what gave rise to it, what will result from it, or what to name it. We simply know that something has changed, and we know that the change has called us to attention. Wisdom calls us to attention by way of a cry, but the cry does not name itself: it is named by the one who hears it and then named again. The first name Ford shares is "blessing." When Elizabeth heard Mary's greeting, the child leaped in her womb. Elizabeth was filled with the Holy Spirit and exclaimed with a loud cry, "Blessed are you among women and blessed is the fruit of your womb" (Luke 1:41–42). But what does this blessing have to do with "wise discernment"? Much of the rest of Ford's chapter 1 serves as a response to this question.

> Discernment of cries and crying out with discernment are near to the heart of the meaning of a prophetic wisdom that is involved in history and oriented to God and God's future. (19)

Ford takes a first step in the movement from "cry" to "discernment" by asking, "What is the difference between something said and something cried out?" (19). He answers that there is "no general answer"—just as a cry has no permanent name, it has no general meaning—*and* that this rule applies both to those who cry out and to the content of the message. The meaning of a cry is not intrinsic to it but appears only through the relation of the cry to the one who uttered it; meaning lies in between the speaker and the spoken. But who hears it, and what is heard?

> These things are not likely to be learnt through normal methods of education or investigation. This is . . . deeply personal understanding that is dependent on trust and other qualities of relationship. . . . It is about something new, a handing over of all things that, when worked out in history, leads to unprecedented things being seen and heard. (22)

To hear what is spoken is to enter into some ongoing relationship with the speaker and what is spoken.[5] This may be why the Spirit lacks any general name in itself: the purpose of its appearing is inseparable from the relationships that are formed in response to its appearing. The fact that the speaker

---

5. Ford's account of discernment, from the cry to a kind of unknowing to a knowing in relationship, corresponds to Charles Peirce's account of *abduction* as the initial, conjectural, yet really possible stage of perceptual, scientific, and religious knowing. It also corresponds to Hardy's study of Coleridgian abduction.

has no permanent name, or the cry any self-evident content, does not therefore lead to a strict doctrine of unknowing, or apophaticism. For Ford, only everyday knowing is inadequate to disclosing what has been spoken,[6] and Luke has this everyday way of knowing in mind when he writes of what is hidden from the wise yet revealed to infants (Luke 10:21). Do not, says Ford, think of infants in only a literal sense; think also of a dimension of us that has the kind of knowledge that precedes our well-formed ways of knowing the world. To be an infant before the Word is to be able to receive it as something new and renewing: a meaning handed over like our ancient traditions are, but as if handed over even prior to them. This is something "handed over to me by my Father" (Luke 10:22): the Father who is author of all words, whose words are all of his creation and all that we are called to perform within it. To be an infant means that if the ways of this world have left you ill, illness cannot define all that you will have, nor poverty if you have been impoverished, nor treasures if you have received too much, nor death if you have been delivered over. The handing over from Father to Son is exhibited and embodied in all the chains of transmission we know here in this world; they belong to its pattern, but it is not exhausted by them. It is the handing over of "handing over" itself, and to receive this is to be transmitted from one chain of transmission to a new or wholly renewed one and is, in that sense, to be like an infant. "Father, into your hands I commend my spirit," Jesus "cried with a loud voice" (Luke 23:46). For Ford the cross both enacts and transforms the archetype of transmission and Sonship.

To answer the question raised a section earlier, Ford appears to argue that every case of speaking and transmitting is ultimately of the form of the relation of Father to Son and Son to Father, realized only in the triune life of God. It is, no less, a lesson about each worldly event of generation, but we will be frustrated if we think that questions we ask about the worldly will be fully answered when we consider the divine. Even the divine leaves us with what appears to be an agonizing question: how can death be God's means of redeeming us? Ford cites Luke 24:5, "He is not here but has risen," as if to answer: Jesus's death is not like ours, except in agony; in this death comes Jesus's appearance to his disciples on the road to Emmaus, his resurrection, and his return in the Spirit. This death is a "handing over," not merely a continuation of the transmission of God's Word but an ultimate display of it: the transmission of God's Word as Christ and, with him, all flesh, to the Spirit.

[On the road to Emmaus (Luke 24:13–53), there is an] extraordinary intensity of life in relationship. . . . The opening of eyes, minds and scriptures is part of a handing over of responsibility by Jesus to the disciples. . . . [T]he decisive event

6. Not that everyday knowing is impoverished. It is how we know the world and live in it, ask for and obtain food, and conduct our business, including the business of academic inquiry and the effort to gain knowledge.

is to be the "power from on high," the sending of the Holy Spirit. That is the ultimate transfer, a sharing of life from God, which is about whole persons and communities being transformed; but first, in immediate proximity to his death, the risen Jesus shares his wisdom. (38)

With these words Ford completes a meditation that began with "Wisdom is a mother of many children, and Jesus . . . is one" (15). Shall we learn that Jesus fulfills his life as Jesus when he too bears the children of wisdom? And does this come through his death and resurrection, as "the risen Jesus shares his wisdom"? And shall we learn that "commending his spirit" is proximate to leaving his disciples to do the work of the Spirit as led by the Spirit? If so, at least three implications follow directly.

Following Jesus after the resurrection means living life in the Spirit. Ford's theology is therefore a meeting place of what we may call Yale Christology and British (Anglican) pneumatology. This is primarily the topic of chapter 5 of CW.

This transformation—of discipleship into life in the Spirit—is enacted by way of a hermeneutic of resurrection. Ford rereads the Gospel according to such a hermeneutic. This is a Christian analogue to the rabbinic hermeneutic of midrash: rereading the plain sense in its relation to the calls and cries of life's new settings. It is a hermeneutic of transfer and transformation, of renewal in infancy and maturity: a verbal tracing of the life of the Word incarnate as it commends its spirit not only to God to receive it but also to the community of disciples to follow after and embody it. Resurrection breeds the transformation of Christology into pneumatology. This is primarily the topic of chapter 2.

The hermeneutic of resurrection is enacted in (and serves as prototype for) the salvation history of worldly death and resurrection. Ford thus takes up the narratives of both Israel and church as types for a christo-pneumatology of life after death in this world. In the life of Israel this comes by way of narrative cycles of destruction and rebirth, from Exodus to Job to recent rabbinic responses to the Shoah. In the church it comes by way of the narrative of death and resurrection, by way of Eucharistic practice. These are topics of chapters 3 and 4. I turn, next, to illustrate these implications through commentaries on selected excerpts from Ford's work, from chapters 5, to 2, to 3 and 4.

Chapter 5: Jesus, the Spirit, and desire—a wisdom Christology

For me this chapter serves as a prototype of Ford's British (Anglican) yet non-non-American postliberalism, capturing the moment where Christology breeds pneumatology and pneumatology breeds future Christologies. The chapter also illustrates how central Ford's account of "cries" is to his theology and how central his analysis of "moods" is to the study of cries: in this chapter, the optative mood or "desire." "Cry" and "desire" are therefore not mere tropes in Ford's work; they provide irreplaceable access to his theology. As noted earlier, the cry is mark of some change, and the mark is known only by what it does rather than what it represents. As Ford portrays it, furthermore, the cry has a double effect, drawing the observer to attention while at the same time awakening the observer's sense of assurance that there is indeed help in this world for those who cry. If and when aid comes, the sign has a third effect: signifying that there is knowledge in the world of how to help this one and that this knowledge is actualized as help comes. This helping need not be direct: while one cry may be for help "to cross this street now," another may be to help "reorganize the health-care system in the next four years." Ford's chapter comes itself as a cry with its own triple effect: hear Jesus's cry on the cross and bear his cross; enter thereby the blessings of the Spirit that Jesus has left with us; and, serving that Spirit, embody, declare, and share its blessings with the world.

> The utterly vital thing to be learnt is the incomparable desirability of God . . . and how to follow Jesus in his realisation of it. (160)

If the central sign of Ford's chapter is the transfer of Jesus from body to Spirit, then the central effects of this sign are the transformation of Jesus's disciples into servants of the Holy Spirit, transferring God's Word from Scripture to ecclesial work. Ford's chapter delivers its message about worldly work in the Spirit through a reading of Luke's desire to share the truth of "the things about which you have been instructed" (Luke 1:4), of God's desire for his Son, whom he fills with the Spirit (3:21–22), and of Jesus's desire that his disciples give up the desires of this world for the desire for God's kingdom and for him (12:29–34; 9:23–25). The leading trope is thus of desire to transform desire, from this world to the kingdom, without leaving life in and care for this world.

> One of the most powerful passages in [the Wisdom of Solomon] links spirit/ Spirit not only to wisdom but also, through her, to creation, the glory of God. . . . "For wisdom, the fashioner of all things, taught me. . . . For she is a breath of the power of God, and a pure emanation of the glory of the Almighty. . . . She renews all things; in every generation she passes into holy souls and makes them friends of God . . . for God loves nothing so much as the person who lives with wisdom" (Wisdom of Solomon 78:22–28). (165–66)

Impressed with scholarly claims that Luke was deeply influenced by the Wisdom of Solomon, Ford reads Luke's portrayal of the transformation of desire (Luke 12:19–34, cited on p. 159) as an account of the transformation of worldly wisdoms into embodiments of the Word. Luke's narrative thereby delivers a lesson in wisdom, as if to say: "Know the Word as it is embodied on earth, but also know each embodiment as it reads and is read by each other embodiment." There is a kingdom of embodied words here, named the kingdom of God, since each member is God's Word incarnate. It is also a

kingdom of Wisdom, since Wisdom is a name for the consequence of reading
the divine Word by way of each of its embodiments. Such reading is action in
the world in imitation of the Word, so that this is also a kingdom of actions
taken in remembrance of Christ: the embodiments of Christ in the everyday.[7]
In this way, Ford's account of the cry comes full circle. Earlier I noted how Ford
read "the cry" as mark of a discernment that surpasses the limits of everyday
knowledge. By this point in chapter 5, he has returned to the everyday as a
place where worldly discernment can be transformed into an embodiment of
divine Wisdom.

> Job, read and reread alongside the Gospel, offers a discipline that might train
> our attention to concentrate on the cries of Jesus and, through him, on the cries
> he hears now. Job helps to draw attention back again . . . to the intractable . . .
> quality of intense suffering as expressed in the cry from the cross. (171)

> Job helps Christian reading that attends to the crucified and risen Jesus Christ
> as himself God's desire . . . whose traumatically tested desires embody God's
> risky involvement in the contingencies of history. (175)

"God's risky involvement" means attention not only to new sufferers, but
also to "new events that challenge past categories" through which Christians understand suffering: "Job's suffering, leading into wrestling with his
friends and God, was such an event, as was the Shoah, which has raised radical questions for both Jews and Christians. So too was the complex event
of Jesus Christ in his life, death, resurrection, and the giving of the Holy
Spirit" (175–76). Ford's reading of Job alongside the Wisdom of Solomon
alongside Luke illustrates the synergistic character of his pneumatology, which
is always also a Christology. In terms I introduced earlier, Ford reads Job's
cry as reemphasizing the "triple effect" of Jesus's cry on the cross. (a) There
is suffering here that commands our attention. While exceeding our comprehension, this suffering immediately moves us to act, enacting previously
unrecognized capacities to respond to the cry in a reparative way. (b) We may
later (even if a mere moment later) experience our engagement in such action
as a new and blessed discovery: that there is energy here to respond to such
suffering. (c) To experience our reparative activity as a blessing is in some way
to replicate the blessing: not only to enact it but also to reflect on it. To observe
one's actions as a blessing received is to introduce into the world not only the

7. "Christian life is participation in the encounter of Christ with the world." Dietrich Bonhoeffer, *Ethics* (London: Collins, 1964), 130–33, quoted in David F. Ford, *Self and Salvation:
Being Transformed* (Cambridge: Cambridge University Press, 1999), 247. Ford's reading of Luke
complements his various readings of Bonhoeffer. "Because Christ stands between me and another,
I must not long for unmediated community with that person" (Dietrich Bonhoeffer, *Life Together*
[London: SCM, 1954], 43). Ford indicates how Christ's participation in the worshiping community—as "kingdom of actions"—enables discernment to emerge within the "ordinary day."

blessed activity but also a witness to it. This representation of blessing might appear only as an icon, an image that signifies "blessing" only to observers already attentive to blessings. But this representation could also emerge as a fully articulated witness that proclaims and instructs others in the character and joy of reparative activity.

Ford's account of this triple effect displays what we might call his "reparative pneumatology": a three-stage narrative of the Spirit's movement in response to the cry. In the next section, I explore the three parts of Ford's narrative in more depth as a three-stage account of our capacity to know the cry of suffering as a call to action and a blessing.

Reparative Pneumatology as a Narrative of Cry-and-Response-and-Blessing

Chapter 5 of CW narrates these three stages of the Spirit's response to the cry: (a) moved by the Spirit, we respond to some cry as a message of suffering; (b) we then reread our response as a message of blessing in the world and thus as a sign of the Spirit's healing work; (c) our witness to this blessing thereby enters the world as a message in its own right. Others may now interpret this as a sign of blessing in the world. If so, our reflection has become a witness to the Spirit's healing work. Here are more extended readings of these stages.

1. The cry that commands us to attention signifies only by what it does, which is to stimulate healing action

In Ford's terms, the cry has an "abundance of meanings" (CW, 3), so that to hear it is not simply to perceive something already known, but to be opened to hear and see in new ways that engender new ways of responding. To hear the cry is thus to "discern," which is to observe something "startling" (37) and "transformative" (38) that becomes a source of renewal for the one who discerns (33–41). For Ford, discernment requires the attentiveness we may associate with the disciplined scientist[8] and the transformative ways of seeing and speaking we may associate with the gifted poet. Ford calls regularly on the works of Irish poet Micheal O'Siadhail to illustrate such transformative capacities. Here, for example, Ford introduces what he calls the "post-Holocaust wisdom" of O'Siadhail's book of poetic reflections on the Shoah, *The Gossamer Wall*: "O'Siadhail uses the whole range of moods inspired by the urgency of complexity of doing justice to the cries of the victims" (142):

---

8. The university nurtures discernment only when it integrates the activities of research, teaching, *Bildung*, collegiality, interdisciplinarity, and responsiveness to the needs of society (see Ford, "An Interdisciplinary Wisdom," CW, esp. 316–36).

> *Destruction turns all their presence into absence*
> *unless some testimony breaks their infinite silence.*
> *In remembrance resides the secret of our redemption. . . .*
> Can how we remember shape what we become? . . .
> Humble siftings, a patient tentative process;
> Angles and tangents of vision, layered witness.
> No closure. No Babel's towering overview;
> With each fugitive testimony to begin anew. . . .
> Never, never again. Pleading remembrance
> Whispers through the gossamer wall:
> *Promise us at least this.* An insisting silence.[9]

I note these lines because they capture Ford's attention to the polyphonous sound of each victim's cry. No cry permits "Babel's towering overview"; meaning and response is there ("Nothing less may insure against our hell"),[10] but there is no closure, no return to the Enlightenment's "rage for everything certain and hierarchical."[11] Ford quotes Kenneth Grayston's characterization: "It is clear from the various words used to describe those who heard Paul's instruction . . . that no fixed terminology was in mind."[12]

2. When we respond, we receive this solitary cry as if it were already part of a communicative process that moves among the cry, our response, and the context of practices and capacities out of which we respond

In the setting of Ford's pneumatology, we may also refer to this process as a community of three interrelated "persons": one who cries, one who responds, and the context of response personified as a living community—or society of communicants. To name each of these "persons" is to emphasize the three-part relations that bind each one to another one as guided by the third, prototypically binding those who cry to those who respond, as guided by the community in which the cry is heard. To name them persons is also

---

9. Micheal O'Siadhail, *The Gossamer Wall: Poems in Witness to the Holocaust* (Newcastle: Bloodaxe Books / St. Louis: Time Being Books, 2002), 112, 118, 121, quoted in *CW,* 143. Used with permission.

10. Ibid., 120, quoted in *CW,* 141.

11. I believe there is a significant dialogue to be heard between Ford's account of the cry and Edith Wyschogrod's manifesto for what she calls the "heterological historian" (that is, the historian "who hears the other"). Wyschogrod's argument is that even the postmodern historian, who was otherwise dissuaded from making truth claims about the past, is called to a higher responsibility when it comes to recording the cries of those who have suffered in the past. Are these "truly" cries of suffering? Wyschogrod responds to this question in her poignant and very detailed book *An Ethics of Remembering: History, Heterology, and the Nameless Others* (Chicago: University of Chicago Press, 1998).

12. Kenneth Grayston, *Dying, We Live: A New Inquiry into the Death of Christ in the New Testament* (London: Darton, Longman and Todd, 1990), 25, quoted in *CW,* 184.

to link these three-part relations to Ford's account of the relations that bind together the three persons of the Trinity.

In the last section of chapter 5, Ford rereads Luke yet again, this time by way of 1 Corinthians, offering a "wisdom Christology" that complements the wisdom pneumatology displayed in his Joban reading of Luke. First Corinthians introduces "Christian wisdom" explicitly as a means of discerning that which "surpasses understanding" in "the message of the cross." Interpreting Isaiah, Paul declares that this is the wisdom that makes the wisdoms of the world "foolish": that which "no eye has seen, nor ear heard."[13] How then is it seen? By way of the Spirit: "these things God has revealed to us through the Spirit; for the Spirit searches everything, even the depths of God" (1 Cor. 2:10, in CW, 182). And how is the work of the Spirit known? Ford says: by the way it "inspires wisdom, knowledge, prophecy, teaching" (183)—in other words, by way of its consequences in the actions of those who attend to Jesus's cry. The Spirit is known in the communicative process—and the active community of persons—that links cry together with response. This is the process and the community of Christian wisdom. Each participant in this process and community is known only in relation to each other. This means that no participant is known discretely (the way we claim to know discrete facts in the world); considered by itself, each participant is known only polyphonically and ambiguously, as "that or that or that." Each is known determinately only in relation to each other. This is why "it is clear from the various words used to describe those who heard Paul's instruction—teleioi, pneumatikoi, sarkikoi (1 Cor. 2:6, 13–15; 3:1, 3)—that no fixed terminology was in mind,"[14] not even to identify the process of instruction in God's wisdom. This does not imply a radical apophasis, however, for God's wisdom can be spoken by other means: by the way all the wisdoms of this world interrelate with each other as all are transformed, bit by bit, into God's wisdom. Divine wisdom is thus neither earthly wisdom nor non-earthly wisdom; it is earthly wisdom transformed by the divine. So, Ford adds, "if Christ is the wisdom of God, then part of what those appeals imply is that Paul and the church are to embody God's wisdom. Indeed, this may be the most important single thing to be said about wisdom christology: that its meaning is found mainly in lives, practices, and communities" (187). Jesus's cry thus acquires its meaning through the lives and practices of the persons—individuals and communities—who hear and respond to it. Through those lives, its singularity is received as if part of a reparative community of interrelated persons.

3. The first stage of reparative pneumatology—the cry that commands reparative action—is characterized as such only by way of the second

13. 1 Corinthians 2:1, 7, 9, quoting Isaiah 64:4—and cited in CW, 181.
14. Graystone, Dying, We Live, 25, quoted in CW, 184.

*stage, in which the cry reappears as participant in a communicative
process and a reparative community*

Analogously, the second stage is characterized as such only by way of a third,
in which those who respond to the cry "reflect on" their actions and proclaim
them to be responses to this cry. This third stage brings hope and promise,
since it names the blessed fact that "our Redeemer lives" so that cries may be
answered in this world. But the third stage brings great danger as well: the
community that names itself in this way may mistake its account of the cry
for the cry itself. In this case, what could have been a source of blessing would
tend to become an idol, a humanly constructed representation that is taken to
be an embodiment of God. In this case, Jesus's cry would be represented as
precisely what it is not, as God's wisdom is reduced to the terms of worldly
wisdom and some hearers are thereby elevated to the status of God's representatives on earth. If these hearers have social influence, they could serve as
false prophets and teachers; if they have political power, they could acquire
totalizing authority over other hearers.

Ford's implicit response to both the danger and the promise of this third
stage is made explicit when the wisdom Christology he presents in chapter 5
is read in relation to his accounts of suffering in chapters 3 and 4. In chapter 3,
"Job!" and chapter 4, "Job as Post-Holocaust Wisdom," Ford identifies the
conditions for a nonidolatrous theology of the cry.

Wisdom out of Affliction

Job 3:20–26, "Why is light given to one in misery and life to the bitter in soul,
who long for death but it does not come. . . . Why is light given to one who
cannot see the way, whom God has fenced in?" [Ford:] Job cries from out of the
depths of the worst imaginable, the fulfillment of what he has dreaded most. . . .
What response can possibly be made to this comprehensive and intensive suffering? . . . [The] book of Job is about wise living before God in the face of
extreme testing. (*CW*, 90–91)

These first words of chapter 3 introduce the condition for a nonidolatrous
theology of the cry: fully recognizing that the cry is not just any cry, but a
cry of Job ("from out of the depths of the worse imaginable") and of Jesus
on the cross and of the Shoah. Any cry is the voice of another that interrupts
one's self-enclosure. But beyond interrupting self-enclosure, the cry of Job, of
Jesus, and of the Shoah interrupts any imaginable means one has to respond,
exposing the finitude and inadequacy of all of one's habits of action and,
beyond them, all of one's inherited traditions[15] and communities of action.

15. Tradition as *mesorah* or "the process of handing on what is more significant for a community—orally in face to face relationships, in writing and in symbolic action. Tradition is

This is why it is a cry of ultimate despair. It calls us irresistibly to attention and leaves us there, ever commanded to act but also incapable of acting.

For Ford, Job's cry therefore marks "the trauma of affliction." In Simone Weil's terms, affliction (*malheur*) is suffering for which there is no answer: "Affliction causes God to be absent for a time, more absent than a dead man."[16] So Job cries, "Why did I not die at birth? . . . I have no rest; but trouble comes" (Job 3:7–26). Weil concludes, "[A]ffliction is not a psychological state: it is a pulverization of the soul by the mechanical brutality of circumstances." The poet O'Siadhail cites the trope of Paul Celan's "black sun": "Unwholesome radiance. A devious implacable will / outpaces all explanation. / The black sun shines."[17] The black sun shines but with no light, calling to attention but with no object of attention. The cry calls us insistently, but we have no idea what to do. The result is frustration beyond frustration, the exhaustion of a tradition of belief and practice; more than the death of individual bodies, it is the death of a communicative process. This is the setting of a potentially nonidolatrous pneumatology of the cry.

If traditions of belief and action are silenced before this cry, then the cry cannot be represented and those who claim to identify it are utterly deceived. To persist in the deception is idolatry, substituting a representation of the cry for the cry itself. The fatalistic alternative is to infer, therefore, that no response is possible and that the cry is a sign of unrelieved affliction. Neither the narrative of Job, however, nor that of Jesus ends in such despair, because each introduces a third something we have not yet considered: neither the stark affirmation nor rejection of a tradition, but the transformation of one tradition and community into a new one. For Ford, this is the birth of "a new Heaven and a new earth": not of a singular and determinate end of days, but of this recurring moment when the Spirit comes and the cry of affliction is followed by the birth of a transformed tradition and community. Ford cites Susanna Ticciati's words in *Job and the Disruption of Identity*. In response to Job 3:5, "Let gloom and deep darkness claim it. Let clouds settle upon it," Ticciati comments, "The cloud which Job invoked in league with darkness to expunge his day (Job 3:5), becomes, in parallel with the 'swaddling bands' of the sea, a procreational and nurturing image (3:9a) being brought into harmony with the womb of 3:8b which is freed once more to play its life-giving role."[18] Job's

---

a function of all trans-generational communities whether religious, cultural, political, legal, scientific, or scholarly. At its best, it is about passing on what is judged to be important, reliable, and essential for a good future for the community" (CW, 195). Ford offers a fuller characterization in CW, chap. 6, 194–207.

16. Simone Weil, "The Love of God and Affliction," in *The Simone Weil Reader*, ed. George A. Panichas (New York: David McKay, 1977), 442, quoted in CW, 104.

17. Micheal O'Siadhail, *The Gossamer Wall*, 25, quoted in CW, 106.

18. Susannah Ticciati, *Job and the Disruption of Identity: Reading beyond Barth* (London: T&T Clark, 2005), 105.

cloud of despair, we may say, is also a cloud of unknowing that marks the birth of a new way of knowing, new light where there was only "black sun."

Ticciati and Ford read what we may call an "eschatological code" out of the movement from Job's loss of family in the prologue to his recovery of family in the epilogue. By way of this code, Ford meets three challenges that Joban theodicy poses to postliberal Christian theology, and the way he meets these challenges reveals the force of his reparative pneumatology. In the next, concluding section of this chapter, I describe the challenges and how Ford meets them.

Wisdom's Reparative Spirit

Three challenges to postliberal Christian theology

Anticipating the afflictions of Christ and of the Shoah, the afflictions of Job challenge postliberal Christianity in three ways.

1. THE CHALLENGE OF IDOLATRY

Job's affliction is, in short, that his religious tradition has failed him. Job's sorry friends cannot identify a way out of his affliction, since they cannot imagine their tradition's taking any form other than the one they know. If theirs is a religion of "measure for measure," then in their eyes it shall always be, and Job's wounds can only be a consequence of his own sins. In the terms I applied to Ford's reparative pneumatology, they have idolized their religious understanding, smoothing over any contradiction between their understanding and the empirical reality they observe. But what if, perceiving the contradiction, another of Job's friends were converted to the opposite conviction: that this and perhaps any tradition is overwhelmed by the current facts on the ground? What if Job's affliction were a sign that suffering simply makes no sense, so that, in response to it, one may equivocally act this way or that? We might label this "the idolatry of fatalism" and observe that fatalism and traditionalism are joined by a *coincidentia oppositorum*. In this case, both share the assumption that religious traditions identify God's will univocally, so that if a religious tradition contradicts experience, then either experience is deceptive, or our tradition—and the divine will—fails us.

2. THE CHALLENGE OF SUPERSESSIONISM

Job's cry offers a paradigmatic opening to the Christian supersessionist, who, I imagine, may reason this way: "Here, after all, is an apparent type of the people Israel's perennial struggle with the rewards and punishments of covenantal justice. Israel's affliction marks the failure of its covenant—either because Israel's punishment is justified but eliminates it, or because its covenant was false. Will Israel not recognize that Christ replaces its covenant and

Christ alone saves it?" For Ford, such reasoning displays what I have labeled idolatry's *coincidentia oppositorum*, since the supersessionist applies the same law of measure for measure to both Israel and the church. By that law, Israel loses its covenant (as punishment), and the church gains it (as reward): either–or. According to Ford's reparative pneumatology, however, both the Joban and the Gospel narratives promise the afflicted a new birth that exceeds the either–or of this law. What if the supersessionist replies that only the church understands this promise? It would be in the spirit of Ford's narrative to answer, "Even if we granted that—which we do not—are you suggesting that Christ's disciples would speak in the manner of Job's friends? No, they would assure Job that his Redeemer lives, and, recognizing their finitude, they would add that he will speak to Job in his own manner."

3. The challenge of schism

Like the American postliberals, Ford perceives in supersessionism a failure of the church to be the church, not first in relation to the Jews but in relation to Christ. The primary failure is hermeneutical. Supersessionism's eschatological code has only two stages, not three: marking the end of this and all traditions, the cry of affliction signals and is replaced by the coming of Christ, which is life in the end-time. For the supersessionist, this means that all cries are signs of the end-time, since all are already answered by Christ. If so, not only Job's cry, but also the entire Old Testament, represents a cry of affliction that is already answered in Christ. The Gospel narrative therefore replaces rather than interprets the Old Testament, since it reads every Old Testament text the same way: as sign of the end-time. The Gospel therefore reads the words of the Old Testament as no longer words (to be read in different ways in different contexts), but as self-evident marks of a known cause (technically, *indices*): Christ has come in place of Israel. In effect, the Old Testament is therefore no longer Scripture, understood as the revelation of God's will; Christ alone is that Scripture. But what then of the Gospel narrative itself? It reveals God's will, but not in the manner of a script to be read and interpreted. The words of the Gospels also become self-evident marks of a known cause: the life of Christ and the end-time it delivers. But *supersessionism* names a vast literature of commentaries and homilies that interpret the Gospel narrative: are these not the products of textual interpretation? One mark of the failure of supersessionism is its self-contradiction. Because the words of Scripture are in fact words, supersessionist readings are often readings but guided equivocally and unpredictably: sometimes by the unacknowledged hermeneutics of reading and sometimes by what we may call their explicit "law of replacement." By this law, reading is replaced by seeing, the text of Scripture by the facts of Christ's life. The defining mark of the whole process is that *these facts are facts as seen by the supersessionist author*. This is the mark of idolatry, since it identifies divine actions with a human representation of them. And this, finally, is why supersessionism leads first to schism. Because the Spirit is not in fact limited by such representations, different supersessionist authors will tend to see and represent the Spirit in different ways. Mistaking their representations for reality, they will tend to read such differences as marks of truth or falsity—most often the truth of "what I see" and the falsity of "what you claim to see." But this is the rule of schism. Supersessionism's rejection of the Jewish account is one case of the larger rule of schism.

In their humanity, postliberals are not wholly immune to schism. As indicated by the two halves of this book, American and British postliberals may at times assert themselves, one against the other, in the fashion of two schismatic churches.

For God's sake! Ford's replies to the challenges

The idolatries we are considering arise out of misdirected efforts to respond to severe trauma. Ford's rereading of Job provides a vocabulary for characterizing postliberal Christian theology as an effort to repair such idolatries, including those that may arise within any level of postliberal repair itself. On one level, he rereads Job as a type of Israel suffering severe trauma and facing the idolatrous temptation of either traditionalism or despair. Job's traditionalist friends smooth over the implications of his suffering in order to preserve tradition as they already know it: "Because their wisdom was radically threatened by Job they could not be content with disagreement. They had to attack Job's whole position. This inevitably involved undermining the credibility of his cry. . . . This is a classic move by ideologies that are challenged by the intensity of human sufferings" (CW, 126). Tempted by despair, Job finds no adequate answer to his cry until God appears in the whirlwind: God alone redeems Israel from its temptations, enabling it to resurrect its religion in a new way, a new heaven, reformed for life in a new world, on this earth.

On another level, Ford rereads Job as a type of the modern church, tempted by antimodern traditionalism and modernist secularism and redeemed by God alone, in the whirlwind, and not by way of humanly constructed mediations (including those dubbed "religious"). American postliberal Christian theologians tend to witness the whirlwind in Scripture; British postliberals tend to witness it wherever the Spirit pleases.

On yet another level, Ford may reread Job as a type of postliberal theology itself, whenever its reparative work is interrupted by the specific temptations to which it is liable: supersessionism or schism and the excesses of which either side of the schism accuses the other. Schismatic Anglicans, for example, accuse the Americans of sectarianism and bibliolatry, while schismatic Americans accuse their complements of naturalism (worldly and political) and conceptualism.

How to respond? Act for God's sake alone! That is Ford's most general guideline. But it is not sufficient in itself, since *there is no way to overcome the temptations of idolatry without God's direct assistance*. There is no "method" of overcoming these temptations, no humanly constructed or received discipline that will keep sufferers and potential human redeemers alike on the straight and narrow path between despair and willful ignorance. As portrayed in the Passover Haggadah, God and God alone brought Israel out of bondage, "not by a ministering angel, not by a fiery angel, and not by a messenger, but by Himself, in His glory, did the Holy One blessed be He do so."[19]

Ford's guidelines:

1. PURSUE KENOTIC OR NEGATIVE ACTIONS THAT MAY, GOD WILLING, REMOVE MERE HUMAN CONSTRUCTIONS AND PREPARE SPACE FOR MEETING GOD:

   (a) Do not smooth over the specific signs of affliction that underlie the postliberal project.

The Joban figure: Job's friends "refused a compassion that endangered the coherence of their system" (126)—their religious tradition and worldview.

A contemporary analogue: The complementary temptation is to fear the Spirit's freedom and hold fast only to trusted images of Christ. In Ford's reading[20] this is, in the face of severe trauma, to cling to an established knowledge of God rather than risk an encounter with God in the unknown. It would be difficult to criticize such clinging were it not performed in the face of someone else's terrible suffering.

Responding to supersessionism: For Ford this temptation is a challenge to the church rather than the synagogue, because it implies that the death and resurrection of Jesus Christ did not introduce any hermeneutical renewal. Supersessionism implies, first, that the Old Testament is limited to the law of measure for measure (the "Deuteronomic theodicy"). It implies, second, that the New Testament retains this law: because of Israel's sin, it is punished with the loss of its covenant. Like Job's friends, supersessionists smooth over the sufferings of the one whose condition would upset their theological peace, objectifying Israel as recalcitrant other and in the process applying to Christianity the law they attribute, derisively, to the religion of Israel.

Responding to schism: Schism is a correlate of supersessionism, since both reduce the gospel message to a hermeneutic of replacement and a theodicy of measure for measure where there is a victor who possesses the gospel truth and a vanquished who has lost it. In the case of postliberalism, schism appears

19. *Passover Haggadah*, new rev. ed., trans. Rabbi Nathan Goldberg (Hoboken, NJ: KTAV, 1993), 14.

20. The reader will kindly assume that each time I attribute something to "Ford's reading," I mean to add "I trust" or "As I read him."

as competition between American and British types, each accusing the other of reenacting rather than repairing the dislocations of modernity. Such accusations are paradoxical, since they are primary symptoms of the either–or reasoning that postliberals attribute to the modern condition.

> *(b) Do not misperceive this affliction as operating in isolation from all established tradition and community.*

The Joban figure: Job also risks freezing his despair into an idol. Ford is particularly attentive to God's "twice-repeated verdict" that the friends, unlike Job, have not spoken what is right *of God* (*CW*, 128, citing Job 42:7–8); for Ford, the book is, after all, about epoch-changing trauma rather than everyday protestations against tradition. At the same time, Ford also notes Job's capacity for excess: "If the verdict of the book is in favour of Job's way of speaking of God, then this might mean that God is pleased with those who refuse to fit new experience unquestioningly into traditional teaching about God, who ask radical questions. . . . [But] that might be . . . too binary an analysis of a complex argument in which both sides are needed and neither simply wins" (129). To put it differently, the friends may be faulted, but tradition should not be. It simply needs to accept change when it truly comes.

A contemporary analogue: The complementary temptation is, swept into the Spirit's movement, to forget or neglect the Logos, as if the way of renewal were not also the way of the Son, nourished by his Word.

Responding to supersessionism: Ford applies his corrective to both sides of supersessionism's false binary (or, in the terminology I employ in this book, false "dyad"): Israel's new law will not be altogether new but will remain in relation to the old.

Responding to schism: Ford applies his corrective to both sides of the schism between British and American postliberalism. On the one hand, Israel's suffering anticipates the emergence of a new world, a corrective to excessive criticisms of the British for following the Spirit where it will. On the other hand, Israel's new law will not be altogether new but will remain in relation to the old, a corrective to excessive criticisms of the Americans for turning to the Word as trusted guide in times of upheaval.

> *(c) Remember that all these representations of affliction and repair are marks of relationships that exceed them; all arise out of specific relations to the world and to its Creator and Redeemer.*

The Joban figure: For Ford, one relationship alone marks both Job's friends' error and Job's vindication: *unmediated relationship to God.* For the time of trauma represented by the book of Job, this relationship has only two visible marks: the sufferer's *fear of God for naught* and *God's presence in the whirlwind.* Gazing on the humanly actionable side of this relationship, Ford cites "fearing God for naught" as Wisdom's emblem in times of affliction:

"And he said to humankind, 'Truly, the fear of the Lord, that is wisdom; and to depart from evil is understanding'" (Job 28:28, quoted on 137). In his suffering, Job experiences his life as for naught. Nonetheless, he fears God within that "naught" and in that fear marks his enduring relationship to the Creator. He does not see Wisdom, he cannot fathom divine justice or mercy, but he fears God nonetheless, and this fear cuts into the unknown and names it still the place of God. The friends, in contrast, fear the knowledge they have of God rather than God. One hears in Ford's writing echoes of Meister Eckhart, "who prayed to the *Gottheit* that He free me from *Gott*": the friends "see God's transcendence as one of indifference, having no need of people and their goodness. . . . [Thus,] 'Eliphaz the Temanite answered: "Can a mortal be of use to God? Can even the wisest be of service?"'" (22:1–3). . . . By contrast, Job finds history, and especially his own story, far less transparent. . . . He is passionate with God, and at the heart of this is his constant crying out to God and against God. Addressing God takes precedence over speaking about him" (130).

A contemporary analogue: Ford's postliberalism carries a protest against the impersonal theologies of his day and thus, we may assume, against any postliberal temptation to insulate one's empirical church, one's tradition of scriptural reasoning, and one's theological doctrines and systems from the vicissitudes of the Spirit and of lived relations to God.

Responding to supersessionism: Theologies of the early church are representations of the life of Jesus Christ as itself a reparative reflection on Israel's affliction. They lose their meaning if they are detached from Israel's life before, during, and after affliction.

Responding to schism: Postliberal calls to "return to Scripture" or to "return to the Spirit" are appropriate to certain times and places in church history. These calls do not address all conditions of the church at all times.

> *(d) Do not mistake representations for factual or doctrinal truth claims. They are essential to the reparative process, but only as sources of context-specific proposals about how to act.*

The Joban figure: Ford reads within Job "a searching wisdom" that includes both the sciences *and* the wisdom that emerges at their limit, and God's own inquiry that "searches out the human heart" (133–38). "Surely there is a mine for silver and a place for gold to be refined" (Job 28:1). Ford argues that the efforts of "the searching self" are not in vain but are the beginning of wisdom (137), since, in Ticciati's words, they "always occur in response to the divine searching."[21] The searching self is "the searched self living before a searching, testing, purifying God" (137). For Ticciati, "the mind of human attainment becomes the human self that lies beneath this activity. . . . God's

---

21. Ticciati, *Job and the Disruption of Identity*, 189, quoted in CW, 137.

searching is the context and presupposition of his address to humankind . . . :
'Then he saw it and declared it, he established it and searched it out (*chakirah*).
And he said to humankind, "Behold, the fear of the Lord, that is wisdom"
(Job 28:27–28).'"[22] Job's affliction marks the meeting point between the human
and divine searches: not the end of science, but the point at which the sciences
specific to his day and place meet their limit and call out, as it were, for divine
repair. "There is no denial of the trauma and its terrible inexplicability; but
alongside it is an affirmation of a creation that cannot be drawn into trauma
without remainder, and of a God who can, through being questioned and
questioning, open the eyes of the afflicted to who he is for his own sake: 'Now
my eyes see you' (Job 42:5)" (115).

A contemporary analogue: These dimensions of wisdom may be adopted
as guidelines for three dimensions of postliberal repair. The first is to acknowledge the reparative force of postliberal inquiry as a human endeavor.
The authorizing occasion for this endeavor is not some event of human will—
such as a guild-specific research project—but a communal and civilizational
affliction that may be a sign of divine searching. In response to this sign,
postliberal theologians generate various representations that may prove to
be of service to the divine search and thereby to repairing this affliction.
Among these representations are, for example, postliberal reflections on "the
errors of modernist binarism," "the inadequacy of 'experiential-expressivism'
and 'propositionalism,'" and calls to "return to Scripture" and to "attend
to the Spirit." The second dimension of wisdom is to recognize that these
representations could turn into idols if they were mistaken for truth claims.
The result would be such potential errors of postliberalism as bibliolatry or
naturalism. The third dimension of wisdom is to recognize that if and when
they arise, such idols can be repaired only with God's help. To seek this help
does not mean to "hope and wait," but to pray for the specific kind of repair
that is needed. This means to investigate the matter, literally pray for God's
help to conclude the investigation, and seek to become agent of whatever
help God appears to offer.

Responding to supersessionism: Theologies of the early church are not
truth claims about the world, but visions of how the world will change. They
cannot therefore serve as the basis of truth claims about Israel as it has been
in this world or as it will be in the next, but only of expectations about what
will guide its change.

Responding to schism: Postliberal claims are not propositions about the
world, but belong to specific programs of action.

> 2. SHOULD REPRESENTATIONS BECOME IDOLS, THE FOLLOWING ACTIONS
> MAY PROVE USEFUL (SINCE THE PROCESS RESTS ON PRAYER, ONE CANNOT

22. Ibid.

MAKE GENERAL PREDICTIONS BUT ONLY CONJECTURE BASED ON PAST
EXPERIENCES)

> *(a) Inspect the representation (cum idol) closely until it reveals*
> *marks of its finitude and inadequacy.*

The Joban figure of Christ and a contemporary analogue: In chapter 5 of
CW, "Jesus, the Spirit and Desire," the Joban type becomes its antitype, Christ,
but without superseding the Joban account: "Job, read and reread alongside
the Gospel, offers a discipline that might train our attention to concentrate
on the cries of Jesus and, through him, on the cries he hears now. Job helps to
draw attention . . . to the intractable, unassimilable, and unconceptualisable
quality of intense suffering as expressed in the cry from the cross" (170–71).
For postliberal Christians tempted to lose the person in the representation of
Jesus Christ, Ford's Job marks the interruptive otherness of the one on the
cross. Emphasized through Ford's reading of Luke-Acts, this is to mark the
human in the divinity of Christ and thus the mutual otherness of humanity
and divinity.

Responding to supersessionism and schism: A first step in repairing either
supersessionism or schism is to rediscover marks of interruptive otherness
within it, traces of something outside the self-referential surface of its now
frozen representations.

> *(b) Interpret those marks, per hypothesis, as signs of the*
> *representation's etiology—in particular, the reparative*
> *activity to which it makes some finite contribution.*

The Joban figure of Christ and a contemporary analogue: To be reminded
of Christ's humanity is, for Ford, to be reminded of the "contingencies of history" that direct representations of Christ and of postliberal theology back
to the historically specific narratives of affliction with respect to which they
have meaning. For postliberal Christians tempted to lose the historicity of
Christ, Ford reads Luke as setting the narratives of Jesus Christ deep within the
contexts of humanity's history since creation, Israel's history since Abraham,
and the history of the emergent ministries of Christ's disciples (153–65). By
analogy, postliberal Christians must read their representations of the modern
and postliberal church only as marks of the histories that underlie them, and
this means as marks of postliberal proposals for renewing the church today. To
repair idolatrous tendencies in postliberalism is therefore simply to remember
the lived context of postliberal inquiry and to respond to it once again, but
with more discipline and more prayer. "Scripture and tradition come together
most explicitly, intensively, and influentially in prayer and worship" (207).

Responding to supersessionism: Examine these marks as signs, on the one
side, of Israel's actual salvation history and, on the other side, of some unrepaired affliction *in the contemporary life of the supersessionist community*.
Ask what has led this community to smooth over its burdens with the veneer

of a triumphant church and replace images of its actual burden with those of a vanquished "Israel."

Responding to schism: Examine these marks as signs, on the one side, of specific crises in modern Christianity and, on the other side, of regional differences in the American and British contexts.

> (c) Note the mood and modality of the representation. When employed as idol, its moods will be indicative and imperative. To repair this, seek to recover its interrogative mood and, with it, its modality as sign of the unknown. Per hypothesis, reread the representation as a mark of some specific event of unknowing (a context of affliction).

The Joban figure of Christ and a contemporary analogue: Ford's writings have, over many years, displayed close attention to moods in scriptural and theological discourses, such as indicative or optative. In the context of our study, this means that he attends to rhetorical markers of personal embodiment, contingency, and historicity in religious discourse. To link representations to moods is to remove them from abstraction, which in this case is a sign of their self-referential and thus potentially idolatrous use. In chapter 1, Ford examined the moods Luke associated with Jesus's life. In the *indicative*, for example, Luke describes a world blessed by Jesus's coming; in the *imperative*, Luke invites the reader "into an obedience of faith rooted in Jesus's own obedience," and in the *optative*, the ultimate desire displayed in Luke is desiring good for the other.[23] Now, when representations freeze into idols they tend to display only indicative and imperative moods, as if they were truth claims about what is, and as if "is" necessarily implied "ought." By way of illustration, Ford notes that Job's

> friends tend to use indicatives and imperatives, and when they use an interrogative the answer is usually clear. Job uses indicatives that raise radical questions and interrogatives that reflect genuine bewilderment, with an optative longing for answers to his questions through direct engagement with God. There is a pervasive subjunctive openness to possibilities regarding God that can hardly be imagined by his friends. His imperatives are in the service of the other moods, all of which are rooted in his cry to God. (128–29)

23. More precisely, Ford examines the moods Luke associated with the various cries that marked Jesus's life. *Indicative*: Luke describes a world blessed by Jesus's coming. "Luke tells of Jesus being surrounded by cries of affirmation," from before his birth through his death (*CW*, 45). *Imperative*: Luke invites the reader "into an obedience of faith rooted in Jesus' own obedience" (46). *Interrogative*: "The life, death and resurrection of Jesus can be seen as an interrogation of his generation, his disciples and the leaders of his people and at the same time their interrogation of him" (47–48). *Subjunctive*: The mood of surprise accompanies Jesus's parables, calling readers to the unexpected movement of the Spirit (48). *Optative*: "In Greek the optative is the mood of desire" (49). The ultimate desire displayed in Luke is desiring good for the other (50).

Postliberal tendencies to idolatry may, analogously, be repaired by transforming imperatives and indicates into interrogatives, subjunctives, and optatives.

Responding to supersessionism: The moods of the contemporary community's supersessionist claims are most likely indicative (with claims such as "Israel has lost its covenant") and imperative (such as "Jews must repent"). Propose ways of transforming these into interrogatives (such as "What conditions underlie this contemporary community's efforts to repair the world and Israel?"), subjunctives (such as "Conditions of unrepaired affliction could do this"), and optatives and cohortatives that gather like-minded colleagues to work for ways to repair such conditions ("We want to help repair these conditions").

Responding to schism: Note the predominance of indicative and imperative moods in postliberal theologies that tend more to schism as well as to supersessionism (see chaps. 5 and 8). Note how the other moods appear more often in postliberal theologies that tend less to schism and supersessionism (see chaps. 2–4 and 6–7).

> (d) To recover the interrogative and optative is to reread the frozen representation of some purported truth claim as the representation of one's relationship to something as yet unknown. To perceive such a relation, even per hypothesis, is to break an idol. The next step is to uncover more and more about this relationship.

The Joban figure of Christ and a contemporary analogue: One primary consequence of idolatry is to hide the uncertainty that prompted it in the first place. Ford's recommendation is to seek to recover this uncertainty and the trauma that may underlie it and then resume the "searching wisdom" (*CW*, 133) that would respond to the trauma in reparative ways (172). In the Lukan narrative, this wisdom *is* Jesus Christ crucified and resurrected, for in Christ God has met humanity in the unknown and has raised humanity from its affliction: "Jesus Christ as the wisdom of God related to all things and people" (204). The wisdom disclosed after affliction is thus knowledge by and of God alone: in Christ God names the unknown after himself and draws the afflicted to knowledge only by drawing the afflicted into direct relationship with God. The unknown of affliction cannot be known the way one knows this world, because affliction ends this world as it has been known. This unknown is known only in the renewal of this world, and this renewal is not beheld, but received by way of relationship. Ford labels the mind drawn to know God in this way "the crucified mind," which, "shaped by the mysteries and depths of God revealed in Jesus Christ, involves wholehearted participation in the radical transformation begun in Jesus Christ" (184).

Responding to supersessionism: Adopting the interrogative mood reopens supersessionist claims to two dimensions of unknowing. One is the unknowing that accompanies Israel's relation to God in times of affliction: the narrative of Jesus Christ belongs to this unknowing and respects it. The other is the unknowing that underlies each claim and community of contemporary supersessionism: What is this really about? What do the claimants really know?

Responding to schism: Ford's greater openness to unknowing corresponds to his lesser tendency to schism.

> *(e) One's representations of something as yet unknown may be read as context-specific faces of one's relation to this unknown. The work of repair is now to offer hypotheses about the etiology of those faces. This is to resume a process of representation somewhat like the one that generated idols.[24] It is, however, now a reparative process of representation, since it is an attempt to obtain fresh representations that, one prays, will not now be put to idolatrous use. The repair is thus a form of corrective repetition. The only difference is that there has been a fall, which, like Adam's, adds a level of caution and explicit warning to the original creation and call to "go forth."*

The Joban figure of Christ: We return now to where this chapter began: with the pneumatology through which David Ford attends to the various faces of God's relation to us. We now see that these faces appear out of the unknown, as the faces of God's redeeming relation to us in times of and after affliction. The face that appears cannot end suffering like magic, but it redeems suffering of the affliction of unknowing. In this case, it is the face of Wisdom, which redeems by drawing the sufferer into a renewed relationship with the Creator, one through which knowing is possible again and thus inquiry, a "mining after silver and gold." For Ford, Paul epitomizes the human knower who is redeemed from affliction only through a relationship with the Redeemer that is so intimate that it seeds imitation (albeit nonidentically): "Paul meets the Corinthian Christians . . . in person and with testimony to his own ministry. Alongside the message of Christ crucified, the most daring and even scandalous element in what he writes is that he claims to embody what he is talking about: 'Be imitators of me, as I am of Christ'" (1 Cor. 11:1) (187).

Responding to supersessionism: Facing these dimensions of unknowing, supersessionist theologians revisit the original occasions for Christ-centered repair: another opportunity to engage Christ in the unknown and see if indeed the afflicted's relation to Christ and to Israel warrants the clarity and distinctness of supersessionist claims. There is no limit to the value of revisiting these occasions.

Responding to schism: Of the theologians examined in this book, Hauerwas and Ford tend to privilege unknowing in complementary ways: the one

---

24. It is, technically speaking, comparable to the process of phenomenological inquiry.

waiting on the Spirit to bring knowledge as the Spirit wills, the other waiting on Christ, and neither urging conceptual clarity before the fact.

> (f) "Repair again!" is therefore the overall guideline, but with the added warning "to recognize, this time, that you are not so innocent. You are no redeemers, but only finite humans who, in imitatio Dei, have heard the cry of your neighbor and have turned to help. But remember, what you offer might kill your neighbor as much as help her: representations can become idols, and redeemers devils. In you, one power is mixed with the other. There is no magic to protect her or you from this, only prayer and discipline, and we cannot predict whether one will succeed and the other will be heard. Therefore, pray harder this time, wait a little longer to hear God's reply, and, by way of added discipline, make a greater effort to see who else may have turned to help and how helpers may also help one another."

A contemporary analogue: Like inquiry after affliction, inquiry after idolatry is the same as inquiry before idolatry: an effort to repair. "Inquiry after" is simply a touch wiser. It is chastened by the narrative of Job and by the Gospels' witness to Jesus's crucifixion and resurrection. Postliberal inquiry after idolatry is reparative inquiry that can no longer presume it has "gotten things right": the categories of repair remain "postliberal" in the ways I have characterized them throughout this book, but the spirit of repair cannot be "postliberal." It cannot be anything of human hand but can be only of the Spirit. To this end, Ford cites Paul Ricoeur's Christology, which seeks "to preserve the classical Christian tradition's balance between . . . the affirmative way of saying positive things about God through the use of analogies within creation and . . . the negative or apophatic way of recognising the radical inadequacy of all affirmations" (215). The model of balance is trinitarian, "as a wisdom worked out before God in the complexities and ambiguities of history that calls for it to be rethought continually if it is to be held wisely" (213).

Responding to supersessionism and schism: To reengage Christ in the unknown is to revisit prayer as the context for reparative inquiry. This prayer includes petition for repairing whatever affliction underlies tendencies to supersessionism or to schism, and it includes contrition, acknowledging that efforts to smooth over the unknown are acts of human will and not of divine instruction.

> (g) The next stage of repair cannot be predicted, since it belongs to the mystery of one's—and one's community's— intimate relationship with God in the Spirit. This is the moment where, we may imagine, the decision to live for

God's sake alone may—if it will—be met by whatever God may do and say for humanity's sake alone.

The Joban figure of Christ and a contemporary analogue: In Ford's commentary on Job, the Satan articulates right from the start the sapiental goal of Job's narrative: "Then Satan answered the Lord, 'Does Job fear God for nothing [*hachinam yare iyov elohim*]?'" (Job 1:9). Ford comments, "The Satan's question about Job in 1:9 indicates what is probably the main point of the book: the wisdom of fearing God for nothing. . . . The whole book might be read as a commentary on this verse" (99):[25] "The Hebrew for 'for nothing' is *chinnam*, meaning gratuitously, for no purpose, without cause, and the Septuagint translation is δωρεάν 'as a gift'" (100). If "the whole book is needed to explicate the meaning of fearing God for nothing" (100), then here too we must say that the whole drama of Job is needed to portray the process of transformation, God willing, from idolatries to new birth. For this kind of repair, the lesson is not Wittgenstein's "the rest is silence," since there is no sitting silent before idolatry. The lesson, one might say, is unspeaking, which, like Meister Eckhart's "decreation," entails a lot of doing, including saying. The wisdom of Job concerns the agency rather than the fact of speech. Within the frame of his investigation, Wittgenstein could not speak of God's speech, but postliberal theologians speak only because they have witnessed God's speaking, and that speaking alone seeds the possibility of lending their voices to God's agency. There is idolatry in the face of such witness, but there are also paths beyond idolatry, and for Ford, Job traces such a path—anticipating the path of Jesus Christ. The reparative lesson for postliberalism is thus "Be prayerful; wait for the Spirit to answer when you ask 'Where is God?'"

Responding to supersessionism: To repair supersessionism is not to proclaim it contradictory, such as some effort to diminish Christian uniqueness or to make Christian witness secondary to Israel's covenant. It is, instead, to recover the degree and manner of unknowingness that accompanies lives lived in *imitatio Christi*.

Responding to schism: To repair schism is, comparably, not to diminish difference, in this case between theologies that specialize either in reparative pneumatology or in reparative Christology. It is instead to remember the unity of God in whom alone these theologies find their purpose and their rest.

---

25. Ford cites this as the lesson of Ticciati and many others.

8

John Milbank

Supersessionist or Christian Theo-semiotician and Pragmatist?

Preface

For five years, I had the great joy of working with John Milbank as a colleague in the University of Virginia Department of Religious Studies.[1] The department's students and staff were not necessarily aware of the joyous part. Secretaries regularly overhead Milbank and me locked in verbal combat, voices raised, hyperbolic criticisms thrown. Students in the seminar we co-taught gave us an ultimatum: "No more arguing in class or we won't come!" What students and staff did not often see was that over tea or beer, we would later talk at great length and in calm but energized voices over wide swaths of ideas, texts, theologies. Our public misbehavior masked our friendship, shared interests, and overlapping theological grounds (for where else to wrestle than on common ground?). In the context of this book, I will suggest that we shared a post-liberalism and that the heat of our exchanges measured the friction between supersessionist and nonsupersessionist ways of practicing postliberalism.

In this chapter I hope, on the one hand, to reaffirm my friendship with Milbank and toward his postliberalism and, on the other hand, to examine his supersessionism as a mark of non-postliberalism. I will argue that this mark

1. I am grateful for extensive comments on this chapter from Chris Hackett, Jacob Goodson, and Daniel Weiss, and, again, very helpful editing by Rodney Clapp.

provides a second indirect argument on behalf of the thesis of this book. The first indirect argument was that, as illustrated in the work of John Howard Yoder, projects of Christian nonsupersessionism are incompatible with non-postliberal theologies. This second argument demonstrates the obverse: as illustrated in Milbank's work, projects of apparent Christian postliberalism are incompatible with supersessionist theologies, and indeed such projects will prove to be non-postliberal to the extent that they are supersessionist. This second argument will be easy to make, since Milbank would most likely agree both that his project includes supersessionism and that he is not concerned to be consistently "postliberal." I will therefore devote little space in this chapter to making this argument and thereby to concluding the thesis of this book. The rest of the chapter addresses a corollary: Milbank's work displays the conflicting influences of postliberal and non-postliberal rules of inquiry. I doubt such conflict would concern Milbank, and I do not examine it as a point of criticism per se. My goal is instead to examine one of Milbank's most consistently "postliberal" studies—the essay "Pleonasm," in *The Word Made Strange*—and show thereby how some of his central arguments would appear if they were made to conform only to his postliberal tendencies. I suggest that contradictory tendencies within that essay demonstrate the persistence of such conflicts in his work, but, at least in this example, Milbank's non-postliberal tendencies are the weaker of the two. By way of experiment, I will suggest what "Pleonasm" would look like if the latter tendencies were elided, and if Milbank therefore made his case within the terms of postliberalism. The result of the experiment is that such a Milbank would work in ways surprisingly close to the philosopher Charles Peirce: offering a pragmatic critique of secular modernism and, in its place, proposing a Christian theo-semiotic that need not employ supersessionism as part of its apologetic for Christianity in the after-modern world. An apology to general readers: this chapter will be more technical than the previous ones, because Milbank's more technical philosophical theology provides the clearest ground for examining his contradictory tendencies.

Introduction: Competing Tendencies in Milbank's Philosophical Theology

Milbank's writings have received a good deal of attention the past decade, from both supporters and critics. The arguments get complex, I believe, not only because of the range and complexity of Milbank's readings in the history of thought, but also because of the conflicting interpretive tendencies that appear to inform his reasoning. I do not draw attention to such conflict as a means of criticizing Milbank. To the contrary, I think inner conflict and outer contradiction often accompany the work of pioneering thinkers, since they inhabit both a former and an emergent universe, whose copresence displays itself as contradiction. What matters here are the public truthfulness and efficacy of the emergent direction, rather than an individual thinker's efforts to display its apparent coherence. My analysis of contradictions in Milbank's work is therefore directed not to Milbank but to his readers and, even there, not to give instruction but to clarify—as if to say, "Okay, you want to claim x. Do you see that it is closely associated in his work with y? Do you also want to claim y? If so, OK, but be up front about it. If not, do you have a plan for separating the x from the y?"[2]

An Overview of the Competing Tendencies

Milbank's writings are rich with textual, historical, and interpretive detail, and I would not presume to account for the details of his argumentation in this short space. My comments therefore focus on only the more general patterns and form of his argumentation, about which I offer only a few selective observations:

- As illustrated in *The Word Made Strange* and in particular the essay "Pleonasm," Milbank's writing displays two dominant and competing tendencies of inquiry. I label one of these Milbank's *pragmatically realist tendency* (or his Christian postliberalism), the other his *foundationalist tendency* (or his Christian triumphalism). I judge the pragmatic

2. As I will illustrate below, the x and y here do not refer only to postliberalism and supersessionism, but also to a family of associated claims that mark his work. As for Milbank himself, I trust that he would affirm much of what I will suggest about his work. He is certainly unapologetic about his supersessionism, and he may also be unconcerned about any "imperfections" in his "postliberalism." Moreover, what I take to be the extrascriptural dimension of Milbank's theology may well have patristic antecedents in Cyril of Alexandria and others. (My thanks to Paul Jones for this suggestion.) I am not about to suggest that this is not a way to practice Christian theology. My claims are, instead, that (a) contrary to some of Milbank's arguments, Christian realism or what you may take to be a "true" or "orthodox" Christianity does not require supersessionism (or require the blanket criticisms offered of Islam); (b) moreover, Milbank's own arguments for Christian realism (or Christian orthodoxy) are logically separable from, and in that sense independent of, his blanket criticisms of Judaism (and probably of Islam); (c) these criticisms are warranted by something indigenous to his sense or experience or intuition of Christ's presence (I am not sure how Milbank would prefer to characterize this sense), but this sense or experience need not—and most likely should not—be promoted as a condition for Christian realism; (d) to adopt such a sense as condition for Christian belief and theology is to promote a Christian foundationalism whose logical form is modern nominalism rather than realism—or at best of a naive realism of the Lockean sort (which is adopted as well by many modern nominalists); (e) a Christian foundationalism of this sort is logically compatible with some features of Christian postliberalism (such as some postliberal criticisms of modern humanism and antihumanism), but logically incompatible with other features, as those illustrated in this essay.

tendency to be by far the stronger of the two, because if it operated alone, considerably more of Milbank's argument would be preserved and without inner contradiction. I focus primarily on "Pleonasm," which I believe is one of the strongest illustrations of Milbank's pragmatism and Christian postliberalism. Correlatively, it shows only modest influence from his foundationalism.

- While each of Milbank's arguments includes an element of supersessionism, the strength of that supersessionism corresponds with the relative strength of his weaker, foundationalist tendency of inquiry. I will argue that if his stronger, pragmatic tendency operated alone, Milbank's arguments would not need to include any supersessionist claims. Since his pragmatism is fully consistent with Anglican postliberalism, I will infer that his supersessionism is correlative to his non-postliberalism.

- Milbank's context of argument is *Christianity amidst European postmodernism*. He argues that this postmodernism has had a corrosive effect on Christian theology and on the realist ontology and account of language that ought to accompany this theology. This postmodernism, according to Milbank, is displayed prototypically in Derrida's account of language and its accompanying technical critique of realist ontologies. He argues that, along with its accompanying defense of radical skepticism, this critique has too many Christian realists backpedaling: not because their realism is unworthy, but because they lack the technical tools to defend it. Milbank offers his "Radical Orthodoxy" in part to give Christian realists reason to stop backpedaling: to criticize Derridean postmodernism on its own terms and thereby fashion a language for promoting Christian realism in the modern and postmodern academy. Up to this point, Milbank's argument remains within the bounds of his pragmatism and postliberalism. He takes the argument a significant step further, however, claiming that Christian realism is not only defensible but also true in general—in other words, that it offers a ground for universal claims that may compete with whatever universal claims modern and postmodern theory offer.

I will argue that this additional step is unnecessary in the terms laid out in Milbank's pragmatic claims and that he can achieve all he needs to achieve without the addition. With that addition, however, his strong defense of Christian realism gets mixed up with a Christian foundationalism that is liable to the same criticisms he makes of Derridean non-ontology and of modern secular ontology. To be sure, Milbank is aware of claims like mine, and he does not agree. He argues that what I am calling foundationalism is simply Christian realism itself and that claims like mine mix in an unnecessary relativism with the postliberalism. I do not agree, since I do not believe postliberalism is relativistic or foundationalist.

Illustrating Milbank's Competing Tendencies:
A Study of "Pleonasm, Speech, and Writing"

Chapter 3 of *The Word Made Strange*, "Pleonasm, Speech, and Writing,"
plays a significant role in Milbank's effort to beat the Derrideans at their
own game. He argues that their game is, in this case, to resuscitate William
Warburton, bishop of Gloucester, as a surprisingly early progenitor of their
own attempt to deconstruct theological uses of biblical language.[3] Milbank's
strategy is to deconstruct the deconstructors—to show that Warburton's
argument neither anticipates Derrida nor succeeds on its own terms, and
thereby to undermine one of postmodernism's potential pedigrees. Turning to
a contemporary of Warburton's, Milbank then examines the work of Robert
Lowth, bishop of Oxford, as what he considers a successful effort to achieve
what Warburton failed to achieve.[4] Milbank thereby sets the genealogical
ground for his critique of Derrida. Having shown that Lowth succeeds where
Warburton fails, he traces two competing lines of argument: the successful
line that leads from Lowth to Vico to Hamann and, by implication, to Milbank, and the unsuccessful line that leads from whatever Warburton-like
ancestor Derrida might want to claim to the Derrideans and to the havoc they
have wreaked in contemporary Christian thought.[5] In this section, I survey
Milbank's basic argument.

Milbank introduces Warburton's *The Divine Legation of Moses* as a surprising object of attention for recent postmodernists:

> [The book] was first set upon by Frenchmen in 1744, when the section of the
> work dealing with the origin of language was removed from its original theo-
> logical context and translated by Leonard de Malpeines as *Essai sur les Hiero-
> glyphes des Egyptiens*. . . . With the revival of interest in the problematic of the
> origin of language in the climate of poststructuralism, Malpeines' edition was
> republished in Paris in 1977, smothered by commentary by Patrick Tort and
> Jacques Derrida. (55)

For the Derrideans, Warburton's study of the origins of language represented *"une étonnante ouverture logique au materialisme,"* errant only

---

3. William Warburton (1698–1779) was an English critic and churchman, bishop of Gloucester,
and author of *The Alliance between Church and State* (1736) and of *The Divine Legation of
Moses* (1737–88). A portion of the latter was translated and published as *Essai sur les Hiero-
glyphes des Egyptiens* (Paris: Maspero, 1977).

4. Robert Lowth (1710–87) was a bishop of the Church of England, a professor of poetry at
Oxford University, and author of *A Short Introduction to English Grammar* (1762) and *Lectures
on the Sacred Poetry of the Hebrews* (1787).

5. In this way, Milbank's genealogical criticism parallels Charles Peirce's method of criticizing John Stuart Mill through a critique of Descartes, whom Peirce considers Mill's prototypical
antecedent.

in Warburton's failing to note that humanity's *very first writing* was meta-phoric—and not only, as Warburton claims, humanity's subsequent efforts to repeat this first writing. Once this one error is corrected, say the Der-rideans, Warburton's study is both materialist and, in Milbank's words, "drastically subversive," since it tends to suggest "that all language, all culture, inevitably involves those concealments . . . and acts of political violence which emerge through specific metaphor as the very matrices of human meaning" (60). From this perspective, language introduces all these subversions because language arises out of *writing*, and writing introduces subterfuge into human life. As a material thing, writing appears to be pres-ent to the reader like any other object of experience (a rock, a rain shower). But as a medium of language, writing redirects its readers' attention from the object of experience (this cuneiform, this scratching on paper) to a meaning that is "distanciated"—which, in the postmodern lingo, means that it lies somewhere else. Writing distanciates because it separates the source of meaning, a linguistic sign, from its reference, the meaning of the sign. Writing deceives because it veils this distance behind the materiality of the sign—this inscribed rock, this scratched paper—so that what is absent appears present. So too, say the Derrideans, all language separates humans from the meaning of language. Since meaning is ultimately about the world humans live in, writing and thus language itself separate humans from their world.

In Milbank's perception, Derrida celebrates this alienation, while Chris-tianity solves and removes it, reuniting humanity with the world God gave them. If Christianity retained the alienating character Derrideans ascribe to it, then its language of salvation would not be salvific but would reinstan-tiate writing's subterfuge all the more viciously, since it had promised to remove it. Milbank's goal is thus to expose the errors in Derrida's assump-tion that language begins in writing and in the inference he draws from it: that all language distanciates. Within this chapter, Milbank pursues this goal in two steps. The first is to show how the Derrideans misread Warbur-ton—for Warburton argued, with reason, that aboriginal writing was not distanciating but an invitation to engage ritually with the created world as the aboriginal place of meaning. Milbank's second step is to suggest that even though Warburton was not as "bad" as he appears in Derridean dress, a contemporary of his, Robert Lowth, offered a much stronger model of the origins of language that can withstand the errors of both Warburton and the Derrideans. From Lowth through Hamann, Milbank then offers his alternative to Derrida: accounts of the aboriginal orality of language and of the nondistanciating force of oral learning. Milbank then reintroduces Christianity as a model of humanity's capacity to reenact the aboriginal reception of creation into language.

Four Central Steps in Milbank's Argument

1. *Milbank introduces Warburton's* The Divine Legation of Moses *as a commentary on the origins of language.*

For Warburton, Egyptian hieroglyphics and biblical Hebrew represent two alternative prototypes: the former leading to an idolatrous practice of naming the word, the latter to a way of redeeming the idolatry. According to Warburton, all human beings first adopted "languages of action" consisting of gestures, pointing, and mimicry. The languages generated fables, which captured relationships between natural events and ritualized human response to them. These fables were then symbolized by brief etchings, each standing for the natural event that was central to a given fable. The etchings may have evolved into hieroglyphics, then into ideographs. Signs of shared qualities rather than of things and actions, the ideographs functioned as metaphors rather than as miniatures or icons. In the last stage, ideographs evolved into alphabetic speech and writing, and what was originally a language of action became a language of metaphor. For Warburton, the effect of this evolution was to distanciate language from its original source and thus from its aboriginal relationship to creation. As Milbank notes, this is the feature that caught Derrida's attention as a prototype of his own work: an Anglican bishop, no less, as source of deconstructionism! For Warburton, the point was that in the evolution of language in ancient Egypt, alphabetic writing separated itself from its origins. Culture was thereby distanced from humanity's primordial knowledge of the natural world. Warburton speculates, however, that the Egyptian rulers, undoubtedly unconsciously, sought to repair the breach by translating their own language of power back into the ancient hieroglyphs (58). In place of their aboriginal meanings, the hieroglyphs were made to bear the new ideologies of the rulers, who thereby imposed their understanding of the world onto Egyptian culture. For Warburton, this last move represents the legacy of Egyptian idolatry: a human order is made to replace the divine creation.

Warburton argues that biblical Hebrew emerged as an antidote to this idolatry. He speculates that Hebrew evolved in a different way. Following Locke, Warburton interprets the words of Genesis—"whatever the man called every living creature that was its name"—to mean that "Adam developed his language according to a rational sequence, in response to clear sense perception. At first, this language was 'extremely narrow,'" but it was "progressively developed by means of the 'natural' tropes" (59). Milbank notes that Warburton inserts "the crudest interventionism" by suggesting that God revealed to Adam the first elements of this natural language in order to speed up the process. Milbank argues that nonetheless, Warburton fails to articulate a clear account of how biblical Hebrew thereby recovered the aboriginal clarity of humanity's language of action. Instead, he refers rather obliquely to the Bible's love of "historical allegory," which means that Warburton's thesis remains simply apologetic: to show that biblical Hebrew achieved what Egyptian language failed to achieve.

Milbank's conclusion is that Derrida's supposed early hero served more as a cipher for Derrida's own conception of the "writing process itself as the extra-human source of error and violence." In Derrida's reading, the hieroglyph represented the linguistic fall: the way that humanity's intimate language was exiled into the distanciation that he associates with writing. As employed by the Egyptian rulers, hieroglyphs acquired the characteristics Derrida associates with modern language: the tendency to display meaning only through the play of difference and difference; because signs and letters lost any intrinsic reference to the world, meaning could be imposed on them only by violence. Milbank concludes that Derrida's account is doubly faulted. One, Derrida misreads Warburton, assimilating his account of the way Egyptian writing obscured its origins to his account of metaphor. Two, Warburton offers a seriously underdeveloped account of aboriginal orality and of metaphor. Unlike Warburton's, however, Derrida's errors seem—in Milbank's reading—to be irreparable.

2. According to Milbank, Warburton's fideistic account of the origins of Hebrew may be repaired and completed through the work of his contemporary Lowth.

For Lowth, "the original 'poetic' speech of human beings was characterized [by] inventive and conjectural powers, [as well as] by an extraordinary mnemonic capacity, whereby the 'minutest circumstances' could be retained in the memory" (64). Milbank comments that "where Warburton emphasized the preserving capacity of *literal* written marks, Lowth insisted rather on the power of oral anaphora, involving a *repetition with variety* as opposed to written literalness" (64). In this "repetition with variety" (pleonasm) biblical Hebrew expressed both the wildness of nature and the spontaneity of spirit where "the . . . inmost conceptions are displayed, rushing together in one turbid stream, without order or connection . . . for to those who are violently agitated themselves, the universal nature of things seems under a necessity of being affected with similar emotions."[6] For Lowth, biblical Hebrew displayed the most exemplary, primitive, and materialist model of this spontaneous merging of expressive spirit with nature (apostrophe) and pleonasm (here repeating the aboriginal syntheses but in ways specific to each context of repetition). In this way, biblical Hebrew enables its leaders to reperform humanity's primordial intimacy with the created world. This Hebrew was oral-cum-written language in which meaning is not distanciated but reenacted in a way that permits growth through participation and thus through learning. The product, in Milbank's

6. Robert Lowth, *Lectures I*, 79, cited in "Pleonasm," 64–65.

terms, is a poetics that ensures "*a certain ontological faithfulness*" (66). It is telling that Milbank makes note of the *humanistic* character of Lowth's poetics: "Lowth inherits a tradition of regarding the grammar and rhetoric of the Bible as unique which stretches far back into the Middle Ages; but now this is ascribed to the peculiar *poeticality* of the Hebrews, and it is his *metaphysical* conception of the Hebrews as co-creators which opens up for the Germans the 'critical' space in which the Bible could be viewed as a human work" (64).[7]

Immune to Warburton's fideism, Lowth is thereby able to identify certain poetic methods that enable the "Hebrews" to preserve such intimacy with nature in their scriptural verses. It is not the literal word per se but these methods of speaking it that capture the power of Hebrew language. This provides Milbank a means of accounting for the metaphorization Derrida found in Warburton, but without losing ontology. At the same time, Lowth's account of Hebrew "materialism" provides Milbank a type of "intimacy with nature" that is not yet ensured by divine revelation per se. Hebrew poetics trumps paganism ("Egyptian hieroglyphics") without the full aid of direct divine intervention.

Milbank concludes that Lowth's and Warburton's theories of scriptural language represent two contradictory types. "For Warburton, pictographs were mere copies of physical things, and mental notions or modes . . . were from the first represented by arbitrary marks. For Lowth, to the contrary, . . . perception of the environment and projection of values spring up together" (68). The two therefore employed two different models of semantics. Warburton maintained a "positivist" view of knowledge, according to which later Egyptian hieroglyphs bore an arbitrary relation to their objects of meaning, and the Hebrew prophets overcame this nominalism only through divine aid. Lowth argued that Hebrew poetics allowed for "mystical allegory," according to which meaning is displayed by way of the mutual relation between two or more textual signs rather than through the reference of a textual sign to its extratextual object. Milbank argues that Lowth's account makes sense of how Scripture works; Warburton's does not. At the same time, Milbank suggests that Warburton's effort is worth redeeming, since he, unlike Lowth, offers a useful account of the errors of pagan—that is, non-Hebrew and non-Christian—discourse. To redeem Warburton would be to replace his account of Hebrew poetics with Lowth's account, as the biblical alternative to pagan discourse.

3. According to Milbank's genealogy, Lowth's insights into Hebrew language were extended by Giambattista Vico and Johann Georg

7. Milbank thereby credits Lowth with contributing to modern biblical scholarship much earlier than may be supposed: "The idea that 'modern biblical scholarship' began when an already established 'historical science' was applied to the Bible, is therefore an illusion." John Milbank, *The Word Made Strange: Theology, Language, Culture* (Oxford: Blackwell, 1997), 64.

Hamann into an epistemological realism that undermines Derridean
nominalism and simultaneously recommends ways of repairing and
completing Warburton's incomplete account.

More than Lowth, Vico emphasized the exoteric character of Hebrew language as key to its realism. According to Milbank's reading of Vico, "all culture and all humanity begins with an original metaphoric tension—manifest through ecstatic bodily gesture—in which the world is symbolically grasped as the story of a divine power whose presence constitutes a teleological imperative for human beings" (73).

Vico then distinguishes between pagan and Hebrew use of metaphor.

> In paganism, Vico believes, this metaphoric tension is immediately collapsed; the absent God is *reduced* to his presence in the inscribed sign. . . . The Hebrews, by contrast . . . preserved both the divine transcendence and awareness of an integrally human activity in the formation of human culture. . . . The Hebrews, like the pagans, continued to inhabit their enabling functional projections, but they did not much mystify the *fictional process* . . . so that history remained for them the work of men, and Genesis records the work of founding fathers and not the intervention of demigods like Orpheus and Hercules. (73)

Introducing his own terms, Milbank suggests that Lowth and Vico offer a means of reading biblical Hebrew as the source of a "non-deceptive and non-violent culture" and that Hamann carries out this reading for us. Biblical Hebrew does this by maintaining humanity's primordial participation in the creative activity of the divine Logos. "For Hamann, the 'naturalness' of the origin of language in fact implies that it is simultaneously humanly produced *and* divinely revealed. . . . In the conscious co-creative work of human beings which 'gives to all creatures their content and their character,'[8] the divine creation is most fully realized, for it is always 'a speaking to the creature through the creature'"[9] (74). Thus "for Hamann 'revelation' *adds nothing* to 'creation,' for the latter is precisely revelatory," and "creation . . . through man and by the power of God, writes an abbreviated, hieroglyphic version of the divine pictograph" (74). But how is humanity cocreative with this logos?

Milbank reads Hamann's response as follows. The fundamental type of humanity's cocreation is not the Hebrew Bible as a whole, but only its vision of Adam's cocreative work. This work enacts the divine gift of logos. After Adam, however, Adam's sin disfigured all human contribution to this repetition. This disfigurement extends also to the Hebrew Bible, whose writings capture the aboriginal metaphoricity of Adamic speech, but only cloaked within the

8. J. G. Hamann, "Aesthetica in Nuce," in Ronald Gregor Smith, *J. G. Hamann* (London: Collins, 1960), 192.
9. Ibid., 199.

fallibility of the written text. The genius of Hebrew poetics was to reenact the primordial metaphoricity of Adamic language, but this reenactment is realized only in oral repetition and then only by dint of fallible, humanly constructed tropes. Adamic language may be recovered only through an indefinite process of rereading the text as strictly a sign of this oral performance.[10] The Bible is therefore not a direct revelation of God's Word but a human engagement with it. The implication is that logos is fully reiterated only in Christ, not in Hebrew. Biblical writing, like all human writing, remains bound to the finite, and this writing always threatens totalization: Hamann sees this as much as Derrida. Only oral speech has the capacity to protect against this totalization.[11]

But by what guidance does oral performance reenact the Adamic activity, and by what means can humanity end the potentially indefinite cycle of imperfectly reparative repetition? Milbank's commentary on Hamann introduces a sharp distinction between Hebrew and Christian sources—a distinction that appears in his study of Lowth and Vico only in faint hints. For Milbank–Hamann, the performances of biblical Hebrew remain within the cycle of repetition and error, but Christ alone brings to humanity the possibility of reenacting the Adamic activity per se and ultimately of completing the cycle of reparative repetition. This christological claim gives a more tangible meaning to the Milbank–Hamann claim that "revelation added nothing" to creation and that in fact the Bible is not revealed, for the Word is merely observed in Scripture and is encountered only in Jesus Christ.

In the concluding section of "Pleonasm," Milbank radicalizes these suggestions about Christ, introducing triumphalist claims that outstrip the greater complexity of the preceding pages. Tracing out the implications of earlier hints, he now argues that the accounts of Lowth and Vico already subtly anticipated the claim of Milbank–Hamann that the Bible's Hebrew poetics was marred by human fallibility. Milbank draws out an even more radical inference: this fallibility is ultimately fatal, since even an infinite series of corrections would fail to remove the stain of sin and error that is implicit in the Bible. There is,

10. Note Milbank's strong tendency to valorize oral performance over written text. Later I will read this as a sign both of Milbank's intuitionism and of his effort to deny what Derrida affirms and affirm what he denies.

11. When guided—as it may be—by direct, cocreative encounter with the divine Word by way of the divine Spirit, it deconstructs this writing: recognizing (re-membering) Adamic activity within the writing, separating it from its errant accretions, and then—beyond deconstruction—reiterating the Adamic writing, nonidentically, within its present and concrete setting. This reiteration corresponds to what Derrida calls "supplementation." For Milbank–Hamann, supplementation is the nonidentical repetition (pleonasm) through which God graces humanity with the capacity to embody the Word in the concreteness of here and now. For its own "reader," each embodiment is a writing that once again displays the Adamic activity only through the disfiguration of human finitude and error. (Milbank's account, we might add, like Derrida's, works well as a model of rabbinic hermeneutics and of the inner-scriptural hermeneutics the rabbinic tradition often reads in the Bible.)

he says, only one way out of the (Jewish) tradition's ultimately futile efforts to repair its source: the grace of God in Christ. For Christ alone is fully human and fully divine, so only in his presence is it possible fully to recover Adam's primordial acts of naming without error. The Word itself redeems the written word, and the Word itself is given, alone, in Christ.

Questions Raised by "Pleonasm"

In this section, I raise a series of questions that are prompted by Milbank's text. In the following section I will explore answers I introduced at the start of this chapter: "Pleonasm" displays the contradictory influences of Milbank's dominant pragmatic tendency and his unpragmatic foundationalist tendency.

1. Overall characterization

According to the argument of "Pleonasm," speech is the mother of writing; the speaker is more present to the intention and object of speech than is the writer, and more present as well to the addressee. In Milbank's christological terms, the speaker participates in the Logos as the Logos joins speaker, speech (the Word), and listener into its ultimately Eucharistic community. Writer and reader remain, however, one step removed from this community. In these terms, we may say that "Pleonasm" hosts a dialogue between two of the dominant influences on European postmodern philosophy, Saussure and Derrida, while drawing their dialogue into the language of a christological realism. Saussure privileges speech as the seedbed of human language use and describes writing as a secondary, external act. Derrida privileges writing, but recharacterized as the assertion of difference in oral as well as literally written signs. Derrida therefore criticizes the presumption that speech is more "present" to the speaker, since speaking and writing are comparably distant from both authorial intention and the meaning of this intention. "Pleonasm" hints at a correspondence, on the one hand, between Saussure and what Milbank takes to be Gospel orality and, on the other hand, between Derrida and what Milbank takes to be the externality of Old Testament écriture. Reversing the terms of Derrida's critique of Saussure, "Pleonasm" characterizes Gospel orality as the "internal" life of the Word, in relation to which biblical Hebrew illustrates the Word's "external" relation to historical contingency. While the argument of "Pleonasm" is ultimately christological, its addressees are by no means confined to those who share the author's Christianity; its critique is addressed to all readers, including Derrideans. "Pleonasm" therefore appears to address human reason as such or, beyond that, being as such. In this way Milbank's work appears to be unlike the other postliberal projects we have seen, since all the others (including Yoder, although with some exceptions) disclaim this kind of universality.

I would classify the essay's dominant methods of argument as *typologi-cal*, *genealogical*, and *associative*. It is typological in the sense that Milbank reads the arguments of Derrida, Saussure, Warburton, and Lowth as types of universal claims against which Milbank promotes countertypes. His argument is genealogical in the sense that he situates each interlocutor within a certain chain of intellectual transmission, against which he promotes arguments that belong to a competing chain of transmission. His argument is associative in the sense that he measures the validity of these universal claims according to no single exoteric standard, but according to the authority of a network of arguments that he introduces through the course of his argumentation. His essay therefore appeals to measures that are internal to it. Any reader may appreciate the apparent beauty of the essay's argument, but the ultimate measure of that beauty lies at another level within the essay. Milbank does not make this level explicit. This last step separates Milbank's argumentation from that of the other postliberals. Their argumentation is also ultimately christological, but for that reason they address "ultimate argumentation" only to other members of a (or their) Eucharistic communion. When they address general readers, they do so with respect to standards of argument that are available in general.

2. Specific questions

(A) MILBANK'S DISTINCTION BETWEEN LOWTH'S "SPONTANEOUS MERGING OF EXPRESSIVE SPIRIT WITH NATURE" AND WARBURTON'S ATTENTION TO THE "PRESERVING CAPACITY OF LITERAL WRITTEN MARKS"

Milbank appears to favor the Platonic character of Lowth's notion of participation, which he therefore defends against Hans Frei's criticisms (64). Frei finds Lowth's analysis theologically neutral, because he fails to argue for the *truth* of Scripture. In reply, Milbank argues that "it is clear that Lowth regards formal, cultural aspects as in some measure *internal* to theology, because so often he relates them to doctrinal points" (63). In this way Lowth continues "the Renaissance account of man's participation in the Divine creative power" (64). Milbank thereby defends Lowth's Christian pedigree genealogically, showing how he shares in a recognized subtradition of Christian thought. Milbank offers a comparable argument for his own positions: they are valid because they clearly belong to a legitimate hermeneutical circle and not because they can be defended according to some more general standard of inquiry that could be applied in any possible context of inquiry. In one way Milbank's argumentation resembles that of postliberals like Frei, who argue that Scripture displays its conditions of truth only within the lives of particular communities of interpreters. Unlike these postliberals, however, Milbank argues for the validity of his community of interpretation against all comers. How are we to evaluate his standard of argumentation if it warrants universal claims on the basis of intracommunal or esoteric conditions of truth?

I would understand Milbank's argumentation if he claimed, in the fashion of classical rabbinic Judaism, that his community knows the truth only of what it knows and cannot presume that God speaks to other nations as he speaks to Israel. I would understand it if, in postmodern fashion, he claimed that we lack standards of truth, per se, and possess standards only of validity (some criterion of local meaningfulness and consistency). Milbank appears to take a third stand, however: that his position has local truth (as the Jews claim for their positions) but universal extension (as in classic patristic claims)—not that just anyone anywhere can observe the truth of his position, but that those who share this truth (those who know Christ as he is known in Milbank's circle) will be able to display its superiority to any other claimant. Here, "superiority" is a species of truth that is comparable to claims for "strength" or for the "best or richest available account."[12] Comparable to methods employed in debate competitions, this kind of truth would be defended against one other claimant at a time. Its "universality" would thus be established by induction; after we have seen its superiority demonstrated against each of a series of other claimants, we would have reason to anticipate that its superiority could be defended against any future claimants. Ours is not the only possible truth; it is simply the strongest we have yet seen, and we have not yet failed in debates against advocates of any other truth.[13]

If this is Milbank's method, then we might read each of his writings or talks as implicitly addressing particular contexts of debate, the way one might read Paul's letters. This also means, however, that to receive his readings and arguments as true is to receive them as if we were members of his hermeneutical circle or, if not, then to receive them as if prophetic—that is, as introducing new standards of truth whose meanings will be displayed only seriatim as we assume their truth and test it against each case of a former way of thinking (that is to say, in the manner of his own debates).[14] I do not see any coherent alternative.

---

12. A cousin to an "inference to the best explanation"; see Peter Lipton, *Inference to the Best Explanation*, 2nd ed. (New York: Routledge, 2004).

13. In this case, we would share the postliberal argument against Enlightenment universalism: a set does not contain itself (the theory of types), or, in other words, we reason according to certain presuppositions that cannot themselves be defined and defended by the same reasoning. At the same time, we would claim that, de facto, there is no evidence that any argument has arisen that is stronger than ours, so in the meantime we have no reason to lessen our commitment to this argument.

14. In Charles Peirce's terms, Milbank's method—to the degree that what I have portrayed is evinced in his work—is to reason according to "what is agreeable to reason." This method, says Peirce, has local validity but otherwise the validity only of abduction (hypothesis making). More generally, it displays a real possibility (if indeed it has been successfully adopted in some locality), but only one of many, even for any given context of meaning. On behalf of Milbank's method, one might argue that he acknowledges this Peircean claim, and that is the reason Milbank argues consistently for grounding epistemology on a logic of nonidentical repetition. From this perspective, Milbank recognizes the locality of his claim and generalizes his claims only by way

(B) Milbank's claim that "revelation adds nothing" to creation

Milbank's claim appears to be either dogmatic or offered in terms that are evident only to those within a hermeneutical circle. Does the fallibility of Hebrew poetics imply that the Hebrew Bible is not revelation? Milbank has shown us that he shares this assumption with Hamann and others, but this is to demonstrate only that a serious thinker *could* entertain such a hypothesis. The claim does not enable us to weigh the hypothesis relative to others, nor to test its strengths and weaknesses. Are we to conclude that what Milbank presents in a form of a general argument is not meant to be an argument, but rather a cohortative expression, a call to like-minded readers to find support for their beliefs within the hermeneutical circle claimed by Milbank–Hamann?

There are many other possibilities we could examine. For the sake of illustration, let us consider just this one. What if we supposed that biblical Hebrew is fallible but this is how biblical revelation is supposed to work? As Milbank notes, the text stimulates an indefinite series of corrective rereadings, and Milbank–Hamann assume that the goal of the series is eventually to eliminate all error or fallibility. As illustrated, however, in the work of the noted Talmudist David Halivni, rabbinic tradition includes a different option, which Halivni labels "continuous revelation."[15] He understands this to mean that God beckons the reader by way of apparent errors in the text ("maculations," in Halivni's terms), not through the text's plain sense alone. Readers enter into the Bible's "revelation" only when they turn their attention passionately to these maculations the way a compassionate human being turns to aid someone lying in distress on the side of the road. To reread the text is, as it were, to help lift it up from its distress. But does the reader's fallibility not imply that any effort to "lift the text up" will belong to what Milbank calls the tradition's "futile effort" to perfect the text? No, suggests Halivni, each reading can indeed fulfill its reparative task within the finitude of this world, provided we recognize that the maculation is not merely "in the text" but also "in the reader" or, otherwise put, in the specific relation that binds this text to this reader (within his or her community of reading at this particular time). In these terms, the text's maculations are also signs of context-specific problems within the reader's community. A reading completes its task when it identifies these problems and contributes to their repair. In rabbinic tradition, this is what it means to "observe a commandment": not to achieve some infinite standard of perfection but to achieve what is commanded here and now in this historical context. If the commandment is to

---

of analogy, as if to say, just as "x is to c" in my locality, so might you observe that "y is to d" in yours, where $f(xc)$ shares a leading principle (a rule of analogy) with $f(yd)$. In other words, there is some $f(n)$ that repeats itself nonidentically in each of these local contexts.

15. David Weiss Halivni, *Revelation Restored: Divine Writ and Critical Responses* (Boulder, CO: Westview, 1998).

begin the Sabbath at sundown, then it is fully achieved when, in this moment of sundown, we observe the Sabbath. If the commandment is to come to the aid of that person in the street, then it is fully achieved when we come to his or her aid. "Perfect and total healing" is God's work; ours is only to "come to the aid" of this person or this text. Meanwhile, the indefinite series of rereadings goes on, since the reading I perform now speaks only now, and the next moment may call for new reparative readings. From this rabbinic perspective, we would label such renewed readings a "futile series" only if we took our lives and efforts in this world to be futile. But we don't, since we do not imagine a wholly alternative world. From this perspective, to pray for the fulfillment of history is not to seek another world, nor to understand the work of this world as tragic. It is, instead, to take deep satisfaction in the fulfillment offered in each and every moment of reparative reading and worldly repair, while awaiting a time in this world when no human would lack such fulfillment.

What then, of Milbank–Hamann's claim that "Christ alone" ends the cycle of reparative readings? Outside of their hermeneutical circle, the reader does not yet know what fallibility may or may not attend human participation in Christ's work. In this case, Milbank's effort is cohortative. But if so, how are we to understand the relation of his writing to the general reader? Furthermore, are there ways to envision nonidentical repetition other than Milbank offers us?[16] Why must we assume that salvation history generates only a single line of saving repetition? Milbank–Hamann argue that nonidentical repetition is not governed by any transcendental a priori rule. If this is so, we have no basis for presuming single rather than multiple lines of nonidentical repetition. The most Milbank can argue is that there is a hermeneutic circle within which some serious and pious thinkers make sense of living according to their understanding of a single line.

(c) Is Milbank's supersessionism unnecessary?

If Milbank's argument cannot preclude the possibility that "salvation history generates more than one saving repetition," then we have reason to ask whether his critique of Derrida as well as his christological alternative could be preserved without also associating them, as he does, with supersessionism. Following my previous line of reasoning, we may imagine more than one way for a human community to embody the aboriginal intimacy that, in Milbank–Hamann's vision, binds human language with the created world. For Milbank–Hamann, this intimacy is embodied only in the salvific activity of Jesus Christ, in whom the primordial orality and perfection of human language are eternally reenacted. But "Pleonasm" offers no general grounds for precluding

---

16. For example, what keeps us from a "dual aspect" account of each repetition: it may in one aspect fulfill this work while in another aspect it leads on to the next repetition?

other embodiments, and we may appeal again to Halivni's rabbinic reading for one illustration of such an embodiment. According to Halivni's hermeneutic, we might argue that the errors of Old Testament performance need not be repaired "once and for all," since they are repaired in each complete act of reading *for the sake of that moment of reading*. This rabbinic alternative could be excluded only if there were a priori grounds for claiming that "God's presence" has been removed (God forbid) from the Jews. According to the rabbinic tradition, there is no more prophecy, but intimate contact with God is possible through prayer, acts of charity and loving-kindness, and the study of Torah for its own sake. To speak of "intimacy with God" is to speak of moments in which humanity's primordial intimacies are nonidentically repeated. The rabbinic tradition does not recognize the requirement of "repairing that error once and for all." The tradition adopts another line of reasoning: until the end of all time, such fulfillment is available but only within the limits of a given historical moment. Since "Pleonasm" does not offer grounds for precluding this alternative to a "once and forever" fulfillment, Milbank's argument for the uniqueness of Christ's embodiment would appear to be made on the basis of intuition or experience rather than of exoteric argument. But that would bring us to what, in the next section, I call Milbank's "foundationalism": the belief that a single experience or intuition can be rationally self-legitimating and that he may be privy to one.

Pragmatic Repair and Nonpragmatic Critique

In this section, I offer a single set of responses to the questions raised in the previous section. I do not argue that this is the only way to respond, but that it is one line of response that is logically coherent and not precluded by the arguments of "Pleonasm." Here is an overview of the entire line of response. The argument of "Pleonasm" is *associative*, which means that it offers a series of claims that are true to its own premises in a way that is transparent only to those who share its premises. This is not problematic. The problem is that the argument is also *typological*. In the case of "Pleonasm," I use this term to suggest that Milbank identifies individual thinkers with general types of argument *and* that he associates these types with universal claims, so that different types compete in a zero-sum game. Combining associative and typological arguments, Milbank makes universal claims on the basis of nongeneral or esoteric premises. His claims may be true, but his reader has no consistent basis for testing them. Milbank's *genealogical* argumentation displays the result: a fascinating associative-and-typological narrative that raises many interpretive possibilities but that cannot perform one additional feat that Milbank asks of it—to demonstrate the truth of his claims and the errors of those who do not share them. Now for a more detailed account.

1. *Pleonasm as measure of religious practice, and analogy as measure of religious reasoning*

"Pleonasm" offers norms for measuring its claims. In this section I argue that the character of these norms and the way Milbank presents them are appropriate in two of three ways to the methods of "Pleonasm." (1) Since norms are immanent in a practice of associative reasoning, it is appropriate for Milbank to embed the two norms of "pleonasm" and "analogy" within the argument of his essay. (2) Milbank also defines the norms in a way that is appropriate to his overall argument. He argues that "non-identical repetition" (pleonasm) is humanity's only means of reproducing in its *practices* the aboriginal copresence of language and the created world. Insofar as the norms of "Pleonasm" are internal to its argument, then, yes, this claim is consistent with Milbank's reading of Warburton and Lowth. He argues, moreover, that "analogy" is the appropriate method of reasoning about pleonastic practice and, therefore, of evaluating its legitimacy. This claim is also warranted within the context of Milbank's argument. It implies, in fact, that analogy is the form that reasoning adopts in service to pleonasm. If some practice, P, nonidentically repeats itself according to some rule $r(p)$, then it stands to reason that the way we practice P in this particular location represents one application of the rule $r_1(p)$. The way we practice P in another location would represent another application of the rule $r_2(p)$, and the relation of $r_2(p)$ to $r_1(p)$ defines the rule of analogy: (p) serves as a rule of analogy according to which the way we practice P here $[r_2(p)]$ is analogous to what we practiced there $[r_1(p)]$. Analogy is pleonasm in reasoning.

Pleonasm and analogy are therefore defined appropriately within the terms of "Pleonasm." The one problem is that Milbank applies these norms as if they were also warranted beyond the limits of his essay and as if the conclusions he reaches by way of them applied universally. The result, I believe, is *an unwarranted reasoning from analogy*. As Milbank defines them, arguments by analogy should be probable or hypothetical means of clarifying what we know within a finite context (such as this essay) or of raising general claims per hypotheses for future testing. Milbank presents the defining analogy of pleonasm, however, as if it were self-evidently universal. The analogy is this: just as Adam's words engaged intimately with the created world, so is Christ as God's Word intimate with the creation—in other words, so does it nonidentically reiterate Adam's intimacy. This analogy holds strictly with respect to axioms that are implicit in "Pleonasm": (a) that we know of Adam's aboriginal language use;[17] (b) that we know that Christ is God's Word, so that our relationship to Christ should nonidentically repeat Adam's relationship to God's Word.

17. It would appear that for the analogy to hold, our knowledge of Adam must be infallible. If so, this would be an exception to Milbank–Hamann's assumption that the Old Testament's witness is fallible.

Milbank's argument should be that Christians who share these beliefs have a realism already implicit in their beliefs and should therefore not feel tongue-tied in front of nominalist Derrideans. It should be an intra-Christian argument against nominalism or skepticism. As indicated in the previous section, however, Milbank forwards his argument as if it were not limited to an interpretive context like this and as if therefore his argument sufficed for successfully debating postmodernists on their own ground—or modernists, for that matter.

A sympathetic reader might reply that the argument of "Pleonasm" is analogous to the ontological argument, since Anselm's meditations on "that than which nothing greater can be conceived" are analogous to Milbank's meditations on "that the nonidentical imitation of which would enable us to reenact the primordial language of Adam." The analogy would not be that what Milbank conceived "could not not exist," for that would be an identical repetition of Anselm's meditation, not an analogy. Milbank's version of the argument would instead be something like this: there is a conceivable human capacity that, if realized, would grant humanity direct knowledge of this world as it is created; this is the capacity nonidentically to imitate Adam's aboriginal intimacy with the creation; only one literary tradition in history identifies its God as one who has come to fulfill this capacity, and this is the New Testament characterization of Christ. In this reading, Milbank would not argue for Christ's necessary existence, but for Christ's irresistible appeal to humanity's rational desire. No other literature would offer its readers the promise that the narratives of Christ offer. And no other literature would offer a stronger warrant for realism.[18]

18. In Milbank's writing we are, however, dealing with knowledge of matters beyond this world, or, more precisely, of God, the infinite, or what we cannot know directly but only by observing its effects and reasoning per hypothesis to what be the source of those effects. Milbank's grounding assumption is that Christ mediated and mediates the ontological and epistemological gap between infinite being and finite knower or between worldly effects and more-than-worldly causes. Christian postliberals share the more general form of this assumption: God has revealed himself in Christ and by way of the church as the body of Christ. If there are differences on this matter between Milbank and other postliberals, they will concern the knowledge of Christ. As illustrated in the first part of this book, American postliberals tend to argue that the primary means of knowing Christ are acquired through the study of Scripture and that this study has many implicit rules, including each individual's participation in communal worship, learning, and practice. The rules of study include a hermeneutic of reading, interpretation, and practice; they may be illumined by philosophic or other forms of conceptual inquiry, but they are not grounded in such inquiry. American postliberals tend, furthermore, to regard products of the individual theologian's "I think" as only suggestive or hypothetical, and they tend to be suspicious of grounding knowledge claims on discrete judgments of intuition (such as "I saw this" or "I experienced that"). Anglican postliberals share the Americans' attention to Scripture but tend to place greater trust in the workings of the Spirit as a complementary source for knowing God's will—the Spirit as working, that is, in history, including social and political history, in various signs of the affections, and in the created world. They are, however, also suspicious

I note this sympathetic reading because it may be the strongest case that could be made for the nonrelativity of Milbank's argument. Even so, the same objection stands: it may be true within the bounds of this literature and its reading community; outside of these bounds, it belongs to the modality of the possible. On that basis, to be sure, one may wager one's life; but one lacks warrant for delegitimizing or preempting other wagers. There are other reasonable wagers, perhaps even with the conditions set by "Pleonasm," and "Pleonasm" cannot provide the conditions for examining them in their own intraliterary terms.

2. *"Pleonasm" evaluated in the terms of postliberalism*

At the risk of overgeneralization, I will suggest that both American and British postliberals also promote nonidentical repetition as a model of practice, and analogy as a model of reason. Their openness to inter-Abrahamic scriptural dialogue rests on their reasoning that God may speak in one voice to us and another voice to you, and in one voice to us here in this context and another voice to us in a different context. For postliberals, such analogies are not displayed within the bounds of propositional discourse, but only in the life of God within each community; and there is no more direct way to observe these analogies than through the hermeneutics of reading Scripture, or of reading the life of the Spirit among and between the scriptural traditions. These postliberals would therefore part company with Milbank when he offers direct and therefore dogmatic claims on the basis of analogy: that, for example, we (of a certain community of believers) know by direct intuition *that* Christ shares the identity of God *and* what constitutes that identity. For these postliberals, we may infer from other evidence that the one we know is indeed Christ, but we cannot claim this knowledge through direct intuition. We offer our inferences, furthermore, with respect to certain axioms that are not shared by members of other communities. In intracommunal conversation, we therefore argue for these inferences only on the basis of analogy, which means only as probable judgments subject to translation and testing by members of the other communities.[19] For American and British postliberals, "Pleonasm" would therefore appear to combine two contradictory modes of argumentation: Milbank argues for analogical reasoning but on the basis of nonanalogical reasonings. He argues against the reduction of religious thinking to universal concepts but then makes universal claims on the basis of his religious thinking.

of efforts to ground knowledge claims on discrete judgments of intuition, except as fallible sources of abduction.

19. This kind of relativity is compatible with the kind of realism that is defined by scriptural reasoning. See Peter Ochs, "Philosophic Warrants for Scriptural Reasoning," in *The Promise of Scriptural Reasoning*, ed. David Ford and Chad Pecknold (Oxford: Blackwell, 2006), 121–238.

3. A pragmatic analysis of the contradictions in Milbank's argument

According to my analysis thus far, there are "two Milbanks" in "Pleonasm": one who argues analogically (and thus nondogmatically) and one who extends this argument dogmatically. In this section I introduce one additional measure of Milbank's reasoning: philosophic pragmatism, defined for our purposes as a method for repairing contradictory modes of reasoning. Like Milbank's approach in "Pleonasm," pragmatism is a form of genealogical criticism. Its method is to read contradictions in a thinker's writing as symptoms of the writing's having sought but failed to repair problems in certain antecedent traditions or systems of thought. Reasoning from a symptom to its possible cause, the pragmatic critic offers hypotheses about the source and character of these problems. The critic's goal is to recommend ways that these problems could be resolved without generating the kinds of contradiction that appear in this thinker's work. Readers interested in this thinker may then choose to reread the thinker's work in light of these recommendations. In the following two subsections I apply this form of criticism to the contradictions I observe in "Pleonasm"; in this chapter's conclusion, I then offer recommendations for rereading Milbank's writing without contradiction. My recommendations also demonstrate why I believe it is worthwhile to read Milbank pragmatically. The contradictions in his work may be reread coherently as signs of a conflicting devotion to pragmatic and nonpragmatic modes of reasoning; his genealogical criticism is free of contradiction when it is reread as pragmatic criticism; his argument is free of dogmatism and supersessionism when its nonpragmatic dimensions are removed. In this section, I briefly revisit what we have already observed in "Pleonasm."

(A) THE PRAGMATIC SIDE

In terms of our definition of pragmatism, Milbank offers a pragmatic critique of Warburton. He traces contradictions in Warburton's argument to his conflicting devotion, on the one hand, to a performative model of language use (applied to Adam) and, on the other hand, to a literalist model of the meaning of written language (applied to biblical Hebrew). Milbank reads Warburton's contradictions as symptoms of his failed effort to repair conflicts between his community's religious and naturalistic standards for reading the Bible—or, in Milbank's terms, between realist and nominalist accounts of our knowledge of God. Milbank then recommends ways of repairing what Warburton failed to repair: adopting Lowth's consistently performative model of language use, extended through Vico–Herder. From this perspective, Milbank's recommendation applies strictly to the terms of Warburton's argument and could be extended beyond those terms only as a speculative exercise.

(B) THE NONPRAGMATIC SIDE

Milbank's nonpragmatic tendency is displayed most simply by the fact that he extends his recommendation beyond the limits of his inquiry. One of many illustrations appears in my previous critique of his drawing more than analogical inferences from analogies. Milbank's tendency is displayed more indirectly through the way he extends his reading of Warburton–Lowth to Vico and thence to Hamann. As noted earlier, he affirms Vico's distinction between the Hebrew Bible's linguistic realism and its idolatrous alternatives (among them the Egyptian hieroglyphs). Then, however, he adds to this distinction the criterion of "violence"/"nonviolence." "Violence" does not appear here as an empirical measure of bodily injury or of some trespass immediately visible to the senses, but as a measure of what, *according to the Christian realism with which he concludes*, accompanies the separation of language from its primordial intercourse with nature. He says that to separate words from their *realia* is to separate humanity from its home in the divine creation and thereby to do violence to humanity as such; whatever preserves or restores humanity's primordial intimacy with nature is "nonviolent." Without any apparent source within the prior discussion of Warburton–Lowth, this criterion of violence/nonviolence appears to enter as a correlate of the distinction between idolatrous/nonidolatrous. Prompted by Hamann, Milbank reads Egyptian idolatry as violent because—as Warburton–Lowth–Vico argue—hieroglyphics veil this primordial intimacy. When contrasted with this idolatry, Hebrew monotheism is nonviolent, since it provides a means of preserving intimacy through its metaphorization of primary language. At the same time, biblical Hebrew preserves this intimacy in an imperfect way and therefore fails to remove violence altogether from its practices. As we saw earlier, this failure is a feature of writing, and the Hebrew Bible metaphorizes by way of writing rather than speech. Christ comes, however, to remedy the imperfections of writing and of the Bible by reinstating the primordially oral performance in which language is immediately present to nature. Only Christ therefore brings perfected nonviolence to humanity; in Christ humanity has direct intercourse with nature.

This Milbank–Hamann narrative of primordial violence and idolatry is self-contained or true to its own premises in a way that is transparent only to those who share its premises—in this case, some of those who participate in Christ. Nonetheless, the entire account would remain pragmatic if Milbank were to claim for it the modality only of abduction, as if to say: here is a self-coherent way of imagining our place in the world; let us treat each of its elemental terms as inherently vague, and let us now assign pragmatic procedures for defining and testing each of these terms within the linguistic code of each literary tradition that purports to offer a realist account of language use. In this case, as noted in the example from Halivni, rabbinic Judaism might be seen to enact this account in its own terms, Islam might enact it in another way, and so on. But Milbank preserves the linguistic code of his Christian realism as if it were nonvague and therefore as if it already defined the means through which all other codes would be tested. In these terms, he offers no alternative to supersessionism and no means for pragmatic testing.

This is not to say that his claim is necessarily wrong, only that God alone knows. Milbank's account illustrates how supersessionism finds a warrant in nonpragmatic practices of corrective reading. It need not be supersessionist to claim that Christ alone repairs contradictions in the Old Testament. Such a claim becomes supersessionist only when this recommendation is presented as self-legitimating and therefore as true for any reader whatsoever. Supersessionism finds no warrant in a strict pragmatism, since pragmatic abductions remain vague and do not permit the kind of a priori clarity and certainty Milbank assigns to his narrative of origins.

Conclusions

What would the argument of "Pleonasm" look like if Milbank stuck to his pragmatic side? As suggested piecemeal through this study, a pragmatic Milbank–Peirce might proceed according to the following directives.

1. *Make your genealogy fully reparative and pragmatic by isolating, as discretely as possible, the specific irritant or concern that stimulates your inquiry.*

Milbank's explicit object of concern in "Pleonasm" is the undue influence postmodernism has had on recent Christian theology. But this does not tell us enough about his irritant, since it does not identify what stimulates him to address Christian postmodernism in a somewhat pragmatic and somewhat foundationalist way. To complete a reparative genealogy, Milbank would need to locate the stimulus within some problematic practice within his own community of belief and inquiry. What could this be? Perhaps Milbank is concerned about his own community's attraction to postmodern criticism, in which case the irritant would not be postmodernism per se but the way it contradicts certain elemental assumptions of this community's Christian orthodoxy.

2. *Trace the irritant, genealogically, to some antecedent practice in which the irritant appears to coexist alongside what may prove to be the source of its repair.*

In "Pleonasm" Milbank identifies the irritant strictly with Derrida and his postmodernism, and he traces this irritant genealogically to Warburton–Lowth's inquiries into the origins of language. For a pragmatic Milbank, the irritant would appear to be an unsettled relationship between Derrida and Christian orthodoxy, not Derrida himself, and the antecedent would be something like an unsettled relationship between Warburton's praise of biblical Hebrew and Lowth's account of the performative or "oral" character of Adamic language use. The pragmatic goal would not be to "get rid of" Derrida or of one aspect of Warburton, but to find a way, without contradiction, to inhabit a Christian orthodoxy and pursue philosophic inquiry into various problems of language, meaning, and so forth.

3. *Offer a reparative abduction. This means, per hypothesis, to propose a way to practice Christian orthodoxy and philosophy without contradiction.*

This is the stage of inquiry that most explicitly separates foundationalist and pragmatic modes of repair. The pragmatic scholar Richard Bernstein suggested that what he called "Cartesian anxiety" might serve as an explanation. He referred to a psychosocial-epistemological syndrome that leads an inquirer at once to believe he or she must urgently propose a solution to some elemental cultural crisis (in particular, a crisis that undermines a society's sense of security in its conventional ways of knowing the world) and also to doubt that such a solution can be found within any of the current institutions of the society. The result is, in Susan Haack's terms, to "doubt more than one has reason to" and then to "believe more than one has warrant to." If, for the sake of illustration, we read such a syndrome into "Pleonasm," then we might conclude that its author overly doubted his Christian community's capacity to respond appropriately to the challenges of postmodernism. Such a Milbank might take responsibility to do the job himself (or we might substitute "a community of Radical Orthodox inquirers" for any one individual). Feeling great urgency to construct a solution, the inquirer might propose this hasty strategy: "Since Derrida's postmodernism is simply wrong, then we might readily locate a model of 'what is simply right' by constructing the logical contradictory to what is wrong! If, for example, Derrida's notion of 'aboriginal writing' is wrong, then 'aboriginal morality' must be right! If Derrida's notion of the 'arbitrary signifier' is false, then we should search for some 'necessary signifier' as a source of the truth! If, finally, it is wrong to ground Christian realism in any series of iterations that include error or imperfection, then such a realism must be grounded in a series of perfect (even if not identical) iterations!" This is at least one way to reconstruct the etiology of the unpragmatic Milbank's foundationalist conclusions. The lesson would be that foundationalist intuitions are offered willfully as the logical contradictories of the errant beliefs that have stimulated his or her inquiry.

A pragmatic Milbank would assume, by contrast, that the world of belief and practice that brings us these irritants has also brought us sources for repairing them. However urgent the need for repair, then, there is no need to achieve it all at once through some instantaneous construction. Milbank might indeed return to Warburton–Lowth, but this time to find in them guidelines for happier relations between Christian orthodoxy and philosophy. These guidelines would not prompt Milbank to construct opposing lines of inquiry (such as Warburton–Derrida versus Lowth–Vico–Hamann). They would prompt him, instead, to reach within his account of Warburton–Lowth for some hint (if not an outright model) of the kind of deconstructive inquiry that would complement a Christian orthodoxy rather than undermine it. At this stage, I would leave it to members of Milbank's hermeneutical circle even to illustrate possibilities. I assume that other circles of postliberal Christian theologians would offer other ways of performing a Christian, nonsupersessionist, and deconstructive inquiry. As a Jewish philosopher, the most I can contribute at this point is to offer analogues within Jewish tradition—illustrations of how to perform a rabbinic and deconstructive inquiry. This does not mean that my critique is a Jewish one per se; I believe it is a pragmatic critique (out of sources of Western philosophy and logic), tested and refined by studies in Christian and Jewish scriptural traditions. After the critique, I turn to rabbinic sources to illustrate, within my area of scriptural practice, that there are other ways to accomplish a scripturally grounded deconstructive inquiry.

4. Consider some rabbinic analogues.

Consistent with the approach to rabbinic Judaism we considered earlier, I could imagine locating rabbinic analogues to the following stages of Milbank's reparative inquiry.

(A) A MODEL OF PRIMORDIAL LANGUAGE

"Blessed be the One who speaks and the world is" (Rabbinic Daily Morning Prayer Service). For the rabbinic-biblical tradition, the One God speaks the world into being. The speech of God (*dibbur*) is thus the source of all things (*devarim*), each of which is a spoken thing (*devar* = *dibbur*). The speech of God is also the source of the written Torah (*torah she b'khtav*), which God spoke to Moses on Mt. Sinai: *vayidaber hashem el moshe lamor*—"God spoke to Moses, saying"—so that each word to Moses is God's spoken word (*dibbur*).

(B) A MODEL OF ISRAEL'S CAPACITY TO PARTICIPATE INTIMATELY IN THE LIFE AND SPEECH OF THE ONE "WHO SPEAKS AND THE WORLD IS"

We may see in classical rabbinic readings of the Song of Songs a rabbinic analogue to Milbank's model of what it means for the church to participate in the primordial Logos:

As Rabbi Akiva taught, "All the books of the Bible are holy, but the Song of Songs is the Holy of Holies" (*Mishnah Yadayim* 3:5). Only a soul as great as Rabbi Akiva could testify that the "Song of Songs is the Holy of Holies" and that "the entire universe is unworthy of the day that the Song of Songs was given to Israel" (Song of Songs Raba 1.1.11).

Solomon composed many songs. And [why is it said, "Song of Songs" in the plural]? Because it contains the praise of God, the praise of Torah, and the praise of Israel. And how do we know it is the praise of God? For it is said, "His head is finest gold" (Song 5:10). And how do we know it refers to the Torah? For it is said, "And his banner of love is over me" (Song 2:4). And how do we know it refers to Israel? For it is said, "Like a lily among the thorns" (Song 2:2). (*Midrash Shir HaShirim*)[20]

Reflecting on verses like these, a medieval poet composed this song, later adopted for daily and Sabbath meditation (here in less satisfying translation):

Yedid nefesh [Soul Mate]

Soul mate, loving God, compassion's gentle source,
Take my disposition and shape it to your Will.
Like a darting deer I will rush to You.
Before Your glorious Presence humbly will I bow.
Let Your sweet love delight me with its thrill . . .

For our purposes, the implication of the song and preceding set of midrashim is that Israel and God sing love songs one to the other. Rabbinic tradition thereby understands the people Israel to engage in direct intercourse with the One whose words create this world. Should we ask how individual members of the people share in this intimacy, then we may look to the rabbinic reading of Hosea 2:21–22: "Thus says the Lord: I will betroth you to Me forever. I will betroth you with righteousness, with justice, with law, and with compassion. I will betroth you to Me with faithfulness, and you shall love the Lord." In rabbinic tradition, this verse is recited as a marital proclamation. And it is chanted each morning while the worshiper wraps the phylacteries, or *tefillin*, around the left hand and middle fingers—performing a kind of marital bond with these virtues of the Holy One. In Milbank's terms, we may say that through the way these words are reiterated nonidentically, the tradition indicates the capacity of members of the people Israel to participate in intimate relation with the One who speaks the world into existence. This is one of many illustrations of what we might call rabbinic pleonasm, among the most evocative of which may be Israel's observance, or nonidentical repetition, of God's resting on the Sabbath, and the hundreds of blessings individuals recite when they enjoy the pleasures and gifts of this world. According to tradition, individuals are to recite the blessing so that the sound of the blessing and the taste of a given pleasure are mingled, thereby disclosing the reality of that pleasure as God's actively spoken word entering into the life and body of that individual. A prototype is the blessing on

20. Ed. Yosef Wertheimer (Jerusalem: 1981), 3–4, quoted by Alon Goshen-Gottstein, "Thinking of/with Scripture: Struggling for the Religious Significance of the Song of Songs," *Journal of Scriptural Reasoning* 3, no. 2 (August 2003).

eating bread: "Blessed are you YHVH, our God, guide of the world, Who brings forth bread from the earth."[21]

(c) A MODEL OF CRISES IN THE LIFE OF ISRAEL (AS A NAME FOR THE PEOPLE OR FOR EACH INDIVIDUAL MEMBER) TO WHICH ISRAEL'S "REDEEMER" HAS, DOES, AND WILL RESPOND

Applied as it is to a doctrine of humanity's primordial relation to the Creator of this world, Milbank's account of pragmatic repair is also a soteriology. In his account, Christ is Savior; according to his foundationalist account, this means Christ and Christ alone. In this analogous, rabbinic account, God is Redeemer. Biblical and subsequent rabbinic literatures offer prototypes of how, when Israel suffers, Israel prays to God for redemption and how God may respond to her call.

The Exodus from Egypt

• Suffering

The Israelites groaned in their bondage and cried out, and their cry for help because of their bondage went up to God (Exod. 2).

The Exodus account portrays Israel's primordial event of loss: exile, enslavement, and the dissolution of the kinship-based Abrahamite religion.

• Redemption

The Lord continued, "I have marked well the plight of my people in Egypt and have heeded their outcry because of their taskmasters. . . . I have come down to rescue them. . . . I will send you." Moses said, "Who am I that I should go?" . . . He said, "*ehyeh imach*, I will be with you. . . . Thus shall you say to the Israelites, '*ehyeh* sent me to you'" (Exod. 3 JPS).

The religion of Abraham died in Egypt, but it was reborn as the Mosaic religion of the One whose Name is with Israel in its suffering, and of the people of Israel that is united under the legislative force of Torah.

Chorban: First Destruction

• Suffering

I reared up children and brought them up,
but they have rebelled against me. . . .
The Lord's anger burns against his people. (Isa. 1)

How solitary sits the city, once so full of people.
Bitterly she weeps at night, tears are upon her cheeks. . . .
Jerusalem has become unclean. (Lam. 1)

---

21. "Upon reciting [this] berakhah [blessing], says R. Levi, the individual is permitted to have, as a member of society, what up to that moment had belonged solely to God." Max Kadushin, *Worship and Ethics: A Study in Rabbinic Judaism* (Binghamton, NY: Global Publications, 2001), 66. "The bread . . . is a concretization of God's love" (65, and see 63–96).

Here is portrayed Israel's paradigmatic destruction: the burning of Israel's Temple, the end of its monarchical theo-polity and political independence, the exile of its priests and intellectuals to Babylonian captivity.

- Redemption
  > But you, Israel, My servant,
  > Jacob, whom I have chosen,
  > Seed of Abraham my friend—
  > You whom I drew from the ends of the earth . . .
  > To whom I said: You are My servant . . .
  > Fear not, for I am with you. . . .
  > This is My servant, whom I uphold,
  > My chosen one, in whom I delight.
  > I have put My spirit in him,
  > He shall teach the true way to the nations. . . .
  > Who formed you, O Israel:
  > Fear not, for I will redeem you. . . .
  > You are Mine. (Isa. 41–43)

The religion of monarchy-and-prophecy died in the First Destruction, as did the religion defined by what the Talmud later called *chateau yisrael*, "the sins of Israel," whose written Torah was maintained only imperfectly through a vicious cycle of meritorious and sinful governments. In the very place of exile, however—in Babylon—the religion of Israel was reborn as the religion of Second Isaiah, Ezekiel, and Ezra: a religion of scribal priests who would redact and reteach the Torah as well as maintain it, and whose reteaching would gradually become the legislative voice of Torah within the Second Commonwealth.

Chorban: Second Destruction

- Suffering

An image dominates even more than a text: the Burnt Temple (70–71 CE), Jerusalem razed and salted (135 CE). But texts also abound:

It was decreed for Israel that they study words of Torah in distress, in enslavement, in wandering and in uncertainty, suffering for lack of food. (*Midrash Eliayahu Rabbah*)

When Rabbi Joshua looked at the Temple in ruins one day, he burst into tears. "Alas for us! The place which atoned for the sins of all the people Israel lies in ruins!" (*Avot de Rabbi Natan* 11a).[22]

These were the defining accounts of destruction for modern Judaism, which is rabbinic Judaism. The biblical promises are broken, so it seems.

---

22. Cited by Jules Harlow, *Machzor for Rosh Hashanah and Yom Kippur* (New York: United Synagogue of Conservative Judaism, 1988), 615.

"Because of our sins, we are exiled from the land" (Galut). It is the end of direct biblical jurisdiction over Israel's life.

• Redemption

All Israel has a place in the world to come, as it is written, "Your people shall all be righteous, they shall possess the land forever; there are a shoot of My planting, the work of My hands in whom I shall be glorified" (Isa. 60). Moses received Torah from Sinai and transmitted it to Joshua, and Joshua to the elders, the elders to the prophets, the prophets to the members of the Great Assembly. . . . Simeon the Just was one of the last members of the Great Assembly. He used to teach: The world rests on three things: on Torah, on service to God, and on acts of loving-kindness. (*Pirke Avot* 1)

Hillel taught: Do not separate yourself from the community.

Rabbi Tarfon used to teach: You are not obligated to finish the task, neither are you free to neglect it. (*Pirke Avot* 2)

The religion of biblical Israel died in the Second Destruction—the religion maintained by Temple service, as defined by the literal word of the written Torah and as lived by Israel only on its holy soil. In its place, directly out of the fires of Chorban, the religion of rabbinic Judaism was reborn: a religion that inherited the Torah teachings of the scribal priests and the central beliefs of their Pharisaic defenders. These are belief in the resurrection of the dead, in life in the world to come (*olam haba*) as well as in this world, and belief that on Sinai God gave Moses two *torot*: the Written Torah (*torah she b'khtav*) and the Oral Torah (*torah she b'al peh*), carried through a chain of transmission to the rabbinic sages. This is the Torah through which, alone, the directives of the Written Torah are disclosed and enacted. As articulated by David Weiss Halivni, this Oral Torah is the fruit of Ezra's reception of the Spirit of God, through whom he redacted and restored Israel's blemished Torah and initiated what would later become the rabbinic practice of midrashic reinterpretation. This is the practice that is reconstituted today as rabbinic pragmatism. In the hour after Israel's Destruction, the rabbis renewed Judaism through the teachings of Mishnah and Talmud, and they recodified the directives of Torah through the legislative activity of the *halakhah*.

5. A nonfinalized and nonperfected model of salvation history

In his foundationalist mode, Milbank understands salvation history to be divided between the stark alternatives of perfection and futility. The second alternative is illustrated in Israel and Judaism's ultimately futile efforts to fulfill a law that cannot be perfected, guided by a written Torah whose errors cannot be perfectly removed. The first alternative is illustrated in the life of Jesus Christ, in whom the law is fulfilled and all errors of the divine Word removed. As I suggested earlier, rabbinic tradition offers a different model. For the rabbinic sages, salvation history is not governed in this world by the law of the excluded middle, which means that it cannot be comprehended in terms of such a stark dichotomy. Instead, as illustrated through this cyclical history of distress and redemption, rabbinic salvation history is informed by what we might call "meantime soteriology": an understanding of God's fulfilling historical time again and again, but within the contexts of historically and spatiotemporally particular worlds. A final end of ends is attained only in the world to come—or what we might call the world of worlds to come—but each world we know has its own end followed by its own resurrection, which is the birth of another world.

My interest here is not with this rabbinic soteriology for its own sake, but only to demonstrate that a realist account of primordial language can be articulated by way of more than one soteriology. As foundationalist, Milbank allows for only one soteriology that supersedes all others. Pragmatic reasoning precludes this kind of foundationalism, however, along with the supersessionism that accompanies it. I assume that a consistently postliberal Christian theology would also avoid this kind of foundationalism and supersessionism and may most likely adopt a pragmatic account of reparative inquiry—and, thus, of salvation history.

Appendix: On Postliberalism and Christological Universalism

In July 2009, University of Virginia graduate students convened a small conference in response to the manuscript of this book.[23] Continuing after the conference, the most spirited discussion came in response to the chapter on John Milbank, especially on questions of universalism and particularism. Was my model of postliberalism relativist? In response to the participants' suggestions, I offer this appendix to clarify my critique of the "unpragmatic" and universalist side of Milbank's work and its relation to what I consider the *relativity but nonrelativism* of Christian postliberalism and my own Jewish postliberalism.

The conference discussion suggested to me why Radical Orthodoxy (RO) appeals to some believing Christians who want to maintain their faith amidst (and not just outside) the perplexities of modern academic thought. I believe RO appeals because it promises classical patristic orthodoxy *and* a christological response to all the challenges of modern philosophy and social thought *within* the terms of that philosophy. *Another Reformation* was not written as a response to this promise per se—that would be another undertaking—but it may assist readers if I offer a brief response here.

The main purpose of this book is to test out the correlation I observed between postliberalism and nonsupersessionism. As a secondary matter, I hoped the book might also suggest how postliberalism achieves a species of Christian orthodoxy without succumbing to either side of the logic of modern universalism: without, in other words, identifying this orthodoxy as either universalist in the modern sense *or* antiuniversalist. I hoped readers would get accustomed, chapter by chapter, to a nonmodern believing Christianity, one whose affirmations are guided by the Bible's intrinsically vague logic and grammar of proclamation and application, rather than by the dyad of modern universalism versus particularism. I hoped readers would see that a biblically based orthodoxy is neither relativist nor triumphalist, because its fidelity to the divine Word means fidelity to a Word that convinces, guides, and redeems

23. The event, "The Gift of Wisdom: A Gathering of Christian Theologians Learning from a Jewish Philosopher," included seventeen young Christian theologians and this one Jewish philosopher. Each of the seven sessions featured a paper on one chapter of this book and its treatment of one of the postliberal Christian theologians: (1) "On George Lindbeck," by Peter Kang, UVA PhD candidate; (2) "On Robert Jenson," by Benjamin Maton, UVA PhD candidate; (3) "On Stanley Hauerwas," by Lindsay Cleveland, Baylor PhD candidate; (4) "On John Howard Yoder," by Tommy Givens, Duke ThD candidate; (5) "On Daniel Hardy," by Andrew Black, University of Dayton PhD candidate; (6) "On David Ford," by Rebekah Eklund, Duke PhD candidate; (7) "On John Milbank," by W. Christian Hackett, UVA PhD candidate. Discussants were Wesley Zell and Dawg Strong (Center for Christian Study, Charlottesville), William Elkins (Drew University), Barry Harvey and Jennifer Howell (Baylor), David Dault (Christian Brothers University), Jason Byassee (Duke), and Scott Yakimow (UVA). Conference organizers were Jacob Goodson (UVA and William & Mary) and Timothy McConnell (Center for Christian Study).

through intimate relation rather than through cognitive affirmation-or-denial. I hoped readers would see that such an orthodoxy is nonsupersessionist not because it relativizes Christian proclamation, but because its proclamation includes biblical Israel in a way that leaves vague (or not fully clarified) the scriptural meaning of Israel in relation to Christ in this time between the times. I hoped, finally, that by the end of the book, readers would be prepared to see why RO cannot maintain its form of universalism and at the same time affirm a scripturally based Christology. I did not want to overstate this claim (as I have elsewhere) but only to open readers to the possibility that RO may achieve its triumphalist kind of Christian universalism by adopting a modern logic of universals that is operative even in claims about Christ's "universal particularity."

Discussions during the conference showed me, however, that some readers might be tempted to associate my critique of Christian universalism with either modern relativism or simply my "Jewish" approach as opposed to a Christian one. While this book as a whole is the most I can offer them in response, I shall note here a few of the assumptions I have brought with me as author of this book; these may help clarify my intentions, even if they cannot strengthen my claims.

- Consistent with my theme of relativity, I cannot presume that the arguments of this book will be pertinent to every community of readers. I believe God's Word is "universally" pertinent, but only as demonstrated directly by the One who speaks it, not by any of our middling efforts. I understand this creation as an activity and a stream of consequences of God's living Word, and I understand sacred Scripture as God's speech to us. I understand the plain sense of Scripture to be inalterable but without clear meaning or force by itself. I understand such clarity to come to us only *within* our various communities of belief and practice *and* specific to the questions we ask of God in the context and space-time of our asking. This is the relativity of our knowledge of God's word and will: he offers these to us *with respect to his relation to us in our space-time.* What we hear in response has binding authority for us, then and there: even in its own temporality, what we hear belongs to the Absolute, not merely to us. *But we are not instruments for transporting what belongs to the Absolute beyond the contexts of our hearing.* We may declare: We have heard directly from the One whose Word is true universally. Yes indeed. But we are not the ones to articulate the universality of this Word. Our responsibility is only to act then and there as prompted. But the next moment we turn to ask again—to ask what we have just done, or what we should do next, or what we shall say to others in other contexts—in that moment we can only ask again. Can we therefore not speak? Of course we can speak, but as human creatures, with experiences and histories and theories, even wonderful and profound and wise theories, but all of them creaturely. The urge to speak as if we spoke God's Word—and thus spoke universally—is a sinful urge.

- The relativity described here is the relativity—or relationality—of God's Word to us, not the relativism of our own words. Our words bear varying degrees of generality. If I say "Camels are brown," I may intend my words to speak generally of all camels, and folks may discover that in fact my words do apply to a whole bunch of camels. What I cannot do is assume that because I intend generality this intention will correspond to a verifiable discovery of equal generality. I might even intend universality. But if so, I cannot assume this will correspond to something verifiable before the end-time. This applies also to what Immanuel Kant labeled *categories of the understanding*. There is no verifiable evidence (short of the end-time) that God created human creatures who *must* think by way of the transcendental categories of universality and particularity. (And I include verification by way of further transcendental inquiry.) Relativity emerges as an appropriate measure of our own words when we seek to measure their actual generality, which is measured in relation to the conditions of our speech, the contexts for testing it, and so on.

- When I refer to the relativity of God's Word, it is to its relativity with respect to space-time and context, not necessarily to specific persons. When I visit an Anglican Eucharistic service, I witness the Eucharist as shared among and thus in relation to that community of persons in the church. It is not offered in relation to me there as Jew, or in relation to those Anglicans down the road in or not in another church service. I therefore do not write this book as one whose Judaism renders him incapable of engaging intellectually and theologically with matters of church doctrine—limited in depth of engagement, yes, but as a matter of degree. Yet I do not understand the word of God that is spoken within the flesh of the body of Christ to be spoken to "me" and thus within "my hearing." These last two sentences voice the distinction I perceive between human understanding (the former sentence) and human participation in God's context-directed speech (the latter sentence). I do not understand individual cognition, by itself, to provide a means of deeper engagement with the divine Word. I understand that for any creature brought into deeper relation with the divine Word, individual cognition offers an instrument for clarifying the meaning and force of that Word within the various dimensions of creaturely life.

- In this chapter I criticize those aspects of Milbank's arguments—and by extension those of RO—that trespass on these differences between God and creature and, in particular, between human participation in the divine Word and any individual thinker's examination of such participation. For what I name the "unpragmatic" Milbank, a certain marriage of participation and cognition gives birth to "universal" claims about the meaning and force of "Christ" and of "knowing Christ." This is the presumption, in other words, that an individual's project of thinking may serve as an appropriate vehicle for transporting the meaning and force of God's Word from the context of its offering (such as a Eucharistic communion) to another context (such as the behavior of other Christians, or Jews, or Muslims in other places).

• Do I offer this critique because I write "outside of Christ"? As applied to the topic of universalism/particularism, one thesis of this book is that postliberal Christian theologians draw the distinction I have also drawn between participation and cognition—and that the "pragmatic" Milbank would draw these distinctions as well.

9

Conclusion

CHRISTIAN POSTLIBERALISM AND CHRISTIAN NONSUPERSESSIONISM ARE CORRELATIVE

Like a laboratory experiment, this book has examined the probability that one phenomenon, the practice of postliberal Christian theology, is correlated with another phenomenon, nonsupersessionism (a critique and disavowal of the Christian practice of reading the Gospel narratives as evidence that God has elected the church in place of Israel as his covenant partner). I believe the book has uncovered sufficient evidence to conclude that there is indeed a strong correlation between these two phenomena. The correlation has been verified in the work of five theologians (Lindbeck, Jenson, Hauerwas, Hardy, and Ford), and its contrapositive has been tested successfully in the work of two additional theologians. In the latter cases, the acknowledged absence of one correlate has been shown to predict the unacknowledged weakness or near-absence of the other correlate (non-nonsupersessionism in Milbank's theology has predicted tendencies to non-postliberalism, and tendencies toward non-postliberalism in Yoder's theology have predicted tendencies to non-nonsupersessionism).[1] The purpose of this chapter is simply to clarify the book's conclusion.

---

1. In the terms of a contemporary quantum physicist, the correlation I have tested corresponds to "an underlying symmetry, which imposes conservation laws that would not allow the detection of one [phenomenon] without the presence of another" (Mehrdad Adibzadeh, University of Virginia, personal correspondence, November 2009). Looked at from one experimental per-

The Meaning of "Postliberal Christian Theology"

In the introduction I was reticent to define what I mean by "postliberalism," choosing to let readers first draw their own impressions from the detailed accounts offered in each chapter of the book. Through the course of this book, I have given myself increasing license to describe major trends in each theologian's postliberal practice and then to risk generalizations about the American and British types in general. In this section I want now to risk a more general summary of these two types and of the overlapping beliefs and interests they seem to share. I am not concerned about misrepresenting what these theologians have already done, since they and I know that I am reading them only from the perspectives of this book and of my own work in Jewish philosophy. My concern is that readers not mistake my characterizations for predictions about where postliberal-like theology may move in the future: at best it will go where the Spirit takes it, and none of us can predict that. To preserve the occasion-specific character of my characterizations, I have not sought to integrate them with characterizations offered by other scholars of postliberalism. James Fodor's portrait of postliberalism has been the single most helpful resource for this part of my study; readers may see that our portraits are complements, with enough differences to preserve the locality of our efforts.[2]

---

spective, I have shown that the phenomena of postliberalism and nonsupersessionism display an "overlapping statistical distribution." Looked at from another perspective, I have shown that there is a symmetry between one phenomenon and the other, so that one cannot be detected without the other. Both these perspectives offer ways of describing the correlation I have observed without invoking notions of causality or determination. I find this approach very helpful.

2. See James Fodor, "Postliberal Theology," in *The Modern Theologians: An Introduction to Christian Theology since 1918*, 3rd ed., ed. David Ford with Rachel Muers (London: Wiley-Blackwell, 2005), 229–48. Readers will want to study the whole essay. For comparative purposes, here is a summary of Fodor's characterizations of postliberalism, which, in my terms, lean more to the American wing:

> Postliberal theology names an internally highly differentiated movement in contemporary English-speaking theology (primarily in North America and Britain) whose aims are chiefly (1) faithful yet creative retrieval of the Christian tradition; (2) ecumenically open renewal of the church; and (3) compassionate healing and repair of the world. George Lindbeck, Hans Frei, Ronald Thiemann and Stanley Hauerwas are among its most well-known advocates. . . . In brief, (1) postliberal theology represents . . . a retrieval and redeployment of premodern sources in characteristically "unmodern" ways to meet today's challenges; (2) it self-consciously engages and reflects upon theology's tasks in relation to its ecclesial settings; . . . (3) it deploys narrative as a key category, promoting thereby a distinctively Christian form of intratextuality and a hermeneutics of social, ecclesial embodiment in service to the practical tasks of living the Christian life . . . (4) it emphasizes the peculiar grammar of Christian faith, concentrating on its scriptural logic and the regulative role of doctrine with a view to sustaining communities of "native speakers" facing diverse pressures (internal and external) that would weaken that competency, threaten the church's identity or otherwise distract it from its central mission as one of

(a) American and British "wings" of postliberal Christian theology

I have observed two "wings" of postliberalism, one attending more to Christology (the "Yale" or "American" wing), the other to pneumatology (the "Cambridge" or "British" wing), with various mixtures. In my own words, the two wings appear to display the following sets of beliefs.

AMERICAN POSTLIBERALISM

- *Semper reformanda.* The purpose of all reformational work is to contribute to the unification of the church, both economically in the unity of the churches and immanently in the unity of the body of Christ.
- *Church doctrines are signposts of moments of radical reformation in the history of the church, moments when the church is called to repair obstructions that have arisen to its perennial work of unification.* The reformational process of doctrinal formation is an ecclesial process of rereading the Gospels' witness to the life of Christ. This rereading uncovers historically specific guidelines for doctrinal reformation.
- *Postliberalism has protodoctrinal force as a reformation of the practice of reading Scripture in the contemporary church.* Its reformational work includes (a) reparative ecclesiology—efforts to repair obstacles to ecclesial unity today; (b) reparative historiography—uncovering sources of the church's inability to repair its disunity; (c) reparative scriptural theology—hermeneutical proposals for recovering scriptural guidelines for the work of reformation; this thesis includes an understanding of the scriptural text as a place where divine and human voices meet, the ineliminable face of a body that extends into sacramental intimacy and sociopolitical practice; (d) reparative trinitarian theology—a critique and repair of onto-theology as separating body and spirit and thereby obstructing ecclesial repair; this thesis includes the warning that human works—including human reasonings—will not suffice to bring Christ's reparative presence.
- *Nonsupersessionism is a corollary of this reformation.* It emerges out of the surprising discovery that ecclesial repair comes to rest in the hand

---

communal witness and service "for the sake of all humanity"; (5) it allocates to theology a primarily corrective rather than constitutive or formative function . . . ; (6) it exhibits a distinctively Protestant flavor that yet is open to Catholic, Anglican and Orthodox inflections in ways that promote comparative work of a reconciling, ecumenical nature within Christianity but also among the Abrahamic traditions; (7) it espouses a non-essentialist approach to religions . . . ; (8) it adopts a non-foundational epistemological posture, committing itself to offering pragmatically superior and theologically fructifying conceptual redescriptions of the Christian faith, instead of attempting to ground those claims on purportedly universal principles or structures that can be accessed in a "neutral" and "objective" (i.e., framework-independent) manner . . . ; (9) [postliberal theology] sees its primary task as descriptive rather than apologetic. (229–31)

of a Redeemer God who not only raised Jesus from the dead but also raised Israel from Egypt.

BRITISH POSTLIBERALISM

- *Living in the Spirit: theology begins in hallelujah, praise, and blessing.* "Blessed are you among women, and blessed is the fruit of your womb" (Luke 1:41–42). "The utterly vital thing to be learnt is the incomparable desirability of God . . . and how to follow Jesus in his realization of it."[3] To follow Jesus in this way is share in the feast of God's Spirit as Wisdom. "Taste and see that the LORD is good" (Ps. 34:9). "For she is a breath of the power of God, and a pure emanation of the glory of the Almighty. . . . for God loves nothing so much as the person who lives with wisdom" (Wisdom of Solomon 78:22–28).[4] To live in the Spirit of wisdom is to inhabit God where one finds him—where one finds God in Scripture and where one finds him in the world and in history. "By wisdom a house is built, and through understanding it is established" (Prov. 24:3).[5]

- *Knowing in the Spirit: Eucharistic pneumatology.* The beginning of knowledge is to be inhabited by God and thus to live in God's light: this is to know God contingently as one finds him in the words of Scripture, the things of the world, and the persons and events of history. The sacraments are pathways to this finding, and the central pathway is the Eucharist. The Eucharist "is an historically particular, theoretically infused practice that is also normative for the social performance of meaning as referred to God through Jesus Christ, and thus an anticipation of God's eschatological purposes. . . . The Eucharist embodies all the dimensions of human existence in the world."[6] The template for life in the church and, more generally, for all forms of social existence, the Eucharist is thereby the source of guidance for the ecclesial work of repair.[7]

---

3. David F. Ford, *Christian Wisdom: Desiring God and Learning in Love*, Cambridge Studies in Christian Doctrine (London: Cambridge University Press, 2007), 160.

4. Quoted in ibid., 165–66.

5. For Ben Quash—adopting a vision of Luke Timothy Johnson's—the Scripture we inhabit is like a house or building, or, better, like "a city of buildings." I take this to mean that the city we visit is already inhabited, so that its words are not directly transparent but carry their own human-filled histories. (Loosely paraphrasing Ben Quash, "Theology on the Road to Damascus," in "Spreading Rumours of Wisdom: Essays in Honour of David Ford," special issue of *Journal of Scriptural Reasoning* 7, no. 1 (January 2008).

6. Daniel W. Hardy, *Finding the Church: The Dynamic Truth of Anglicanism* (London: SCM, 2001), 243–44.

7. Ibid., 238. Hardy adds, "The Church is a society, [which] is meaning—potentially wisdom—structured in social terms." As the template for the church, the Eucharist is therefore the template for society. Hardy does not mean by this that Christian understanding of the Eucharist is the only means by which humanity truly understands society. He means that given his Christian faith, his understanding of Eucharistic communion is the template for his understanding

- *Repairing in the Spirit: redemptive ecclesiology.* Theology begins in praise, but its end is to respond to the cries of human affliction, each of which is the cry of Job, which is the cry of Christ on the cross. In his death, Jesus handed over the balm for such cries: "He is not here but has risen" (Luke 24:5), the transmission of God's Word as Christ to the Spirit."[8] The Spirit heals. But humanity also raises up obstacles to this healing. The theologian's work of repair—Christian reparative reasoning—is to respond to humanity's cries indirectly by attending to the obstructions that arise in each generation to the Spirit's reparative work. Postliberal theologians attend in particular to obstructions caused by intra-Christian schisms, the Jewish–Christian schism, and intra-Abrahamic schisms.

(b) Overall characteristics of "postliberal Christian theology"

The following beliefs and goals seem to be shared by postliberal theologians, whatever their relative leanings toward the American or British types of inquiry.[9]

- *Unity.* Whatever else it accomplishes, a theologian's work must also contribute to the unification of the body of Christ.
- *Reformation.* Reformation is the effort of each generation of Christians to remove the specific obstacles to church unity that characterize their age. In these fading years of the modern epoch, the greatest obstacle is a "second order" one: the church's having neglected its ancient practices of Scripture study, which include sacramental practices of communal formation as well as text-interpretive practices of communal study. When it lacks these practices, the church lacks adequate guidelines for its reformational work.
- *Scripture, community, and sacrament.* The place of Scripture in the ongoing history of the church is not merely formational but *reformational.* For each generation, Scripture should serve as the source of ultimate guidelines for identifying the aspects of contemporary life that obstruct church unity and the reformational practices that would repair

---

of any form of society—including, as he has said to me, the society of atoms in a molecule. If, for example, he found a rabbinic account of society very compelling, he might say to me, "That is a Eucharistic understanding."

8. Ford, *Christian Wisdom,* 35. This is something "handed over to me by my Father" (Luke 10:22).

9. In shaping my overall characterizations of postliberalism, I have been helped very much by personal correspondence with Scott Bader-Saye. In addition to the work of James Fodor (cited in n2), readers may want to compare the following list with treatments by Gary Dorrien, "The Future of Postliberal Theology," *Christian Century,* July 18–25, 2001, 22–29 (also available at www.religion-online.org/showarticle.asp?title=2115); Douglas Harink, *Paul among the Postliberals* (Grand Rapids: Brazos, 2003); and William C. Placher, *The Triune God: An Essay in Postliberal Theology* (Louisville: Westminster John Knox, 2007).

or remove such obstructions.[10] To receive such guidelines is not a matter of cognition or of individual study alone. It is a consequence of being *formed into reformational practice* through the presence of the Word and the work of the Spirit in sacrament, in lives of *imitatio Christi*, and in communities of reformational inquiry.

• *Critique.* In the modern church, the greatest obstacle to this reformational work has been the neglect of scriptural study as the setting for reformational inquiry—in particular, the study of the Gospels as a perennial rereading of the Old Testament. In the absence of this study, ecclesial scholars are tempted to look for guidance from such false substitutes as evidentialism and inerrancy. Here, *evidentialism* refers to the belief that statements about the church are true when there is irrefutable empirical evidence for them. *Inerrancy* refers to the belief that such statements are true when they express the irrefutable authority of their sources (the literal word of Scripture or the voice of ecclesial authorities). Trust in such substitutes breeds irremediable disagreement and schism rather than reform.

• *Retrieval.* The reformers' scholarly task is not first to "study Scripture again," since it is not obvious how to reinstitute such study in ecclesial and academic environments that are shaped by false substitutes. The task is in part genealogical: to uncover possible sources of the desire for false substitutes and to uncover antecedent models for repairing such desires. The task is in part experimental: prompted by the genealogy, to propose and test models of what should be repaired now and how. Inspired especially by patristic and Reformation patterns of scriptural hermeneutics, the current generation of postliberal scholars has proposed, tested, and refined two sets of models. As described above, one is more christological, one more pneumatological, and as I will suggest below, they work best when adopted as complements.

Postliberalism as "Another Reformation"

I label postliberal theology "another Reformation" as my way of characterizing the postliberals' effort to reform as well as renew the practices of the

10. Scripture does not perform this function magically, as if any line-by-line recitation would automatically serve a reformational purpose. Instead, say the postliberals, the early church acquired a *practice* of scriptural study from late Second Temple Judaism. It both accepted and reformed this practice, and the product was both the New Testament/Old Testament canon of the church *and* the church itself as a scripturally shaped community of liturgical and social practice. Among the practices of the early church was a reformational practice of Scripture study, which included communal patterns of reading, commentary, and what we may label "reparative interpretation." This is interpretation that disclosed newly clarified levels of scriptural meaning and previously unseen ways of repairing the church of that day.

Reformers. In this section I briefly state the conclusions I have reached about the relation of postliberalism to the Reformation. I then test these conclusions against statements by three postliberal Lutheran theologians.

(a) It is another Reformation

I conclude from this study that the current movement of postliberal theology bears at least four relations to the Reformation per se.

Direct influence. The theologians examined in this book are Lutheran, Methodist, Mennonite, and Anglican. In a literal sense, their ecclesial work continues many aspects of the work of the Reformers. There are, however, also Roman Catholic theologians we may label postliberal, for example David Burrell, James J. Buckley, Paul Murray, Kevin Hughes, Chad Pecknold, Rusty Reno, Ann Astell, and Robert Wilken. I have yet to gather the characteristics of their work to see if it represents a third "wing" or opens new dimensions of the other two. In the meantime their work may illustrate, on the one hand, that Christian postliberalism also reforms some key features of the Reformers' project (see below, "Reform") and, on the other hand, that some aspects of postliberal theology apply without significant distinction to recent trends in both Catholic and Protestant theology. Among these trends are shared criticisms of dyadic thinking in the modern church and shared efforts to retrieve the nondyadic practices of medieval and patristic scriptural theology.

Retrieval. Postliberal theology appears to retrieve significant guidelines for its work from four earlier sources. (a) Reformation: Postliberals retrieve certain aspects of the Reformation doctrine of *sola gratia* to guide their critique of mechanistic, positivistic, and deterministic (in that sense works-righteous) directions in modern theology and modern biblical studies. Postliberals retrieve aspects of *sola scriptura* as a model for *reformational* (rather than formational) practices of Scripture study. Karl Barth's significant influence on the postliberals illustrates this aspect of their retrieval. (b) Medieval and patristic scriptural theologians: Postliberals do not construct new guidelines for removing obstacles to scriptural study or, then, for reformational scriptural study. Instead, they uncover successive layers of premodern prototypes for their work and then reread and reinterpret these prototypes so that they may yield refined and renewed guidelines for postliberalism's contemporary work. I have not taken time in this study to examine the postliberals' medieval and patristic sources in any detail, but a broad array of recent books perform this task, citing, for example, the influences of Clement, Augustine,[11] Gregory of

---

11. See, for example, C. C. Pecknold, *Transforming Postliberal Theology: George Lindbeck, Pragmatism, and Scripture* (London: T&T Clark / New York: Continuum, 2005); and Jason Byassee, *Praise Seeking Understanding: Reading the Psalms with Augustine* (Grand Rapids: Eerdmans, 2008).

Nyssa,[12] the Cappadocians broadly,[13] Thomas Aquinas,[14] Bonaventure,[15] and many others. (c) Rereading the Gospel narratives and Pauline letters: This is, of course, the primary retrieval, as illustrated throughout this book. (d) Rereading Tanakh or the Old Testament: And this is the coprimary retrieval, comparably illustrated.

Reform. Postliberalism also practices "another Reformation" in the sense that it consciously reforms the work of the Reformers. As Lindbeck argues most clearly, the doctrine of *sola scriptura* was flawed because it failed to include a complementary doctrine of nonsupersessionism. The postliberals supplement the Reformers' work in another way as well: turning to medieval and patristic sources for richer prototypes of scriptural interpretation (as noted above).

From historical to perennial type. Postliberalism practices another Reformation, finally, because it renews "reformation" as Christian theology's perennial responsibility, to be enacted only periodically, in epochs of inordinate stress when, in the judgment of potential reformers, the dominant practices of theology obstruct rather than enable efforts to unify the body of Christ. As I read them, all the postliberal theologians examined in this book identify this as such an epoch.

(b) Reformation in the work of Lindbeck, Jenson, and Sauter

In the course of preparing the book, I interviewed three postliberal Lutherans—the German theologian Gerhard Sauter, as well as Lindbeck and Jenson—to learn what "the Reformation" means to them and whether or not they consider their work part of "another Reformation."[16] There is space here for only a brief summary of their profound and complex responses.

The three offered fairly overlapping accounts of both the Reformation and of their affirmation that, yes, reformation is a periodic activity in church history and, yes, we live at a time of another reformation, a significant one. I learned that for all three Lutherans, postliberalism offers a means of renewing, extending, and reforming the Reformers' work. The three offered similar ac-

---

12. See Placher, *Triune God.*

13. See, for example, ibid.

14. See, for example, Bruce Marshall, "Aquinas as Postliberal Theologian," *Thomist* 53, no. 3 (1989): 353–402. And for more general treatment of the period, see Peter M. Candler Jr., *Theology, Rhetoric, Manuduction, or Reading Scripture Together on the Path to God* (Grand Rapids: Eerdmans, 2006).

15. See, for example, Kevin Hughes, *Constructing Antichrist: Paul, Biblical Exegesis, and the Development of Doctrine in the Early Middle Ages* (Washington, DC: Catholic University of America Press, 2005), and Kevin Hughes, "The Mystical Pedagogy of St. Bonaventure: A Reappraisal of the Collations on the Six Days of Creation" (ms).

16. The interviews with Robert Jenson and Gerhard Sauter took place at the Center of Theological Inquiry in Princeton, Fall 2003. The interview with George Lindbeck took place in New Haven and by phone during Fall 2003.

counts of Luther's goals, but with varying emphases. For Lindbeck, the Roman Catholic Church's misunderstanding of justification by faith was paramount. For both Jenson and Lindbeck, the Reformers' turn to *sola scriptura* was for the sake of reformation, not formation. Christian formation remained, in other words, the work of the church as a whole—tradition, sacraments, congregational life, the imitation of Christ in all aspects of living—not only of scriptural study and scriptural doctrine. Scripture's privileged place is as *norma normans non normata* ("the norm of norms that is not normed") in times of extreme change. For Sauter, Luther's primary concern was to overcome the Roman Catholic Church's self-isolation, turning to the witness of God's Word and action in order to subordinate any self-referring creeds or practices of the empirical churches to the promise of God that is displayed in his Word. For Sauter, the doctrine of justification also protects against any mechanistic or deterministic notions of God as first cause of action rather than author of grace. God's grace alone is the source of reconciliation and thus of any ecclesial efforts to repair schism and recover the unity of the church. Sauter did not address the problem of schism, however, with as much urgency as do the American Lutherans. While Sauter and Jenson are devoted to the work of Lutheran–Catholic reconciliation, Sauter was not convinced that the time has yet come for this: the differences remain as yet too great.

All three theologians seemed to speak with one voice, however, when it comes to "another Reformation." They said, yes, the church requires reformation whenever times of great change lead the churches to the wrong changes, and this is such a time. All agreed, furthermore, that recovering close relations with the people Israel—of today and of the Old Testament—is a condition for achieving today's reformation. Among the reasons for reform today are modern Christianity's attractions to both conceptualism and emotivism and its neglect of the practices of scriptural reading and interpretation that characterized both the early church and the work of the Reformers. For these three theologians, the Reformers' work needs reform as well as renewal in at least two areas: Luther's neglect of ecclesiology[17] and all the Reformers'—as well as the church fathers'—tendencies toward supersessionism. Not the only but the first sin of supersessionism is hermeneutical, since it veils the Gospels' everrenewed relation to the Old Testament texts and thus, in effect, encourages strictly literal or one-leveled readings of the gospel message. Such readings encourage naive and potentially idolatrous attachments to the mere appearances of things, obstructing the Gospels' capacity to generate practices of nuanced and context-related reading, not only of scriptural texts but also of human faces and hearts.[18]

17. This was emphasized only by Lindbeck, but I assume the others share his judgment.
18. I read Hauerwas, Hardy, and Ford as sharing—albeit in different words and with differing emphasis—comparable judgments about the current epoch of reformation.

And for Jewish Readers?

Within the framework of this book, I have not attempted to draw out the implications of Christian postliberalism for Jewish life per se, for rabbinic study, or for Jewish theology. While it is because of those implications that I have undertaken this inquiry, it would require a book-length study for me to share what lies in that "because." I shall merely open the subject by introducing some of these implications.

(a) Hopes for better health

I do not believe that the religion and spirit of Judaism is in good health, nor do I believe that it has been in good health in any part of the modern period, especially since the Shoah. One persistent feature of this poor health has been Judaism's relation, as a religion, to Christianity as its dominant neighbor and the religion of its dominant host civilization. Among the unhealthy features of that relation have been (a) the images Judaism has had of itself in Christian eyes: primarily as superseded, either through the coming of Christ or through the coming of secularism and universal enlightenment, and (b) the temptation Judaism has had to assimilate into its various identities the dyads that are characteristic of modern Christianities, such as nature versus spirit, individual versus community, public versus private spheres, universalism versus particularism. Postliberal Christianity illustrates how it is possible for a significant movement in Christian theology to repair Christianity's contribution to these unhealthy features: (a) by offering in its own mirror images of Judaism as beloved of God and loved by the church (and not out of generosity but for the sake of the church), as enacting its covenant with God for God's sake and not to serve the will of other societies or peoples, and as a valued dialogue partner; (b) by working to repair those dyads in favor of the scriptural, interpretive, and relational practices that were described in this book. I imagine that the first set of features ("a") would help strengthen the capacities of Jews in these lands to treasure their own covenantal, scriptural, and rabbinic heritage; to revisit that heritage as a source of gifts and wisdoms for the nations (rather than as an opprobrium of the nations and a burden for the Jews); and to revalue their religion as capable of unanticipated renewal and growth and of entering into new relationships with its neighbors and its God and its own people. I imagine that the second set of features ("b") would help these Jews recover latent practices of careful hearing and reading, including carefully "reading" the created words or things of the world and carefully hearing the spoken words of other humans.

(b) Partners for reparative work

Postliberal Christian theologians are already among the most active Christian dialogue partners with Jews on matters of theology and belief. Their most sustained dialogues are with those we might label "postliberal Jewish scholars," including, but not limited to, members of the Society for Textual Reasoning (Jewish scholars of texts and philosophy) and Jewish participants in the Society for Scriptural Reasoning.[19] One consequence of this partnership is that without compromising their distinct beliefs and practices, an expanding circle of Jewish and Christian scholars strengthen and reinforce each other's efforts to repair schismatic or dyadic tendencies within modern academic and religious institutions. Some circles include postliberal Muslim scholars as well, further expanding the work and influence of these reparative approaches.

(c) Partners in tikkun olam

These partnerships contribute to what many Jews today, from a wide range of denominations, like to call *tikkun olam*, now understood as "repair of the world"—humanity's effort to contribute to the divine work of mending the creation itself, including but not limited to the ill effects of human sin. In the company of these partnerships, Jews need not consider themselves alone.

19. See chapter 1.

Index of Subjects

abduction (hypothesis-making), 99, 101, 156, 176, 177, 193, 194, 199, 236, 242, 244–46

Abraham, 29, 76–78, 84–86, 114, 115, 132, 142, 149, 158, 174, 189, 191, 216, 242, 249, 250, 259, 261

Adam, 60, 77, 137, 219, 229, 232–34, 240, 241, 243, 245

Adams, Nicholas, 29, 64, 65, 101, 198

Amos (book of Bible), 93–96, 101, 102, 104, 106, 111

Anabaptists (Free Church, Mennonite Church), 114, 127–68, 263

anti-Semitism, 1–2, 9, 131

apophaticism, 136, 186, 199, 200, 209, 217–19, 221

Aquinas, Thomas. See Thomas Aquinas

argument, 1–7, 12, 13, 24, 27, 30, 31, 36, 42, 43, 45, 49, 50, 73, 77, 87, 93–97, 101–2, 104, 126, 128–32, 140, 143, 146, 149, 150, 152, 154, 184, 190, 191, 205, 213, 224–27, 229, 234–43, 245, 255

Aristotle, 86, 97, 107

Augsburg Confession, 38, 75

Augustine, 13, 15, 65, 76, 85, 263

Bader-Saye, Scott, 29, 261

being, 16, 63, 69, 77, 79, 83–90, 107, 108, 118, 121, 134, 136, 138, 170, 171, 175, 182, 196, 241, 247

Bernstein, Richard, 10, 50, 186, 246

Bible, 21–23, 45, 46, 48, 49, 51, 53, 115, 134, 135, 148, 149, 157, 174, 184, 193, 196–98, 221, 228, 229, 230–34, 237, 239, 243–45, 247, 253. See also Tanakh

Black, Andrew, 127, 167, 253

body, 52, 63, 65, 89, 90, 116, 126, 128, 139, 153, 199
and spirit, 67, 69, 75, 82, 83, 102, 105, 107, 110, 113, 123, 138, 162, 198, 202, 248
See also Christ: body of

Bonhoeffer, Dietrich, 91, 203

Borowitz, Eugene, 26, 72

Braaten, Carl, 73, 74, 86, 88

Buber, Martin, 21, 72

Buckley, James, 29, 30, 36, 74, 80, 84, 263

Burrell, David, 21, 29, 98, 263

Byassee, Jason, 29, 253, 263

Calvin, John, 37, 56, 57, 125, 157, 168

Cartesianism. See Descartes, Rene

Cartwright, Michael, 19, 30, 96, 127–29, 149

Center of Theological Inquiry, 27, 30, 65, 71, 264

Christ, 1, 35–37, 39, 40, 43, 44, 48, 52, 68, 81, 85–88, 89, 94, 97, 98, 101, 106, 108–11, 113–23, 126, 129–31, 133–38, 140–44, 147, 154, 156, 157, 160, 161, 170, 173, 180, 184, 195, 196, 198, 200, 201, 203, 206, 207, 214, 216–21, 233, 238, 252, 260, 261
body of, 1, 37, 39, 40, 53, 54, 65, 75, 81, 83, 89, 90, 102–3, 105–6, 108, 109, 113, 118, 123, 124, 126, 130, 134, 136, 137, 139, 167–72, 178, 179, 181, 184, 185, 187, 189, 190–92, 196, 241, 255, 259, 261, 264

Christology, 1–5, 20, 52, 70, 85, 106, 174, 190, 201, 203, 206, 207, 220, 221, 254, 259
wisdom Christology, 201, 203, 206, 207, 220, 221

Church (*ecclesium*)
  American, 28, 36, 38
  Anglican (and Church of England), 27, 28, 124, 167–73, 177, 181, 183, 184, 187–92, 194, 196, 227, 255, 263
  Lutheran, 38, 65, 71–73, 78, 90, 135, 140, 168, 263, 265
  Mennonite, 127, 133–66, 263
  obstructions to spirit and, 38, 41–51, 69, 124, 131, 182–89, 192, 259, 261, 262
  Orthodox, 65, 84, 113, 114, 129, 181, 259
  repairing, 6, 36, 39, 40, 53, 55, 58–60, 70, 110, 114, 129, 130, 136, 145, 156, 172, 182, 187, 190, 191–93, 216, 261, 262
  Roman Catholic, 36, 38–40, 47, 65, 71, 90, 91, 103, 124, 181, 263, 265
Clapp, Rodney, 1, 93, 127, 167, 195, 223
Cleveland, Lindsay, 93, 253
Cohen, Aryeh, 26
Cohen, Hermann, 72, 177
coincidentia oppositorum, 209, 210
Coleridge, Samuel Taylor, 171, 172, 193
community, 4, 5, 14, 17, 20, 23, 24, 26, 29, 35, 37, 46, 75, 77, 82, 86, 90–93, 99–110, 114, 116–20, 122, 131, 133, 138–53, 171, 174, 178, 183, 188, 196, 199–208, 213–20, 234–55, 261, 262, 267
  ecclesial, 55, 57, 58, 171
  religious, 19, 47, 58, 78, 144, 145, 174, 208, 242, 243
  wounded, 117, 122
  See also Church (*ecclesium*)
conceptualism, 27, 66–73, 89, 155, 159, 211, 265
Constantinianism, 119, 129, 130, 131, 139, 151, 156, 159, 160, 167–69
contradiction, 6–18, 38, 66, 69, 72–75, 80, 86, 88, 128, 147, 187, 209, 210, 221–46
correlation, 2, 8, 43, 50, 68, 72, 95, 107, 127, 136, 146, 177–81, 212, 226, 244, 253, 257–67
covenant, 1, 18–20, 30, 43, 48, 62, 63, 87–91, 108, 109, 113–18, 126–30, 140, 141–43, 150, 151, 158, 161–63, 174, 191, 209–21, 257, 266
cry, 42, 106, 152, 195–221, 249, 261
  of Jesus, 201–7, 216–21
  of Job, 203–21
  of the Shoah, 203–9, 266
  of wisdom, 196–207
Cyril of Alexandria, 90, 225

deconstruction, 227–30, 233, 247
Derrida, Jacques, 226–47

Descartes, Rene (Cartesianism), 10, 50, 155–58, 186, 227
Dewey, John, 10, 11, 81, 95, 182, 186
dialogue, 19, 20, 24–31, 40, 41, 98, 153–58, 162, 169–74, 190, 191, 205, 234
  interreligious, 118, 145, 146, 163, 242, 266
discernment, 134, 199, 203–4, 134, 138, 197–204. *See also* wisdom
disciple, 109, 114–21, 133–39, 163, 168, 169, 182, 194, 197–203, 210, 216, 217
doctrine, church, 1, 2, 15, 27–31, 35–62, 69–91, 114–58, 171–73, 180, 185, 192, 200, 214, 235, 249, 255, 258–65
drama, 62, 67, 81, 84, 87–91, 103, 104, 109, 122–26, 147, 180–82, 221

ecclesiology, 74, 124, 167, 174, 175, 183, 189, 191, 194, 265
  reparative, 65, 66, 71, 259, 261
Edwards, Jonathan, 21, 64, 81, 182
Eklund, Rebekah, 195, 253
Eliayahu Rabbah, 250
Enlightenment, 1–4, 82, 83, 120, 180, 205, 236, 266
ethics, 4, 24, 27, 82, 97, 103, 110, 115–18, 135–39, 203–5, 249
Eucharist, 81, 89–91, 109, 116, 168, 171–74, 179–82, 187–91, 194, 201, 234, 235, 255, 256, 260, 261
Exodus (book of Bible), 13, 61, 70, 108, 201, 249
Exodus Rabbah, 177
Ezra (book of Bible), 249, 250–51

face-to-face, 19–20, 108, 126, 147, 148, 176, 193, 195, 196, 207, 212, 219, 259, 265
Fishbane, Michael, 21, 45
Fodor, James, 3, 4, 29, 258, 261
Ford, David, 2, 3, 27–30, 82, 106, 167, 172, 174, 194–221, 242, 253, 257, 258, 260–62, 265
foundationalism, 50, 87, 155–62, 225, 226, 234, 239, 245–52, 259
Fraade, Steven, 21, 24
Frei, Hans, 7, 19, 21–27, 49, 50, 102, 103, 167, 235, 258

genealogy, 42, 43, 50, 51, 66–73, 89, 143–46, 156–60, 192–94, 227–45, 262
Genesis (book of Bible), 76, 77, 148, 229, 232
Gibbs, Robert, 26, 29, 177
Givens, Tommy, 127, 253

God
  absence of, 65, 66, 152, 208, 232
  and blessing (grace), 77–80, 128–30, 150,
    160–62, 197, 234
  and creation, 14, 17, 72, 170, 171, 186, 187,
    229, 241, 247–51
  fear of, 142, 213–15
  for God's sake, 197, 211–14, 221
  of Israel, 30, 63–92, 95, 111, 147, 151
  knowledge of, 84–85, 89, 96, 105, 118, 124,
    128, 161, 243–45
  love of, 8, 18–19, 198, 248, 266
  power of, 260–62
  presence of (*shekhinah*), 1, 16, 17, 30, 35, 37,
    38, 41, 43, 44–49, 63, 68, 82, 83, 87, 89, 90,
    106, 109, 110, 113–17, 120, 121, 122, 126,
    136, 137, 148, 153, 177, 178, 189, 196, 207,
    217–19, 239, 252
  and society, 183
  Son of. *See* Christ: Christology
  Spirit. *See* theology: pneumatological
  as Trinity. *See* theology: trinitarian
  unity, 5, 20, 122, 123, 128, 179, 247
  will of, 104–5, 118, 160, 161, 209–11
  word of (voice, speech), 14, 21, 22, 37, 38,
    41, 44–49, 69, 70, 75, 94–96, 101–3, 107–9,
    111–12, 114–17, 119, 134, 191, 197, 221,
    233, 236, 237, 240, 242, 247–51, 254–56, 265
  work of, 30, 60, 82, 86, 101, 102, 126, 136–38,
    168, 181, 193, 194, 220, 238
  and world, 12, 13, 16, 17, 63, 97, 102–3,
    170–76, 193, 194, 207, 228, 248–51
  YHVH, 30–31, 249
  See also Christ; holiness; redemption; suffering
Goodson, Jacob, 1, 93, 127, 195, 223, 253
gospel, 1, 18, 19, 35–62, 67–75, 79–91, 98, 99,
    108, 109, 117, 120–26, 129–31, 135, 136,
    141, 143, 144, 161, 173, 196, 198, 201, 203,
    210–16, 220, 234, 257–65
grace, 13, 16, 60, 76–78, 89, 98, 117, 120–23,
    233, 234, 265
Greenburg, Moshe, 21–26
Greggs, Tom, 29, 195, 197
Gregory of Nyssa, 37, 84, 86, 264
Gustafson, James, 96, 124

Hackett, W. Christian, 223, 253
haggadah (Passover), 24, 35, 67, 212
halakhah (Jewish religious law), 115, 147, 150,
    251
Halivni, David Weiss, 21, 82, 143, 237–39, 244,
    251

Hamann, J. G., 227, 228, 232, 233, 237–41, 244,
    247
Hardy, Daniel, 2, 27, 167–94, 199, 253, 257,
    260, 265
Harink, Douglas, 30, 36, 116–23, 128, 133,
    135–39, 261
Hauerwas, Stanley, 2, 19, 21, 27, 81–83, 93–126,
    128, 129, 132–39, 167–69, 219, 253, 257,
    258, 265
Heidegger, Martin, 84, 171
hermeneutics, 7, 9–13, 21–30, 37–62, 66–85,
    115, 123, 126, 129, 130, 139, 143, 148, 154–
    63, 168, 173, 192, 201, 210, 212, 233–47,
    258–65. *See also* Scripture, interpretation of
historical criticism. *See* Scripture, interpretation
    of
historiography, 43, 46, 52, 65–72, 143–47, 157,
    158, 168, 259
  depth-history, 144, 145, 156, 160, 191
  plain-sense history, 56, 144, 145, 156
holiness, 28, 56, 64, 113, 118, 152, 173, 182,
    193, 196, 199, 201–3, 212, 247, 251
Holocaust. See *Shoah*
Hosea (book of Bible), 95, 248
Hughes, Kevin, 30, 263, 264
hypothesis, 1–4, 9, 22, 42, 71, 72, 100, 102,
    107, 112–13, 135, 142, 146, 157, 160, 176,
    216–19, 237, 243, 246

idolatry, 76, 153, 208–10, 212, 218, 220, 221,
    229, 244
individualism, 120, 135, 139
Isaiah (book of Bible), 102, 111, 112, 143, 168,
    206, 250
Islam. *See* Muslim
Israel, 1, 13–18, 20, 29, 30, 35–63, 67–78, 86–90,
    95, 101, 108–18, 128–34, 140, 143, 145–54,
    161–63, 168, 172–74, 179–83, 193, 197, 201,
    209–21, 236, 247–51, 254, 257, 260, 265
  exile (diaspora, *galuth*), 75, 147, 148, 150,
    151, 161, 249–51
  land of, 76, 147, 150–52, 251
  people of (*am yisrael*), 1, 13–18, 20, 30,
    35–63, 69, 72, 77, 78, 87–89, 95, 109, 110,
    112–14, 116, 129, 132, 145, 147, 150, 151,
    154, 161, 163, 173, 181, 209, 214, 218, 248,
    249, 250, 251, 265
  state of, 18, 151, 152

James, William, 97, 111
Jefferson, Thomas, 169, 183
Jenson, Robert, 2, 63–91, 134, 153, 264

Jeremiah, Yoder's reading of, 131, 147–63
Jesus. *See* Christ
Jews, 1, 4, 17, 18, 24, 39, 44, 52, 61, 68–72, 108,
    110, 113–16, 128–32, 138, 140–63, 169, 173,
    174, 190, 191, 203, 210, 218, 236, 239, 256,
    266, 267
Job (book of Bible), 30, 195, 196, 201–21, 261
joy, 195, 196, 199, 204, 223
Judaism, 3–5, 21, 24, 25, 29, 44, 61, 71, 72,
    84, 108, 111, 114, 116, 125, 128–31, 140,
    149–56, 159–62, 189, 191, 236, 244, 247,
    250, 251, 255, 266
  civilizational, 144, 152, 266
  diasporic, 114, 142, 147–51
  Maccabean, 151, 152
  messianic, 131, 148, 151, 154, 159–62
  Pharisaic, 129, 251
  Rabbinic, 5, 24, 84, 114, 131, 144, 146, 147,
    151, 153, 154, 160, 236, 244, 247, 250, 251
  Second Temple, 154

Kadushin, Max, 24, 25, 72, 249
Kang, Peter, 253
Kant, Immanuel, 5, 7, 8, 41, 42, 79, 88, 101, 121,
    174, 176, 255
Kepnes, Steven, 21, 26, 29
Knight, Douglas, 88, 89
Kuhn, Thomas, 12, 124

land, 76, 130, 139, 146, 149–162, 251, 266
language, 6, 12–14, 27, 36, 58–59, 76, 79, 84,
    89–91, 97–101, 106–9, 124, 151, 161, 177,
    187, 226–52
  Adamic, 232, 233, 245
  alphabet, 143, 229
  Egyptian, 229–31, 244
  of God (*dibbur*). *See* God: word of
  Hebrew, 1, 101, 119, 148, 149, 155, 198, 199,
    221, 229, 230–34, 237, 239, 243–45
  hieroglyphic, 229, 231, 232, 244
  icon, 34, 204, 229
  ideograph, 229
  metaphor, 46, 104, 111, 113, 149, 162, 228,
    229–33, 244
  primordial, 229–34, 238, 241, 244, 247, 252
Lash, Nicholas, 158, 159
law, 7, 13, 20, 61, 75, 78–83, 89, 107, 111, 115,
    116, 120–22, 126, 130, 138, 142, 152, 153,
    173, 177, 182, 187, 210, 212, 213, 248, 251,
    252, 257
Levinas, Emmanuel, 84, 176–78, 195

Lindbeck, George, 2, 19–31, 35–62, 65–66,
    71, 94, 114, 123–26, 129, 132–35, 139–41,
    143–44, 157, 169, 253, 257–58, 263–66
liturgy, 20, 45, 58, 65, 78, 103, 262
Locke, John, 23, 84, 155–58, 225, 229
logic, 2–20, 31, 57, 66, 90, 98–102, 111, 120,
    135, 152, 155, 236, 247, 253–54, 258
  diagram (graph), 15–17, 182
  dichotomous/dyadic, 8–19, 26–28, 40–43,
    47–53, 74–78, 83, 100–114, 118, 125, 145,
    156–62, 182, 185, 190, 213, 252–53, 263,
    266–67
  excluded middle, 7–8, 20, 90, 252
  of suffering, 8–12, 15
  See also abduction (hypothesis-making)
love, 1, 121, 134, 157, 170, 185, 195–202, 229,
    248–50, 260. *See also* God: love of
Lowth, Robert, 227–48

Magid, Shaul, 26, 29
Marcion/Marcionite, 44, 45, 155
Marshall, Bruce, 25, 30, 115–16, 264
memory. *See* remembrance
Messiah, 45, 91, 114, 129–32, 137, 144, 148–55,
    159–61
midrash, 15, 24, 67, 115–16, 162, 177, 201,
    247–51
Milbank, John, 3, 50, 135, 167, 223–56, 257
Mishnah, 141–42, 149, 153–55, 160, 247, 251
mission/missionary, 75, 79, 91, 103, 117, 134–
    38, 146, 148–50, 154, 160, 171, 185, 258
modernism. *See* theology: modern
mood (grammatical or emotional), 52, 196,
    201–18
Mouw, Richard, 157–58, 168
Murray, Paul, 174, 263
Muslim, 20–21, 29, 160, 169, 173, 174, 189, 191,
    225, 244, 256, 267

name, 13–14, 17, 21, 28, 31, 40, 51, 87, 96,
    106–7, 179, 184, 188–90, 196–200, 210–18,
    229, 249–51
nation, 4, 30, 76–77, 82, 89, 101–5, 110–15,
    130, 137–39, 144, 146–47, 151–54, 169, 236,
    250, 266
Nation, Mark Thiessen, 127–29, 132–35
Nazarenes, 130, 144, 160–61
Neuhaus, Richard, 64, 81, 90
New Testament, 25–26, 30, 43–45, 57, 62,
    68–70, 87, 108, 115–23, 129, 142, 146, 155,
    173, 192, 205, 212, 214, 262
Nicaea (council/doctrine), 56, 113, 129–30, 147

nonsupersessionism. *See* supersessionism
nonviolence. *See* violence

Ochs, Peter, 2, 9, 13, 21, 25, 29, 30, 72, 129, 143, 194, 242
Old Testament, 17–18, 20, 36–37, 40, 43–45, 48, 51, 62, 69–70, 108, 114, 129–30, 143, 149, 192, 210–12, 234, 239, 240, 245, 262, 264–65
O'Siadhail, Micheal, 167, 204–5, 208

Palestine, 140–41, 148
Pannenberg, Wolfhart, 85–91
patristics, 1, 17, 29, 46, 64, 66, 81, 90, 108, 114, 143, 158, 225, 236, 253, 262–65
Paul (apostle), 18, 35–36, 69, 76, 83, 94, 103, 108, 115–26, 129–63, 205–6, 219, 236, 261, 264
Pecknold, Chad, 29, 242, 263
Peirce, Charles Sanders, 10–16, 25, 36, 41, 57, 64–66, 71, 81, 98–102, 105–7, 111–12, 120, 189, 193, 199, 224, 227, 236, 245
Pentecostal, 87–88, 109, 114, 172–73, 182
philosophy, 5–19, 21–28, 36, 71–72, 80, 84, 86, 96–101, 120, 125, 143, 150, 175–79, 224, 235, 246–48, 253, 258, 267
Placher, William, 29–30, 103, 261, 264
Plato, 85, 191, 235
pleonasm (non-identical repetition), 224–48
pneumatology. *See* God; theology: pneumatological
politics, 7, 27–30, 43, 69–71, 81–91, 103, 110–63, 167, 170–83, 190, 207–8, 211, 228, 241, 250, 259
postmodernism, 2–10, 17–20, 27–29, 84, 96, 155, 205, 226–46
pragmatism, 2–10, 17–29, 41–43, 58, 64, 66, 70, 81, 94, 98–126, 182, 192–93, 224–26, 234, 239–56, 259, 263
prayer, 14, 18, 27, 31, 42–43, 69, 74, 80–81, 115–18, 132, 148, 171, 173, 193–94, 195, 214–16, 220–21, 238–39, 247–50. *See also* liturgy
Preller, Victor, 98–100, 106
proclamation, 74–82, 102, 108–9, 120, 126, 136, 139, 161, 168, 248, 253–54
promise, 70, 74–89, 95, 97, 114, 142, 150, 191, 205, 207, 210, 241, 250–51, 265
prophets, prophecy, 12, 63, 93–126, 150, 152, 156, 162, 199, 206–7, 231, 236, 239, 251
proposition, 5–9, 13–18, 24–26, 48, 98, 120, 125, 159, 161, 243
propositionalism, 50, 56, 215
psalms, 57, 149, 173, 176, 177, 263

Quash, Ben, 30, 260

Rabbinic Daily Morning Prayer Service, 247
Rabbinic literature and tradition, 5, 14, 18, 21, 24–27, 56, 61–62, 67, 72, 78, 81, 84, 89, 108, 115, 131, 144–60, 173, 201, 233, 236–39, 244, 248–52, 261, 266–68. *See also* midrash; Mishnah; Talmud (*Gemara*)
Rabbinic sages, 56, 67, 84, 108, 147, 151–54, 160, 177, 251–52
Radical Orthodoxy, 226, 246, 253
reasoning, 2, 8–22, 27–30, 36–40, 64–67, 70, 79, 94–126, 128, 133, 143–47, 155–63, 169–76, 191–92, 196–98, 210, 213–14, 224, 236–44, 248, 252, 259, 261
    dyadic, 9–19, 25–28, 40–41, 83, 103–7, 111–14, 145–46, 156–63, 182, 190, 263, 267
    reparative, 8, 13–17, 64–65, 100–126, 133, 145, 192–95, 261
    scriptural, 14–20, 27–30, 36, 169, 174, 191, 196–97, 214, 248, 260
    textual, 20, 26, 29, 143, 267
    theopractic, 93–126
    transcendental, 40–43, 58–59, 66, 87, 101, 134, 171, 176, 182, 194, 239, 255
    triadic, 25, 26, 145, 156
    See also scriptural reasoning
redemption, 8, 18, 30, 37, 47, 51–52, 64–78, 89–91, 100, 107–17, 126, 129–30, 148–53, 175–90, 200–220, 229–34, 249–54, 260–61. *See also* Messiah
Reformation, reformational (process, logic), 6–7, 35–62, 64–83, 91, 103, 114–15, 123–25, 129–30, 135, 144, 151, 157, 173, 178, 185, 192, 196, 259–66
relation, 4–27, 36, 39, 42–53, 56, 61, 62, 66, 72, 75–91, 95–97, 101–14, 122–26, 129–35, 143, 150, 154, 161, 167–94, 198–221, 229–31, 240, 249, 254–56, 263, 265–67
remembrance, 51, 78, 109–14, 151, 180, 203, 205, 213, 216, 220–21, 230
Reno, Rusty, 30, 163, 263
repair, 6–18, 26–29, 36–62, 64–83, 99–126, 129–37, 143–45, 156–57, 160, 168, 172–74, 178–94, 195–221, 229–34, 237–46, 249–50, 258–62, 265–67
representation, 47, 70, 159, 204, 207–21. *See also* sign
resurrection, 35, 63, 67–70, 75–80, 88–91, 115–16, 122–26, 129–30, 134, 140, 155, 181, 200–203, 211–12, 217–20, 251–52

retrieval, 27, 48, 146, 258, 262–64
revelation, 4, 13, 23, 56, 84–85, 98, 108, 140,
    178, 210, 231–33, 237–38
righteousness, 76–79, 113, 135, 143, 151, 248,
    251, 263
Rogers, Eugene, 28, 29, 134
Rome, 72, 103, 132, 151, 170–72, 246
Rosenzweig, Franz, 61, 72, 177

sacrament, 89–91, 109, 126, 130, 136–40, 180–
    81, 190, 193–94, 259–65
salvation, 76, 122, 124, 130, 148, 152, 228
    history, 5, 19, 25, 43–44, 52, 54, 60, 64, 68–84,
        94, 109–16, 201, 216, 238, 251
Sauter, Gerhard, 264–65
schism, 37–44, 46, 65, 127–63, 168, 183–85,
    190–91, 210–21, 261–65
    church, 37–40, 46, 65, 168, 183–85, 190, 210,
        261–65
    intra-Abrahamic, 191, 210–221
    Jewish-Christian, 37–44, 127–163, 190–91,
        210–21, 261–65
Schwöbel, Christoph, 89–91
science, 9–17, 27, 41, 50–51, 66, 71–72, 84,
    97–102, 124, 167, 171–76, 186–87, 193,
    214–15, 231, 257
scriptural reasoning, 13–21, 27–31, 36, 169, 174,
    191, 197, 214, 242, 249, 260, 267
Scripture, 4–5, 12–31, 35–62, 65–91, 97–126,
    128–63, 167–79, 185–94, 195–221, 225,
    231–35, 241–42, 248–52, 254, 258–67
    commentary on, 13, 19, 24, 29, 121, 143–44,
        196–98, 221, 262
    homiletic interpretation, 25, 45, 57, 60, 210
    See also Bible; gospel; midrash; New
        Testament; Old Testament; Tanakh
        (Hebrew Bible); Torah
Scripture, interpretation of, 15–31, 43–53,
    64–72, 77–91, 108–116, 141–43, 146, 191,
    210, 241, 251, 262–66
    academic, 8–17, 27, 36–54, 72, 104, 197, 200,
        253, 262, 267
    depth-historiographic, 143–46, 156
    factualist (propositionalist), 23–24, 49–51,
        214–15
    fundamentalist/literalist, 45, 48–50
    historical-critical, 22, 23, 48–49, 52, 57,
        73–78
    propositional, 5–18, 23–25, 48–50, 56, 98,
        124, 159–61, 215, 242
    Reformational, 35–62, 64–80, 123–25, 259,
        261–63

semiotics (sign), 13, 25–27, 36, 46, 57–62, 72,
    137, 169, 202, 204, 208–9, 215, 217, 223–24,
    228, 231–33
semper reformanda, 35, 36, 52–55, 71,123, 259
Shir HaShirim (Song of Songs Rabbah), 247,
    248
Shoah, 1–5, 17–19, 72, 160–62, 201–9, 266
Sider, Ron, 116–21, 128, 135
sign, 7–9, 24–26, 57, 75–76, 136–37, 169, 202–
    21, 228, 231–34. See also representation
sin, 16, 30, 42, 60, 65–68, 76–78, 85, 95, 101–5,
    112, 116, 151–53, 157–58, 168, 212, 232–33,
    265, 267
sola gratia, 35, 39, 56, 263
sola scriptura, 28, 35–39, 47–52, 56–57, 61, 65,
    103, 114, 123, 125, 168, 263–65
Soulen, Kendall, 2, 29–31
suffering, 7–18, 42, 65, 76–78, 100–104, 112–23,
    132–34, 149, 157, 173, 177–81, 195–221,
    249–52, 261
supersessionism, 1–5, 154–63, 168–70, 189–91,
    209–21, 223–26, 238, 243–45, 252, 254–66

Talmud (Gemara), 15, 24–29, 67, 82, 143,
    153–54, 160, 188–89, 237, 250–51
Tanakh (Hebrew Bible), 45, 132, 148, 149,
    196, 198, 221, 228, 229, 230–34, 237, 239,
    243–45, 264
Temple (First and Second), 130, 142, 148–49,
    152, 154, 161, 179, 251, 262
    destruction of (chorban), 111, 142, 149, 162,
        250–51
textual reasoning, 20, 26–29, 143, 267
theology, 1–34, 43, 46, 48, 53–55, 63, 71, 89, 94,
    96, 117–19, 124, 128, 196, 224–26, 235, 245
    Anabaptist, 114, 129–63
    Anglican, 27–28, 167–94, 196, 201, 226, 242,
        255, 260, 263
    apocalyptic, 116–26, 132, 135–42
    found, 168–75
    Jewish 28–31, 169, 266–67
    modern 2–10, 13, 18, 26, 28, 37, 40–52, 56, 64,
        68–75, 82, 84, 87–90, 97–104, 108, 114, 121–
        25, 135, 155–62, 173, 182–90, 197, 211–17,
        224, 226, 241, 253–54, 261–67
    narrative 18, 23, 37, 40–62, 67–70, 87, 90, 108,
        110, 114, 125, 129, 147, 161, 163, 181, 192,
        196, 201–21, 241, 257–58, 264
    philosophical 5, 96–98, 150, 224
    pneumatological, 1, 27–29, 66, 85, 134, 167–
        193, 196, 200–204, 206, 259–62

political, 81–91, 103, 110–26, 133–63, 167
postliberal, 1–34, 36, 39–40, 71–91, 94, 134, 146, 192–94, 209–16, 252, 257–67
pragmatic. *See* pragmatism
reformational, 65, 74–91, 158
replacement, 1, 42, 47–49, 69, 210
scriptural, 48, 66, 126, 167, 196–221
trinitarian, 28–29, 56, 63–91, 109, 123, 134–35, 167, 175–79, 180, 184, 188, 200–202, 220, 259
Thomas Aquinas, 79, 80, 84, 90, 98, 264
Ticciati, Susannah, 29, 208, 209, 215, 221
Torah, 24, 56, 61, 70, 78, 106–9, 129–30, 141, 149, 152–55, 161, 179, 239, 247–51
  Written and Oral Torah (*torah she b'khtav, torah she b'al peh*) 161, 247–51
tradition (*mesorah*), 4–5, 10, 13, 18–26, 37, 40, 45–59 111, 119–20, 141–42, 155–63, 172, 178–82, 189–91, 198–200, 207–33, 236–48, 252, 258–59, 265
Trocmé, André, 110–11

unknowing. *See* apophaticism

vagueness, 16–18, 60, 107, 124, 146, 158
Van Buren, Paul, 21, 61
Vico, Umberto, 227, 231–33, 243–44, 247
violence, 9, 84, 123, 145–46, 152–53, 228–230, 244

Wainwright, Geoffrey, 89–91, 175
Warburton, William, 227–35, 240, 243–47

Weaver, Alain Epp, 126–28, 131–32
Weiss, Daniel, 1, 127, 131, 137, 151, 156, 223
Wilken, Robert Louis, 29, 87–88, 263
wisdom, 23, 50, 59, 78, 82–84, 96, 110, 115, 140, 144, 161, 168–71, 175–82, 195–221, 253, 260, 266. *See also* discernment
Wisdom of Solomon, 202–3, 247, 260
Wittgenstein, Ludwig, 35, 98–100, 106, 124, 155–56, 220–21
world, 8–12, 15, 19, 25–29, 46, 49, 58, 67, 86, 88–91, 97–100, 103, 104, 107–15, 118–19, 123–26, 134–39, 151–61, 167–94, 195–221, 228–52, 258, 261, 266–67
  this world/the other world, 35, 63–66, 77, 136–39, 180–83, 198–202, 206, 211, 218, 237–38, 248, 251
worship, 24, 30, 75, 115,149–51, 161, 178–85, 193, 203, 216, 241, 248–49. *See also* liturgy
wound, 13, 101, 132–33, 117–23,133, 209–11, 252. *See also* suffering

Yale, 21, 23, 25, 73
Yale school (American postliberalism), 3, 26–30, 172, 174, 182–84, 189–94, 196–201, 210–13, 217, 241–42, 258–66
Yeago, David, 90–91
Yoder, John Howard, 3, 19, 30, 112, 114, 118–22, 127–64, 167–68, 224, 234, 253–54, 257

Zionism, 151–52, 154, 162
Zoloth, Laurie, 26–29
Zweig, Stephan, 147–53, 163

Index of Scripture
and Other Ancient Sources

Old Testament (*Tanakh*)

Genesis

12 78
15:6 76

Exodus

2 249
2:23 106
2:25 76
3 177, 249
3:12 76
3:13–14 13
22:1–2 153
24:7 67

Leviticus

19:16 153
25:36 153

Numbers

1:51 152

Deuteronomy

26:8 67

Joshua

24:19 183

Isaiah

1 249
8:2 152
10:5–8 112
28 101
41–43 250
52:5 152
59:16 151
60 251
60:21 151
64:4 206

Jeremiah

29:7 130, 147–49, 158

Lamentations

1 249

Hosea

2:21–22 248

Amos

1 93–96, 101, 102
3:2 95
3:8 104
4:1 93, 95
9:14–15 95

Micah

3:12 152

Zechariah

8:4 152

Job

1:9 221
3:5 208
3:7–26 208
3:8b–9a 208
3:20–26 207
22:1–3 214
28:1 214
28:27–28 214, 215
42:5 215
42:7–8 213

Psalms

34:9 260
137:3 149

Proverbs

24:3 260

Song of Songs

2:2 248
2:4 248
5:10 248

Old Testament Apocrypha

Wisdom of Solomon

78:22–28 202, 260

New Testament

Matthew

7:16 63, 71, 98, 100, 101

Luke

1:4 202
1:41–42 199, 260
3:21–22 202
4:1 196
7:35 198
9:23–25 202
10:21–22 200
12:19–34 202
23:46 200
24:5 200, 261
24:13–53 200

John

2:22 196
3:11 175–76
8:56–58 114

Romans

7:4–6 115
8:18–21 117
13:8 121

1 Corinthians

2:1 206
2:6 206
2:7 206

2:9 206
2:10 206
2:13–15 206
3:1 206
3:3 206
6:12–20 105
11:1 219
12:3 80
14 118

2 Corinthians

5:16–17 117, 163

Galatians

1:1–5 122
1:7 117
2:19 115
2:20 188
4:7, 9 118
4:25–26 158
5:1–5 120, 122
5:2–6 115
6:15 122

2 Timothy

3:16 197

Hebrews

2:8–9 157
11:1 76
13:14 120

Rabbinic Literature

Mishnah

Avot

1 251
2 251

Yadayim

3:5 247

Babylonian Talmud

Bava Metzia

62a 513

Berakhot

58a 153
62b 153

Makkot

2b 151
24a–b 152

Megillah

29a 152

Sanhedrin

37 151
72a 153
72b 153
73a 153
74a 153
98a 151

Sukkot

52b 151

Midrash

Avot de Rabbi Natan

11a 250

Song of Songs Rabbah

1.1.11 247